THE ULTIMATE G
Strange
CINEMA

Michael Vaughn

Schiffer Publishing Ltd®

4880 Lower Valley Road • Atglen, PA 19310

Copyright © 2017 by Michael Vaughn

Library of Congress Control Number: 2017935610

Designed by Justin Watkinson
Cover design by Justin Watkinson
Type set in Bodoni MT/Univers LT Std/Minion Pro

ISBN: 978-0-7643-5428-1
Printed in China

Published by Schiffer Publishing, Ltd.
4880 Lower Valley Road
Atglen, PA 19310
Phone: (610) 593-1777; Fax: (610) 593-2002
E-mail: Info@schifferbooks.com
Web: www.schifferbooks.com

For our complete selection of fine books on this and related subjects,
please visit our website at www.schifferbooks.com.
You may also write for a free catalog.

Schiffer Publishing's titles are available at special discounts for bulk purchases for sales promotions or premiums. Special editions, including personalized covers, corporate imprints, and excerpts, can be created in large quantities for special needs. For more information, contact the publisher.

We are always looking for people to write books on new and related subjects. If you have an idea for a book, please contact us at proposals@schifferbooks.com.

Other Schiffer Books on Related Subjects:

World Gone Wild: A Survivor's Guide to Post-Apocalyptic Movies, david j. moore, 978-0-7643-4587-6

It Came from the Video Aisle!: Inside Charles Band's Full Moon Entertainment Studio, Dave Jay, William S. Wilson & Torsten Dewi, 978-0-7643-5410-6

Lights, Camera, Game Over!: How Video Game Movies Get Made, Luke Owen, 978-0-7643-5317-8

I would like to dedicate this book to my entire family, including my mother Debra, my stepfather Clyde, and sister Nicole. A special dedication goes out to my father Roger, who passed away way too young, as well as my grandfather Ray and Aunt Ruth. I love you all and miss you every single day.

Special Thanks: Bob Jacobs, Eric Schmitt, Alan Bender, Vincent Deamon, Joe Flood, Larry Cohen, Rufus Seder, Gorman Bechard, Alex Essoe, Frank Murgalo, Chad Crawford Krinkle, Tim Ritter, Frank Henenlotter, Jeff Lieberman, Adam Rehmeir, Chuck Cirino, Brandon Marrgart, Glenn M. Benest, Valorine Hubbard, Eric Stanze, Tim Burd, Tim Bartell, Brian Yuzna, Richard Elfman, Michael Felsher, Nick Zedd, Vito Trabucco, Chad Crawford Kinkle, and Grindhouse Releasing.

CONTENTS

Welcome, seekers of the odd and the strange! What you hold in your hands is not merely a book but a map to the sublimely weird, the wonderful, and the grimy side of cinema from all over the globe. It's a labor of love and the result of a lifelong love affair and obsession.

I have always had a huge love for films. For me they are pure magic and a fun way to escape to another time and place. As a kid I'd watch a movie, rewind it (prehistoric VHS days), and re-watch it all over again. I'm sure my parents thought I was a strange kid. My father, Roger, unknowingly changed my life when he bought me a secondhand VHS copy of *Little Shop of Horrors*, the Corman version. After my young eyes viewed the strange plight of Jonathan Haze's Seymour and the man-eating plant that demanded humans for his supper, something inside me just clicked and I knew I'd never view films the same again.

After I got a little older I graduated to other main stream horror films like the Friday the 13th series, Halloween series, etc. And sure, it was a strong love affair, but I grew bored of slick Hollywood films and sought out things that were a little bit on the fringe. Luckily my town had a wonderful mom and pop VHS rental store and, much to the chagrin of my parents, I would race to the horror section and stand in awe over the lurid covers that promised me all sorts of unbridled terror and ecstasy. And of course the cover art was just amazing. *Psychos in Love* was a cover that always got my attention, as well as *Dead Alive* with the brilliant photo of the woman pulling a little skull out of her mouth. With a cover like that how could you not want to see it? Of course most of the times the cover art was so much better than the actual film itself, but it did take me down a path that I'm still happily on today.

Then there was *Henry: Portrait of a Serial Killer.* Its stark realism and documentary-like grit made it far more disturbing than the run-of-the-mill thug wearing a mask killing naughty teenagers. And, of course, later I would discover classics like *Night of the Living Dead, The Last House on the Left,* etc. Now I feel like a total dinosaur, but back in my day, before the Internet made it incredible easy to find and buy movies, you had to rely on mailing lists and catalogs to get the really weird offbeat stuff. *Blackest Heart Media* was one that I remember very vividly. Fanzines like *Fangoria* and *Gorezone* were also extremely important in a pre-Internet era. I'd devour every issue and try and track down every film I possibly could. But now, discovering them is as easy as a few clicks. And while it is no doubt a helpful resource, I can't help but yearn for those old days of reading fanzines and books to uncover rare gems.

I put this book together because. while online articles on movies are alright, and I do enjoy writing my blog, *Gorehound Mikes,* it's hard to reproduce the feel of a real book in your hands, and I refuse to believe printed material is dead. In doing research for this book I found many new films and with it came that old surge of excitement all over again. Hopefully, in some small way, you will feel the same thrill I did in the early days of my underground film education, pawing through fanzines and mail order catalogs and finding hidden treasures just begging to be enjoyed again and again.

Each chapter is organized alphabetically by film title, except the chapter on horror, which is organized alphabetically by country and then film title. Most reviews have bonus content such as trivia and in some cases even exclusive interviews, mini interviews, or quotes from some of the people involved in said movie. My hope is that this extra content makes for better reading and gives fans more insight from primary sources. I also took pains to track down obscure titles so every fan can discover something totally different.

I'm not saying this is the most complete film guide, but I feel like I have enough movies and obscure stuff to make it interesting for those new to offbeat cinema and even the more seasoned lover. Lastly, I hope you enjoy this book as much as I enjoyed writing it. And thank you for supporting an independent writer and the idea that real books will never die.

CHAPTER 1

Explosions, fights, cannibal tribes, and killer cyborgs that run amok is just a taste of the weird and wonderful bits to be found in the Action/Adventure chapter. Think of all the energy of a Michael Bay film with not even a quarter of the carting budget. When you watch these movies it's good to keep in mind that these balls-to-the-walls mavericks didn't have the luxury of millions of dollars and CGI; hell, some of them didn't even have the money for real stunt men. The in-your-face grit and electric energy in these low-budget films is why, for me, they will always be more exciting than today's billion-dollar transforming eye sores. When you look at the stunt/wire work in say *The Devils Sword* it may look cheap by today's standards, but when you factor in the limited resources it's pretty impressive. The films run the gambit from a trashy *Terminator* rip-off, *Lady Terminator*, man-eating-zombie sushi in *Dead Sushi*, and so on. Like the other chapters, I try to provide an interesting cross section of films from different countries and not a major studio production in sight. Yes, this is the wild, wooly, go-for-broke stuff I just love as a film fan, and I hope you do to.

Action/Adventure

Battle Wizard, The, aka Tian long ba bu (1977)

DIRECTED BY	Pao Hsueh-li
WRITTEN BY	Kuang Ni, Louis Cha (story by)
STARRING	Danny Lee, Tanny Tien, Wai Wang, Lam Jan-kei
COUNTRY	Hong Kong

Bad-er-tainment is a term that is defined as anything that's bad yet still retains its likeability and charm, making it an overall enjoyable experience. *The Battle Wizard* is most definitely a film that falls into that category. Danny Lee plays Prince Tuan Yu, a young man who, despite his family's wishes, isn't too keen on learning the art of Kung Fu. This, however, changes when a villainous maniac with the ability to breathe fire seeks revenge against the prince. He meets a mysterious woman who trains him and helps him defeat the evil that seeks to destroy them. While doing research, I stumbled upon this film, and it certainly met every single criteria for this book. You have mystical creatures, villains that seem to come right out of an acid trip, and oh yeah, let's not forget about the trained gorilla assassin who just happens to know Kung Fu. And that's not even all of the weirdness that's in store for you here. Now, I said from the start that this isn't a good film. While the plot isn't terrible, it is needlessly convoluted and doesn't explore anything you haven't seen in a hundred other better films. Also, the special effects are laughably dated, sometimes using flat 2-D animation to represent 3-D objects. Worst yet, the kung fu is just passable, and if you're looking for real high-flying intense action this is not it. However, it is the perfect amount of bat-crap-crazy fueled with no-shame cheese. The result is a rip-roaring psychedelic romp that will have you shaking your head in disbelief but loving every minute of it. Sadly, this movie gets overlooked, but even with its flaws it's a fun flick and perfect to pop on, unplug, and let the insanity wash over you. But really, need a say more than trained assassin gorilla.

Battlefield Baseball (2003)

DIRECTED BY	Yudai Yamaguchi
WRITTEN BY	Yudai Yamaguchi, Ryuichi Takatsu, Isao Kiriyama, Gatarô Man (Comic by)
STARRING	Tak Sakaguchi, Atsushi Itô, Hideo Sakaki, Alex Revan, Akiko Mishiro, Shôichirô Masumoto
COUNTRY	Japan

From the director of *Versus* comes a highly weird take on the great American pastime done the way only the Japanese can. In regular baseball you may get your feelings hurt, however, in battlefield baseball, your very life is at stake. A group of misfits must face off against a team of blue faced zombie-like players. All seems bleak until a secret weapon with a killer throw comes to save the day. *Battlefield Baseball* is a high-octane action comedy that plays like a Manga comic done by way of *Troma*. The concept is great; however, the film strikes out more than it hits home runs. I really wanted to love this film and, while I found some parts genuinely entertaining, it's hard not to ignore its issues. Sure, I could gladly forgive sketchy character motivations and even gaps in logic because, after all, this isn't exactly high art. However, the plot holes are so huge that it feels like you've missed chunks of the movie when you didn't. Often, things are needlessly incoherent and confusing, and it seems as if the writers were simply making up the story as they went along. Worst of all, the titular event is never fleshed out, and the audience has no idea what the rules are, how points are scored, and what we get is just goons fighting on a baseball field. I get that the film is supposed to be a silly-crazy action film, but that doesn't excuse the lazy writing that seems to drop the ball instead of knocking it out of the park. Thankfully, things are kept just weird enough to be mildly entertaining despite its severely under-developed screenplay. *Battlefield* is a promising action comedy that could have scored big but fails miserably. You'rrrrre out!

Burst City, aka Bakuretsu toshi (1982)

DIRECTED BY	Gakuryû Ishii
WRITTEN BY	Jûgatsu Toi
STARRING	Michirô Endô, Shigeru Izumiya, Takanori Jinnai, Kou Machida, Shinya Ohe, Shigeru Muroi, Yasuto Sugawara
COUNTRY	Japan

This totally full throttled film is said to be a favorite of visionary filmmaker Takashi Miike. Set in a dystopian Japan, a group of punk-rockers fight back against the construction of a power plant. There is no denying that this is a high-energy, visually popping hyperkinetic ride fueled by pure testosterone and rage. We, the audience, get an interesting and up-close glimpse into the '80s Japanese punk scene and, wisely, it is filmed partly in a documentary style. This coupled with plenty of sleaze, blood, and gritty *Mad Max*-like vibes makes this a real stand-out experience. The scene involving a dead hooker is truly unnerving stuff. It also manages to sneak in sly (but not so subtle) social commentary. I can certainly see the artistic and satirical merit here, but at nearly two hours, things start to get a bit tedious. Still, despite the bloated runtime, contained within *Burst City* is a wildly insane and highly caffeinated romp. Recommended.

Dead Sushi (2012)

DIRECTED BY	Noboru Iguchi
WRITTEN BY	Noboru Iguchi, Makiko Iguchi, Jun Tsugita
STARRING	Rina Takeda, Kentoaro Shimazu, Takamasa Suga, Takashi Nishina, Asami
COUNTRY	Japan

The thought of consuming raw fish can be scary enough; I include myself in such sentiments. However, in Noboru Iguchi's wild action-horror-comedy *Dead Sushi* the fear goes far beyond the idea of eating raw seafood. Keiko (Rina Takeda) is a meek but skilled sushi chef that is forced to take a job at an inn. She is forced to take constant abuse by her boss and the guests. As fate would have it, she puts her talents to the ultimate test when a legion of undead and hungry seafood is  unleashed on the unsuspecting patrons. Without a doubt, the best way to approach this film is as if you were watching a live action Manga (comic book) and, of course, not take anything too seriously. *Dead Sushi* has a nice balance of high-flying chaotic action, bizarre set pieces, and of course lots of blood and nudity. As you might expect, it has plenty of great WTF moments such as a totally icky scene in which two lovers swap raw egg via kissing. Also, I've never seen two zombie sushi humping and moments later expelling babies. For the most part the film is able to rise above its own novelty premise, but some scenes feel as if they only exist to pad out the runtime. I was, however, pleasantly surprised by the fact that characters are fleshed out a lot more than you would expect from this kind of story. The special practical effects are well executed but, sadly, the addition of poorly done CGI doesn't help. Normally I'd say it would take you out of the film, but it's not as if we're dealing with reality here. Cheese, splatter, plenty of skin, and all-out cartoon-style gonzo makes *Dead Sushi* a fun goofy spectacle you'll want to serve at your next get-together. Recommended.

Devil's Sword, The (1984)

DIRECTED BY	Ratno Timoer
WRITTEN BY	Imam Tantowi
STARRING	Barry Prima, Gudi Sintara, Rita Zahara, Enny Christina, Advent Bangun, Yos Santo, Kandar Sinyo
COUNTRY	Indonesia

Are you a fan of *Conan* but wished it was made by someone tripping balls? Well look no further than *The Devil's Sword*. Deep inside a cave is a mystic object, a sword which is said to possess unlimited power for those who wield it. This leads to a host of evil warriors hell-bent on gaining the weapon for themselves. It's up to a young hero with the aid of his master to reach it before the others do. While it may lack a coherent plot, this Indonesian outing packs a real punch in the action department. Surprisingly, there is some nicely done fight choreography, and the use of wires impressed me, especially considering the film's bottom-of-the-barrel budget. Like most films of this type, director Ratno Timoer plays everything totally straight, which results in pure campy goodness. Every inch of this production is hyper-surreal and just totally daffy, giving it a wonderful cartoon-like quality. One highlight is, of course, Barry Prima's character fighting off a hoard of (crudely done) man/croc hybrids. Or, let's not forget the incredibly hilarious and cheap-looking Cyclops. Definitely a film sure to put a big goofy grin on every trashy action-lover's face.

Encounter of the Spooky Kind, aka Spooky Encounters, aka Gui da gui (1980)

DIRECTED BY	Sammo Kam-Bo Hung
WRITTEN BY	Sammo Kam-Bo Hung
STARRING	Sammo Kam-Bo Hung, Fat Chung, Lung Chan, Ha Huang, Po Tai, Ma Wu, Ching-Ying Lam, Biao Yuen, Billy Chan
COUNTRY	Hong Kong

A man named Cheung (Sammo Hung) is known around town for his legendary bravery, which is put to the ultimate test when he crosses the wrong side of an evil sorcerer. Writer, director, and actor Sammo Hung fuses funhouse-style horror, martial arts, and comedy with surprisingly good results. The action sequences are well crafted with lots of great ass-kicking scenes, but I just wish there were more of them. And, while the supernatural element is not actually scary, the set pieces Hung creates do manage to evoke a nice haunted mood even if it's a bit silly. But the real wicked magic of *Spooky* is Hung himself, who brings to life the lovable yet dimwitted Courageous Cheung character. He has nice comedic timing coupled with physical humor, and he's so damned likeable you can't help but be endeared to him. This is certainly no masterpiece; however, it's pure brain candy with enough entertainment value to help gloss over some of the film's more glaring faults. *Spooky Encounters* makes the perfect lazy Sunday-type movie if you're willing to embrace its low-budget cheesiness. A fun weird little romp and makes a great alternative Halloween-season flick.

GOES WELL WITH: *House*, aka *Hausu* (1977)

For Your Height Only (1981)

DIRECTED BY	Eddie Nicart
WRITTEN BY	Cora Caballes
STARRING	Weng Weng, Yehlen Catral, Carmi Martin, Anna Marie Gutierrez, Beth Sandoval
COUNTRY	Philippines

For Your Height Only boldly answers the question: What if the ultra-cool super-spy, 007, was a tiny Pilipino man? And it's just as amazing as it sounds. A villain named Mr. Gaint plans to hold the world hostage with the N-bomb. Enter our hero Agent 00 (Weng Weng) who, standing at just three feet tall, proves size isn't everything when it comes to kicking ass and saving the day. Big fun really does come in small packages in this action-packed parody of the insanely popular James Bond films. Even though the film does rely way too heavily on the novelty of its tiny star you can't help but love the delightfully shameless way it rips off the famed franchises while injecting its very own weirdness. The action itself isn't brilliant, as you might expect, but it's entertaining nonetheless, and there is hardly a dull moment to be had. Of course the real magic of this film is its pint sized star, Weng Weng, who, in recent years has become something of a cult icon, and his likeness has spawned a line of merchandise as well as a feature-length documentary. Whether he is flying on a jet pack, fighting kung fu-style, or seducing the ladies, it is nearly impossible not to fall totally in love with the actor. Though it may not reinvent the wheel genre-wise, this film is redeemed by its smooth-talking action hero and its dime store charms that go with it. *For Your Height Only* is *seriously* glorious and needs to be watched at once. Required viewing.

Golden Bat, The, aka Ôgon batto (1966)

DIRECTED BY	Hajime Satô
WRITTEN BY	Susumu Takaku, Takeo Nagamatsu (Creator)
STARRING	Sonny Chiba, Wataru Yamagawa, Osamu Kobayashi, Chako van Leeuwen, Andrew Hughes, Kôsaku Okano, Kôji Sekiyama
COUNTRY	Japan

A grown man in a bat suit fighting crime and protecting the innocent . . . it could only be Golden Bat? Cult star Sonny Chiba of *Kill Bill* fame stars in this far-out action superhero flick. An amateur star-gazer named Akira (Wataru Yamagawa) discovers a planet dubbed Icarus hurdling towards Earth. A group of scientists  headed by Dr. Yamatone (Sonny Chiba), while searching for a mineral to use in a comet destructor machine, stumbles upon a tomb containing . . . you guessed it—the Golden Bat. Only the Bat can save the world from both the planet and a band of aliens.

If you're like me no-budget Japanese space adventures put a great big grin on your face. Well, it doesn't get as cheap, cheesy, and wonderful as *The Golden Bat.* All the hallmarks of crazy J-Action/Sci-Fi are present from the spaceships with visible wires, cheap-looking laser beam effects, and a villain that looks like a plush Beanie Baby reject (serious, this thing is hilarious). You also gotta love the evil henchman who looks like a no-budget *Wolf Man*. For the most part, the movie clips along at a steady pace, but gets bogged down in some repetitiveness and standard clunky sci-fi plot devices. *Golden Bat* is not at all what I'd call a good movie, but it's just bad and endearing enough to be worth watching. All the fun of a terrible Japanese movie with the smooth charms of Sonny Chiba; how could you go wrong?

Hanzo the Razor: Sword of Justice, aka Goyôkiba (1972)

DIRECTED BY	Kenji Misumi
WRITTEN BY	Kazuo Koike, Takeshi Kanda (story by)
STARRING	Shintarô Katsu, Yukiji Asaoka, Mari Atsumi, Kô Nishimura, Akira Yamauchi, Kôji Kobayashi, Daigo Kusano
COUNTRY	Japan

In the mountain of remakes, reboots and, "re-imaginings" few movies stand apart as those nobody in their right mind would have the balls to update. Such is the case with this oddball early-seventies outing based on a Manga by Kazuo Koike whose work *Lone Wolf and Cub* was also turned into a successful film series. Hanzo Itami (Shintarô Katsu) is an Endo officer who sets himself apart from the pack with his upright incorruptible values. He learns that an infamous murderer has escaped from an island prison and, even more disturbing, the cover-up goes all the way to the top. Now it's up to the long "arm of the law" to unravel this mystery and bring order back. *Hanzo* is made up of a trilogy of films so I decided to focus on the very first one, *Sword of Justice*. What sets this film apart from pretty much

every single action/kung fu film is the strange over-the-top sexual overtones.

This stems from our hero's legendary genital, which he beats with a stick (presumably to strengthen it), and has intercourse with a bag of rice. Even stranger than his quirky habits is the way he interrogates his female suspects; namely by forcing them into sex. Once they become instantly hooked on Hanzo's "sword" he withdraws, leaving the girls wanting more, but not until he gets the information he wants. Warped morals aside, the film has a good amount of in-your-face action and some decent twists. The plot itself is far from perfect and could have used more polish and direction. As you may have guessed there is plenty of violence and, of course, copious amounts of bare flesh on display. Despite its twisted values and tepid screenplay, *Hanzo* still manages to set itself apart from the pack and serves up a deliciously weird slice of kung fu eye candy. Not for the easily offended, and you're not likely to find another one like this (expect, of course, for the two sequels). Recommended.

Harry Knuckles and the Pearl Necklace (2004)

DIRECTED BY	Lee Demarbre
WRITTEN BY	Ian Driscoll
STARRING	Phil Caracas, Nancy Riehle, Emma Maloney, Jeff Moffet, Josh Grace, Ian Driscoll, Shana Betz, Patricia Bellemore
COUNTRY	Canada

Director Lee Demarbre followed up his 2001 cult film *Jesus Christ Vampire Hunter* with *Harry Knuckles and the Pearl Necklace,* a film based on two previous short films. Harry Knuckles (Phil Caracas) is tasked with recovering a valuable pearl necklace, which was snatched by a giant Bigfoot creature. But, of course, something more sinister is at "foot," and Knuckles must navigate this mystery as well as countless foes. Despite its shortcomings, I really enjoyed *Jesus Christ Vampire Hunter,* but sadly, the same cannot be said about *Harry Knuckles and the Pearl Necklace.* Lee wisely carries over his Grindhouse style from his previous outing and it perfectly sets a funky retro mood. This film also amps up the weirdness to new heights and pushes the envelope in delightfully tacky humor with some genuinely funny bits. Where this movie really falls apart is its bloated runtime of nearly two hours, Lee's aimless wading through a sea of needless padding, and a totally incoherent plot which goes far beyond convoluted. Scenes go on too long, getting repetitive, and it's hard not to reach for the fast forward button. The humor works at times, but mostly falls flat with running gags that again only serve to stop the plot dead in its tracks rather than move it forward. The whole thing feels like the filmmakers are in on the joke but forget to let the audience in on it as well. I have to admit I was excited when this film first came out as I enjoyed JCVH, but instead of growing and maturing as an artist, the filmmaker's taking a major backslide. The result is a tedious and self-indulgent romp which tries to pile on too many subplots and scenes that simply go nowhere. This film is as entertaining as a Harry Knuckle punch to the face.

Hell Comes to Frogtown (1988)

DIRECTED BY	Donald G. Jackson, R. J. Kizer
WRITTEN BY	Randall Frakes, Donald G. Jackson
STARRING	Roddy Piper, Julius LeFlore, William Smith, Cliff Bermis, Nicolas Worth, Rory Calhoun, Lee Garlington, Sandahl Bergman
COUNTRY	United States

By the late eighties Corman's legendary New World Pictures was sadly going under, but it still managed to produce *Hell Comes to Frogtown*—a wildly absurd little cult classic. After atomic war leaves America a burnt-out wasteland, there is a desperate need for highly fertile males to re-populate. Enter Sam Hell (Roddy Piper) who just so happens to be the man for the job. In exchange for a clean slate from charges, Hell must mate with a group of women. Sounds like quite a sweet deal. The catch is Hell has to help save said women from Frogtown, as they are being held captive by an evil Toad overlord. A movie this wild and silly could only come out of the eighties and, of course, its chock full of cheesy goodness. Surprisingly though, the writing is above what you might expect (despite ripping off *Escape from New York),* and the film manages to not only have great action but some good comedy, which cleverly plays with social and political satire. Wisely, it knows exactly what it is and plays up the camp aspects, always keeping its tongue firmly planted in its cheek. However, as solid as the first two acts are, it begins to get a bit sloppy writing-wise. Once we get to the titular Frogtown things just seemingly happen without any real aim. It is also not immune to some sizeable plot holes; for example, why would they send Hell in in the first place if he was so important? On second thought, I'll let that one slide, since without it, we wouldn't get the machismo brilliance of Sam Hell. Roddy turns in a hammy but solid performance and has charm; good comedic timing coupled with great stunt work no doubt honed from his day job. I was actually surprised that the special effects work holds up well considering the time it was made and the budget. However, some of the villainous toads look rather sloppy. Is this a flawless masterpiece? Sadly, no, but despite its uneven story and effects, it still manages to be a wonderfully weird and entertaining thrill ride. And I dare you not to fall in love with Sam Hell. It's impossible. Come on down to Frogtown.

GOES WELL WITH: *A Boy and His Dog*

Ilsa: Haremkeeper of the Oilsheiks (1976)

DIRECTED BY	Don Edmonds
WRITTEN BY	Langston Stafford
STARRING	Dyanne Thorne, Max Thayer, Jerry Delony, Uschi Digard, Colleen Brennan, Richard Kennedy, Su Ling, George "Buck" Flowers
COUNTRY	Canada, United States

Everyone's favorite well-endowed blonde Ilsa is back for another round of sadism. Ilsa (Dyanne Thorne) has found work as a warden/assistant to a brutal Arab sheik named El Sharif (Jerry Delony). She helps with finding women for Sharif's harem of sex slaves as well as dishing out punishment when needed. A plot is brewing to bring down the sheik that is stock piling valuable oil. Fans of the previous Ilsa film will no doubt notice that the violence has been toned down considerably. This is largely due to the director wanting to achieve a wider release. So, if you're expecting the same level of over-the-top outrageous violence you might be sorely disappointed. The plot isn't exactly brilliant and rehashes elements from the previous film, but thankfully (like *She Wolf*) it plays up the dark humor, camp, and twisted irony. Of course it still has some pretty demented gross-out scenes, even if they are watered down. Highlights include a gruesome castration and a very unlucky girl losing an eyeball. Though I will say these scenes aren't nearly as memorable as *She Wolf*. Dyanne Thorne once again steps into the main role, this time trading her SS uniform for skimpy desert wear. As always, she tackles the role with great sinister vigor, and it's fun to watch her perform. Even though it falls a bit flat at times *Haremkeeper* is just sick and sleazy enough, mixed with black comedy to keep it entertaining.

Ilsa: She Wolf of the SS (1975)

DIRECTED BY	Don Edmonds
WRITTEN BY	Jonah Royston, John C.W. Saxton
STARRING	Dyanne Thorne, Gregory Knoph, Maria Marx, Tony Mumolo, George 'Buck' Flowers, Nicolle Riddell
COUNTRY	Canada, United States

I always cringe when the "producer's disclaimer" pops up before the film claiming this movie is meant to educate us to the horrors of Hitler. Let's get real: this movie is total exploitation-period. The film takes place in the final days of the Third Reich in a place called Camp 9. There, SS officer Ilsa (Dyanne Thorne) sets out to prove, in a series of ghastly experiments, that women can withstand pain better than any man. But, she also has a huge sexual appetite and any man that can't satisfy for gets his . . . member revoked. This all changes when she meets a young man named Wolfe (Gregory Knoph). For anyone brand-new to the Ilsa series, all I can say is strap yourself in for one hell of a wild, trashy, gore-soaked ride. It features grotesque set pieces straight out of a sexual sadist's darkest fantasy. Nothing about this movie is in the least bit subtle and that's more than alright with me. The story isn't exactly brilliant, with a clichéd "escape plot," plot holes, and laughable dialogue, but what the film has going for it is a shameless level of sleaze that is off the charts. Dyanne Thorne gives a tour de force performance as the beautiful, buxom, tough-as-nails SS pussycat. She really lights up the screen in the role and is the stuff of cult infamy. I'm going to mention something most reviews of *Ilsa* fail to mention, which is it's well-shot with some nice compositions, slick camera tricks, and moody atmosphere. And, despite its nasty grisly nature, it has a dark sense of humor and obviously plays up some of the more campy aspects. For example, in Ilsa's room we pan from a picture of an old frowning lady (we assume a relative, maybe a mother) over to her making vigorous love. The ending also has a humorous bit of wicked irony. Fans of splatter will not be disappointed, as this film features plenty of blood, gore, and just plain nasty bits. The violence is so over the top it's almost cartoon-like. Yeah, its not a great movie, but it revels in its own filth, wicked comedy, and over-the-top splatter. In the annals of grimy Grindhouse cinema *Ilsa She Wolf of the SS* ranks as the greatest.

TRIVIA: The producers of *She Wolf* got permission to use the *Hogan's Heroes* set which, at the time, was cancelled. After learning that the script entailed the camp being set ablaze the producers of the show allowed them to use the set in order to save the cost of demolition.

Rob Zombie pays direct homage to this film in his fake trailer for *Werewolf Women of the SS* made for the Tarantino/Rodriguez film *Grindhouse*.

Infra-Man, aka Super Infra-Man, aka Zhong guo chao ren (1975)

DIRECTED BY	Shan Hua
WRITTEN BY	Kuang Ni
STARRING	Danny Lee, Terry Liu, Hsieh Wang, Man-Tzu Yuan, Dana, Wen-Wei Lin, Lu Sheng, Chien-Lung Huang
COUNTRY	Hong Kong

There are scores of ultra-weird superhero films made in Hong Kong and Japan, so much so that one could fill an entire book on those alone. But, how could I not include this colorful action adventure made in the seventies? The evil Princess Dragon Mom (Terry Liu) and her army have risen and are hell-bent on taking over the world. Only Infra-Man can save the day. Director Shan Hua pulls out all the stops with this high-flying superhero movie, which seems like it almost leaped right out of the panels of a comic book. Once you get past its shoddy dialogue and razor-thin plot, which is stripped down to bare basics, there is a lot of fun to be had, even if it's of the so-bad-it's-good variety. Because it's hard not to love an eye-popping, ultra-trippy outing populated by cheap rubber-suited monsters and, of course, a hilarious-looking hero. The look of the film is also pretty great, and the sets (cheap as they are) only enhance the overall hyper-surreal otherworldly quality. It's also worth noting that this movie was very important in its native country of Hong Kong and has spawned countless imitators. Fans of the nineties show *Power Rangers* will no doubt see the influence it must have drawn from this (Princess Dragon Mom and Rita Repulsa could be sisters) and other movies like it. Shortcomings aside, *Infra-Man* has a lot of heart even if it's lacking in other departments, and fans of psychotronic action movies filled with dime-store monsters will find this oddity endlessly watchable. This makes the perfect lazy weekend movie and a must see.

TRIVIA: *Infra-Man* was the first superhero movie made in Hong Kong.

Killing of Satan, The, aka Lumaban ka, Satanas (1983)

DIRECTED BY	Efren C. Piñon
WRITTEN BY	Joe Mari Avellana
STARRING	Ramon Revilla, Elizabeth Oropesa, George Estregan, Paquito Diaz, Cecille Castillo, Charlie Davao
COUNTRY	Philippines

For my money any ultra-low-budget Pilipino movie is at least worth a look, because chances are it's going to be weird and sleazy with some blood thrown in for good measure. *The Killing of Satan* meets all of those standards and then some. A man must take arms against a deadly band of men after the untimely death of his uncle. He must face many deadly foes including the ultimate evil-Satan himself. Fans of the so-bad-it's-great will no doubt find some delirious fun in this bottom-of-the-delete-bin action/adventure "epic" made in the Philippines. As you might expect there is plenty of fist-pounding action, grimy sleaze, and mystical battles between good and evil. In the splatter department it's on the tame side, however, there are some nice nasty bits, the highlight being a gruesome face ripping. The effects, both special and practical, are of course, laughably terrible, making the overall experience all the more satisfying. My biggest issue with this film is the pacing, which at times can be tedious, and movies like this shouldn't be is boring. Thankfully, things do pick up and provide some truly strange and enjoyable moments. *Satan* also utilizes its shooting locations, giving it some production value for its dime (and I really do mean dime). *The Killing of Satan* is recommended only for those truly interested in ultra-trash-action cinema.

Lady Terminator (1989)

DIRECTED BY	H. Tjut Djalil
WRITTEN BY	Karr Kruinowz
STARRING	Barbara Anne Constable, Claudia Angelique Rademarker, Christopher J. Hart, Adam Stardust, Joseph P. McGlynn
COUNTRY	Indonesia

Here is a question for you. What's better than watching a great film? A totally trashy Indonesian knock-off of a great film, that's what. An evil queen vows to get revenge on the relative of the man that defeated her. Flash forward and a peppy anthropology student named Tina (Barbara Anne Constable) ventures where she shouldn't and becomes possessed by the queen's spirit. Now she has her sights on a young pop star named Erica (Claudia Angelique Rademarker), who, you guessed it, is related to the nemesis of the ancient hag. Mayhem ensues as the now-demonic leather-clad Tina goes on an epic killing spree and, of course, lures men to their deaths after passionate sex. Because even a possessed woman on a mission needs to get her grove on. How to describe *Lady Terminator*? Well, imagine someone just finished watching *The Terminator,* then suffered massive head trauma, and shortly after decided to make a movie based on their hazy delirium, taking only key elements from the original source material and adding strange Indonesian folklore, loads of bizarre sexuality, and enough fire power and explosions to excite even Michael Bay.

The plot of what there is is not entirely original and is filled with stock character dialogue that makes no sense and lots of clichés. What this film does right, however, is its sheer hyper-energetic action scenes that are genuinely satisfying to watch and keep the film from becoming dull. The blood and gore is also off the charts and, as the film slips further down the rabbit hole, the manic action and splatter only gets more intense as does the pure insanity. Three words: laser beam eyes. The entire film is coated in these really weird sexual overtones, which only add to

its totally off-the-wall nature. Say what you will about this film, yes it's trashy, sure it's a shameless copy of a much better film (even famously "borrowing" a line), but for pure so-bad-it's-great fun it's hard to find a film that truly tops this. Gather up your friends and some adult beverages because this makes the ultimate guilty pleasure film. Come with me if you wanna be entertained!

Mercenary, The, aka Cannibal Mercenary, aka The Jaguar Project (1983)

DIRECTED BY	Hong Lu Wong
WRITTEN BY	George Lam
STARRING	Alan English, Paul John Stanners, Harry Myles, David Borg, Nian Watts, John Brown
COUNTRY	Thailand

It may not be the first movie to mix the horrors of war with cannibalism but it certainly ranks up there as one of the weirdest. Needing money for his daughter's operation, a man named Wilson (Alan English) leads a group of men into jungles of Vietnam in order to defeat a dangerous drug lord and his men. Little do they know that the drug lord's army is made up of flesh-hungry cannibals looking to put Wilson and his men on the menu. This is the kind of movie I love, as it knows exactly what it is and embraces its own nasty charms. The result is a wonderfully shameless, mindless movie perfect to unwind to. The action is almost nonstop and, considering it's ultra-low-budget, is actually pretty effective with some decent stunt work and fight chorography. And, of course, the film is chock full of nasty filth which just oozes from every frame. For example, there is the infamous scene of lovemaking gone horrible gone. Those who love early '80s cheese and lots of whacky dialogue will find plenty. Where the film falls short is the carnage. While there is some blood, I feel they could have really played up the splatter aspect, and fans of ultra-gore may feel slightly cheated. By no means a classic, *The Mercenary* is a tasty little dish that serves up plenty of cheap thrills and exciting action and, because it's in this book, lots of strangeness. Basically this has everything fans of trashy Grindhouse cinema love. Recommended for lovers of grimy bottom-of-the-barrel fare.

GOES WELL WITH: *Cannibal Apocalypse, We're Going to Eat You*

Mountain of the Cannibal God, aka Slave of the Cannibal God (1979)

DIRECTED BY	Sergio Martino
WRITTEN BY	Sergio Martino
STARRING	Stacy Keach, Ursula Andress, Claudio Cassinelli, Antonio Marsina
COUNTRY	Italy

Italian maestro Sergio Martino takes a bite at the ever-popular cannibal adventure film and it's a cut above the rest. Susan Stevenson (Ursula Andress) is the distressed wife of an anthropologist who went missing in the jungles of New Guinea. She assembles a rag tag team including her brother, Arthur (Antonio Marsina), Dr. Edward Foster (Stacy Keach), an expert in the area, and guide Manolo (Claudio Cassinelli). They believe that the missing man is on a remote part of the jungle which is rumored to be home to a blood-thirsty tribe of cannibals. Now it's a struggle for survival in the harsh landscape as they must worry about dangerous wildlife, not to mention trying not to end up on the menu of a cannibal feast. Martino follows the standard cannibal film blueprint, but like many of his films he takes the DNA of the genre and gives it his very own polished flare. This rousing adventure is better-written than what you might expect, with decent character development and plenty of twists and turns to keep you entertained. The cast is stellar with cult favorite Stacy Keach in the lead. As always, he is fun to watch, and while he may get just a tad bit hammy, overall he gives a solid performance. Sex kitten Ursula Andress adds some much-needed titillation, and Martino takes full advantage of her beauty. Gore-wise the film may be tame compared to say *Cannibal Ferrox,* but fans of hardcore gruesome brutality will not be disappointed. Regrettably, the film has some mild gratuitous animal violence, a typical staple of the genre. Sergio himself has stated in interviews he tacked these on due to a demand from the distributors. To Martino's credit, most of it was simply footage of natural wildlife activity, something that happens if the cameras are rolling or not. However you feel about it, there is no denying it certainly adds an extremely uncomfortable element. Martino's film may follow a familiar formula, but he improves upon the standard flesh-munching fare with a more refined script, filled with adventure, bloody violence, and some weird set pieces. *Mountain of the Cannibal God* is a fun and underrated little morsel that should be consumed by all film fans.

Oldboy, aka Oldeuboi (2003)

DIRECTED BY	Chan-wook Park
WRITTEN BY	Chan-wook Park, Chun-hyeong Lim, Jo yun Hwang, Joon-hyung Lim, Nobuaki Minegishi (based on Manga by)
STARRING	Min-sik Choi, Ji-tae Yu, Hye-jeong Kang, Dae-han Ji, Byeong-ok Kim, Dal-su Oh, Jin-seo Yoon, Yeon-suk Ahn
COUNTRY	South Korea

Remakes? We don't need no stinkin' remakes. Chan-wook Park's original epic doesn't hold a candle to the pointless re-hash made in 2013. A man named Dae-su Oh (Min-sik Choi) is kidnapped one rainy night and put inside a strange prison. He doesn't know why he is imprisoned but only that he must fight to keep both his strength and sanity. After fifteen long years he is released, and what plays out is a strange game of cat-and-mouse as he tries to unravel the mystery of why he was put into confinement and, more importantly, who did it. But things only get worse as he gets closer to the truth. Park's ultra-brutal meditation (based on Nobuaki Minegishi's successful Manga) elevates itself above merely showcasing mindless violence by injecting a harrowing and thought-provoking story filled with rich and complex characters. He effortlessly builds a spider web-like mystery while creating a great deal of tension and emotional weight through lines. Much like his Italian counterparts, Bava and Argento, Park has a distinct visual flare that enhances the already brilliant screenplay and gives the film a dark poetic vibe. *Oldboy* features possibly one of the greatest fight scenes ever committed to celluloid. Its amazingly raw, brutal, and exciting, yet takes a less stylized matter-of-fact approach. The film also features plenty of nasty violence, the most infamous being the hammer scene, which you're unlikely to forget anytime soon. Grim, disturbing, exciting, and thought-provoking, Chan-wook Park further cements himself among the greats with this action thriller. So forget the remake and go straight for the real deal. *Oldboy* is required viewing as is most of Chan-wook Park's body of work.

Riki-Oh: The Story of Ricky (1991)

DIRECTED BY	Ngai Choi Lam (credited as Simon Nam)
WRITTEN BY	Ngai Choi Lam, Masahiko Takajo (story) Tetsuya Saruwatari (based on Manga by)
STARRING	Siu-Wong Fan, Mei Sheng Fan, Ka-Kui Ho, Yukari Oshima, Kan-Wing Tsang, Kwok-Pong Chan
COUNTRY	Hong Kong

The world can be a harsh place, so sometimes it's necessary to escape by popping in an action film, switching off your brain, and letting its high-octane carnage carry you away. This is certainly that kind of movie. Set in the year 2001 AD, prisons are now privatized corporations and teeming with greed and corruption. Enter a savior in the form of a young inmate named Riki-Oh (Siu-Wong Fan), who seems to be destined to topple the evil regime using his special super-human strength. I call this a mindless film, but I don't mean that in a negative way. In fact, I think this is a wildly entertaining film. Director Ngai Choi Lam manages to taps into the ultra-weird that rival the likes of early Peter Jackson, all while outdoing him in terms of outlandish violence. It's not hard to believe this film was based on a popular Manga, and indeed the film feels like you're watching a live-action comic book filled with loads of gore, crazy villains, and nonstop kung fu action. One thing is clear: nothing is subtle about this film. Part of its fun is the absurd, over-the-top nature. It also does a novel attempt at developing character background and motivations, and this provides a nice balance to the mad cap slaughter and goofy bad guys. Though, sadly, it doesn't go as in-depth as the Manga does. As I stated above, the mayhem is cranked to eleven and, considering this was done on a low budget, the gore is rather effective-looking. Some of the practical effects, however, are a bit dated but, for me, it doesn't detract and only adds to its B-film charm. I'm always impressed when a movie can show me something new. For example, I've never seen someone literally punch someone apart before. *Riki-Oh* doesn't aim for high art but merely acts as a wonderfully insane escape from humdrum life. Highly recommended for anyone with eyeballs.

Robo Geisha (2009)

DIRECTED BY	Noboru Iguchi
WRITTEN BY	Noboru Iguchi
STARRING	Aya Kiguchi, Hitomi Hasebe, Shôko Nakahara, Takumi Saitô,Suzuki Matsuo, Cay Izumi, Kentarô Shimazu
COUNTRY	Japan

From the director of *Machine Girl* and *Mutant Girl Squad* comes another highly bonkers female-driven action comedy. Two sisters find themselves as strange cybernetic Geishas run by a businessman and his son. They are tasked with killing terrorists only to find out the real danger lies with their employers. Butt swords, acid-spraying breast milk, and blood-spewing buildings; it must be a Noboru Iguchi film. The whacky premise, at times, slightly gets away from itself, but surprisingly Iguchi is able to rein in all the crazy into a workable, mostly coherent screenplay. Much like *Dead Sushi,* the insane story is given a much needed balance with some emotional weight and character development. At times, however it goes a bit too overboard with the sappy, especially the ending, which is so sweet it may hurt your teeth. Also, it tends to get a bit repetitive at times and would have benefitted greatly from a trim. But, of course, the saving grace is the ever-increasingly insane set pieces which help keep things entertaining. Iguchi delivers pulse-pounding, full-throttle action sequences that are equal parts outrageous and satisfying. The violence, of which there is plenty, is as you might have guessed: cartoon-like, keeping with the movie's overall feel. Sadly, poor-looking CGI tends to take one out of the action. Like a lot of Noboru's films, *Robo Geisha* manages to take a somewhat all-over-the-place script and make it work (mostly), and viewers are in for a ride that is clever, bizarre, and engaging. This is the droid you're looking for.

Turkey Shoot, aka Escape 2000, aka Blood Camp Thatcher (1982)

DIRECTED BY	Brian Trenchard Smith
WRITTEN BY	Jon George, Neil D. Hicks, George Schenck (story), Robert Williams (story), David Lawrence (story)
STARRING	Olivia Hussey, Steve Railsback, Michael Craig, Carmen Duncan, Roger Ward, Noel Ferrier, Lynda Stoner
COUNTRY	Australia

Legendary cult director Brian Trenchard Smith puts a delightfully crazy spin on *The Most Dangerous Game*. Set in a future society that is run by a cruel corrupt form of government which rules with an iron fist, anyone who doesn't conform to their standards is shipped off to a re-education camp run by Charles Thatcher (Michael Craig) and his brutal warders. A group of such society "misfits" are rounded up and soon learn that beatings, rape, and brutal treatment are an everyday way of life. As if it couldn't get any worse, a select few are chosen to be hunted as sport by wealthy weirdos to slate their bloodlust. With tongue planted firmly in cheek this action film offers plenty of thrills but also injects a lot of sly social commentary about how the rich powers that be target the everyday working stiff, and it's certainly telling that the main villain is named Thatcher. Wisely, the message never gets too preachy, and Smith delivers his usual level of action and enough strangeness to keep film junkies glued to the screen. And, while not super gory, the film does have a lot of cartoon-style violence with some really memorable nasty bitse. *Turkey Shoot* does suffer from wildly uneven story and tone, but when you consider the troubled production and numerous re-writes it's a miracle it ended up being as entertaining as it is. The cast is interesting with character actor Steve Railsback giving a solid (albeit strange) performance as the male lead. But it's the prim and proper Olivia Hussey who is really surprising, as you'd never expect to see her in a film like this. Hussey gives the material her all, especially considering she reportedly hated doing it. I think she's great and her unexpected presence further enhances the film's odd vibes. With lots of in-your-face action, black comedy, and a healthy dose of brutality, this film is never dull and endlessly watchable.

Virgins from Hell, aka Maidens Revenge (1987)

DIRECTED BY	Ackyl Anwari
STARRING	Enny Beatrice, Yenny Farida, Harry Capri, Nina Anwar, August Melasz, Yetty Loren, Debby Ratnam
COUNTRY	Indonesia

Indonesian cinema is pretty wild, and they certainly don't mess around when it comes to producing a high-octane thrill ride—even if it's on a laughable budget. What it may lack in money it makes up for in mind-blowing, groin-kicking action. After a drug lord brutally kills their mother and father two sisters form an all-girl gang with the sole purpose to get revenge upon him and his henchmen. However, the gang is captured, and they must use everything they got, including seduction, to free themselves and bring down his evil empire. The film wastes zero time in cranking up the explosive action but, sadly, this is one of the film's major flaws. It's no doubt fun to watch, but with too much action happening at the beginning, the result is a film that is top heavy, leaving the third act stagnant. It also doesn't exactly try and re-invent the wheel with a stock character bad guy with evil henchmen and a groovy-yet-totally-impractical lair/hideout which just happens to be outfitted with a cave-like dungeon, as they always do. Flaws aside, I found *Virgins from Hell* to be great fun. Imagine a wonderfully lurid comic book come to life and smashing into your living room with female fury and guns 'a blazing. I also dug the fact that, while this is part exploitation, it does feature a lot of female empowerment and, even though there is a "hero" male scientist character, the women are solely responsible for bringing down the drug lord. Even with a somewhat sluggish third act this film still manages to be highly entertaining with enough action, sleaze, and heaping helpings of explosions, cat fights, and splatter to keep fans coming back for more.

Warrior, The, aka Jaka Sembung (1981)

DIRECTED BY	Sisworo Gautama Putra
WRITTEN BY	Darto Juned
STARRING	Barry Prima, Eva Arnaz, Dana Christina, Dicky Zulkarnaen, Rukman Herman, W.D. Mochtar, Dorman Borisman
COUNTRY	Indonesia

Barry Prima, the go-to actor for gonzo action adventure, stars in *The Warrior*, another kick-to-the-face action flick in the vein of *The Devil's Sword*. Indonesia is a country torn by conflict, with its citizens in poverty and desperation. A rebel by the name of Djaka Semboeng (Barry Prima) rises as a savior. The powers that be do not like this and hire a deadly assassin to kill him. As you might expect, *Warrior* delivers on some great ass-kicking action and plenty of nice splatter. The story itself, while not heavy on plot, has more substance than you might expect, with some attempts at character development. Pointed social and political commentary blends surprisingly well with the film's more fantastical elements, giving it a somewhat grounded feel. The practical and special effects range from decent to downright laughable, but fans of Indo action (myself included) wouldn't have it any other way. With that being said, I was delighted by some really slick-looking trick photography, such as the headless villain. It, of course, has a generous helping of LSD-like weirdness, such as a wonderful human-to-pig transformation, floating heads, etc. Without spoiling a thing, I will say that the finale ends on a tragic, even operatic, note, which really took me by surprise in a good way. *The Warrior* is a fist-flying, blood-spewing bit of Indo cheese that deserves, no, demands you to watch it.

We're Going to Eat You!, aka Di yu wu men, aka Hell Has No Gates (1980)

DIRECTED BY	Tsui Hark
WRITTEN BY	Tsui Hark
STARRING	Norman Chu, Eddy Ko, Melvin Wong, Fung Fung, Kwok Choi Hon, Mo Lin Cheung
COUNTRY	Hong Kong

What do you get when you take a dash of *Cannibal Holocaust,* a pinch of over-the-top slapstick, and a generous helping of knuckle-crunching kung fu? Well, you have a recipe for a very strange genre-bending film. Secret Agent 999 (Norman Chu) is on the hunt for a criminal named Rolex (Melvin Wong). His search leads him to a mysterious island populated by men and women who have an insane craving for human flesh. The leader of this group, known only as Chief (Eddy Ko), keeps the people in line with an iron fist and gives them only small rations of the sweet meat when they are lucky enough to get tourists. Soon, the hard-boiled agent must form an unlikely alliance with Rolex in order to make it off the island in one piece and not in a pot of stew.

This was director Tsui Hark's second film and the first I had ever seen. It seemed like this had the makings of a really great film but, sadly, like so many new filmmakers, Hark seems to have had a lot of great ideas but didn't know how to make them mesh well. What we get is a film with an identity crisis. It's a cannibal film comedy with lots of kung fu, and it also has elements of detective work, and why not include a giant psycho-nymphomaniac for good measure? True splatterheads will be disappointed, as this film has gore, but not nearly as much as you'd want to see in a movie of this kind. What gives this film a much needed boost is the extremely well-done kung fu fight sequences that never disappoint.

I'll be honest. Even though this movie is a great big mess it's also hard to outright hate it. And what it lacks in direction it makes up for in quirky charm which falls under the so-bad-it's-fun category. I can also say that it had my head spinning by the end which is an admirable feat. So if it's a tasty treat you're seeking, filled with high-flying action, gore, and some strange humor, get your fill Hong Kong-style.

TRIVIA: Corey Yuen, the film's martial arts choreographer, has gone on to an amazing career working on such films as *Bulletproof Monk, The One,* and *Transporter 2,* just to name a few.

CHAPTER 2

Who doesn't enjoy an awesome car or biker film? The sound of the roaring engine, the images so vivid you could swear you can smell the exhaust fumes rolling off the blacktop pavement. Seriously, who wouldn't want to drop everything and watch something like the satirical *Deathrace 2,000* or *Race with the Devil?* I felt like the car movies deserved their very own chapter because lumping them in elsewhere would seem to me to be a huge injustice. Inside, you'll find the leather-clad, drag-racing honeys from Russ Myers' skin-tastic *Faster, Pussycat! Kill! Kill!* or the all-female biker gang The Maneaters in H.G. Lewis's off-the-rails biker film. Everything from Jean-Luc Godard's classic *Weekend* to a mostly naked David Carradine in the laughable *Deathsport,* truly a diverse group of films gathered here. I only wish I could have found more movies to fit into this chapter, but I think it's a nice break from the standard genre chapters. Much like the action chapter, I want to stress just how badass and fearless these stunt drivers were, and without people like Grant Page these movies wouldn't have the magic that they do. They truly are the unsung heroes of Grindhouse cinema. So hop in, get your motors going, rev those engines, and try not to hit anyone unless you're racking up points in *Death Race*. And for Godzilla's sake, enjoy the ride! (Bonus points if you get that reference)

Cars, Trucks, and Choppers

Car, The (1977)

DIRECTED BY	Elliot Silverstein
WRITTEN BY	Dennis Shryack, Michael Butler, Lane Slate
STARRING	James Brolin, Kathleen Lloyd, John Marley, RG Armstrong, John Rubinstein, Roy Jenson, Kim Richards
COUNTRY	United States

Move over Christine, you're not the only evil car to come barreling out of hell firing on all cylinders. The peace of a sleepy Utah town is rocked when a mysterious sleek black car drives into town, leaving in its wake a trail of death and destruction. But, can the simple cop Wade (James Brolin) restore the law and order of the small town, or is the evil-in-chrome unstoppable? *The Car* is a nonstop action-packed thrill ride and a deliciously guilty pleasure. Heading up a solid cast is a pre-*Amityville* James Brolin who really brings his A-game to material which can admittedly be hokey at best. His brand of seventies sex appeal and swagger makes him a perfect choice for the officer. Of course, the main star is really the car, which was custom built by the legendary George Barris. Unlike the sleek and sexy Christine, Barris's steel mean machine is a wonderfully sinister presence paramount to the film. I love how this film plays with the concept of Satanism but never really gives a clear-cut answer to why these attacks are happening. Much like Hitchcock's *The Birds* it seemingly comes out of the blue to judge the citizens. It's also full of totally bizarre dialogue like when a rather large angry woman shouts, *"Cat pooh!"* at the villainous car. Who says something like that? Clearly, Elliot Silverstein can handle not only the film's pulse-pounding action but the more surreal aspects as well, making for the perfect hot rod hybrid. Elliot wisely highlights the desert locations which help give the film a heavy sense of dread and foreboding. Sure, the film is cheesy with some large gaps in logic, but it's really hard to hate it because it's so damned entertaining in a basic way. So if you're looking for an evil car movie with plenty of mayhem and some damn good acting, park your butt right here and take this car for a spin. If you dare!

TRIVIA: The look of the titular car has been spoofed in the hit show *Futurama* in the episode "The Honking."

Not only is director Guillermo de Toro a huge fan of this film, he had a replica of the car made for his personal use.

GOES WELL WITH: *Duel, Spasm*

Cars That Ate Paris, The, aka The Cars That Ate People (American Re-issue) (1974)

DIRECTED BY	Peter Weir
WRITTEN BY	Peter Weir, Keith Gow (story), Piers Davies (story)
STARRING	John Meillon, Terry Camilleri, Kevin Miles, Rick Scully, Max Gillies, Bruce Spence, Danny Adcock
COUNTRY	Australia

The Cars that Ate Paris, later re-titled The Cars that Ate People, is often cited as the first in a series of car-based movies made in Australia, which would reach its zenith in popularity with the Mad Max series. In the small town of Paris, Australia, the people have a rather morbid way of earning a living, notably causing horrific car wrecks and selling the scraps. Arthur Waldo (Terry Camilleri) and his brother fall victim to this scheme, leaving Arthur banged up and his brother dead. Now it seems he must remain in the small town, which he begins to realize is deeply disturbed. Peter Weir, probably best-known for The Truman Show, rolls out a darkly funny film that gleefully satirizes Australia's love affair with cars, while also injecting some smart social commentary. Weir often explores stories about outsiders or off-beat characters, and this definitely has them in spades. Another Weir trademark pops up in the form of pitch-black, even cynical, humor played up by the quirky residents, and it's this aspect that really gives the movies its wry charm. The film seems to suggest an allegory on small town community yet it's too muddled by other subplots to fully realize this idea. Still, its ever-increasing insanity ensures that there is never a dull moment to be had. Kick it into high gear and prepare yourself for this brilliantly quirky black comedy that is wildly entertaining and endlessly re-watchable.

TRIVIA: Paying homage to kicking off the Car series, Mad Max: Fury Road features a car very similar to the spiked vehicle featured heavily in the film.

Crash (1996)

DIRECTED BY	David Cronenberg
WRITTEN BY	David Cronenberg, J.G. Ballard (based on novel by)
STARRING	James Spader, Holly Hunter, Elias Koteas, Deborah Kara Unger, Rosanna Arquette, Peter MacNeil
COUNTRY	Canada

I have a fondness for nineties cinema, not only because it was a decade I grew up in, but it was a time when a lot of exciting new filmmakers were coming onto the scene. However, David Cronenberg, someone who has been making his own brand of strange art for thirty some years at this point, made some of the ballast films to come out of the decade, such as *Naked Lunch* and, of course, *Crash*.

Film producer James Ballard (James Spader) is in a horrific auto accident. While recovering he meets Vaughan (Elias Koteas), who introduces him into an underground world where crashes aren't something to fear but rather a source of extreme sexual pleasure. Part of what makes Cronenberg such a dangerous director is he boldly and unashamedly takes the audience into some very dark places that many of us would rather not go and holds up a mirror to our deeply hidden ugly inner selves. He brilliantly injects his trademark  "Body Horror" into an exhaust-fueled nightmarish landscape of twisted managed steel and hot sweaty orgasms. He wisely uses Spader as a sort of viewpoint character, and we enter this fetish-laden world viewed through his eyes. But of course even Ballard takes the plunge. After this point there is no sane character left, which may be unsettling for some viewers. Most mainstream film-goers will notice the film has no real story arc; rather it's a snapshot into the lives of some really disturbed people who find satisfaction in horrible things. And really, who doesn't love a twisted movie about perverts? Cronenberg constantly proves himself to be one of the boldest filmmakers working in the medium and, while this film may never be as popular or "mainstream" as *The Fly*, it's still every bit as good as anything he's done to date. Screw *Fifty Shades of Grey*—this is the real deal.

Dead End Drive-In (1986)

DIRECTED BY	Brian Trenchard Smith
WRITTEN BY	Peter Smalley, Peter Carey (story)
STARRING	Ned Manning, Peter Whitford, Dave Gibson, Natalie McCurry, Wilbur Wilde, Ollie Hall, Lyn Collingwood
COUNTRY	Australia

If it's weird, full-throated, metal-crunching action, it's gotta be Brian Trenchard Smith. In a burnt-out future overrun by roving gangs, the only escape is the Star Drive-In. A young man named Jimmy "Crabs" (Ned Manning) and his girlfriend, Carmen (Natalie McCurry), go out one night for a double bill and some physical activity. They find out too late that they just drove willingly into a concentration camp for outcasts and troublemakers. Even stranger is that most don't want to leave, as they are supplied with drugs, booze, junk food, and of course, films. Of all the films to emerge in the wake of *Mad Max* success, Brian Trenchard Smith's *Dead End Drive-In* is a wonderfully wild, darkly humorous, and action-packed thrill ride.

The whole premise has a wicked irony, especially when you consider that all the subjects not only willingly trap themselves, but that their lives are seemingly so much better that they make no effort to escape. This is where its brilliantly pointed social commentary comes into play. It's this and its slick style which really saves the film from its sometimes-underwhelming plot. I also loved Smith's *Turkey Shoot* playing at the drive-in, which makes for a nice inside joke, but also works as foreshadowing. And, of course, it has plenty of twisted metal crashing to please any Ozzy fans. *Drive-In* is by no means perfect, but it's damned entertaining and has something to say to boot.

Death Race 2000 (1975)

DIRECTED BY	Paul Bartel
WRITTEN BY	Robert Thorn, Charles Griffith, Ib Melchior (based on story by)
STARRING	David Carradine, Sylvester Stallone, Mary Woronov, Louisa Moritz, Martin Kove, Roberta Collins, Fred Grandy
COUNTRY	United States

Roger Corman produced this wildly entertaining sci-fi action helmed by Paul Bartel, a bright talent in the Corman family. Cult fans will no doubt recall his roles in such classics as *Eating Raoul, Gremlins 2, The Usual Suspects,* and his stepping behind the camera for *Private Parts, Lust in the Dust,* etc. Though he did many great things, Bartel's crowning achievement has to be *Death Race 2000.* In a dystopian future the national sport is not baseball, but rather a deadly game called Death Race. The game is simple: racers hit pedestrians, which are worth an allotted point. Whichever driver kills the most people wins. Its brightest star, known as Frankenstein (David Carradine), is hell-bent on bringing down the corrupt government and the game. The biggest strength in *Death Race 2000* is its wickedly dark humor which elevates a good concept into a brilliant one. Taking this a step further is its clever satirical and sardonic comment on politics, religion, and society at large. But like any good Corman-produced film, the entertainment is front and center. Pulse-pounding driving stunts, cartoon-style violence, as well as a host of colorful characters guarantees there is never a dull moment to be had. The cast is incredible, with genre favorites David Carradine, Mary Woronov, and an early role for Sylvester Stallone. While the remake, *Death Race,* is fun in its own way, it doesn't really capture the magic and energy of Bartel's film. Required viewing.

TRIVIA: Cowriter Charles Griffith penned such classic Roger Corman films as *Little Shop of Horrors, It Conquered the World, Attack of the Crab People,* etc.

The role of Frankenstein was first offered to Peter Fonda who promptly passed.

Roger Corman actually drove in certain scenes.

Deathsport (1978)

DIRECTED BY	Allan Arkush, Nicholas Niciphor
WRITTEN BY	Nicholas Niciphor, Donald Stewart, Frances Doel (story)
STARRING	David Carradine, Richard Lynch, Claudia Jennings, William Smithers, Will Walker, Jesse Vint
COUNTRY	United States

Producer and king of the B's Roger Corman wanted to cash in on the unexpected hit of *Death Race 2000* and rushed out this weird science fiction action film starring a loin-clothed David Carradine. Set in a future devastated by war and now ruled by a totalitarianism form of government, the citizens play a game called Deathsport, where prisoners fight for their very freedom. Fans of *Death Race 2000*, expecting more of the same exhaust-fueled action, biting satire, and wonderful carnage will be sadly disappointed with this horribly uneventful film. *Deathsport* muddles through a needlessly convoluted plot that is a strange sword-and-sandals "epic" blended with biker apocalyptic science fiction. You can't help but feel a tad bit sorry for Carradine and Lynch; even these solid actors can't seem to muster up even a phoned-in performance. Clearly they knew how terrible it all was, but obviously the paycheck wasn't.

As you might expect the special effects and makeup are super dated and cheesy and some are so laughable you can't believe someone behind the camera actually said, 'yeah that's good, perfect, print it!' Even its sound design is borrowed heavily from *Star Wars*. But I think all of this could have been easily forgiven but for the fact that it takes itself far too seriously without ever injecting humor or any political satire that the plot suggests it would be rife with. But surely there are enough badass riding scenes to make this watchable? Sadly, it doesn't even get that right with tepid stunts that wouldn't thrill an eight-year-old child. This film is truly strange, though, and features mutants, laser motorcycles, and of course, some really weird and random fetishes like torture scenes. All of this seems like it would equal so-bad-it's-good gold, but it's so terribly boring and uninteresting that it even fails on that level. It's like the filmmakers went out of their way to make every single thing unremarkable. If you're a hardcore trash fan and dare to view it anyway I'd recommend a couple cold drinks to help ease the hurt. Better yet, just watch *Death Race 2000*—a far better film.

TRIVIA: According to co-director Allan Arkush, actor David Carradine was high on pot for most of the filming.

The motorcycles used in the film were modified Yamahas.

Faster, Pussycat! Kill! Kill! (1965)

DIRECTED BY	Russ Meyers
WRITTEN BY	Jackie Morgan, Russ Meyers (story)
STARRING	Tura Satana, Lori Williams, Haji, Sue Bernard, Ray Barlow, Paul Trinka, Dennis Busch, Michael Finn
COUNTRY	United States

It's really impossible to stress just how amazing and ahead of its time Russ Meyers' leather-clad female flick *Faster, Pussycat! Kill! Kill!* was. Decades after its release it's still being talked about and, more importantly, watched. Three go-go dancers hold a young girl hostage after the leader, Varla (Tura Satana), kills her boyfriend. Out in the desert, however, they discover an old man living with his sons and, rumor has it, he has a large sum of money hidden. Now the girls set their sights on the old man and his loot. Sexploitation master Russ Meyers' drive-in epic explodes like a powder keg of in-your-face sexuality and revved-up action unlike anything before it. The plot seems fairly straightforward and even predictable until the addition of the creepy desert-dwelling family, and the film almost slides into full-on horror territory. But, of course, Meyers gives his target audience what they really want, which is copious amounts of gyrating flesh, heavy petting, violence, and exhaust fumes. It also has a sly bit of commentary on the growing feminist movement, and indeed it straddles a weird line between exploitation and female empowerment. Besides some great action it has some wonderful dark humor and unintentional camp, especially from some of the performances. And speaking of acting, Tura Satana really shines in the role which made her an icon among genre fans. Often copied but never duplicated *Faster, Pussycat! Kill! Kill!* is without a doubt one of the greatest Grindhouse films ever made. Period.

TRIVIA: The band *The Cramps* covers the title song on their live album *Smell of Female.*

Director Quentin Tarantino is a huge fan and included a nod to the film in 2007's *Death Proof* in which the character named Shanna wears a shirt with Tura Satana on it.

Actor Tura Satana legally owned the rights to her likeness and image. This was smart as she received money from merchandise as well as re-releases, etc.

Dialogue from the film is sampled in White Zombie's song *Thunder Kiss '65* as well as *Black Sunshine.*

Killdozer (1974)

DIRECTED BY	Jerry London
WRITTEN BY	Theodore Sturgeon, Ed Mackillop, Hebert F. Solow
STARRING	Clint Walker, Carl Betz, Neville Brand, James Wainwright, Robert Urich, James A. Watson Jr.
COUNTRY	United States

Dear people of the seventies, what exactly were you smoking when you came up with the idea for *Killdozer*? Also, did the people who green lit it share? On a Pacific island a small construction crew finds themselves being hunted by a large bulldozer. Why? Because of space-related reasons, or something. Okay, I'm having a bit of flippant fun with this film but it's one of those oddball movies you just cannot wrap your mind around why it exists. But you're happy it does nonetheless. Its zero budget mixed with hilarious melodrama, poor acting, and ridiculous plot make up for the lack of an actual story. There really is nothing to this movie expect for men fighting and talking interspersed with a loud killer bulldozer and some mild action. This makes for some great mindless entertainment and the perfect thing to watch on a rainy weekend. So, if you need to turn off your brain for some cheesy seventies cinema this dozer's for you. Contact high from its fumes not included.

Mad Foxes, aka Los violadores (1981)

DIRECTED BY	Paul Grau
WRITTEN BY	Paul Grau, Hans Walthard, Jaime Jesús Balcázar
STARRING	José Gras, Laura Premica, Andrea Albani, Peter John Saunders, Hank Sutter, Garry Membrini, Ana Roca
COUNTRY	Spain, Switzerland

Director Paul Grau may have directed only two films in his career but he certainly gave us something wild with his nasty biker thriller *Mad Foxes*. A man's girlfriend is brutally raped by a Nazi biker gang. It's made all the more horrific as it happens on the girl's 18th birthday, and she was a virgin. What ensues is a chain reaction of savage revenge, leaving many bloody bodies in its wake. Grau really amps of the sleaze in this in-your-face biker-rape-revenge action flick. It not only doesn't shy away from vile and uncomfortable moments, it seems to revel in them. He certainly caters to the gore crowd as the film features lots of nice gross-out, splattery moments. This, coupled with some decent stunts makes this a must for the Grindhouse set. It also features a perfectly bleak ending which fits the film's nihilistic tone. As entertaining as the film is it does have a lull in the action and, seeing how the entire runtime is just under eighty minutes, it doesn't help. Grimy, action-packed, kinky sex, and biker mayhem—what more could a Mondo fan ask for? *Mad Foxes* is a biker film worth taking for a spin.

TRIVIA: Actor José Gras is no stranger to cult films having roles in Bruno Matteri's *Hells of the Living Dead* and Lucio Fulci's *Conquest* among others.

Pink Angels, The, aka Pink Angels (1972)

DIRECTED BY	Larry G. Brown
WRITTEN BY	Margaret McPherson
STARRING	Bruce Kimball, John Alderman, Tom Basham, Henry Olek, Dan Haggerty, Michael Pataki, Maurice Warfield
COUNTRY	United States

Biker films have been a time-honored tradition in American cinema and pop culture since they first roared into cinemas, exciting teenagers and frightening their parents. Could this be the weirdest biker film yet? Well, I honestly haven't seen one that tops this one. A band of transvestite bikers are blazing across the country to a drag show in L.A. As they go on their journey they meet various people like other bikers, police, etc., who give them plastic hassles. Many times after I watch a film it's crystal-clear who the target audience is. But it's rare when a film baffles me as to who they were marketing it towards. Such is the case with the 1972 biker oddity *Pink Angels,* which seems to be a film without an audience. Sure you'd think it was targeted towards the chopper community, however, most rough-and-tumble bikers at the time wouldn't be interested in a plot about effeminate men traveling cross-country, so it's not for them. But of course, it's made for the LGBTQ community. Think again. The depiction of gay men is highly insulting and overly stereotypical with everyone as flaming drag queens. Further more, any notion it was geared towards a gay audience is totally stomped out by its pitch-black whiplash ending. But you might be saying, "Hey maybe it's meant to be a sly satire of the biker genre?" Well, sadly, no, it doesn't work as either a parody or satire, which is a shame because it's a genre that would be ripe for ribbing. The film aimlessly goes from one outrageous scene to the next while stretching its plot to the limit with some very dated humor.

So why watch *Pink Angels*? Because it's so off-the-charts nuts that it's something you need to see to believe. Adding to the weirdness is seeing Dan Haggerty of *Grizzly Adams* fame makes an appearance, but sadly not as a pink angel. Also, I can't stress how truly jolting the ending is, which comes completely out of left field and crushes any of the lighthearted tone of the entire film. *Pink Angels* is not a good movie with a weak plot, and its caricature of gay men is about as shameless as Mickey Rooney's Mr. Yunioshi stereotype of Japanese Americans in *Breakfast at Tiffany's*. It does manage to have some redeeming value with loads of insanity, camp, and an overall so-bad-it's-good quality. Who is this film for? As it turns out it just might be for the truly adventurous trash seeker who is brave enough to climb aboard and take it for a joy ride.

Psychomania, aka Death Wheelers, The (1973)

DIRECTED BY	Don Sharp
WRITTEN BY	Julian Zimet, Arnaud d'Usseau
STARRING	George Sanders, Beryl Reid, Nicky Henson, Mary Larkin, Roy Holder, Robert Hardy, Patrick Holt
COUNTRY	Britain

In the wake of George A. Romero's seminal horror classic *Night of the Living Dead* many horror directors took a bite at the undead subgenre. After all, George himself simply (and brilliantly) re-invented an already-existing horror premise dating back to the dawn of cinema. Hammer director Don Sharp put his own 'spin' on the living dead with his 1973 film *Psychomania*. Tom (Nicky Henson) is the leader of the gang, "The Living Dead," whose chief activities include semi-destructive mayhem to outright murder. But, like any young man, he longs for the day him and his girlfriend, Abby (Mary Larkin), can die together and come back, untouchable to the law of man. It just so happens that his mother is a spiritualist and has the key to coming back from the dead. "Just believe really hard and it'll work." Yep, that's all it takes. Seriously. So you pretty much know where the film goes from here. Bad boy Tom comes back from the dead and invites his gang members to join in, but of course Abby has reservations. Before I get down to business, one thing: upon reviewing a film I go into it with high hopes. However, it's really hard to put a positive spin on a film this unremarkable, wasting a lot of untapped potential. The plot is wildly contrived with uneven tones and plot holes. I could forgive all that, but it's so lazily done. The idea of undead bikers brought back from the dead to raise hell suggests a wild gory and fun romp, however . . . what we have here is cinematic wallpaper, because even when things are happening they're not really happening. Even the murders that take place are so uninteresting that it's comical. It doesn't attempt to shock, or, at the very least, pander to the gore crowd. Worse yet, it tries to shoehorn in a romantic subplot which doesn't work, largely due to Henson and Larkin having zero chemistry. *Psychomania* doesn't play up its weird card that it sets up in the beginning and, instead, we get a dull and tepid film that is confused in its message and bogged down in its own ineptitude. I really wanted this film to be a rip-roaring high-flying take on the zombie genre but it's not nearly as fun as its poster art might suggest. Dead on arrival and not worth digging up.

She-Devils on Wheels (1968)

DIRECTED BY	Herschell Gordon Lewis
WRITTEN BY	Allison Louise Downe, Fred M. Sandy (story idea)
STARRING	Betty Connell, Nancy Lee Nobel, Christie Wagner, Rodney Bedell, Pat Poston, John Weymer
COUNTRY	United States

The "Godfather of gore," H.G. Lewis, was known for his outrageous and groundbreaking splatter cinema like *Blood Feast,* but he also broke into other genres and tried to keep up with the cinema trends. At the time, motorcycle films were all the rage. Of course, Lewis puts his own personal spin on the subgenre and the result is something altogether weird, wild, and trashy goodness. Lovely, stylish, and deadly Queen (Betty Connell) is the leader of "The

Maneaters," an all-female gang of bike-riders, and they prove that they are tough enough to hang with the big boys. We observe their club rituals, including a drunken orgy and, of course, lots of racing. But, it's all-out war between their rival gang, "The Hot-Riders." Herschell Gordon Lewis pokes a bit of fun at the normally male-dominated genre and wisely plays up the role reversal for all it's worth. A line that sums this up comes from a female biker who laments that they treat men just like slabs of beef. Betty Connell hams it up as Queen, the ultra-fierce leader and, in my opinion, is every much a female B-Icon as Tura Satana. While there is some violence, it's relatively tame when you compare it to Lewis's other films; however, there is some blood and a very nice decapitation to keep splatterheads' motors going. *Devils* lacks a lot in the story department, setting up dramatic elements and never fully realizing them. The ending also feels terribly anticlimactic. Still, I have an incredible fondness for this film, warts and all. The concept of an all-female biker gang is way ahead of its time and something you rarely see even today. And because it was made for a general audience it's racy, yet it retains a kind of innocence which is appealing. *She-Devils on Wheels* is a pure kitsch sixties time capsule and its motor doesn't purr—it roars. I must not be alone as the film has a small but loyal cult following and its theme song, *Get Off the Road,* has been covered not once but twice. Blood, orgies, and motorcycle sixties sleaze H.G Lewis-style.

TRIVIA: According to the *Something Weird* DVD commentary director Herschell Gordon Lewis explains the audition process. He ran an ad looking for women bikers who had a little acting experience. He expected only three or four replies but ended up with more than one hundred. He goes on to explain that he had each girl read a few lines then ride around to showcase their abilities on a bike.

All of the members of The Maneaters were proficient in riding bikes expect for Nancy Lee Noble who played Honey Pot. She learned how to ride during the making of the film.

The actors wore their own clothes for the film.

ORIGINALLY TITLED: *Maneaters on Motor Bikes,* which can be heard in the title theme.

Weekend (1967)

DIRECTED BY	Jean-Luc Godard
WRITTEN BY	Jean-Luc Godard, Juilo Cortázar (based on the short story "La autopista del Sur" by)
STARRING	Mireille Darc, Jean Yanne, Jean-Pierre Kalfon, Juliet Berto, Michèle Breton, Michel Cournot, Lex De Bruijn
COUNTRY	France

When a film opens with that the words "*. . . it's adrift in a cosmos,*" you know you are in for a totally nuts ride, which is certainly the case in this late-sixties art film. A couple's trip to the beautiful countryside is turned into a nightmare of burnt rubble and vicious murder in this epic from French new-wave director Jean-Luc Godard. *Weekend* marks an interesting time in the director's career and personal life, reflected in the film's dark tone, which acts as a nihilistic nightmare of depravity and moral anarchy. Such a thing can be very off-putting for viewers not used to a film that spews this much mean-spirited venom. Even the humor, which helps off-set this, is pitch-black sprinkled with some very clever satire. Now, I don't claim to be an expert in Jean-Luc's body of work, and I won't bore you with a detailed essay about the symbolisms and subtext, but I will say this film is littered with very pointed (and not subtle) social commentary about war, politics, and society in general, which drives the film's very loose plot. Even someone like me, who is fond of art-house-style cinema, found this to be a bit daunting with scenes that, at times, aimlessly stretch on as to purposely test the audience's patience. Despite this, I found this film to be totally engrossing in its surreal disjointed linear narrative. Boldly and quite humorously it breaks the fourth wall on numerous occasions, further highlighting its more strange aspects. While we're on the subject, *Weekend* tips the weird-o-meter, as it explores such taboos as cannibalism. And I, of course, was in utter awe of the infamous tracking shot, which is considered to be not only the longest ever done but the best ever committed to celluloid. Is this film for you? Well, I think it really boils down to whether or not you enjoy this kind of cinema. While not without a strong message it definitely is more style over grounded reality. Even with some dull spots I enjoyed it and I think, if given a chance, you may as well.

Werewolves on Wheels (1971)

DIRECTED BY	Michel Levesque
WRITTEN BY	Michel Levesque, David M. Kaufman
STARRING	Steve Oliver, Donna Anders, Gene Shane, Billy Gray, Gray Johnson, Barry McGuire, Owen Orr, Anna Lynn Brown
COUNTRY	United States

It seemed it would only be a matter of time before the biker film would crash head-on into the ever-popular horror genre, and the result is among the weirdest of the motorcycle outings, beaten only by *The Pink Angels*. But, does it live up to its title? A gang of rough-and-tough bikers stumble upon a monastery where they encounter a group of robe-wearing Satanists. The devil worshippers try and use the female biker Helen (Donna Anders) as a sacrifice, but that backfires as the riders put a nice beat-down on the cultists. Of course the devil has other plans for the rowdy bikers and things are about to get hairy.

The fun title and poster art suggest a wild, full throttled horror fest but what we really get is a rather dull outing. Director Michel Levesque clearly should have picked one genre or the other because he just doesn't seem able to balance both well while also providing enough action. Worst of all is the lack of actual werewolves, which seems like the very least you would expect from this film. This mixed with a confused plot that doesn't play up its fun camp aspects makes for an unremarkable film. Even still the movie has just enough ultra-cheese and funny low-budget performances to keep it passable despite its aimless plot. The idea of hairy wild bikers becoming, well, hairy wild werewolves on choppers is a pretty awesome one, but sadly, the film never realizes its full furry potential. *Werewolves on Wheels* is alright for an evening with friends and some cold suds but keep your expectations in check as the film offers a puppy instead of a wolf.

TRIVIA: Director and co-writer Michel Levesque went on to have a successful career directing on the small screen for such shows as *Renegade* and *Silk Stalkings* among others.

Rob Zombie sampled the line, *"We all know how we're gonna die, baby/We're gonna crash and burn,"* in the song "Sick Bubblegum" on his album *Hellbilly Deluxe Part 2*

The film can be seen playing in a hotel during Quentin Tarantino's *Pulp Fiction*.

CHAPTER 3

I love horror movies but give me a good gut-busting comedy any old day. If you're like me you're pretty tired and, frankly, bored of the Hollywood crap that passes for humor. Okay, I'm going to sound like a cranky old man here, but for my money, people acting raunchy and cursing every other sentence isn't a substitute for actual jokes, clever wit, and physical timing. Actors like Keaton and Chaplin had this gift, now compare them with say Adam Sandler, and you start to see my point. Inside you'll find comedies with a horror element like *Bloody Bloody Bible Camp* and *Student Bodies* or those with dark humor like *Eating Raoul.* Or if you're into more over-the-top fare, there is Trey Parker and Matt Stone's *Orgazmo.* Working on this chapter I discovered the brilliant writer/director Quentin Dupieux, and I'm now a lifelong demented fan. Just like the other chapters I wanted a nice cross section of films from a diverse group of filmmakers. George Kuchar can now mingle with Rainer Werner Fassbinder, Nick Zedd, and John Waters in some twisted LSD-laced cocktail party. Some of these are art house, some are definitely not. Some are great, some are crap. It's a wide range of films that I think would appeal to all walks of cinema viewers. But, as always, I urge you to (like I had to with writing this book) break out of your cinematic comfort zone and try new things, because, hey, you just might find something you like.

Comedy

Aliens Cut My Hair (1992)

DIRECTED BY	Michael McIntosh
WRITTEN BY	Gentry Johnson
STARRING	Stephen Maxine, Racine Manson, Cherrod Cooke, Leigh Crow, Lucille Carmichael, Gentry Johnson, Michael McIntosh
COUNTRY	United States

Imagine if RuPaul and John Waters got together in a mushroom-fueled haze and one of them had the bright idea to gather some friends, bust out the crazy makeup, and costumes, and make a *Star Trek* parody. The result might come close to *Aliens Cut my Hair*. Aboard the ship SS *Penetrator* Captain Priapus (Gentry Johnson) and his boyfriend Lt. Biff (Michael McIntosh) are having relationship issues which result in Biff getting a zombie love slave. This unknowingly leads to a run-in with Priapus's former nemesis. Now the hair will fly as the crew is led into a trap which is literally a drag. Some may find *ACMH* either an annoying, cheesy, student-like film or a brilliantly witty but flawed work of the so-bad-it's-great variety. Personally, I fall under the latter. The filmmakers are obviously in on its own joke and wisely play up the crappy low-budget production values and intentional camp factor which coats every single frame. It's also wonderfully self-aware, constantly breaking the fourth wall, even incorporating it into the plot itself. As great as that is, sadly the jokes are more miss than hit and the meta moments tend to get terribly repetitive. I will say that the visuals, while crude (due to the budget), give the production a nice shot in the arm. Even with its flaws, *Aliens Cut My Hair* is just odd and clever enough to be enjoyable, and I'm a sucker for '90s shot-on-video schlock. Not a film for everyone's tastes; however, if you get your kicks from shoestring-budget fare chock full of insanity, this might just be the perfect time-waster for you. Not a bad little effort, even if it could use a slight makeover.

Anniversary, The (1968)

DIRECTED BY	Roy Ward Baker
WRITTEN BY	Jimmy Sangerster (based on the play by Bill MacIlwraith)
STARRING	Bette Davis, Sheila Hancock, Elaine Taylor, Jack Hedley, James Cossins, Christian Roberts
COUNTRY	Britain

Larger-than-life mega-star Bette Davis gets to sink her finely manicured nails into her family in this pitch-black British comedy based on the hit stage play. Mrs. Taggart (Bette Davis) is the matriarchal ruler of three boys, Tom (Christian Roberts), Henry (James Cossins), and Terry (Jack Hedley), all of whom work at her construction company left to her by her late husband. She demands

the boys, along with Terry's wife, Karen (Sheila Hancock), gather at her home once a year for a perverse celebration of their wedding anniversary. However, the day is rocked when Tom brings his fiancée, Shirley Blair, a mousey blonde, to the affair. What ensues is a vicious battle of words and wits and a power struggle for dominance over Mum. As soon as Davis makes her epically grand entrance wearing a garish red eye patch you know you're in for a strange and bumpy ride. Being a British comedy the humor is snappy, witty, and of course, on the dry side with plenty of obvious camp value. While of course the film has laughs, it smartly injects some harrowing drama. For example, the origin of how Mother lost her eye is truly heart-wrenching stuff. These moments really help give the film some weight and substance yet thankfully doesn't get too heavy-handed, striking a nice balance, because, after all, this is a comedy. Ms. Davis is a cinematic force of nature and it's a delight to watch her dive into the role with a lot of gusto while retaining a great deal of class, and one can't help but be in awe of her. This film features a host of great supporting actors such as Jack Hedley, James Cossins, and Christian Roberts. However, while the male leads are great, I gotta say the ladies really steal the show. Shakespearian-trained actress Sheila Hancock has some very memorable moments battling it out with the Duchess of Mean Bette Davis. Elaine Taylor may not have been given any great lines but her performance is solid as well. Which leads me to my one compliant, which is Elaine Taylor's character is not very interesting aside from her deformity (no spoilers), and it's a shame they didn't give her more to do because she's a good actor. When I'm in the mood for a wickedly funny spot of high camp I turn to this film, because after all, who doesn't like to watch a film with a bitchy monster played by a legendary star? *The Anniversary* is a wonderful movie that doesn't get the attention it should.

GOES WELL WITH: *Whatever Happened to Baby Jane, House on Haunted Hill* (1959)

TRIVIA: The making of this film was, from all accounts, a nightmare, and Davis had her first director fired and did not like certain cast members.

Bette Davis's second film (and last) for Hammer. She had previously done a brilliantly creepy film for them called *The Nanny*.

According to the DVD director commentary, Bette Davis could in fact see out of her specially made eye patch. He even went on to say she had all of her wardrobe made in New York and brought over with her.

Barton Fink (1991)

DIRECTED BY	Joel Coen
WRITTEN BY	Joel Coen, Ethan Coen
STARRING	John Turturro, John Goodman, Judy Davis, Tony Shalhoub, Jon Polito, Steve Buscemi, Michael Lerner, John Mahoney
COUNTRY	United States

File this film not under B for Barton but C for criminally, as in a criminally underrated gem by Hollywood geniuses the Coen brothers. Writer Barton Fink (John Turturro) is the toast of Broadway and his latest play about the common man has earned rave reviews, and Hollywood is knocking on his door. He is contracted to write a B-wrestling picture for Capital Pictures, which is something he has very little knowledge or interest in. Now staying in the Earl, a strange hotel, he tries to overcome his writer's block, meeting quirky characters along the way like Charlie (John Goodman), a lovable insurance salesman. *Barton Fink* is definitely a movie you'll either love or hate with little to no middle ground. I think it boils down to those who have an affinity for off-beat comedy, and this is, at its very core, a blisteringly dark one at that, possibly the darkest comedy the duo has made. Like all of Coens' the script is masterfully written with weird characters and lavish production values which take great pains to transport us back to Hollywood circa 1941. It also features their patented brand of hilarity and, of course, pointed social commentary which, thankfully, never gets in the way of the story but serves as beautiful background music. Why do some not like this film? Well, at a certain point the film seems to take a totally different turn with a huge shift in both story and tone, which may be off-putting to viewers not used to that kind of unconventional switch. And for most filmmakers this would spell disaster, but the Coens' brilliant writing saves it, and is kept tightly focused with a strong lead character to keep it on track. I also think audiences were turned off by the bleak ending. The cast is superb with John Turturro playing the narcotic writer with a funky hairdo straight out of David Lynch's *Eraserhead*. It's truly remarkable how he throws himself into the role without ever becoming hammy or stereotypical and most importantly remaining sympathetic throughout. Equally good is John Goodman, and watching the two act together is nothing short of magical. The extremely odd Earl Hotel that our anti-hero stays in is very much its own character. Much like the Overlook Hotel in *The Shining* the place has a strange surreal feeling, with its faded and peeling wallpaper and weirdly lit hallways. *Barton Fink* may not be everyone's poison but, for me, it embodies everything I love about the comedy duo. While it may be skipped over for their better-known comedies I feel it's every bit as good, albeit maybe not as commercially satisfying. I implore everyone to give this film a chance, as it's outstanding.

TRIVIA: The Earl Hotel Hell theory: Not only is the hotel extremely creepy there is a theory that the Hotel is actually hell. For example, some have noted that Chet, the bell boy, comes out of a door on the floor after it takes a long time to come up, perhaps from the underworld? Also, you'll notice when Chet and Barton are in the elevator he says the word 'six' three times: 666, the mark of the beast. Finally, the place is sweltering hot, the walls peel, and the place is literally engulfed in flames at one point. Unsettling stuff.

The idea of a sequel has long been tossed around, supposedly taking place in the sixties with Fink teaching at Berkeley College.

Big Feast, The, aka La Grande Bouffe (1973)

DIRECTED BY	Marco Ferreri
WRITTEN BY	Marco Ferreri, Rafael Azcona, Francis Blanche (dialogue)
STARRING	Marcello Mastroianni, Michel Piccoli, Ugo Tognazzi, Philippe Noiret, Andréa Ferréol, Solange Blondeau
COUNTRY	France, Italy

Food, love, and death are all natural parts of life, and in *The Big Feast* it wraps up all those elements in one crazy cinematic stew. Much like *The Discreet Charm of the Bourgeoisie* the film deals with the relationship between food and death which is a major theme throughout. A group of men go to a beautiful villa with the sole purpose to screw prostitutes and ultimately eat themselves to death. What ensues is a wild nonstop deviant and decadent orgy of gluttony. At times gross-out and raunchy, this movie doesn't shy away from the absurd and, like a glorious train wreck, it's hard to look away. It also isn't afraid to get into the surreal with strange moments, like one of the characters dancing with a severed cow's head. The unique concept has a weird way of sucking you in, even if it's hard to really identify with the characters. Director Marco Ferreri and cinematographer Mario Vulpiani really know how to fill the frame, and there is some inventive camera work coupled with excellent use of lighting which captures a nice mood. As interesting as the film is, at over two hours long, it does begin to feel bloated and gets terribly repetitive. This could have easily done with a good twenty minutes of trimming. For better or worse *The Big Feast* is certainly something totally different and, even through it tends to drag, it hardly ever gets outright dull with plenty of bizarre set pieces to stay entertaining. Bon appétit.

GOES WELL WITH: *The Discreet Charm of the Bourgeoisie; The Cook, The Thief, His Wife & Her Lover*

Bloody Bloody Bible Camp, aka Sin (UK) 2012

DIRECTED BY	Vito Trabucco
WRITTEN BY	Shelby McIntyre, Vito Trabucco
STARRING	Reggie Banister, Tim Sullivan, Ron Jeremy, Ivet Corvea, Jessica Sonneborn, David Hayes
COUNTRY	United States

 What horror fan doesn't love a good old-fashioned slasher set in a camp? It's a time-honored tradition in the vein of *Sleepaway Camp, The Burning*, etc. Trabucco cooks up a comedy throwback to the bygone days of sunscreen, cheesy camp songs, and of course, brutal carnage. The year is 1977, and a group of wide-eyed Christian campers are up to more than just praying. You know what teens do in these kinds of films like fooling around, drinking, and doing drugs. A mysterious killer armed with an axe and dressed as a nun soon teaches the young people about God's wrath. Flash forward a few years later, and Father Richard Cummings (Reggie Banister) takes a group of wayward teenagers to the camp with the prospect of buying the place if the weekend goes smoothly. And as you might expect, the psycho is lurking and hoping to teach these campers a deadly lesson they'll never forget.

One of the exciting things about being a film journalist is discovering strange little gems like this, and I can honestly say I've been a fan of this since day one. Vito Trabucco and Shelby McIntyre craft a laugh-a-minute slash-

er that, in my book, beats the pants off *Broken Lizard's Club Dread*. It's part *Friday the 13th* with a mixture of *Alice Sweet Alice* all played for laughs.

Eighties slashers are prime for parody, but few have pulled it off like this. What could have been just anoth-er *Scary Movie*-style spoof is greatly elevated by interesting characters, genius over-the-top moments, and most im-

portantly, a blisteringly clever script that is funny yet injects plenty of social and religious satire. It also has a solid cast of newcomers and fun cameos by fan favorites Reggie Banister and Ron Jeremy. For a sinfully good time *Bloody Bloody Bible Camp* is a high-energy horror comedy send-up which never takes itself too seriously but still delivers the goods.

Blown (2005)

DIRECTED BY	David Hayes, Bill Noning, David Sabal, Kevin Moyers
WRITTEN BY	David Hayes, Bill Noning, David Sabal, Kevin Moyers
STARRING	Carina Lira, Jeff Dolniak, Kevin Moyers, David Hayes, Corey Busboom, Dan Erbach, Joanna Green, Mike Heenan
COUNTRY	United States

Imagine Edward D. Wood Jr., and Russ Meyers were given a hundred dollars to make a kill-er sex toy movie (ouch my brain!) and you might have *Blown*—a movie for lovers of bad but

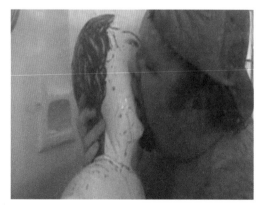

enjoyable films. Bobby (Jeff Dolniak) is getting married and his horny buddies decide to throw him a wild bachelor par-ty. Sick of their loud parties, a voodoo priestess who lives next door takes the form of a blowup doll in order to reek for bloody revenge.

It would be really easy for me to pick apart every glaring flaw in this film made by a group of friends for pretty much no money. However, I have to admit it's actu-ally not terrible, even clever at times. Wearing its dime store status proudly on its mustard stained sleeves, there is a cer-

tain endearing charm to it, and you can obviously tell these guys are having a blast making an overtly bad film. To my delight, the comedy is more hit than miss with some really great bits that made me laugh out loud. The tender shower love scene between actor David Hayes and a blood-covered doll is hilarious. And while the jokes are mostly good some tend to fall flat. But it's a movie after my own sick heart and it is clearly in on its own joke. Not a great movie but really fun and surprisingly a lot more entertaining than you might think. Gather up your friends, crack open some cold drinks, and get ready for a crass, bloody, and funny ride. No hot air here. *Blown* is worth a watch.

TRIVIA: The ugly-looking blowup doll was not made for the movie; but rather was the cheapest model from the Adam and Eve catalog.

Bone (1972)

DIRECTED BY	Larry Cohen
WRITTEN BY	Larry Cohen
STARRING	Yaphet Kotto, Andrew Duggan, Joyce Van Patten, Casey King, Jeannie Berlin, Brett Somers, Dick Yarmy
COUNTRY	United States

Larry Cohen is always an interesting director, and even when his films are sometimes off point they still manage to be wildly entertaining and endlessly re-watchable. The same is certainly true with his first effort, *Bone*. A man named Bone (Yaphet Kotto) breaks into a rich couple's house looking for money. To his dismay they are not as wealthy as he first thought, or it seems as happily married. A series of strange events ensue as the wife and Bone turn the tables on her awful husband. I have to say I was blown away by this powder keg of dark satirical social comedy that pulls no punches. While the film is not what you'd call plot-heavy it is just so delightfully bizarre and makes a perfect snapshot of the turbulent time in which it was made. However, the film is not weird for weird sake, and it has a lot of say about equality, class system, and stereotyping. Thankfully, the message never gets too self-righteous and puts the entertainment value first. The writing sizzles with freshness and is wonderfully frank and in your face especially considering the time it was made. Future star of *Alien* and *Homicide Life on the Streets* Yaphet Kotto gives a raw and uncompromising performance as the titular character, and it's some of his best work. Equally good is Joyce Van Patten, who also puts herself out there in a bold way. Both play off each other well, and it's clear they have chemistry together. *Bone* is a pitch-black absurd tale that doesn't shy away from taboo subject matter yet embraces it. The result is a brilliant and blisteringly funny comedy. It offers enough clever twists and turns to keep its viewers glued with an unforgettable ending. Right out of the gate Cohen proves that he is a fresh voice in cult cinema. Required viewing.

Larry Cohen on the Look of *Bone*

We started off to make the picture in 16mm with a slightly different cast than we had in the final motion picture. After three days of shooting in 16mm I decided it wasn't good enough, that the story and the script was so good that it deserved the first-class treatment so I just stopped shooting and I changed the cast. We switched to 35mm with a top-notch cinematographer named George F. who has had sixteen Academy Award nominations and worked on such movies as Meet Me in St. Louis *and so many other great MGM films. He was an older gentlemen who was retired, but I drug him out of retirement and he was happy to go back to work, and he called up some of his cronies from MGM and most of them were retired as well and they all said 'Hey let's make a movie' and they all came up and joined him and made this picture together. And it was a great experience working with people who photographed such people as Greta Garbo, Clark Gable, Spencer Tracy, etc. These were people who had the most experience in the period of motion picture which I loved the best, so it was a marvelous experience. I must note that many of them had never worked with a black actor before with Yah Kotto playing the lead in a very explosive comedy about a rapist entering a house; it was something shocking to these older gentlemen but they got over it and they did a great job for me and I was very pleased with the final product, and the picture has caught on over the years and became a cult classic, so it just goes to show you that time catches up with movies and they find their own audience, so I am very happy with that picture and I'm happy I stopped with the 16mm version and went on with the final 35mm Panavision version. The three days of 16mm footage is available on the DVD (Blue Underground) as an extra and you can actually see those days we shot.*

Calamari Wrestler, The (2004)

DIRECTED BY	Minoru Kawasaki
WRITTEN BY	Minoru Kawasaki, Masakazu Migita
STARRING	Kana Ishida, Nobuo Kameko, Osamu Nishimura, Akira Nogami, Miho Shiraishi, Yoshihiro Takayama
COUNTRY	Japan

I wasn't a huge fan of Minoru Kawasaki's *Executive Koala,* a film with a clichéd plot only made "different" by some actors being played by people in furry costumes. So imagine my surprise when *The Calamari Wrestler* turned out to be an entertaining film. A champion is just given the belt when, out of nowhere, a giant squid rips it away from him and proceeds to take him down with a move that is oddly similar to a former legend that disappeared from the sport. The squid gains a great deal of celebrity until an octopus bursts onto the scene and challenges him to a fight. Now the stage is set for one of the strangest match-ups to ever ink up the ring. If you're a fan of Japanese monsters in purposely cartoonish costumes flung into the "real world" then you'll find a lot of fun to be had in this outlandish Japanese comedy. In order to enjoy this film you'll need to just throw logic right out the window and roll with the absurdity. Part of the genius of the film is everyone plays the humor straight and nobody in the film is in on its own whacky lack of reality. "Oh, a giant squid is doing commercials? Sure, why not?" The film also acts as both a pointed commentary on sports and its inherited greed but also plays like a parody of the sports genre in general. Though I wished they would have taken the parody theme just a little bit further. Also, it tends to stray from its own premise at times and is bogged down by some needless padding and subplot. I have to give huge props to the special effects team for making some really detailed yet cartoon-like costumes that perfectly fit the films crazy tone. Playing like a live-action Manga (comic) with bright colors and outrageous monster fights, *The Calamari Wrestler* is able to rise above its seemingly novelty premise with a decent plot that is completely nuts. A totally fun and humorous knock out.

Cannibal!: The Musical, aka Alfred Packer the Musical (1993)

DIRECTED BY	Trey Parker
WRITTEN BY	Trey Parker, Matt Stone
STARRING	Trey Parker, Matt Stone, Toddy Walters, Dian Bachar, Ian Hardin, Stan Brakhage
COUNTRY	United States

Trying to survive the brutal winter conditions while fighting off starvation and disease doesn't sound like it would make for a rousing musical, but flittered through the twisted minds of Matt Parker and Trey Stone and you got one funny and strange film. Alfred Packer (Trey Parker) joins a group of men who set out for Breckenridge seeking gold. Their trip starts out lighthearted and full of promise until Packer's beloved horse takes off, and to make matters worse she was carrying their food supply. Things only get worse as they get hopelessly lost and increasingly hungry. Will they have to break the ultimate taboo to stay alive?

Four years before Stone and Parker would find mega-success with a little show called *South Park* and, later, the smash Tony-award-winning musical *Book of Mormon* they made this wonderfully weird and catchy comedy horror musical. *CTM* really sets the stage for the later projects the duo would do and it really showcases their subversive and smart humor that has become their trademark. As you might expect, the humor is smart but delightfully low-brow at times and the jokes often hit the mark. Parker obviously has a love for over-the-top cartoon-style gore as evident by the opening scene were the crimes of Parker are reenacted for the court. There is also a fun little nod to the original *Friday the 13th*. But you may be asking yourself, "Sure, it's funny, but does it work as a musical?" Oh hell yes, it does. The numbers are extremely well-written and hilarious, and you'll be loathed to admit that you'll catch yourself humming them. I'm sure I'm not the only one who does, right? You can really see why *Book of Mormon* was such a hit after seeing this. So get your "Shpadoinkle" on and belly-up to this gut-busting film. You'll be asking for seconds for sure!

TRIVIA: LISTEN: At the 16 minute, 3 second mark you can hear Cartman singing! Yes, a pre-South Park Cartman-style voice can be heard.

According to the audio commentary the story of Liane the horse was a metaphor for Trey Parker's former fiancée. SPOILER AHEAD* Also, if you watch/listen closely at the end (because it happens off-camera) it's clear that the horse meets with a bad end.

An off-Broadway musical based on the film ran for many years.

Creature from the Hillbilly Lagoon (2005)

DIRECTED BY	Richard Griffin
WRITTEN BY	Richard Griffin, Lee Smith, Andrew Vellenoweth
STARRING	Andrew Vellenoweth, Tanith Fiedler, William DeCoff, Patrick Pitu, Ben Chester, Leigh Radziwon, V. Orion Delwaterman
COUNTRY	United States

I have a huge soft spot for B-horror of the '50s and '60s. Something about a mad scientist hell-bent on world domination, poorly fabricated creatures, and of course terrible dialogue just puts a big goofy grin on my face. *Creature from the Hillbilly Lagoon* is a loving spoof of those bygone days with a much needed update.

Deep in the back woods toxic chemicals are turning people into huge hideous creatures that have a thirst for more than just beer, and soon they start preying upon the local hillbillies. Meanwhile, a group of wide-eyed college students doing research run into the slimy beast and a doctor whose mad plan smells a bit fishy. Without an ounce of shame I'll say I really enjoyed this low-budget film that is a love letter to my favorite guilty pleasure genre. *Creature* plays like a comic book with nicely done panels at the beginning, and this theme is further echoed by its very stylish use of bold colors such as greens, purples, and blues. It really gives the film a polished look while also perfectly setting the mood. Early on, the film builds a fast momentum and thankfully, it never lets up and

the result is a fast-paced story with very little padding. The titular monster is not the greatest but, considering its budget, I think it's solidly crafted, as are the practical effects. What it may lack in budget it more than makes up for in high-energy hilarity and over-the-top gore gags that reminded me of old school Troma in the best way. *Creature from the Hillbilly Lagoon* never goes full-blown parody but its bloody heart is obviously beating for classic monster films with an updated edge. So get yerself a beer and get ready to laugh with this over-the-top and delightfully offensive hickploitation hillbilly hoot!

Dark Backward, The (1991)

DIRECTED BY	Adam Rifkin
WRITTEN BY	Adam Rifkin
STARRING	Judd Nelson, Bill Paxton, Wayne Newton, Lara Flynn Boyle, James Cann, Rob Lowe, King Moody, Danny Dayton
COUNTRY	United States

The '90s was an exciting time for indie cinema, with cutting-edge films like *Clerks, Reservoir Dogs,* and Adam Rifkin's ultra-crazy *The Dark Backward.* Marty Malt (Judd Nelson) and his sidekick, Gus (Bill Paxton), are two losers who work as garbage men, but Marty has a dream of being a stand-up comic. The only problem is that his jokes fail to make people laugh. Through a bizarre turn of events Malt grows a full-length arm on his back, and suddenly a big-time agent, Jackie Chrome (Wayne Newton), is interested. But can this gimmick land him in the big-time, or will he remain a stand-up without a leg to stand on? Playing like a cross between a vintage sideshow carnival and an underground comic this highly creative film packs a punch right to the funny bones. The production values are outstanding, and Rifkin creates a dystopia-like world that seems to exist in some kind of Lynch-like nightmare world where everything is dirty, creepy, and just plain insane. Purposely, he goes for an old-school Hollywood-like feel lovingly wrapped in a circus-like atmosphere. Judd Nelson heads up an all-star cast which includes Bill Paxton, Wayne Newton, and even heavy hitters like James Cann and Rob Lowe. Nelson is great, and he seems to be channeling his inner Crispin Glover. Wisely, he downplays the character while Paxton chews every bit of scenery he can get ahold of. This allows them to play off each other's differences beautifully, and they have a great chemistry together. *The Dark Backwards* is like a wonderful hybrid of David Cronenberg-style body horror and a generation X-style attitude. It certainly ranks right up there with some of the best alternative cinema to come out of the decade. I give the film two thumbs up as does the hand behind my back. Required viewing for those interested in the totally far out.

GOES WELL WITH: *Freaked, Society*

Desperate Living (1977)

DIRECTED BY	John Waters
WRITTEN BY	John Waters
STARRING	Edith Massey, Susan Lowe, Mink Stole, Liz Renay, Jean Hill, Mary Vivian Pearce, Turkey Joe, Brook Yeaton
COUNTRY	United States

John Waters' *Pink Flamingos* could have been in this book, but I decided to go with the lesser known but equally brilliant *Desperate Living*, a film that marked an interesting turning point in his career, having moved in a more mainstream direction with his next features *Polyester* and *Hairspray*. And while he always kept his penchant for the weird throughout his entire body of work, it certainly wasn't as crazy or underground as his early stuff. Peggy Gravel (Mink Stole) is a high-strung mentally ill woman who is released to her home for care (against the strong advice from her doctor) and ends up accidently murdering her husband. Along with her nurse, the large-and-in-charge Grizelda Brown (Jean Hill), they flee to a town called Mortville, a place where the lowest of the low go and killers fear not prosecution. The pair must navigate the strange town, which is ruled by the evil Queen Carlotta (Edith Massey). According to Waters, this is his least favorite film he's done, but I must respectfully disagree, and it easily holds up as well as anything he's done. *Desperate Living* is his most overtly political with the Queen obviously being a fascist allegory (paintings of various dictators can be seen inside the Queen's castle). It's not at all subtle but it's a great bit of commentary that you might not expect from this filmmaker. Even more brilliant than the biting satire on politics is how the entire film is played like a twisted fairy tale and even Stole's character at one point is in a Disney-inspired outfit. Taking this theme one step further is the purposely fake-looking sets (most notably the castle) not unlike something out of an old German expressionist film. John's usual suspects join in for this outing with favorites Mink Stole, Edith Massey, and Mary Vivian Pearce (just to name a few) wonderfully chewing up the cardboard scenery. New faces Susan Lowe, sex pot Liz Renay, and larger-than-life Jean Hill, all bring something delightfully over-the-top and altogether entertaining. Of course there are plenty of deliciously weird and gross-out moments that are anchored with some very creative writing. Like a demented Disney film made by the Prince of Puke himself this wildly enjoyable political satire marks the end of an era for Waters fans and, while he made many other great films after this, none had the kind of raw surreal in-your-face trashter-piece quality. Highly recommended.

Discreet Charm of the Bourgeoisie, The (1972)

DIRECTED BY	Luis Buñuel
WRITTEN BY	Luis Buñuel, Jean-Claude Carrière
STARRING	Fernando Rey, Paul Frankeur, Delphine Seyrig, Bulle Ogier, Milena Vukotic, Stéphane Audran, Jean-Pierre Cassel
COUNTRY	France

Director Luis Buñuel wonderfully and masterfully blends the theater of the absurd while taking a delightful stab at the upper class in this surreal comedy. Six friends, through a series of weird events, are never able to enjoy a meal together in both dream- and reality-based form. *The Discreet Charm of the Bourgeoisie* is a comedy; not what a mainstream audience would call laugh-out-loud but rather the humor is dry and often on the darker side. Fans of more physical or punch line-style of comedy may be put off by this, but (and not to sound stuffy) if you're a fan of higher brow wit than you will enjoy its discreet charms. The film is also rich with metaphors and symbolism and, while I won't bore you with them, I will point out a few of them. Buñuel purposely draws a link between food and death, and after each planned meal a death usually occurs. It's not surprising that Luis and other filmmakers like Hitchcock have drawn this parallel, since food is the essence of life and without it we would surely die. Food is also used as a kind of metaphor for the hunger of life and each person never fully slates that desire, leaving them empty. Strange and surreal with a wry and black sense of humor this film is certainly not for everyone, but for those who enjoy a comedy that challenges with food for thought, this tasty satirical morsel is something sure to please.

Eating Raoul (1982)

DIRECTED BY	Paul Bartel
WRITTEN BY	Paul Bartel, Richard Blackburn
STARRING	Paul Bartel, Mary Woronov, Robert Beltran, Susan Saiger, Lynn Hobart, Ben Haller, Richard Paul, Mark Woods, and Ed Begley Jr.
COUNTRY	United States

Eating Raoul is the film that still makes me wonder what exactly a basket job is. Never mind, I probably don't want to know. Paul (Paul Bartel) and Mary (Mary Woronov) Bland are typical squares that live in a kitschy '50s-decorated apartment, which is slowly being invaded by a terror too hideous to imagine—swingers! Mary is a nurse and Paul is a wine collector that was recently let go at his job working at a spirits shop. But there dream is to open their very own restaurant, and they are willing to do anything to make it happen. Through a weird set of circumstances the duo find out that murder really does pay, and their targets are the loose moral perverts running amok in Los Angeles. Black comedy doesn't get any more delicious and wonderfully absurd than this gem from the genius that was Paul Bartel. On paper this seems like the kind of film premise that would be doomed to be stretched to its limit but, with brilliant writing chock full of hilariously wicked humor and quirky characters, it works. Part of its brilliance is its smart "biting" satire that not only sends up L.A. swinger culture but a pointed social commentary in general. You also have to admire the many details in the production value (for example, putting the very straightlaced Mary and Paul in a '50s-style apartment sleeping in separate beds, which not only further echoes how uncool they are, but makes the irony of the depraved world they are flung into even more delightful). Another aspect that makes this film really work is the amazing chemistry between the always-brilliant Mary Woronov and Paul Bartel and it's evident they've worked together before, as they are so natural together. Both bring their own unique set of acting skills and charms to the table, yet put them together and it's nothing short of magical. Robert Beltran, best known for role on *Star Trek*, also shines as the titular character. Ed Begley Jr. also makes a screamingly funny cameo. Zany and pitch-black in comedy, this film makes a satisfyingly juicy meal for any film fan.

TRIVIA: An off-Broadway musical version was produced in 1992.

A sequel was planned entitled *Bland Ambitious,* with a script written by Paul Bartel. It was just a mere ten days from production when the funding fell through. Even though it never happened the main characters make a brief cameo in the cult classic *Chopping Mall.*

GOES WELL WITH: *Silence of the Lambs, Chopping Mall, Kentucky Fried Movie*

Even Dwarfs Started Small (1970)

DIRECTED BY	Werner Herzog
WRITTEN BY	Werner Herzog
STARRING	Helmut Döring, Paul Glauer, Gisela Hertwig, Hertel Minkner, Gerturd Piccini, Marianne Sarr
COUNTRY	Germany

Werner Herzog is an incredible filmmaker known for his bold style and deep philosophical views on life and humanity. *Even Dwarfs Started Small* was his second feature and certainly a brain-melting film experience. Off a remote island inhabits of a mental institution liberate themselves. They left behind Pepe (Gerd Gickel), a member of their group who was captured and held by the director of the faculty. Their acts of rebellion start out as wildly absurd but turn more and more disconcerting as time goes on. What's striking right from frame one is the beautiful black-and-white photography and the clinically cold documentary-style approach, which is no surprise seeing how he would go on to do some amazing documentary films later in his career. The film employs nothing but little people actors, a feat that is virtually unheard of (done once in 1938's *Terror in Tiny Town*), but Werner does not make them the butt of jokes or demean them in any way. In other words, if you'll pardon the pun, he never looks down on them. Herzog also isn't afraid to play with the juxtaposition of stark realism and the surreal which can be, at times, jarring for the audience. I love how it walks a razor-sharp line between hilarious absurdities like a mock bug wedding and the harrowing and disturbing. First and foremost, *Dwarfs* is a comedy, but it also taps into deeper messages like the rebellious nature of repressed people. It's no accident that Herzog cast little people to represent the little or common man. *Even Dwarfs Started Small* is an engrossing and hypnotic comedy that acts as an allegory for imprisonment and the fact that you can never fully cage the spirit of a man. It's certainly a bizarre film but it's also a powerful one and I give it my highest recommendation.

FP, The (2011)

DIRECTED BY	Brandon Trost, Jason Trost
WRITTEN BY	Brandon Trost, Jason Trost
STARRING	Jason Trost, Brandon Barrera, Art Hsu, Caitlyn Folley, James DeBello, Bryan Goddard, Nick Principe, Sean Whalen
COUNTRY	United States

Up-and-coming directors Brandon and Jason Trost come out swinging in this laugh-a-minute throwback that has its tongue firmly planted in its cheek. Set in a post dystopian world, two rival gangs don't settle their differences with guns or knives but with a game called Beat Beat Revelation. After his best friend, BTRO (Brandon Barrera), dies during a dance off, JTRO (Jason Trost) vows never to play the game again and leaves. But it seems he can't run away from fate and he finds himself avenging his fallen friend in the ultimate Beat Beat showdown. One of the most fun and original films to come on the scene, *The FP* perfectly parodies '80s turf war films like *The Warriors* with a decidedly more edgy update. Throwing every wonderful film cliché at us the Trost brothers capture the spirit of the films they are paying homage to right down to the synthesize score, and make sure to include plenty of cheese and over-the-top moments. They really have run with their whacky premise but thankfully never go too overboard and really balance the humor and action like seasoned pros. But make no mistake, the film is a comedy first and foremost, and they succeed in rolling out plenty of laughs. *The FP* features some truly genius material. One such scene involving Stacy's father (played brilliantly by Sean Whalen) had me in utter stitches. You also can't help but be impressed by the film's great-looking production design which I'm sure was done on a budget, and it helps give it a more expensive and polished look. Highly creative and entertaining as hell, this film dances to its own beat and was music to this film buff's ears. I can honestly say I had a big goofy grin the entire time. So don't be a chump, and see this right away.

Freaked (1993)

DIRECTED BY	Alex Winter, Tom Stern
WRITTEN BY	Tim Burns, Alex Winter, Tom Stern
STARRING	Alex Winter, Mr. T, William Sadler, Brooke Shields, Megan Ward, Lee Arenberg, Randy Quaid, and Keanu Reeves as Ortiz the Dog Boy (uncredited)
COUNTRY	United States

Ricky Coogin (Alex Winter), a former child star and Hollywood douche bag, makes a very lucrative deal with the evil cooperation EES (Everything Expect the Shoe) to be the spokesperson for Zygrot 24, an extremely toxic sludge. While on an outing Coogin, his friend Ernie (Michael Stoyanov), and protestor Julie (Megan Ward), stumble upon a strange freak show owned by Elijah C. Skuggs (Randy Quaid). Once inside Skuggs shows the gang his freak-making machine using Zygrot 24, of course, and turns them into oddities for his sideshow. Now locked away with other freaks including Worm (Derek McGarth), Cowboy (John Hawkes), the Bearded Lady (Mr. T), etc., they must find a way to escape and return to normal. I still find it hard to believe a far-out movie like this managed to get a decent budget from a major studio. *Freaked* is equal parts crude, outrageous, and hilarious. It also works as a side-splitting satire on the Hollywood system, media violence, and corporate America. Even actor Alex Winter obviously has a sense of humor about himself, and *Ghost Dude,* the film within the film, is no doubt poking fun at his slacker role in *Bill and Ted's Excellent Adventure.* The film boasts a really interesting mix of actors such as Mr. T, Randy Quaid, Brooke Shields, Morgan Fairchild, and even Keanu Reeves under lots of fur playing the Dog Boy. Seeing how the film deals with freaks the special effects better be spot-on. Thankfully they hired makeup and effects legends Screaming Mad George (*Predator, Society*) and Steve Johnson (*Spider-Man 2, Species*). They really bring their insane talents to the screen and showcase why they are top in their respected fields. While the writing is mostly solid some of the jokes tend to fall flat and the plot gets needlessly convoluted. This funny gross-out film plays like a live-action grimy eye-popping underground comic book, and fans of *Airplane* and *Naked Gun* will dig this pitch-black comedy which is refreshingly well-done.

TRIVIA: The look of Alex Winters's half-human, half-freak look is inspired by 1967's *She Freak.*

The Ren and Stimpy Show creator John Kricfalusi has praised *Freaked* for its humor.

Does the Human Flame look familiar? Well, he played Pintel in the Pirates of the Caribbean series.

Funky Forest, aka Funky Forest: First Contact (2005)

DIRECTED BY	Katsuhito Ishii, Hajime Ishimine, Shunichiro Miki
WRITTEN BY	Katsuhito Ishii, Hajime Ishimine, Shunichiro Miki
STARRING	Andrew Alfieri, Hideaki Anno, Tadanobu Asano, Ryô Kase, Maya Banno, Kazue Fukiishi, Shihori Kanjiya
COUNTRY	Japan

How do you toast your brain nicely in just one cinematic experience? Simply find a copy of *Funky Forest,* pop it into your media player, and kiss your sweet sanity goodbye. In researching this book, this title kept coming up as something truly strange, and after viewing it, I can certainly agree. I have never seen another film like it. Told in a series of short segments, the film takes a look at such characters as "The Guitar Brothers" and a dog that directs anime.

At a whopping two-and-a-half hours I was worried that this would be dull and tedious, and at the beginning it is, with segments that tend to drag on. Thankfully, though, the film really picks up speed after the first hour, and after that, it's a nonstop psychotropic ride. The writing is highly creative and very funny, playing out like a bat-crap-crazy skit show. But what really impressed me is how they interwove stories and char-

acters from the other segments, bringing it all together as a whole and giving it a more unified feeling. I was especially impressed with the film's look, which utilizes many different techniques which range from CGI to animation. Furthermore, the practical effects are spot-on and are some of the best stuff I've seen from a lower-budget production. The phrase, "you need to see this to believe it" definitely applies to a film such as this. Despite its rocky start *Funky Forest* manages to craft something brilliant with not only a clever interlocking storyline but an extremely versatile and boundary-pushing visual style that uses every trick in the cinematic bag to full effect. So strap in for a wild and side-splitting time and let yourself get lost in this psychedelic forest.

Geek Maggot Bingo, aka Geek Maggot Bingo or The Freak from Suckweasel Mountain (1983)

DIRECTED BY	Nick Zedd
WRITTEN BY	Nick Zedd
STARRING	John Zacherle, Robert Andrews, Richard Hell, Donna Death, Brenda Bergman, Tyler Smith, Bruno Zeus, Gumby Spangler
COUNTRY	United States

Nick Zedd pays tribute to Russ Meyers, William Castle, and early Universal horror in this deliciously insane ultra-low-budget sex fright comedy. Doctor Frankenberry (Robert Andrews) has a mad dream of creating beings, which is complicated when a suave vampire makes the moves on his daughter. Much like *They Eat Scum,* the film wears its ultra-low budget proudly as a badge of honor, and the homemade sets evokes an early German expressionistic vibe. And it, of course, helps give the overall film a wonderfully broken down, filthy film anarchy feel which is spewed over every single frame. The humor is on par with *Scum,* and is both outrageous and wickedly black. The highlight is an appearance by none other than the Cool Ghoul himself Zacherle, who gives a devilishly hammy performance, which fits the creature feature homage. Admittedly the narrative does sway wildly and tends to get away from itself and could have benefitted with a tighter structure. Fans of depraved sex, monsters, and gore will find *Geek Maggot Bingo* an unparalleled treat. True balls-to-the-wall art from the depths of the underground.

GOES WELL WITH: *Pink Flamingos, Eraserhead*

TRIVIA: Original editor of *Fangoria Magazine,* Robert (Uncle Bob) Martin, makes his first of only two screen appearances; the other is as an uncredited zombie in *Day of the Dead* (1985).

Girls Will Be Girls (2003)

DIRECTED BY	Richard Day
WRITTEN BY	Richard Day
STARRING	Jack Plotnick, Clinton Leupp, Jeffery Roberson, Ron Matthews, Eric Stonestreet, Dana Gould, Chad Lindsey
COUNTRY	United States

Girls Will Be girls taught me a lesson in never judging a movie by its title, as I nearly declined to watch it when a friend suggested it as a movie night rental. Thankfully, I came to my senses and watched it, and seventy-nine minutes later I had a new favorite comedy. Self-centered has been actress Evie (Jack Plotnick) and her roommate Coco's (Clinton Leupp) lives, which are turned upside down when they take in a younger aspiring actress as a roommate. Now the female fury flies as Evie tries to sabotage her career while trying to claw her way back to the top with a matinee in hand. Had John Waters directed a remake of *All About Eve* it would be something like *Girls Will Be Girls,* a pitch-black comedy that features an all-male cast. The film's novelty of all the men playing women seems like it would hinder more than help, but Day pulls it off masterfully with a cleverly written script that perfectly pays homage to over-the-top aging actress films such as *Sunset Boulevard, Whatever Happened to Baby Jane?,* and of course, *All About Eve.* The jokes fly fast and furious and, for the most part, zing you right in the funny bone. A film like this lives or dies on its makeup, and thankfully it's top-notch. Honestly, there are times I totally forgot that this is an all-male cast. And speaking of the cast, this film is populated with some wildly funny actors. While everyone in the cast is great, it's Jack Plotnick who ends up stealing the show as the aged bitter has-been Evie. His physical comedy as well as timing makes him wickedly hilarious and just spellbinding to watch. Considering this was Robert Day's first film he keeps a nice handle on the plot and, while it goes over the top (which is fitting for the material), it thankfully never strays away from its own premise. Also, he clearly knows how to stretch a budget, and the film looks like every dime went up on the screen. Similar to *Die, Mommie, Die!, Girls Will Be Girls* perfectly satires Hollywood both in film and the industry as a whole, and the end result is a hilarious and wonderfully weird comedy. This film is no drag, and if given the chance, it may just become one of your favorite films as well.

GOES WELL WITH: *Psycho Beach Party; Die, Mommie, Die!*

Happiness of the Katakuris, The (2001)

DIRECTED BY	Takashi Miike
WRITTEN BY	Kikumi Yamagishi
STARRING	Kenji Sawada, Keiko Matsuzaka, Shinji Takeda, Naomi Nishida, Kiyoshirô Imawano, Tetsurô Tanba
COUNTRY	Japan

Visionary director Takashi Miike never ceases to amaze me with his seemingly boundless imagination, and *The Happiness of the Katakuris* tops the list of some of his best works. Like his other films, such as *Audition* and *Visitor Q*, the major theme is the family unit. As a last ditch effort to bring his family closer together Masayuki (Shinji Takeda) buys a house to run as an inn. However, guests have a funny way of dying tragically, putting a damper on their fresh start. But could this be just the thing to bring them together? Miike brilliantly crafts a work of art that is totally insane yet surprisingly touching, and *Happiness* walks a fine line between the two. The film is also part musical and, even though I'm not a fan of the genre, the songs are catchy enough to get stuck in your brain with stylishly choreographed numbers that even I couldn't take my eyes off of. Visually, the film is stunning with many interesting and wild techniques, including impressive use of claymation that is mind-bending and awe-inspiring. It's clear that a ton of hard work and creativity went into the artistry and it really helps drive the film forward and keep it ever entertaining. The minor problem with the film is that it tends to drift away from the premise, but thankfully there is a strong message at its core which manages to hold the film together and adds a nice balance to the craziness. Miike outdoes himself with this dark comedy that is visually impressive but also has a tender side, which I'll admit had me a bit choked up at the end. Not to be missed.

I'm a Cyborg But That's Ok, aka Ssa-i-bo-geu-ji-man-gwen-chan-a (2006)

DIRECTED BY	Chan-wook Park
WRITTEN BY	Chan-wook Park, Seo-Gyeong Jeong
STARRING	Su-jeong Lim, Rain, Hie-jin Choi, Byeong-ok Kim, Yong-nyeo Lee, Dal-su Oh, Ho-jeong Yu
COUNTRY	South Korea

Want to watch a strange yet harrowing comedy set in a psych ward that's not *One Flew Over the Cuckoo's Nest*? Well, you're in luck, as visionary filmmaker Chan-wook Park serves up a film to go nuts over. A young girl named Cha Young-goon (Su-jeong Lim) is put into a mental hospital after she appears to attempt suicide. But she is hiding a secret from everybody—namely that she isn't a girl at all but rather a highly advanced cyborg. When she stops eating (for fear food will break down her system) it's a race to save her before she starves to death. Help comes from an unlikely source in the form of a fellow patient. The screenplay, written by Park and Seo-Gyeong Jeong, is highly inventive and provides depth in both characters and situations. They also inject a rich fantasy world which greatly helps give the film a bigger scope and break up the monotony. The quirky humor wisely never goes too far and really helps take the sting out of what might be considered depressing subject matter. Like many of Park's work *Cyborg* has an outstanding visual style which really shines when characters go off into their own little worlds. It also helps that the CGI segments are used sparingly and has aged surprisingly well. My one complaint is that certain scenes felt as if they didn't really need to be there, and the film feels like it ends a few times. What could have easily been a whacky over-the-top comedy in the hands of a lesser writer/director is instead transformed into a thought-provoking, strange, and, yes, even touching, meditation on what it means to be human. Highly recommended.

Jesus Christ Vampire Hunter (2001)

DIRECTED BY	Lee Demarbre
WRITTEN BY	Ian Driscoll
STARRING	Phil Caracas, Murielle Varhelyi, Maria Moulton, Tim Devries, Ian Driscoll, Josh Grace, Johnny Vegas, Tracy Lance
COUNTRY	Canada

Looking for a vampire film, but tired of the same old Gothic horror chamber piece? Well how about the world's only blood-sucking comedy/kung fu/action/religious film? A rash of disappearances has been occurring, targeting lesbians. It seems a cult of vampires is responsible, and they found a way to move in the daylight. Enter the kung fu fighting savior, Jesus Christ, who along with his trusty sidekick, Mary Magnum (Maria Moulton), must save the day from the evil bloodsuckers. Lee Demarbre's first feature film is a high-energy genre-bending outing that feels a lot like a mixture of John Waters and Russ Meyers ran through an extreme Troma filter. I love that he constantly plays with weird juxtapositions like the punk priest with a mohawk. It's a fun way to defy the audience's expectations in a clever and humorous way. It's clear from the start that Lee has a refreshingly bold flare, which obviously pays homage to Grindhouse films of the past with film scratches, retro-style music, transitions, etc. As great as the film's concept and visuals are, sadly the screenplay, which at times is brilliant, does suffer from sizable plot holes, the biggest of which actually happens at the film's end. Important plot points are also glossed over or outright ignored leaving the viewer feeling cheated. Also, a strangely random musical number at the beginning feels horribly out of place. Problems aside, I really like this film and I applaud it for its balls-to-the wall action-packed anarchy-style filmmaking which accomplishes a lot on a shoestring budget. Mexican wrestlers and a talking bowl of ice cream are just a few of the totally weird moments in this high-flying, fang-sinking homage to B-Grindhouse films of the past. Take a bite out of this outrageous underground hit.

Lord Love a Duck (1966)

DIRECTED BY	George Axelrod
WRITTEN BY	George Axelrod, Larry Johnson, Al Hine (based on novel by)
STARRING	Roddy McDowall, Tuesday Weld, Ruth Gordon, Lola Albright, Harvey Korman, Lynn Marshall, Max Showalter
COUNTRY	United States

Lord Love a Duck is another wonderful hidden gem I unearthed while researching this book. Told mostly in flashback, high-schooler Barbara Ann Greene (Tuesday Weld) meets the eccentric and smart Alan (Roddy McDowall) and his alter ego Mollymauck. He claims Mollymauck can grant any wish Greene desires, but the problem is that she wants it all. But the old saying, "be careful what you wish for" is never truer as Barbara gets what she wants at a cost. Axelrod takes the '60s teen beach culture of California and shoves it down their

throats in this blisteringly dark satirical comedy.

Axelrod and Johnson's screenplay really shines with smart and witty dialogue and hilarious pointed commentary which perfectly sums up the decade. It's also cleverly self-aware with the addition of a director character, who makes, you guessed it, teen beach bikini movies. The late great Roddy McDowall heads up an impressive cast and gives a delirious high-energy performance and, as always, throws himself head-long into the role. Steaming up the screen is sex pot Tuesday Weld who sizzles in the role of Barbara Ann. And of course, screen icons Ruth Gordon and Harvey Korman also light up the screen and do what they do best—being hilarious and stealing every scene. *Lord Love a Duck* is an intelligent, funny, and twisted film which was ahead of its time, paving the way for other quirky teen flicks such as Wes Anderson's *Rushmore*. So put on your favorite cashmere sweater, summon up Mollymauck, and enjoy this ultra '60s stinger.

TRIVIA: Though George Axelrod only directed two films in his career he was most known for screenwriting. His most famous work includes *Breakfast at Tiffany's, The Seven Year Itch,* and *The Manchurian Candidate,* among others.

Tuesday Weld has said out of all the movies she's done, this is her favorite.

Meet the Feebles (1989)

DIRECTED BY	Peter Jackson
WRITTEN BY	Peter Jackson, Fran Walsh, Danny Mulheron, Stephen Sinclair
STARRING	Danny Mulheron, Donna Akersten, Mark Hadlow, Ross Jolly, Mark Wright, Peter Vere-Jones, Brian Sergent
COUNTRY	New Zealand

Multi-Oscar-winning director Peter Jackson may be known for his landmark hits like the *Lord of the Rings* trilogy and *The Hobbit* but I'll always have a soft spot for the time when he made balls-to-the-wall indie films like *Bad Taste, Dead Alive,* and of course *Meet the Feebles.*

Young Robert's (Mark Hadlow) dream comes true when he is accepted in the chorus in the Feebles Variety Hour, a popular show featuring musical numbers and skits. But the dream soon turns into a nightmare as he quickly learns that behind all the glitter lies a cesspool of depravity, kinky sex, and drugs. This highly creative and gross-out film packs more craziness and humor into five minutes than some films do in their entire run time. It's a bold choice to use nothing but puppets as the main cast, yet it's that very thing that sets the film apart from anything else made at the time or since. Brilliantly, Jackson weaves a pitch-black comedy satire that takes a stab at show business and the corruption that runs amok. I find it interesting how the film is able to tackle some very mature subject matter yet still retain both its humor and endearing charm. Being a variety show, there is bound to be some musical numbers, and thankfully they are wonderfully written and will have you in stitches. For example, one bold and sassy number is entirely dedicated to sodomy. From all accounts, Jackson himself seems to have disowned this as a lesser work; however, I, like many others I know, see it for what it is—an irreverent comedy satire that takes aim at the inherent ugliness of show business. Gloriously grotesque and should be seen by every person interested in alternative cinema.

Micmacs, aka Micmacs à tire-larigot (2009)

DIRECTED BY	Jean-Pierre Jeunet
WRITTEN BY	Jean-Pierre Jeunet, Guillaume Laurant
STARRING	Dany Boon, André Dussollier, Michel Crémadès, Dominique Pinon, Marie-Julie Baup, Yolande Moreau
COUNTRY	France

Micmacs comes to us from the extremely talented director of *The City of Lost Children* and *Delicatessen* and joyfully celebrates the quirky outsiders in all of us. A mild-mannered video store clerk named Bazil (Dany Boon) is shot in the head, an innocent bystander of a ruthless arms dealer. Incredibly, he survives and is taken in by a band of trash-collecting yet lovable misfits who treat him like family. With the help of his new friends Bazil decides to take down the dealer's criminal empire. Brilliantly, the film balances wild action and hyper-surreal comedy all while managing to be heartwarming and totally engrossing. In such a short amount of time you really get to care about the characters and, in turn, root for them. I was also impressed by how it handles sight gags in such clever ways. Writer/director Jean-Pierre Jeunet truly has an unlimited imagination, which is showcased in the film's rich and overwhelming attention to detail in set design, really creating a distinctive world. Taking this a step further is his use of wonderfully inventive visual techniques that really propel this into a feast for the eyes. For example, the title credits done like an old forties-era film is great and also works within the story. It also features some slick camera work. *Micmacs* is the kind of brilliant film that is sadly overlooked by a lot of American audiences but it's overflowing with creativity, action, and laughs, and it really deserves a chance. The film is not hard to find and is very much worth your time. It's almost impossible not to fall in love with this movie. Required viewing.

Microwave Massacre (1983)

DIRECTED BY	Wayne Berwick
WRITTEN BY	Thomas Singer
STARRING	Jackie Vernon, Al Troupe, Loren Schein, Anna Marlowe, Marla Simon, Claire Ginsberg
COUNTRY	United States

Jackie Vernon (Voice of *Frosty the Snowman* . . . yes, you read that right) stars in this micro "epic" about a man hungry for . . . a cannibal feast. Donald (Jackie Vernon) is a back-breaking construction worker, and when he comes home from a hard day's work he just wants a simple meal. Seems reasonable, right? Well his wife, May (Claire Ginsberg), does not feel that way and insists on making him ridiculous gourmet meals or "Q-zine," as she calls it. Things go from bad to worse when she gets . . . you guessed it, a microwave oven! Finally pushed to the breaking point timid Donald goes on a rampage.

    In the wake of the video boom would-be directors came out of the woodwork looking to make their own personal statements and cash in. So it should be no surprise that some

very nutso things came out of it, namely this fried little morsel.

    "The worst movie ever made," boasts the video release. Well, I wouldn't go that far; however, it's not a classic either. It's obvious that the filmmakers were not going for high art and it wears its B-movie status proudly on its ketchup-stained sleeve. This does lead to some so-bad-it's-good charm that might get a few chuckles. However, the major problem with *Microwave Massacre* is that the gimmick is fun for a little bit but is stretched painfully thin to make the allotted run time of seventy-six minutes. It also doesn't help that the jokes aren't very good. As I stated above, Jackie Vernon is best known for lending his voice to Frosty in the beloved 1969 classic *Frosty the Snowman*. For people that grew up with the Christmas film it's kind of jarring to hear Frosty's voice in a large working-class cannibal. Childhood ruined. Vernon isn't the greatest actor, but he brings a certain blue collar self-deprecating appeal to the role and even a certain sweetness to it. Without a doubt, he's a reason why the film is still talked about and watched decades later. Overall it's a film with one or two jokes spread dangerously thin but with Jackie in the lead as well as some over-the-top camp. It might just make for the perfect cinematic side dish.

TRIVIA: Prop and special effects legend Robert Burns, whose work includes the original *The Texas Chainsaw Massacre, The Howling*, etc., worked on this film. He was given a budget of $1,000 and made all the props, including the titular microwave.

The severed head of May (Claire Ginsburg) once belonged to the famed Forest J. Ackerman until his passing.

CRAZY CONNECTIONS: The house in which the majority of the film was shot once belonged to the *Monkees'* Micky Dolenz.

Mister Lonely (2007)

DIRECTED BY	Harmony Korine
WRITTEN BY	Harmony Korine, Avi Korine
STARRING	Diego Luna, Samantha Morton, Denis Lavant, James Fox, Werner Herzog, Leos Carax, Richard Strange
COUNTRY	Britain, France, Ireland, United States

While performing in Paris, a young Michael Jackson impersonator (Diego Luna) seeking something different in his life happens to meet a Marilyn Monroe look-alike (Samantha Morton), and she takes him to a commune in Scotland completely made up of other impersonators. Harmony Korine's comedy drama is a totally engrossing film that explores some powerful themes like destiny, identity, and finding your place in the world. He perfectly balances the more harrowing moments with some delightfully quirky humor, which is played off the cast of impersonators that includes a foul-mouthed Abe Lincoln (Richard Strange) and a little boy Buckwheat (Michael-Joel David Stuart), who has an obsession with chickens. And while the comedy isn't what you'd call side-splitting it is brilliantly done in a darkly wry kind of way. I was really surprised not only by how engaging the film is but also that it is genuinely touching without going too overtly sappy. You really get to like and care about the characters and, I won't lie, I found myself getting choked up toward the end. The cast is incredible, and it's impossible to single one actor as they all do an impressive job. I will say that Denis Lavant is great and is quickly becoming a favorite actor of mine. Even maverick director Werner Herzog has a small role. Blending together a dreamy and surreal world Korine's *Mister Lonely* is a delightfully weird and wonderful celebration of the strange in all of us. Highly recommended.

Mondo Trasho (1969)

DIRECTED BY	John Waters
WRITTEN BY	John Waters
STARRING	Divine, Mink Stole, Mary Vivian Pearce, David Lochary, Bob Skidmore, Margie Skidmore, Lizzy Temple Black, Pat Moran, Susan Lowe
COUNTRY	United States

Following in the footsteps of such filmmakers as Andy Warhol, Kenneth Anger, and Jack Smith, John Waters released *Mondo Trasho* as his first feature film and blazed a trail in a new movement of artist trash. The film follows Divine and an unnamed blonde (Mary Vivian Pearce credited as Bombshell) whose lives quite literally collide during a hit and run accident. The biggest issue with *Mondo Trasho* is it tends to "drag" in spots and Waters himself has admitted that he wished he would have cut this down to a short film. John displays a great raw Warhol amateur quality and it has enough wonderful gutter trash glamour and psychedelic weirdness to keep it always interesting. And of course it's hilarious, over the top, and raunchy (with shades of Jack Smith's *Flaming Creatures*)—basically everything you've come to know and love from his body of work. It's also interesting, as this is a mostly silent film except for small bits of dialogue and a great soundtrack (almost dizzying at times) which features some great vintage rock and roll. Catholic imagery, which would factor in Waters' later works, is also front and center and used in a wonderfully delirious bit with Mary (played by Margie Skidmore) and Divine. *Mondo* really sets the stage for better and more complete works like *Multiple Maniacs* and his later epic *Pink Flamingos*. And while it's not quite as good as his later works it's just odd and artistic enough to warrant a viewing, and it's great to see the seeds of Waters' talents. In the words of the immortal actor, "It isn't easy being Divine!"

TRIVIA: The song *The Girl Can't Help It* is featured in both this and *Pink Flamingos* and both serve as a theme for the larger-than-life star Divine.

Mink Stole, Pat Moran, and Susan Lowe would all reunite to make *Desperate Living* (1977) also directed by John Waters

GOES WELL WITH: *They Eat Scum, Eraserhead*

Orgazmo (1997)

DIRECTED BY	Trey Parker
WRITTEN BY	Trey Parker
STARRING	Trey Parker, Matt Stone, Dian Bachar, Michael Dean Jacob, Robyn Lynn Raab, Ron Jeremy
COUNTRY	United States

The same year *South Park* premiered and forever changed television, the duo released this delightfully twisted film about the world's most unlikely superhero. Mormon Joseph Young (Trey Parker) is sent to Hollywood for his mission work and he longs to be married to fiancée Lisa (Robyn Lynn Raab). They want a wedding in a temple but Young doesn't have the money. He knocks on the door of Maxx Orbison (Michael Dean Jacob), a shady producer of adult films, and as fate would have it he is offered a job as the leading man in his current project. He says "no" but is made an offer he can't refuse. Given a stage name and a superhero outfit he plays the crime-fighting Orgazmo. In another twist of fate, it seems Young is really meant to be the hero he portrays, and with the aid of his sidekick they set out to clean up L.A. As much as I love *Cannibal! The Musical* I feel this film is an improvement in the writing, and you can see a more polished skill behind the camera as well. Parker and Stone still bring their patented brand of clever yet outrageous comedy that is the key behind their continued success. I dare you not to laugh during the title song, *Now You're a Man*. It's impossible! As I said, this is a more developed screenplay that delightfully pokes fun at the porn industry and, to a degree, Mormonism. What's compelling is the fact that the movie plays very innocent for being about a sex superhero, and even when things get really bad for our heroes it never gets too mean-spirited, and considering our main character is Mormon it's rather fitting. But make no mistake, this movie is everything you'd expect from the makers of *South Park*; raunchy jokes, nudity, and dildo fights. It's also awesome to see real-life porn star Ron Jeremy playing, well, a porn star. Big stretch. He and other industry people make various cameos, and the film is littered with inside jokes. Speaking of jokes, while most of them work, some just fall flat and it seems that it would take them a little longer to hit their stride in terms of feature films. I'd say *Baseketball* (yes, I said it) and *Team America* are their best in that department. Fans of the smash show *Book of Mormon* will no doubt see the seeds from this film. Bottom line is, if you don't laugh while watching this far-out comedy check your pulse, because you may be dead. *Orgazmo* is an underrated comedy from two geniuses in their field.

TRIVIA: This was Trey Parker's second feature film.

Look for a nice little nod to Troma who distributed *Cannibal! The Musical*. Several titles from the studio can be seen in a video store. Also, Lloyd Kaufman makes a cameo.

Phantom of Liberty, The (1974)

DIRECTED BY	Luis Buñuel
WRITTEN BY	Luis Buñuel, Jean-Claude Carrière
STARRING	Adriana Asti, Julien Bertheau, Jean-Claude Brialy, Adolfo Celi, Paul Frankeur, Michael Lonsdale, Milena Vukotic
COUNTRY	France

Largely considered one of Buñuel's most free formed works, *Phantom of Liberty* is a delightfully eccentric bit of cinema, but also has a great deal to say in a way that only French director Luis Buñuel could. Throwing the traditional form of narration right out the window, the film is done using a series of interconnecting stories which feature different aspects of life and society in very wacky ways. There is no doubt that this film is strange, even crossing over into the surreal, but like a lot of Buñuel's, work he injects a great deal of satire which this film is dripping with. Everything from religion, class system, and politics, is not safe in the hands of Luis. Probably the best and most famous bit is the scene where the social elite sit on toilets and excuse themselves to the "dining room" to eat privately in stalls. Like *Discreet Charm* he pokes fun using the ritual of food coupled with the upper class. But it's certainly not weird for weird sake with social commentary like the segment with the sniper and the trial that follows, which is an obvious pointed message about the legal system. And thankfully, the film isn't too heavy-handed in its commentary, and it still allows for an entertaining experience. Anyone interested in getting into the films of Luis Buñuel (which I strongly recommend) may find this a good starting place in his filmography, as it's more accessible but still showcases his brilliant trademarks. I'm someone who has come a little bit later to Buñuel's work but he is quickly becoming a favorite director. Highly recommended.

Please Don't Eat My Mother! (1973)

DIRECTED BY	Carl Monson
WRITTEN BY	Eric Norden
STARRING	Buck Kartalian, Lynn Lundgren, Art Hedberg, Alice Friedland, Adam Blair, Ric Lutze, Rene Bond, Dick Burns
COUNTRY	United States

It's a film about a female talking plant that gets her human to feed her human flesh . . . I feel like I've seen this before. A lovable peeping tom named Henry (Buck Kartalian) buys a plant to keep him company. However, he gets a lot more than he bargained for when it starts speaking to him in a sexy voice. Now head-over-leaf, he starts finding various things for it to eat, such as flies, frogs, and dogs. But soon it grows a taste for bigger cuts of meat—namely humans. *Please Don't Eat My Mother!* is a great example of a fun movie on paper that doesn't translate well to screen. It's not that I mind that it plays out like an even cheaper (if that's even possible) remake of the Roger Corman film *The Little Shop of Horrors,* but it's just plain tedious. For example, the lunchtime peeping scene, while alright in small doses, goes on well too long, and the effect is more yawn-inducing than exciting. Also, unlike *Shop* it doesn't retain any of the charm or clever humor. While we're on the subject, the humor is on the corny side, and to make things worse, is terribly outdated to modern eyes. This is made painfully clear by the extremely stereotypical gay guy who owns the plant shop. Lead actor Buck Kartalian does bring a certain dopey charisma which is one of the things the film has going for it. From its title and plot it seems like this would be a heap of trashy no-budget fun, but in reality it's unfunny and horribly repetitive and brings nothing interesting to the table. Skip it and just watch the classic '60s Corman film instead.

Psychos in Love (1987)

DIRECTED BY	Gorman Bechard
WRITTEN BY	Gorman Bechard, Carmine Capobianco
STARRING	Carmine Capobianco, Debi Thibeault, Cecelia Wilde, Frank Stewart
COUNTRY	United States

In my foreword you'll recall my VHS-renting days and how the amazing artwork made a huge impression on my young horror addled mind. *Psychos in Love* had a practically lurid and amazing cover, and it actually lives up to the promotional material. Joe (Carmine Capobianco) is a regular guy who owns a sleazy strip joint and happens to like butchering women. Kate is an attractive young woman who works as a manicurist and enjoys randomly killing men. Fate brings the two together and they find out they have things in common such as their shared hatred for grapes and savagely killing people. Now it's happily ever slaughter as the pair kills and enjoys each other's warped company.

However, it seems the honeymoon is over when a cannibal plumber named Herman (Fran Stewart) comes between them. If you're so inclined for a wacky slasher comedy that wears its low-budget heart on its sleeves then look no further. I love how the film constantly breaks the fourth wall and Joe and Kate talk directly into the camera, sort of like a confessional—a device now used in reality shows. The jokes, for the most part, work really well, giving off an edgy National Lampoon-style raunchy humor, something that is more the norm now than when it was made. The acting is also surprisingly good. Carmine Capobianco has a natural ease behind the camera and his everyman charms easily endear the audience. He and Debi Thibeault have a nice chemistry together and we actually buy them as a deranged couple. It's not all wine and roses, though, as some of the jokes are a bit too hokey and the plot is spread dangerously thin. However, I firmly and unashamedly admit that I love this film. Its low-budget charm and sincerity wins me over more than a billion-dollar crapbuster. And of course, it harkens back to the days of mom and pop stores—you know, before Blockbuster and the death nail of online streaming. Gorman stabs right at the funny bone with this old-school oddity, including all the staples horror fans come to love, while also incorporating smart parody of the slasher genre. There is a lot of fun to be had in this overlooked trash-ter-piece. And how can you not love a movie with its own psychotic theme song? But please, no grapes.

Rubber (2010)

DIRECTED BY	Quentin Dupieux
WRITTEN BY	Quentin Dupieux
STARRING	Stephen Spinella, Jack Plotnick, Wings Hauser, Ethan Cohn, Roxane Mesquida, Daniel Quinn, Haley Ramm
COUNTRY	France, Angola

It's a Saturday night and you're in the mood for something quirky and weird yet cerebral. How about a movie about a sentient killer tire that has telepathic powers? In the middle of nowhere a tire named Robert springs to life and sets out on a journey that includes killing anything in its path, showering, watching TV, and possibly finding that special someone. It's up to a band of not-very-bright cops to find a way to put the brakes on this menace for good. I read a review by an amateur critic that called this film pretentious. Sadly, I feel this person totally missed the point and failed to see the humor and the film's subtext. Dupieux is simply having a laugh at the horror genre as a whole while not stooping to more conventional methods of parody. It wears its wackiness on its sleeve and couldn't be less pretentious about it. What is jarring from the start is how Quentin delightfully smashes down the fourth wall, first by having an actor introducing the film with rather labored metaphors, second and more prevalent is the crowd of spectators that literally serve as a point of view character (one even interacts with the action). As I stated above, the whole film serves as a cheeky satire of horror and nothing embodies this more than the bait scene in which a plastic mannequin stands in for a potential victim, complete with purposely terrible dialogue. It's true the film's plot does "tread" a little thin but, for the most part, it's very brisk in its pacing and I was never bored. Love it or hate it, you certainly have to respect the filmmakers for being adventurous enough to take a crazy idea and "roll" with it instead of just giving us the same old same old. Quentin Dupieux's *Rubber* is a loving homage to not only B-horror but outrageous exploitation films in the same vein as *Death Bed: The Bed that Eats* and isn't afraid to break the fourth wall in a hilarious and smart way. So if you're "tired" of the same old give this film a spin.

Satan's Brew, aka Satansbraten (1976)

DIRECTED BY	Rainer Werner Fassbinder
WRITTEN BY	Rainer Werner Fassbinder
STARRING	Kurt Raab, Margit Carstensen, Helen Vita, Volker Spengler, Ingrid Caven, Ulli Lommel, Armin Meier, Peter Chatel
COUNTRY	Germany

I admit *Satan's Brew* was my first foray into the wild weird world of Rainer Fassbinder and I was not disappointed. Walter (Kurt Rabb) is an erratic poet and anarchist always short on money. He lives with his portly wife and mentally ill brother who is obsessed with dead flies. He tried various ways of making money and fulfilling his creative and sexual appetite. This includes murder and channeling a long-dead poet named Stefan George. Fassbinder takes a devilish glee in taking pot shots at not only politics—mainly fascism—but he also satirizes himself by way of his main character, Walter Kranz. The plot (of what there is) is a delirious mixture of pitch-black comedy fueled by cartoon-like sleaze and sexual fetishism. For the casual movie watcher this film may come off as confusing, too over-the-top, and dry. However, the best way to take *Satan's Brew* is to toss all logic out the window and keep in mind that this is a surreal comedy, which is subject to its very own rules. If I had to voice one complaint it would be that at nearly two hours the film does get a bit tedious and could have used a slight trim. *Satan's Brew* is like spending the entire runtime in a mental ward and not minding a bit. With equal parts brilliant wit, grotesque debauchery, and theater of the cruel it's not hard to see why this is one of Fassbinder's finest films. Required viewing.

Scotland, Pa. (2001)

DIRECTED BY	Billy Morrissette
WRITTEN BY	Billy Morrissette, William Shakespeare (based on play by)
STARRING	Maura Tierney, James Le Gros, Christopher Walken, Kevin Corrigan, Amy Smart, James Rebhorn, Andy Dick
COUNTRY	United States

Taking William Shakespeare's *Macbeth* and setting it in '70s food culture and filling it with great character actors such as Christopher Walken, Kevin Corrigan, and James Le Gros is a surefire recipe for deep-fried cinema goodness. Joe "Mac" (James Le Gros) works at a fast food restaurant; however, he is filled with good ideas to expand the business which are, of course, ignored by his boss, Norm Duncan (James Rebhorn). Mac and his wife, who also works there, plot to steal money and kill Duncan. After the deed is done the couple opens up Macbeth's. But a sly detective is hot on their trail. Writer/director Billy Morrissette conjures up a wickedly funny and smart adaptation of the immortal bard's tragedy. People familiar with the play will no doubt find the update clever, but Morrissette wisely doesn't alienate those who are not, so fear not, you don't have to have read it (though you should) to get the full effect. I love how seamlessly the play translates to '70s food culture, which the film devilishly satires, along with small-town quirk and suburban life. The cast is amazing and features James Le Gros who I also consider an extremely underrated actor. But of course, Christopher Walken steals the show, because, well, he's Walken. It also has a host of great supporting actors such as Kevin Corrigan, James Rebhorn, etc. *Scotland, Pa.* is a wonderfully dark comedy with an awesome soundtrack. Order's up on this fully baked comedy classic.

CRAZY CREDITS: Before writer/director Billy Morrissette directed this dark quirky comedy, he starred in *Ghoulies III: Ghoulies Go to College.*

Screamplay (1985)

DIRECTED BY	Rufus Butler Seder
WRITTEN BY	Ed Greenberg, Rufus Butler Seder
STARRING	Rufus Butler Seder, George Kuchar, Katy Bolger, Bob White, James M. Connor, Eugene Seder, Basil J. Bova
COUNTRY	United States

THE BOSTON MOVIE COMPANY PRESENTS

SCREAMPLAY

Screenwriters are paramount in the film process but sadly, many of these twisted geniuses seldom get the praise they deserve. Rufus Butler Seder's mad cap tale deals with Hollyweird and the lengths some writers will go to cook up a killer screenplay. Edgar Allan (Rufus Butler Seder) is an ambitious young writer fresh off the bus, arriving in Hollywood with stars in his eyes and the dream of writing the greatest screenplay—or at least one that will pay the bills. As twisted fate would have it, he ends up at the Welcome Apartments, a dive owned by a psychopathic man named Martin (George Kuchar). There he meets the quirky residents including a horny aging B-actress and her young protégé named Holly (Kathy Bolger) and a loony old former rocker who constantly spouts religious damnation. The young man strikes up a deal with Martin to stay rent-free as long as he works like a slave around the place. He feverishly works on his horror script in his free time and the wacky goings-on fuel his inspiration. But it seems that the murders he writes have a deadly way of coming true. Is there a butcher prowling or has Edgar finally lost touch with reality? *Screamplay* is a visually striking and surreal film done in black and white and is heavily influenced by German expressionism of the silent era. With tongue jammed firmly in its cheek the film wears its raunchy and weird status proudly but cleverly while avoiding the pitfalls of other such films and retaining a strange kind of innocence about it. It's sort of like early John Waters light. But is this a case of style over substance? Well, yes and no. While the film is no doubt a fiendish and highly creative little film it suffers from uneven tones, loses its focus at times, and relies on tired police clichés. Some scenes also go on a little too long and others may have been better to cut altogether. The film nearly works well as a Hollywood satire but the jokes and concepts don't go quite far enough for it to actually get there. This does not mean it's a bad film by any means, with many of the jokes that perfectly tickle the funny bone. The cast is great, with director and cowriter Rufus Butler Seder playing the lead. He has a perfect psycho-like look which is even not so subtly pointed out in the film. He is actually really good in the role and wisely hams it up, further heightening the films surreal art house aspect. Equally good is Eugene Seder and Katy Bolger who both give naturally good performances. And let's not forget the legendary late great George Kuchar who is amazing to watch. It's like he is channeling some demented Brando from *A Streetcar named Desire*, a truly wondrous sight to behold. While this film may not be perfect it's still damned entertaining with a bold and fascinating style and a delightfully insane concept. It's a real shame that this was the one and only film for Mr. Seder because I could tell he had a lot of talent in all the facets of the production. This mad cap film struck a key with this fellow wordsmith because after all, all of us writers are a bit mad . . . .

Series 7: The Contenders (2001)

DIRECTED BY	Daniel Minahan
WRITTEN BY	Daniel Minahan
STARRING	Brooke Smith, Mark Woodbury, Donna Hanover, Tom Gilroy, Michael Kaycheck, Glenn Fitzgerald, Angelia Philips
COUNTRY	United States

I think we're all guilty of watching what I call garbage television. Sure, it may make you feel not great about yourself, but it's hard to look away. Future A-list television series director Daniel Minahan's first feature film knocks this sly satirical comedy out of the park. *Series 7* follows a marathon of a reality show. The rules are simple: a group of random strangers are pitted against each other and the last man or woman left alive wins. It's literally do or die. Things get complicated when reigning champion Dawn (Brooke Smith) must face off with a former friend Jeff (Glenn Fitzgerald). Will she be able to kill him? *Series 7* is not only still relevant, but it may have been even more so when it was first released. At first glance the film's thin premise seems destined to run out of steam; however, a wonderfully clever and layered script helps carry it nicely. Maybe most surprising is the depth the characters show, and Minahan wisely knows just how far to push them without becoming caricatures. He also provides exposition without it feeling phony or forced, and the harrowing moments work because we actually get invested in the characters. Thankfully, this being a film about a group of people, they zeroed in on three main characters with the focus being largely on two: Dawn and Jeff. It makes sense storywise, and it also keeps it from getting too congested with multiple storylines. Maybe most impressive, though, is how it does such a great job at being a believable reality show, that at one point I felt a bit guilt for getting into it, as if I could really see watching this, had it been a real. Darkly funny and, at times, moving this film squarely points its fingers at America's detached glut of senseless violence and mindless television in a frightening but all-too-real Orwellian future where *Big Brother* isn't just a series, it's a sad "reality".

Student Bodies (1981)

DIRECTED BY	Mickey Rose, Michael Ritchie (uncredited)
WRITTEN BY	Mickey Rose
STARRING	Kristen Ritner, Matthew Goldby, Jerry Belson, Joe Flood, Peggy Cooper, Carl Jacobs, Kevin Mannis
COUNTRY	United States

Long before *Scary Movie* was ripping on the horror genre, another film was taking a stab at the genre's funny bone. Get your rubber chicken and get ready for this body count comedy. Toby (Kristen Ritner) seems to be the last virgin in her over-sexed high school. When frisky teenage guys and gals start getting bumped off, the finger is squarely pointed at her as the number one suspect. Now aided by her friend Hardy (Matthew Goldby), she must clear her name, because surely it could not be innocent Toby. Or has she finally snapped on her horny peers? Some movies can instantly get me out of a funk and *Student Bodies* is most definitely

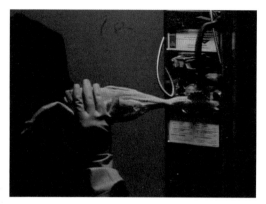

one of them. I'd describe it has a wonderful fusion between *Friday the 13th* and *Naked Gun*. Frequent Woody Allen collaborator Mickey Rose makes the jokes and sight gags zing, and thankfully the humor never feels forced, providing some genuinely hilarious moments coupled with ingenious slasher observations. It's also not afraid to delightfully burning down the fourth wall in a gut-busting and brilliant scene.

The result is a film that is sure to make even the most jaded hardcore horror fan giggle and roar with laughter, and it includes truly memorable lines that are endlessly quoted between my warped circles of friends. Still, what really makes this film work is the amazing cast. The leads, Kristen Ritner and Matthew Goldby, have a natural ease between the camera, not to mention great comic timing. Hammy at times, sure, but I've honestly never showed this to someone who didn't love it by the end. So grab your horse head bookends and get ready for some low-brow yet highly wacky comedy. "Funerals get me hot."

Interview with Actor Joe Flood (Mr. Dumpkin)

MV: How did you get cast in *Student Bodies?*

JF: At the time I had an agent and I had no experience at all, I didn't go to acting class or nothing, but I managed to book a couple of commercials and she was surprised, so she called me up one day and told me there was a movie being shot in Texas and the director was Michael Richie. So she asked if I wanted to go and read for a movie I said, "Sure." I went over to his house and I went in and shook his hand he said, "here's your scenes," and it was for the role of the Sheriff. So I went in and I looked at it and he asked if I was ready and I read for the role. He said "Ok, read this," and it was for another character, one of the teachers, and I read that and then he told me to wait outside for a little bit. About ten minutes later he comes in and says, "What are you doing tomorrow?" "Nothing," I said, and he said, "Want to meet me at Paramount Studios tomorrow?" I almost shit my pants. I said, "Yeah, sure." So I got outside and I sat in the car, leaned my head out the window, and started puking in the streets I was so excited. A buddy of mine took me over to Paramount. When I arrived there was Michael Richie and Mickey Rose. Do you know who Mickey Rose is?

MV: Yes, he wrote a lot with Woody Allen, correct?

JF: Yes, they actually went to school together. So they had me there and I was auditioning for an hour and a half, running up and down the stairs screaming and yelling like a complete madman and later he said, "That should do it, thanks Joe." I called my buddy up and he drove me to the airport and the next day I get a phone call at ten o'clock in the morning with, "Joe this is Michael. Look, the way it stands now, we'd like to have you in the movie but unless someone better comes along it's yours. I'll let you know in a couple of days." A couple days later he calls me and says, "Alright you ready to come to Texas?" So this was mid-February. They arranged my airfare, and I flew down to Houston. That was it, and they completely changed the character and I ended up playing Mr. Dumpkin, the woodshop teacher.

MV: What was the shooting schedule like, do you recall?

JF: We were there for about eight days. We rehearsed the movie before we shot it which is always a brilliant idea. The longer I'm alive the more I realize how good of an idea that is. When you walk on the set you're ready to work.

MV: I'm curious what the mood was like on set, because when I watch the film it looks like everyone is having a blast.

JF: I can't speak for the others, but I had one of the greatest times of my life. I had a lot of fun. We shot all the woodshop scenes in Southern University in Houston in this big woodshop.

MV: What was the first day for you like?

JF: My first day I wasn't actually nervous but excited. Someone had told me a few years earlier that when you do the comedy you can't take it seriously because you're not in on the joke, you are the joke but you're not in on it. I got on set and the cast are there and I go through my horse head book end speech and the whole cast and crew was in stitches. Michael Richie was on the floor almost peeing his pants. I mean, he was roaring. I turned around and said, "What the fuck was so funny?" They went back on their knees again, because I was taking it very seriously. I didn't find the humor in it at all and Jerry Belson, who was one of the producers, he did *The Odd Couple, The Lucy Show,* the list goes on, what a track record he had. What a great guy. He put his arms around me and said, "Don't ever forget what you just did because you got it right." And Michael Richie walked over to me and said, "I have just one direction." I said, "What's that?" "Don't once furrow your brow." I just gave him a strange look but if you watch me in the movie I never furrow my brow once. Overall it was a blast, I had a wonderful time. Mickey Rose became one of my best friends.

MV: Do you recall the reviews?

JF: Gene Siskel gave me a write-up, which was awesome. Two friends of mine flew in from Chicago and brought me three or four Chicago newspapers. At the time, he [Siskel] wrote for the Tribune, and they gave this to me, and I looked at it and I said, "Is he the tall one or the fat one?" and they looked at me like, "You moron, he's the tall one." I said, "Oh, that was a nice review. I'll have to send him a letter." And Charlie Martell said, "Joe, call him up." I said, "Really?" He said, "Yeah." I thought actors didn't call critics, at least that was my understanding. I got the information and I call the Chicago Tribune. I get the switchboard and I asked for Mr. Siskel's office and they said, "Hold on." Moments later I finally get someone and I explain that I want to talk to Siskel and the lady says, "What for?" I said, "He did a review on my movie I did and I wanted to talk to him about it." She says, "He's filming [the TV show *At the Movies*] right now. Why don't you call back in twenty minutes." I waited another twenty minutes and I dial it again and I get the switchboard and I get this voice saying, "Hello?" I say, "Mr. Siskel please." And the voice was a guy and said, "Ahh shit!" I said "Excuse me?" He said "I want you to talk about the horse head book ends. Hi, Joe. This is Gene." I go, "Oh, Mr. Siskel, how are you?" He replied, "Call me Gene." I said, "It was very kind of you . . . " and he said, "Joe you were the best thing in the movie." But he said, "You aggravated the crap out of me." Shocked, I said, "What did I do?" "Every time you came close to going over the top and you didn't and you had me pissed off." [Laughs] And we talked for about twenty, twenty-five minutes and he said, "Look, if you do another movie, call up the office, tell them the name of the movie, or get ahold of me, and I'll review it on the air for you." I thanked him and I said, "I'm kind of dumbstruck you took my call." He goes, "Why's that?" I said, "You probably get these calls all the time," and he paused and said, "Joe you're the first person who has ever taken the time to call me up and say thank you."

MV: Wow.

JF: He was a good man, very kind to me.

Swiss Army Man (2016)

DIRECTED BY	Dan Kwan, Daniel Scheinert
WRITTEN BY	Dan Kwan, Daniel Scheinert
STARRING	Paul Dano, Daniel Radcliffe, Mary Elizabeth Winstead, Richard Gross, Aaron Marshall, Andy Hull, Jessica Harbeck
COUNTRY	United States

I, like many people, was more than just a little skeptical when going into *Swiss Army Man*. I wasn't sure if it was somewhere between a quirky Wes Anderson flick or hipster schlock. A hapless young man named Hank (Paul Dano) is stranded on a deserted island, and in an act of desperation decides to hang himself. Just before he can go through with it he sees a body wash up on the shore. It is a man he comes to know as Manny (Daniel Radcliffe). When he discovers the body has some faint signs of life (namely farting) they strike an unlikely friendship and Hank finds the will to survive. What is incredible is how the Dans could take just a sophomoric thing as fart jokes and transform it into not only a valid comedy but also something richly complex and, yes, even deep. This movie is definitely one that will sharply divide people, with some seeing this as mere pretentious garbage while others, like myself, can see the humor as well as the cleverly inserted metaphors. *SAM* touches upon a range of personal and painfully relatable issues such as all the things we leave unsaid and how we bottle up our emotions much like, well . . . gas. Actors Paul Dano and Daniel Radcliffe give outstanding performances in their respected roles. Dano masterfully showcases a skilled range and it's easy to identify with his character. It's great to see Radcliffe continue to take edgy roles that only further prove this wizard is no one-trick pony. It's really depressing to think that people at Cannes actually booed this film and some even walked out. If you go in with an open mind and open heart, you'll find this hilarious and strangely endearing. In a time of remakes and endless superhero flicks this movie is a breath of fresh air despite the constant farting.

Taxidermia (2006)

DIRECTED BY	György Pálfi
WRITTEN BY	György Pálfi, Zsófia Ruttkay, Lajos Parti Nagy
STARRING	Csaba Czene, Gergely Trócsányi, István Gyuricza, Marc Bischoff, Gábor Máté, Piroska Molnar, Géza D. Hegedüs
COUNTRY	Hungary, Austria, France

I have to say, few films leave me as speechless as György Pálfi's *Taxidermia*, a gross-out symphony of madness and meat. The film details three generations of men—one of whom is a competitive eater, and his son, who works in taxidermy. While not an anthology, the film is masterfully broken down into three segments, which is an interesting way to convey its totally bat-shit-crazy narrative. Pálfi most definitely shows a keen eye with a polished and detailed production design coupled with inventive camera work which is simply incredible. He seamlessly stitches together naturalism and the surreal, not unlike Svankmajer's *Faust*. If bodily fluid (more to the point, vomit) makes you ill, this movie is not for you, as it's unabashedly gross-out and nothing is held back. The film does blend different genres flirting with drama and even horror, but at its rotten core it's a pitch-black comedy. Pálfi also uses the medium to examine a whole host of social and political commentary about Hungary in post World War II. Some have even theorized that it acts as a clever take on the seven deadly sins, which is not hard to believe, seeing how Sloth and Gluttony are major themes. It takes balls to unleash a work of art like this that is darkly humorous, hyper-sexual, surreally grotesque, and an altogether refreshingly different movie-going experience. Without any spoilers, I will say the ending will leave you, like me, totally gobsmacked. *Taxidermia* is a wonderfully bizarre little treat sure to leave a lasting impression. Highly recommended.

They Eat Scum (1979)

DIRECTED BY	Nick Zedd
WRITTEN BY	Nick Zedd
STARRING	Geoffrey Carey, Donna Death, Roy Dillard, Sandy Light, Jim Giacama, Brett Powers, Roberta Reitz
COUNTRY	United States

Often, when people think of offbeat cinema, names like David Lynch, Kenneth Anger, and even Jack Smith might spring to mind. However, one that doesn't get nearly the attention he deserves is Nick Zedd, whose work has been praised by such icons as Jonas Mekas, John Waters, and Jim Jarmusch. The plot of *They Eat Scum* revolves around a dysfunctional family consisting of a pompous religious-nut father, two boys—one mentally ill, the other a cross-dresser—and a punk-rock daughter named Suzi (Donna Death). Suzi is tasked with killing her family while maintaining her drug fueled lifestyle. Zedd's first feature film is a pure balls-smashed-against-the wall piece of cinematic anarchy. Think of a mixture of Herschell Gordon Lewis, Andy Milligan, and early John Waters. The result is a delightfully gross-out, deranged, and depraved outing. His wicked humor comes out in full force like the cannibal scene played with the song "Good Vibrations" in the background, and who could forget the force-fed rat scene? Its utterly amateur nature only adds to its grimy filthy underground quality. Like an issue of *Midnight* or *Tattler* come to life in blazing color *They Eat Scum* is pure punk and something you can show the entire demented family. Infectious flies and rabid poodles are just some of the delicious outrageousness to be had. Highly recommended.

GOES WELL WITH: *Multiple Maniacs, Liquid Sky*

Thundercrack! (1975)

DIRECTED BY	Curt McDowell
WRITTEN BY	George Kuchar, Curt McDowell (story by), Mark Ellinger (story by)
STARRING	George Kuchar, Marion Eaton, Melinda McDowell, Rick Johnson, Maggie Pyle, Ken Scudder, Curt McDowell, Billy Paradise
COUNTRY	United States

Just a word of friendly warning: *Thundercrack!* contains scenes of graphic sexuality. If this offends you I'd advise you to skip it. If you're still on board, let's take a gleefully insane skip into the realm of the nightmarish and the sublime. Your mind may never be the same again. Various people are forced to stay the night at an old creepy house on the hill during a horrible thunderstorm. Their hostess is a mentally ill shut-in who has a few skeletons in the closet and one very real one buried in the wine cellar. As the guests get settled in and get out of their soaked clothes, they soon realize some very strange things are going on, like what is behind the locked door? What dark secrets is their host hiding? The '60s and '70s were a magical time for filmmakers to push the medium to new delirious and artistic heights with filmmakers like Jack Smith, Kenneth Anger, and John Waters crawling up from the underground. Curt McDowell and the Kuchar brothers were certainly very important in the scene, and in *Thundercrack!* they join forces. McDowell and Kuchar combined classic horror tropes and the old dark house style horror mystery and hurl them into more modern and sexually liberating times. The result is a wild ride of pitch-black comedy with wacky characters, strange dialogue, and a wedding scene that will be sure to be burnt into your gray matter for decades to come. And I haven't even mentioned the sex crazed gorilla on the loose. Visually this film is really interesting as it's done totally in black and white which further echoes the *Old Dark House* classic horror vibes. Its low budget is worn proudly on its sleeve and though the sets and editing techniques may be crude it only adds to the charm and other worldly feeling that encompasses the entire film. Sure, the talking scenes may be a little drawn out but the writing is so wonderfully bizarre you can't help but be transfixed. By far too off-the-wall for the mainstream, but it's perfectly suited for the midnight crowd. This is certainly a movie of its time, when anarchy filmmakers blazed a trail for generations of up-and-coming artists like Gaspe Noes, Guy Maddin, etc. Enter if you dare, and experience this funhouse of psychedelic madness, horror, and comedy.

Trailer Town (2003)

DIRECTED BY	Giuseppe Andrews
WRITTEN BY	Giuseppe Andrews
STARRING	Bill Nowlin, Stan Patrick, Walt Dongo, Vietnam Ron, Ruth Estes, Bill Tyree
COUNTRY	United States

Enjoy watching ultra-trashy mentally ill people? Well, come on down to *Trailer Town,* a film written, produced, and directed by actor-turned-director Giuseppe Andrew. Follow the lives, loves, and deaths of the demented residents of a trailer park. Done in a documentary style this outrageous comedy flirts with greatness, but a few fundamental flaws hold it back. But before I get to that, let's talk about what works. Regardless of what you think of him and his films, nobody can say Andrews plays by the rules or cares what other people think about his work, and there is something refreshing about a filmmaker who has zero hang-ups or restraint. He just arms himself with a camera, a thin plot, and a cast of people so weird they seem like they only exist in the shadows. It's what makes films like this so exciting and dangerous. And while I do applaud his raw anarchist style it's the writing that sinks this film like a stone. *Trailer Town* has moments of genius but a good ninety percent of it feels like it was written by a sexually stunted teenager who thinks using dirty words is the same as crafting real humor. Don't misunderstand me; I love comedy that pushes the limits of social acceptance. However, Andrews' excessive raunchiness gets old really fast and its repetitive nature only serves to takes the edge out of humor. And it's not the crude humor that bothers me, I'm all for it, but what does is the lack of any clever jokes. As a positive, the cast is brilliantly populated with some really interesting and strange people who seem like they came fresh out of an early Warhol/Waters film. This is no doubt a very strange film and that's why I thought it deserved to be included in this book; however, I can't say I recommend it, which pains me, because I respect Andrews' raw in-your-face style. And while I thought there were glimmers of genius, the film is aimless and the lazy writing makes the film feel like one long sex joke that goes on for eighty minutes.

Wetlands, aka Feuchtgebiete (2013)

DIRECTED BY	David Wnendt
WRITTEN BY	David Wnendt, Claus Falkenberg, Sabine Pochhammer, Charlotte Roche (based on the novel by)
STARRING	Carla Juri, Christoph Letkowski, Marlen Kruse, Mercet Becker, Axel Milberg, Peri Baumeister, Edgar Selge, Clara Wunsch
COUNTRY	Germany

There are in-your-face vulgar comedies, and then there is *Wetlands,* which may be hands down the boldest and nastiest I've ever seen in the genre. *Wetlands* follows the misadventures of a quirky girl named Helen (Carla Juri) who has an interesting way of looking at things like sexuality and personal hygiene. After a shaving accident lands her in the hospital, she cooks up a scheme to reunite her divorced parents, all while toying with her male nurse named Robin (Christoph Letkowski). I will say from the start that if you are the kind of person easily offended by things of a sexual natural, which tends to get pretty graphic, you may want to skip this film altogether. If you're still with me, let's proceed. Director David Wnendt certainly pulls no punches in delivering a raunchy, even gross-out, film; however, he brilliantly flips convention on its head by having our focus be a woman. This may actually make some viewers all the more uncomfortable, but in my opinion, it's part of what makes this such an interesting and daring little movie. From the outset I feared that this would be all shock and no value, but to my surprise, the story has real heart and deals with a subject that is relatable to a lot of people: divorce. The more weighty drama helps give a nice balance to the more outrageous aspects but thankfully, for the most part everything is kept light. Another thing that really propels this is some fine camera work and wonderfully done visual effects which gives it a more polished look. Sadly, the film does tend to lack direction at times and some scenes are pointless while others go on a bit too long. Actor Carla Juri really does an amazing job at capturing Helen, and her performance helps bring multiple layers to the character. And even if she is a bit bizarre you still totally feel in love with her nonetheless. *Wetlands* may not be for everyone but past its taboo nature lies a work of art that is a refreshingly fearless gender-defying and, of course, funny film. Worth seeking out.

TRIVIA: Actor Carla Juri, who plays Helen, is set to star in the upcoming *Blade Runner* sequel.

Withnail and I (1987)

DIRECTED BY	Bruce Robinson
WRITTEN BY	Bruce Robinson
STARRING	Richard Grant, Paul McGann, Richard Griffiths, Ralph Brown, Michael Elphick, Michael Wardle, Noel Johnson
COUNTRY	Britain

London 1969. Two down-and-out actors, Withnail (Richard Grant) and friend and flatmate Marwood (Paul Grant), decide to get out of there miserable existence and have a holiday at Withnail's uncle's country house. What ensues is a blisteringly weird odyssey in the English countryside. The best way to describe *Withnail and I* to someone who's never seen it is, totally manic yet something oddly poetic about it. The plot is thin yet it's filled with quirky characters and brilliant dialogue dripping with sharp tongued wit. The comedy is wickedly dark with lines that are endlessly quotable for underground film buffs. I can't recall the last time I laughed so hard I could hardly see the screen because of the tears in my eyes. *Whitenail* is also a biting satire on English life as well as the so-called 'swinging '60s. As humorous as this film is it also has a great deal of drama that doesn't feel contrived and hits one like a gut punch. The cast is amazing and Richard Grant and Paul McGann give star-making performances. The late great Ralph Brown is equally amazing as the portly and flamboyant uncle. *Withnail and I* is equal parts side-splitting comedy and drama and is anchored by an incredible cast. Required viewing.

CRAZY CONNECTIONS: Harry Potter and Doctor Who fans will no doubt recognize actor Richard Griffith who plays Uncle Vernon in the *Harry Potter* film series and Paul Grant as the Doctor in *Doctor Who*.

Wrong (2012)

DIRECTED BY	Quentin Dupieux
WRITTEN BY	Quentin Dupieux
STARRING	Jack Plotnick, Eric Judor, William Fichtner, Reagan Burns, Steve Little, Alexis Dziena, Arden Myrin, and Flat Eric (as himself)
COUNTRY	France

From the director of *Rubber* comes another blisteringly funny and brain-melting film. Dolph Springer (Jack Plotnick) is just a regular guy going to a job and loving his furry pal, Paul. One day he wakes up horrified to find that Paul is missing. He learns that a mysterious man named Master Chang (William Fichtner) kidnapped his dog as part of a strange public service. What ensues is a strange odyssey of twists and turns, but will Dolph be reunited with his dog? As always Dupieux throws his audience headlong into a totally bananas world where it constantly rains inside an office building, the dead can, for no reason, come back to life, and people say exactly what they feel like without any filter. For people not used to far out films it can be quite jarring to say the least, but since you're reading this book I assume you're prepared for this. I love how this film teeters on the real and the surreal and walks such a masterful line between the two. It's something that is difficult to pull off but Dupieux does it well. One way he achieves this is having our hero Dolph grounded in, let's call it semi-reality, and helps to anchor the far-out plot and at the same time serve as a viewpoint character. While there is no doubt the film is wickedly clever and smartly written his later work is stronger in concepts and execution. The cast is amazing with Jack Plotnick in the lead. He seems very comfortable in the role and his natural comedic timing really shines through. William Fichtner is also great and the two play well off of each other and it makes for some ultra-weird and funny moments. Equally good is Arden Myrin in a small but hilarious role as Dolph's awful boss. Like his other films Quentin loves to play with subtle sight gags and weird little details, which is yet another reason why multiple viewings is a must. A psychotronic cinematic journey that hits a right note on all accounts and has genuine heart and a refreshing blast of fresh air from the Hollywood glut that keeps getting churned out. This film deserves a pat on the head and is a treat for man and man's best friend alike. You'll be begging for more.

Wrong Cops (2013)

DIRECTED BY	Quentin Dupieux
WRITTEN BY	Quentin Dupieux
STARRING	Mark Burnham, Jack Plotnick, Eric Judor, Steve Little, Eric Wareheim, Alexis Dziena, Arden Myrin, and Flat Eric (as himself)
COUNTRY	France

I'm loathe to admit I am fairly new to the wildly offbeat world of Quentin Dupieux, but, as they say, better late than never, right? This time he tackles cops as a spinoff of sorts to his previous film *Wrong* with Officer Duke (Mark Burnham) returning to his role. In a series of misadventures, Officer Duke accidentally shoots a guy and must find a way to get rid of the body. Meanwhile, Officer Holmes (Arden Myrin) blackmails a fellow officer while dimwitted pervert de Luca (Eric Wareheim) is obsessed with making various females strip while he takes photos. It's just a typical day in the lives of some very Wrong Cops. Once again, Dupieux constructs a film that walks a fine line between reality and absurd, and he does it in a very smart way. Writing-wise this feels more mature than his previous film, *Wrong,* and having the different storylines intersect was a stroke of genius. What I find most interesting about Quentin's films is they deal with dark subject matter, yet his humor softens it and, while it's still pretty weird, it's not as bleak as it might seem on paper. It, of course, features his unique brand of irony and satire and numerous sight gags and inside jokes that fans are sure to pick up on.

Let's talk about the extremely talented cast of actors. Mark Burnham bears almost all and he nails the role of the out-of-his-mind cop who we briefly meet in *Wrong*. His presence is the stuff of comedy gold and even when he does some pretty loathsome things you still kind of like the guy. The supporting cast is equally brilliant with veteran actors like Eric Roberts, Grace Zabriskie, and even shock rock god Marilyn Manson making gut-busting cameos. Also returning (in a different role) is Arden Myrin and, thankfully, she has a bigger role, proving she clearly has the comedic chops to hang with the big boys. Screen icon Ray Wise steals the show with his one scene which has to be one of the greatest funeral speeches ever. Eric Wareheim of *Tim and Eric Awesome Show* fame also turns in a solid performance. No offensive meant to the Broken Lizard gang but this is far superior in my opinion to *Super Troopers,* as it has a sharper wit and edgier comedy. While I loved his previous outing, *Wrong Cop* really shows a lot of growth in terms of writing while retaining the same clever concepts and outrageousness that fans have come to love. It's a film that is criminally underrated and is destined to becoming a cult classic.

Yeti: A Love Story, aka Yeti A Gay Love Story (2006)

DIRECTED BY	Adam Deyoe and Eric Gosselin
WRITTEN BY	Adam Deyoe and Eric Gosselin, Jim Martin, Moses Roth
STARRING	Adam Malamut, David Paige, Joe Mande, Laura Glascott, Loren Mash, Eric Gosselin, Leo Boivin, Noah Wolf
COUNTRY	United States

If Andy Milligan and John Waters made a rom-com together this might be what you get. Troma for me is very hit or miss. Some titles are great but it seems like for every *Toxic Avenger* (the first one anyways) there's a pile of unwatchable steamers.

One exception is *Yeti: A Love Story*. Frat boy Adam (Adam Malamut) and a group of friends go camping seeking fun, drinking, and lots of fooling around. But for Adam, it's love he ends up finding in the form of a yeti he finds in the forest. Soon the gang find themselves embroiled in a twisted plot perpetrated by a sinister cult that uses the beast for their own sick ends. *Yeti* reminds me of *Cannibal! The Musical* in terms of strange subversive comedy with a bold and independent spirit. The humor is aimed at the Adult Swim crowd and is so out-of-its-mind zany it's hard not to chuckle and, at times, full belly laugh. Critics that pan the film obviously are not the intended audience. Because its not high-brow they were aiming for but rather off-the-wall, edgy, and at times, downright stupid humor. They also fail to see this is in fact a well constructed film with slick editing, original music, and a creative, albeit weird, plot. It's very clear the filmmakers are working with a shoestring budget; however, it only adds to the gory gross-out goopy charm that made early Troma films so enjoyable. This film is far from perfect and while some of the jokes work others fall flat. Furthermore, the plot tends to lose focus of the bigger picture. What really saves the film though is how utterly sincere it is and it never apologies for itself. A highlight is the character known only as Sex Piss, a guy who terrorizes the young female campers. His lines are pure underground comedy gold. While not the greatest comedy in this guide it is criminally underrated and deserves to be re-discovered. Praise the Yeti!

CHAPTER 4

Similar to the cars chapter, I wanted to break slightly from the traditional genres and get a little more specific, and I was finding a lot of films fitting the crime and thriller genre. From neo-noir to gangster to more psychosexual fare, there is a little something for everyone here. Inside you'll find a mixture of oddities like a gas-huffing Dennis Hopper in Lynch's nightmarish neo-noir *Blue Velvet* or Jennifer Jason Leigh in the criminally underrated *Heart at Midnight*. There is also something so perverse and deeply unsettling about these films, which I feel lends itself perfectly in this book. In doing research for this chapter I discovered some grimy little gems like the twist-and-turn filled *The House of the Yellow Carpet* and the wonderfully in-your-face madness of *Gone with the Pope*. As always I compiled a wide range of sickos and psychos, femme fatales, and even some mutant chickens for good measure. Enjoy!

Crime/Thrillers

Bad Lieutenant: Port of Call New Orleans (2009)

DIRECTED BY	Werner Herzog
WRITTEN BY	William M. Finkelstein
STARRING	Nicolas Cage, Eva Mendes, Val Kilmer, Fairuza Balk, Xzibit, Shawn Hatosy, Jennifer Coolidge, Tom Bower
COUNTRY	United States

It's hard to believe anyone would do a follow-up to Abel Ferrara's 1992 classic *Bad Lieutenant*, which was a raw and unflinching piece of cinema with an Oscar-worthy performance from its star, Harvey Keitel. Now imagine that very thing happening with Herzog directing and the off the-wall acting style of Nick Cage. The end result is something, well . . . interesting. Terence McDonagh (Nicolas Cage), a newly promoted lieutenant, is a heavily drug-addicted, gambler who plays by his own set of loose rules. After a family of five is senselessly gunned down Terence is on the case, fueled on little sleep and lots of coke. I always found Werner Herzog to be a really interesting director but not someone without flaws in his career, and *Port of Call* is for me a misstep, but not entirely awful. At just over two hours the film tends to drag and it bogs itself down in needless subplots while it gets further away from the main thread, which is the investigation into the five slain victims. The film feels like one big excuse to have Cage acting high out of his mind and while that's certainly entertaining to watch it doesn't totally make up for its sometimes aimless plot. Speaking of Cage, to say he is over the top really does the phrase no justice (though nothing tops him in *Vampire's Kiss*), and his off-the-wall antics seems to anchor the entire film. Because it's just hard to outright hate the film when he is so damned entertaining to watch. Besides Cage chewing every bit of scenery, there are some stellar performances by Eva Mendes, Val Kilmer, and smaller roles by cult stars Fairuza Balk and Brad Dourif who are always enjoyable to watch. One thing that Herzog does right is injecting some delightfully absurd black comedy that greatly helps the sometimes plodding plot. Why does this film exist? Well if it's merely to watch some epic Nick Cage freak-outs like when he terrorizes an elderly lady in a nursing home it's worth it, even if it's pointless. *Port of Call* is very much worth your while if only for the so-bad-it's-great variety.

Bare Behind Bars, aka A Prisão (1980)

DIRECTED BY	Oswaldo de Oliveira
WRITTEN BY	Oswaldo de Oliveira
STARRING	Maria Stella Splendore, Neide Ribeiro, Danielle Ferrite, Márcia Fraga, Meiry Vieira, Sonia Regina, Marta Anderson
COUNTRY	Brazil

In the time honored tradition of women in prison films comes *Bare Behind Bars* which is best described as pure brain candy for the warped cinephile. Sylvia (Maria Stella Splendore) is an evil warden who treats the prisoners like cattle and, worse yet, she sells young girls on the black market. The prisoners have had enough of this and rebel. Similar to *Ilsa: She Wolf of the SS* this movie doesn't know the meaning of subtlety and follows the standard WIP formula. This means it's chock full of sadism via guards, lots of shower scenes, more violence, and, oh yeah, lots and lots of eroticism. *Bare* is indeed pure exploitation but it's also out of it's flipping mind and it's deliriously campy and over the top in every way. The addition of dark humor also makes for some great moments. For example, there is a bit of business where so many women die at this prison the graveyard is literally overflowing. And then of course there is the insane blonde nurse (credited as Barbara the Insane Nurse) who is pure comedy gold. She actually tries to take someone's blood pressure from around their neck. Let's not forget about the ending which is so out-of-left-field and different from what preceded it, it feels like you're watching a totally different movie. Some would say it's a huge minus; however, for me, the perfecting capping of an already out-of-its mind film. It's grimy, it's low-budget, and has a mindlessly simple plot but it's also fun, entertaining, and a wonderful guilty pleasure. So good it should be criminal.

Blue Velvet (1986)

DIRECTED BY	David Lynch
WRITTEN BY	David Lynch
STARRING	Dennis Hopper, Kyle MacLachlan, Laura Dern, Isabella Rossellini, Dean Stockwell, Hope Lange, Priscilla Pointer
COUNTRY	United States

David Lynch's films could easily populate this entire book but I took great pains in picking his very best and weirdest. Enter *Blue Velvet,* a film which is seriously disturbed and also brilliant. In the tiny town of Lumberton everything seems like a little slice of cherry pie until a young man named Jeffery (Kyle MacLachlan) discovers a severed human ear. As he investigates he is flung into a dark underbelly of sex, crime, and insanity. But can Jeffery escape with all his limbs intact? David Lynch peels back the picturesque small town facade and exposes something sinister and rotten like no other filmmaker can do. Lynch's films have a dangerous feeling because he forces us to experience the very worst of human nature, and in this film we get put into the very heart of darkness. *Blue Velvet* is part neo-noir and psycho sexual thriller conceived in a fever-like nightmare world, and it's both engrossing and jarring for the audience. This is considered one of his more traditionally structured narratives unlike more experimental outings like *Inland Empire* and *Rabbits,* but that's not to suggest it's any less weird or at times surreal. The cast is outstanding with Kyle MacLachlan doing a great job perfectly capturing a level of innocence and Isabella Rossellini giving an incredible raw and heartbreaking performance. But it's character actor Dennis Hopper that steals every scene he's in as the gas-huffing psycho Frank Booth. Over the top, you bet, but considering the off-kilter subject matter it seems fitting. There are also wonderfully deranged moments from Dean Stockwell and, of course, the always awesome Brad Dourif and veteran actors like Frances Bay and Priscilla Pointer. What I love about Lynch's films is they take us sometimes kicking and screaming into some very uncomfortable places and do so in a very stylish and extremely well-written way, and *Blue Velvet* ranks among my favorite of not only his films but in the neo-noir genre. Everyone who considers themselves a film buff needs to make this a must-watch.

TRIVIA: *Blue Velvet* has been parodied and referenced in numerous films and TV shows, including *Clerks* and *Mystery Science Theater 3000.*

Cul-De-Sac (1966)

DIRECTED BY	Roman Polanski
WRITTEN BY	Gérard Brach, Roman Polanski
STARRING	Donald Pleasence, Françoise Dorléac, Lionel Stander, Jack MacGowran, Iain Quarrier, Jacqueline Bisset
COUNTRY	Britain

Criminals Dickie (Lionel Stander) and Albie (Jack MacGowran) are stranded by the road. Albie is injured and stays behind as Dickie explores a nearby seaside castle. The home is owned by George (Donald Pleasence) and his young bride Teresa (Françoise Dorléac), and to their dismay they are overrun by the crooks until their boss comes for them. What ensues is a bizarre battle of wit and wills in this tense and extremely odd flick. Roman Polanski weaves a tapestry of psychological twists and turns in the gauze of a crime thriller with undertones of a Samuel Beckett play. Cul-De-Sac explores themes that are ever present in many of Polanski's films such as fear and paranoia, sexual frustration, and ultimately madness, but he also has a wonderfully wry and dark sense of humor which acts as a great counterbalance. There are some great absurd moments like the cross-dressing scene at the beginning involving Donald's character, which coincides nicely with the arrival of the criminals. While this is not an outright horror movie it does flirt with certain tropes of the genre, and indeed the gloomy castle evokes an almost weird Gothic like vibe and leads to a feeling of dread and tension, which builds as the plot unfolds. Polanski is just masterful behind the lens and sets up shots with laser-like percussion and employees some great camera work which becomes part of the narrative. The cast is top-notch with veteran actors Lionel Stander and Jack MacGowran giving seamless performances as the two thugs, but of course, it's Pleasence who ends up stealing the show. He works his cinematic magic as the mild mannered kind of dorky George and brings a wonderfully layered complexity to the character. Equally good is his on-screen wife Françoise Dorléac who is not only talented but a knock-out. With moments that range from weird, funny, tense, and harrowing Cul-De-Sac is an enthralling film that gripped me by the throat and held me until the end credits. Required viewing for anyone serious about films.

Death Laid an Egg (1968)

DIRECTED BY	Giulio Questi
WRITTEN BY	Giulio Questi, Franco Arcalli
STARRING	Gina Lollobrigida, Jean-Louis Trintignant, Ewa Aulin, Jean Sobieski, Renato Romano, Vittorio André
COUNTRY	Italy

In 1964, Mario Bava released Blood and Black Lace, the film that single-handedly created the Giallo genre (which is considered the forefather of the slasher genre in America), unleashing a slew of black gloved killers painting the silver screen red, and as always, ramping up the perversion. Death Laid an Egg, released a mere four years after, ranks up there as one of the strangest to come out of the original cycle. Anna's (Gina Lollobrigida) husband Marco (Jean-

Louis Trintignant) owns a chicken farm, and their seemingly happy marriage is put to the test when her cousin Gabrielle (Ewa Aulin) moves in with them. Soon Marco begins an affair with the young cousin leaving the scorned wife in the wings. When prostitutes begin turning up dead it's a murder case most "fowl" in this Italian outing. This film certainly wastes no time in churning out the sleaze and perversion, which only grows. As the film progresses we get into bizarre fetish territory. Fans expecting an ultra-splattery Giallo will be sorely disappointed as the film doesn't even begin to compare to later, more gore-soaked entries, but what it lacks in the carnage it more than makes up for in sheer strange, even downright surreal, moments. There is even a wonderfully absurd and totally random subplot about genetically altered chickens. Why? Because there just is. The film is also an interesting and sly commentary on the working class labor system in Italy at the time. With hardly a dull moment the film is anchored with some clever twists and turns that keep you on your toes. While *Death Laid an Egg* may not be the greatest or best-known Giallo it is a very odd and engaging outing which deserves to be re-discovered.

Double, The (2013)

DIRECTED BY	Richard Ayoade
WRITTEN BY	Richard Ayoade, Amina Dasmal
STARRING	Jesse Eisenberg, Mia Wasikowska, Wallace Shawn, Noah Taylor, Cathy Moriarty, Craig Roberts, James Fox
COUNTRY	Britain

Simon (Jesse Eisenberg) is a feeble young man, just another faceless cog at his job. While he is a hard worker he seems to just fade into the background. He lives in a world of isolation, no real friends, a mother who loathes him, and the girl he loves doesn't seem to know he exists. Basically, nobody seems to know he exists. But his world is turned upside down when a new employee joins the workforce that looks exactly like him in every way. Soon he works his way into Simon's life and takes over, replacing him. Richard Ayoade, known for the brilliant *Garth Marenghi's Dark Place*, takes a stab at thrillers and it's amazing. *The Double* is a real departure from his usual stuff and, while there is a small amount of dark humor, this is anything but a comedy. Part of the power of this thriller is how many can relate to the character of Simon, a loser in life that seems to get stepped on even though he is good guy. He really taps into some primal fear like death and ultimately being replaced and forgotten about. Bringing to life Simon is Jesse Eisenberg who gives his best performance to date playing not only the painfully shy and lonely Simon but his evil counterpart James. He does so with little effort, and I was really blown away by just how good he is in this. Mia Wasikowska plays the object of Simon's affection and, while I love her as an actor, I feel she plays things very wooden. This brings me to my one complaint with this film, which is how her character is written. It isn't very likeable and it's hard to understand her appeal. Visually, this film is stunning and production designer David Crank has worked on such films as *Lincoln Hannibal* and *There Will be Blood* to name a few. He carefully picks a color scheme that invokes a feeling of neverending dread and gives it a neo-noir-like feeling. *The Double* is a tense ever winding twist-filled thriller with standout performances, dark humor, and an almost oppressive sense of doom. Worth a watch.

Gone with the Pope (Grindhouse re-release title), aka Kiss the Ring (1975/2009)

DIRECTED BY	Duke Mitchell
WRITTEN BY	Duke Mitchell
STARRING	Duke Mitchell, Lorenzo Dardado, Jim LoBianco, Peter Milo, John Murgia, Giorgio Tavolieri, Bill Boyd, John Bruno
COUNTRY	United States

Before I get into the review, it behooves me to give you a little background information on this film. Duke Mitchell, bit actor in the '50s turned filmmaker in the '70s, sadly only made two films before his life was cut short at only fifty-five years old. Well, make that one finished film and one mostly finished one. Originally titled *Kiss the Ring* and later rescued by the good folks at *Grindhouse Releasing* and re-titled *Gone with the Pope* the film was nearly three hours long. To make matters worse its editing was done using no script (none known to exist); only notes and scrapes of paper. Paul (Duke Mitchell) is a recently released gangster, and even though he has a checkered past he believes utmost in friendship and loyalty. He is offered a job to kill seven guys; however, it's the score of a lifetime he's after. While on a sea voyage with his friends he cooks up a plan to kidnap the Pope and ask a ransom; one dollar from every single Catholic in the world. What follows is a whacked-out journey of murder, mayhem, and self-discovery.

Editing without a script would definitely explain some glaring problems with the film. Like the hitman plot at the beginning which has very little significance later in the film, and the main pope kidnapping plot seems jammed in there haphazard. It's also surprisingly not a huge part of the film. The acting, and I'm using that very loosely here, is an unholy mess, and Duke has some great freak-out moments that are both awful and hilarious. But all that can be forgiven because Duke Mitchell with his frizzy hair, giant sideburns, and crooning voice emerges as an unsung cult icon and his film certainly embodies a free-spirited rebellion that is both strange and entertaining. This film isn't very bloody, but there are some murders that are done very matter-of-factly and thankfully not over-stylized. On an obviously low budget Mitchell uses great shooting locations to his advantage. He also shows a keen visual flare; for example, the way the faces are lit during the kidnapping sequence gives a great ominous vibe. *Gone with the Pope* is a gritty, funny, and bizarre exploitation crime drama that is sure to offend and please just about everyone. Despite its flaws I give this outrageous '70s oddity my full blessing.

Heart of Midnight (1988)

DIRECTED BY	Matthew Chapman
WRITTEN BY	Matthew Chapman
STARRING	Jennifer Jason Leigh, Brenda Vaccaro, James Rebhorn, Frank Stallone, Steve Buscemi, Peter Coyote
COUNTRY	United States

In the world of odd and disturbing thrillers *Heart of Midnight* is one of the most overlooked, despite its stellar cast including Oscar-nominated actor Jennifer Jason Leigh and an early role for Steve Buscemi. An already mentally unstable girl named Carol (Jennifer Jason Leigh) inherits a sleazy sex club called "The Midnight" from her Uncle Fletcher (Sam Schacht), but it seems that The Midnight holds dark secrets inside its many rooms, and strange noises leads her to think she's not alone. Writer/director Matthew Chapman delivers a truly off-putting psycho sexual neo-noir thriller that explores heavy subject matter like madness, rape, sadomasochism, and incest. The story weaves an engaging twist filled mystery that keeps you on the very edge of your seat. Chapman masterfully keeps a nice level of tension and suspense, which only grows as the film spirals into some very twisted and unnerving places. *Midnight* also has a wonderful stylish flare that, at times, reminded me of early Mario Bava. Film buffs will also notice the clever visual nod to Kubrick's *A Clockwork Orange*. One of my favorite actors, Jennifer Jason Leigh, does a great job in playing a woman who is deeply damaged and vulnerable but also has an inner strength. She also has a classical noir beauty which really plays up the film's themes of eroticism. Equally brilliant is Peter Coyote who can swing from charming to downright weird with little effort. A few problems I had were some plot holes and some rather large gaps in logic, which I won't mention, as it would spoil one of the film's twists. Also, while it does play a role in the reveal I thought the apple theme was a bit labored for such a minor plot point in the film. Putting this aside, it still manages to be a utterly disturbing and nightmare-inducing film which cranks the creep factor up and never lets up until the final frames. A very impressive tension-filled and stylish neo-noir that mirrors the work of David Lynch. Highly recommended.

Honeymoon Killers, The (1969)

DIRECTED BY	Leonard Kastle
WRITTEN BY	Leonard Kastle
STARRING	Shirley Stoler, Tony Lo Bianco, Mary Jane Higby, Doris Roberts, Marilyn Chris, Kip McArdle, Barbara Cason
COUNTRY	United States

Leonard Kastle loosely based his film on the 1940s real-life killer duo Raymond and Martha, also dubbed The Lonely Hearts Killers. Martha Beck (Shirley Stoler) is an ample woman who works as a nurse but is lonely and wanting to find the love of her life. As fate would have it her best friend, Bunny (Doris Roberts), puts her information in a Lonely Hearts pen pal list, or an early form of Match.com. She soon hears from Ray (Tony Lo Bianco), a charming man who, through letters, sweeps Beck right off her feet. Her deep devotion to him is boundless, even if it involves murder. *The Honeymoon Killers* is a rare gem of a film which walks an interesting line between disturbing and darkly funny. Its inherit camp value is further boosted by its larger-than-life star Ms. Shirley Stoler. She is absolutely amazing in the role, and her performance (like the film itself) straddles a fine line between serious and absurd. Equally good is the suave and handsome Tony Lo Bianco, who, like Stoler, plays everything with just enough earnest to keep things from getting too over-the-top. He also oozes charisma with a measure of sleaze that is perfect for the character. Kastle wisely gives the film a gritty realism by utilizing a documentary-like feel that includes the use of natural lighting and opting for less slick handheld camera shots. The murders themselves are surprisingly tame but made hugely effective by the clinically cold manner in which they are executed. There are a handful of films that I can go back to and rewatch over and over and never get tired. *The Honeymoon Killers* is certainly one of those.

TRIVIA: Feature film debut of Doris Roberts, later known for her role on the hit show *Everybody Loves Raymond.*

Martin Scorsese was originally going to direct this film.

A sequel was in the works but sadly never happened.

House of the Yellow Carpet, The, aka La Casa del Tappeto Giallo (1983)

DIRECTED BY	Carlo Lizzani
WRITTEN BY	Filberto Bandini, Lucio Battistrada, Aldo Selleri (based on play by)
STARRING	Erland Josephson, Béatrice Romand, Vittorio Mezzogiorno, Milena Vukotic
COUNTRY	Italy

The fun yet hard part of this book was researching and tracking down these little-known films, and while some are pretty bad others really blindsided me by how good and criminally underrated they were. *The House of the Yellow Carpet* is certainly one such film. It's a typical Saturday for married couple Antonio (Vittorio Mezzogiorno) and Franca (Béatrice Romand). They are selling their yellow carpet, which was a gift from her stepfather. A mysterious man comes over interested in the item, but things go from awkward to downright weird as the man starts to press the woman for personal information. What ensues is a psychological game of tug of war that turns deadly. It's not often that a film has such a wonderfully creepy and tension-filled start and is able to constantly maintain it throughout its runtime. The small cast of actors helps keep things simple, and intimate, and surprising. This, and the fact that most of the action takes place in one room, doesn't hinder the film with pacing issues. There are enough twists and turns to keep even the most jaded film buffs guessing until the very final frame. It's certainly not your typical Giallo and at a certain point it feels almost like a neo-Gothic with psycho-sexual overtones and a sprinkle of dark humor at the end. It is often compared to *Wait until Dark,* and indeed the film does have an almost unbearably claustrophobic feeling of dread with the addition of bizarre eroticism that adds a nice level of sleaze to the mix. Aldo Selleri's play-turned-film is a great example of the school of less is more with lots of eerie, tense-filled moments and plenty of surprises to keep it constantly engrossing. It's a real treat to have discovered this film and hopefully now you can as well.

Kidnapped Coed, aka Date with a Kidnapper (1976)

DIRECTED BY	Frederick R.Friedel
WRITTEN BY	Frederick R.Friedel
STARRING	Jack Canon, Leslie Rivers, Charles Elledge, Bob Martin, Susan McRae, Larry Lambeth, Skip Lundby
COUNTRY	United States

From the director of *Axe* comes another grimy outing. A young girl named Sandra (Leslie Rivers) is kidnapped by a small-time thug named Eddie (Jack Canon) and through a series of strange events the pair end up in love. Just your typical boy meets girl, boy kidnaps girl, girl develops Stockholm Syndrome. *Date with a Kidnapper* starts with a bang and features a very solid first act full of action, and oozes plenty of sleaze and perversion to keep any Grindhouse fan happy. I was also pleasantly surprised that more attention was paid to fleshing out the story than Friedel's previous outing. For example, Jack Canon's character has some depth with a decent amount of backstory that doesn't feel phony or forced. Also, there is no denying that Frederick Friedel has skills behind the lens, and both this film and his previous film *Axe* feature some wonderful photography and interesting camera work. But the problem with this, like his other film (he only made two), is it feels terribly underdone. It's like he writes a first act and forgets to finish it, and the result is things just happen with no clear drive or point. I also thought the ending was going for something really clever but it just fizzles out, leaving me unsatisfied. Even with its virtually nonexistent plot I still enjoyed this film purely for its strangeness, which keeps it from getting dull. Frederick Friedel certainly has his very own charm, and his quirky stories and offbeat approach make his films a must for anyone interested in alterative cinema.

Killer Joe (2011)

DIRECTED BY	William Friedkin
WRITTEN BY	Tracy Letts (based on his play)
STARRING	Matthew McConaughey, Juno Temple, Thomas Haden Church, Gina Gershon, Emile Hirsch, Marc Macaulay
COUNTRY	United States

Anybody who tells you Friedkin has lost his touch is extremely misinformed. Sure, he may never make another movie has good as *The French Connection, Boys in the Band,* or *The Exorcist,* but he still makes quality films, especially for a man his age. Chris Smith (Emile Hirsch) is in deep with a man named Digger (Marc Macaulay) for a large sum of money. Of course he doesn't have it and, along with his dim-witted father Ansel (Thomas Haden Church), they cook up a scheme. The plan is simple: hire someone to kill Ansel's ex-wife for the insurance money, which will be left to Dottie (Juno Temple), her daughter. Who yah gonna call when you need mama dead? Why, detective Joe Copper (Matthew McConaughey), of course. Shortly after Joe is hired the whole plan starts to unravel, and what seemed like a simple case of murder for hire spirals into some very dark and twisted areas, leaving no one untouched. Take an amazingly weird and provocative screenplay by Pulitzer Prize-winning writer Tracy Letts, mix that with the keen directing of Oscar winner William Friedkin, and blend in some very talented actors, and you got a recipe for a wickedly funny southern fried redneck noir. Matthew McConaughey gives a bone-chilling and (for the most part) understated performance as the titular character. He plays Joe as an almost blank and empty person and allows the audience to project unto that. Giving an equally strange and solid performance is Juno Temple, and the two have such an odd but brilliant chemistry in their scenes together. At its core this is a crime drama, but Friedkin injects a lot of black comedy that gives the film a nice balance, keeping it from being too bleak and allows for some incredibly bizarre juxtaposition. It takes a mad genius to underscore a violent scene with Clarence Carter's song *Strokin*, something few directors would be bold enough to attempt or talented enough to pull off successfully. And while we're on the subject of the violence, the film surprisingly holds back, and that restraint makes the savagery all the more shocking when it happens. He doesn't shy away from the blood, and it is done in a very non-stylized way, making it all the more uncomfortable for us the watch. Letts and Friedkin make a wonderful team having previously worked on *Bug*, another film that is vastly underrated. This southern gothic examines the darkest parts of the human condition in a very real gritty way but also combines the very blackest of comedy, and the result is a deeply disturbing and at times humorous slice of fried thriller. Also, you'll never look at chicken legs the same way ever again. So saddle up and get yourself a big heapin' helping of this extremely well-made thriller.

Mulholland Drive (2001)

DIRECTED BY	David Lynch
WRITTEN BY	David Lynch
STARRING	Naomi Watts, Laura Harring, Jeanne Bates, Robert Forster, Brent Briscoe, Dan Birnbaum, Maya Bond, Michael Cooke
COUNTRY	United States, France

If it's David Lynch, you know you're in for a wild, strange, and, of course, perplexing journey into a cerebral carnival of souls. After a horrible car crash leaves a young woman with amnesia she worms her way into the life of an inspiring actress named Betty (Naomi Watts). Together they start to piece together the clues of her identity. But this, of course, leads to more questions rather than answers and takes them to some very dark and deadly places. Brilliantly, Lynch uses the film noir as a template for what is best described as a surreal nightmare world and among his most baffling. As always, his visuals are on point and create a world teeming to the brim with haunted eroticism and a thick sense of foreboding. Much like *Lost Highway* Lynch starts out with a somewhat traditional narrative and at the last minute dumps the audience in a strange unknown world filled with strange characters and confusing twists and turns. There have been countless theories floating around online about what the film means but, honestly, I firmly believe it's not supposed to have a clear-cut answer, and looking for or needing one is pointless. This may be frustrating to those not used to a more freeform style, but if you embrace it as one long poetic nightmare it becomes wholly more satisfying. Plus it will save you a few headaches trying to figure it all out (much like *Lost Highway*). A seriously creepy and mesmerizing film that every buff should consider required viewing.

Neon Demon, The (2016)

DIRECTED BY	Nicolas Winding Refn
WRITTEN BY	Nicolas Winding Refn
STARRING	Elle Fanning, Jena Malone, Karl Glusman, Bella Heathcote, Abbey Lee, Keanu Reeves, Desmond Harrington
COUNTRY	United States

Walking out of the theater for *The Neon Demon* I was reeling from the nearly two hours of eye-popping, pulse-pounding, total assault on good taste which had me spellbound the entire time. Fresh off the bus, Jesse (Elle Fanning), an aspiring young model, quickly sets the industry on fire with her looks, much to the dismay of other more seasoned girls. But as the shy girl becomes full of herself the competition is waiting in the wings to pounce. Some critics have been quick to label this film as shallow as the models it depicts and, while I can't really argue with that point, I still think this is an incredible film that tells a more visually driven story rather than a standard narrative. Refn himself is almost daring you to hate it, not caring one way or the other because ultimately this is his film, not made for stuffy critics. The cinematography is, simply put, the most stunning I've seen since *The Hateful Eight,* and I would even go as far as to say it's near Kubrick-like in its bold and meticulous design. This coupled with some truly insane and beautiful visuals makes for a totally unique movie experience that totally washes over its audience in one cool psychedelic wave. I also have to give a quick mention about the ear-thumping and trippy score, which is a perfect union with the images on the screen and is as progressive as the rest of the film. Elle Fanning is brilliant as Jesse and she shows a mature range which has improved from her previous work. Equally good is its supporting cast, which includes Jena Malone, Desmond Harrington, and of course, Keanu Reeves in a small but sleazy role as a motel manager. I gotta give Mr. Refn a great deal of credit for having the balls to not only run with his surreal crazy premise but to depict numerous taboos without an ounce of shame or self consciousness. This cements the filmmaker as one of the gutsiest person working in the medium today. Not for the easily offended or disturbed but highly recommended for someone looking for a bizarre thrill ride.

GOES WELL WITH: *Maps to the Stars*

Pi (1998)

DIRECTED BY	Darren Aronofsky
WRITTEN BY	Darren Aronofsky
STARRING	Sean Gullette, Mark Margolis, Ben Shenkman, Samia Shoaib, Pamela Hart, Stephen Pearlman, Ajay Naidu
COUNTRY	United States

At a tender age of thirteen I saw *Pi*, which opened up my eyes to alternative independent cinema and to the amazing direction of Darren Aronofsky, which even at such a young age I knew was somebody really special in filmmaking. I've been following his career ever since. Maximillian Cohen (Sean Gullette) is an extremely shy mathematician who stumbles upon the key that will unlock the secrets of the universe which leads him down a deadly path of paranoia as he quickly learns other people are interested in Max's discovery. Can he escape with his life and his sanity? What made this film stand out for me even at such a young age was the fact that it's a thriller that aims a lot higher in terms of its lofty ideas that explore mysticism, math, and insanity all wrapped up in a surreal and at times kinetic candy coated shell. And it all actually meshes perfectly. The film at its core explores a man risking his very sanity to delve deep into his obsession with the ultimate goal of knowledge, and Aronofsky takes a premise that is convoluted and makes it work with skills behind the camera and well written characters that are well fleshed out. Further anchoring the plot is some great performances. Sean Gullette plays the lead and gives a wonderfully subtle performance, and it's clear that he is up to the task, playing a complex character like this without going hammy. He strikes a perfect balance of obsessed genius and lonely man that longs for love. Equally good is Mark Margolis who plays Max's mentor and, like Gullette, doesn't get carried away and shows different layers of his character in subtle ways. If you're looking for a thriller that plays by its own set of rules and injects a lot of deep themes yet still remains pulse-pounding *Pi* is the perfect equation for you.

Repulsion (1965)

DIRECTED BY	Roman Polanski
WRITTEN BY	Roman Polanski, Gérard Brach, David Stone (adaptation by)
STARRING	Catherine Deneuve, Ian Hendry, John Fraser, James Villiers, Valerie Taylor, Helen Fraser, Renee Houston
COUNTRY	Britain

Roman Polanski is known for his tense American thrillers like *Rosemary's Baby*, but it's his British film *Repulsion* that is regarded as his finest achievement. The problem with Carol (Catherine Deneuve) isn't just that she is frigid; she utterly loathes the touch of a man, all men. When her sister and her man leave for a holiday she is left alone. As time goes on her mental state of mind begins to rapidly decay, which leads to deadly consequences. Nobody has captured the pure nightmare of mental illness coupled with sexual repression and frustration quite like Roman Polanski. *Repulsion* plays out like a perverse carnival of dread-filled days and horrific nights. He effectively achieves this with a slow and methodical progression into madness, thereby creating a decent amount of suspense that becomes almost unbearable. Part of the brilliance comes from the outstanding and haunting black-and-white photography, which right off the bat instills a thick sense of foreboding that intensifies as the film reaches a terrifying finale. It also can be seen as a feminist film, as our heroin is not bound to any man and isn't a victim. Actress Catherine Deneuve is great in the role of Carol and she brings a wonderful venerability and depth in her performance. Polanski's masterpiece of paranoia, fear, and murder is a watershed moment in the thriller genre and a must-see.

Shallow Grave (1994)

DIRECTED BY	Danny Boyle
WRITTEN BY	John Hodge
STARRING	Kerry Fox, Ewan McGregor, Ken Stott, Christopher Eccleston, Keith Allen, Gary Lewis, Colin McCredie
COUNTRY	Britain

Released two years before his break-out hit *Trainspotting*, Danny Boyle unleashed his first feature film and, even at such an early point in his career, it's clear to see that he was a cinematic force to be reckoned with. Three friends and flat mates are looking for another person to house with them and, after an exhaustive interview process that includes mostly torturing the poor applicants, they finally decide on a shady businessman named Hugo (Keith Allan) who almost immediately flashes some cash their way. All seems to be going well with their new charming flat mate until he shockingly turns up dead in his room. Unknown to three friends Hugo is being sought after by some very bad men and, to make matters more complicated, they find a suitcase full of money. Right out of the gate Boyle establishes himself as a master filmmaker with this crime thriller. Screenwriter John Hodge, who would later go on to write *Trainspotting*, really crafts a multi-layered neo-noir with interesting characters and dialogue that zings. But the really brilliant thing about *Shallow Grave* is that Boyle sets up an expectation and masterfully misdirects its audience the entire time and it's like having the rug pulled out from under us. Like Boyle's later work the film is also a pitch-black comedy that wonderfully flies in the face of the rather morbid plot. And of course he ever-so-subtly ratchets up the tension, which only intensifies as the film spirals into some very bleak places. This also boasts an amazing cast that includes a young Ewan McGregor giving a wonderful and high-energy performance and the lovely Kerry Fox. Actor Christopher Eccleston is incredibly creepy as David, a seemingly mild mannered young guy pushed to the breaking point. While it may never get the attention that *Trainspotting* does this film is equally great and shows the beginning of Boyle's genius as a storyteller. Highly recommended.

Skin I Live In, The (2011)

DIRECTED BY	Pedro Almodóvar
WRITTEN BY	Pedro Almodóvar, Agustin Almodóvar, Thierry Jonquet
STARRING	Antonio Banderas, Elena Anaya, Jan Cornet, Marisa Paredes, Blanca Suarez
COUNTRY	Spain

The Skin I Live In is based on the 1984 novel *Tarantula* by French crime writer Thierry Jonquet and brought to the screen by award-winning Spanish director Pedro Almodóvar who is well-known to tackle a number of taboo subjects in a bold and unflinching manner. This film is no doubt his strangest to date. Plastic surgeon Robert Ledgard (Antonio Banderas) is on the cutting edge of skin grafting and top in his field. Little do his peers know he has a mysterious woman locked up in his house/private clinic who is acting as a human guinea pig. But who is the lady in the room and what strange events lead to her being there? Director

Pedro Almodóvar, known for his stylish and irreverent form of filmmaking, purposefully challenges the audience by hitting us right off the bat with many questions and only slowly unravels the mystery done in a mostly non-linear format. I will say this film is not something you can just turn on and tune out, as it requires your constant attention, but for the patient viewer you are certainly rewarded. Fans of Almodóvar will see his usual themes present including women, identity, betrayal, and death, but in something totally different he injects science fiction and even flirts with the horror genre in a *Frankenstein* meets *Eyes Without a Face* hybrid done like a neo-noir. Also front and center is his keen visual flare that plays as an homage to Italian directors like Argento and Bava with hints of Alfred Hitchcock and even David Cronenberg. *The Skin I Live In* is the kind of film that holds you in its icy grip and carries you through the many twists and turns. A stylish noir thriller in the vein of De Palma's *Dressed to Kill* and Hitchcock's *Vertigo* that most definitely requires a second viewing after the big twist is revealed. Highly recommended.

Sonny Boy (1989)

DIRECTED BY	Robert Martin Carroll
WRITTEN BY	Graeme Whifler
STARRING	David Carradine, Brad Dourif, Paul L. Smith, Sydney Lassick, Conrad Janis, Michael Boston, Alexandra Powers
COUNTRY	United States

I never thought I'd ever see the late great David Carradine in drag. But lo and behold *Sonny Boy* has provided the mind-melting answer to what that would be like and, yes, it's just as bizarre as you might imagine. A baby is kidnapped and taken in by a drug lord named Slue (Paul L. Smith) and his wife Pearl (David Carradine). Slue chains him up and raises him as a killing machine to tears up anyone on his master's command. However, unknowingly Sonny Boy (Michael Boston) has a mind and soul of his own, and one day he escapes and discovers the wide world. Of course the locals aren't too keen on this and chaos ensues. *Sonny Boy* is an utterly weird and captivating crime drama that acts as a metaphor for the horrors of child abuse and how monstrous parents can raise a monster. As bleak as it seems on the surface the film actually has a strong message of hope and that even an abused person can still cling to his humanity and soul. Indeed the film also works as a brilliant retelling of Mary Shelley's *Frankenstein,* and *Sonny Boy* very much embodies the monster, misunderstood by everyone but has mind and tenderness. He's even referred to by the townsfolk as "the monster". The acting is top-notch with character actor Brad Dourif, as always, giving a masterful performance and managing to steal every scene he is in. Equally good is Carradine in a—excuse the pun—ballsy gender-bending role, giving it his very all. Going into this film I thought it would be more exploitation but there is a surprising amount of depth in story and characters and a good deal of heart that I wasn't expecting. Wildly entertaining and may even choke you up by the end of it.

Tattoo (2002)

DIRECTED BY	Robert Schwentke
WRITTEN BY	Robert Schwentke
STARRING	August Diehl, Christian Redl, Nadeshda Brennicke, Johan Leysen, Florian Pazner, Joe Bausch, Monica Bleibtreu
COUNTRY	Germany

Some movies baffle me how they seem to get lost in the shuffle while lesser yet more outrageous movies get all the attention, most of the time undeservedly. Such is the case with the extremely underrated and neglected *Tattoo* by future Hollywood player Robert Schwentke. Veteran cop Minks (Christian Redl) teams up with rookie Marc (August Diehl) when a burnt body is uncovered. It is later discovered that she had her tattoo forcibly removed before her death. Soon this leads them down a twisted underbelly of shady people who deal in human flesh inked with art.

A pair of detectives hunting for a serial killer is a common staple of thrillers and they are incredibly difficult to do well, because even the best directors can fall head first into tired clichés. So when I read the plot synopsis for *Tattoo* my expectations were admittedly on the

lower side. Well, I am more than man enough to say my fears were totally unfounded because this was an amazing little film. First off, the screenplay is wonderfully written and allows the action to cool (only slightly) while he digs deep into the characters. I liked how the rookie wasn't a bright eyed do-gooder and, in fact, he's the very last person we

would expect to take the mantle of hero. He starts out as a party boy who just wanted a desk job with the police, but we really see his character evolve over the course of the film which is something you don't see often in these kinds of films. Purposely, they cast two polar opposites for the veteran and the rookie. One is young, the other old; one is bald, the other has hair; you get the picture. It's something you pick up on an unconscious level and it also plays into a mirror/reflection motif present throughout. The overall look of the film is very somber and bleak yet has some very wonderful understated visuals. For example, the rain scene with our femme fatale played brilliantly by Nadeshda Brennicke is so stunning and yet very erotic. You can tell that a lot of pain was taken to make this realistic and, even with a few familiar stand-bys, this film does everything it can to not be a typical detective thriller. In fact, I would easily call it a neo-noir. I think it's rather ironic that Schwentke now makes Hollywood films considering this film is almost anti-Hollywood in its sheer defense of conventions. *Tattoo* is Germany's answer to *Seven* and I'll even be bold enough to say in some ways it actually surpasses it. It's not hard to see why Hollywood has snatched up Robert Schwentke, and his first feature length film is an amazing exercise in the right way to do a crime/thriller horror film.

Tokyo Tribe (2014)

DIRECTED BY	Sion Sono
WRITTEN BY	Sion Sono, Santa Inoue (based on Manga by)
STARRING	Ryôhei Suzuki, Shôta Sometani, Yôsuke Kubozuka, Tomoko Karina, Riki Takeuchi, Yui Ichikawa, Motoki Fukami
COUNTRY	Japan

Tokyo Tribe is a film people seem to either love or hate. The fact that it's a nearly-two-hour hip-hop musical will certainly split a lot of fans. Set in a futuristic Japan, Tokyo is ruled by gangs otherwise known as tribes. The leader of the Wu-Ronz tribe isn't content to rule just his tribe and plans to conquer them all; now it's all out war. I admit the hip-hop thing grated on me at first as it's not a genre of music that I really enjoy. Thankfully, I was able to get past it and focus on the plot. Writer/director Sion Sono really takes the Manga template and plays it for all it's worth, and his cinematic landscape is a trippy neon-colored explosion for the eyes. It tips its hats to classics like *Blade Runner* and *A Clockwork Orange* and even squeezes in a clever *Star Wars: A New Hope* reference. For ass-kicking, high-flying action the film also delivers in spades. Not only are there great fight sequences but impressive and seamless wire use as well. Even with a lot going for it, it sadly lacks a lot in the story department. Similar to his film *Exte: Hair Extensions* Sono has trouble finding the film's emotional center. It also doesn't help that his characters lack depth, which makes it really hard to connect with them. This, coupled with a needlessly convoluted plot makes for a rather uneven viewing experience. *Tribe* does pack just enough punch both in action and visuals to make up for the missteps in writing. And you gotta give Sono props for having the stones to do the film as a musical, something I'm sure was not a popular idea. Flawed but fun and an altogether different outing that deserves a watch, unless you hate hip hop, then stay clear.

Trouble Every Day (2001)

DIRECTED BY	Claire Denis
WRITTEN BY	Claire Denis, Jean-Pol Fargeau
STARRING	Vincent Gallo, Béatrice Dalle, Tricia Vessey, Alex Descas, Florence Loiret Caille, Nicolas Duvauchelle
COUNTRY	France, Germany, Japan

Newlyweds Shane (Vincent Gallo) and June (Tricia Vessey) Brown travel to Paris for their honeymoon and what seems like a blissful stay turns nightmarish. Shane, a doctor, makes mysterious trips to a clinic leaving his new bride to explore on her own. Meanwhile, a woman with a lustful hunger stalks locals in the area. The concept of sexual desires, food, and cannibalism, and how each are closely, even chemically, connected is an interesting one, on par with the themes of Cronenberg. So I went into this film with a lot of excitement and came out rather disappointed. Unfortunately, the theme of a sexual desire leading to cannibalism is never explored at any length, which is a tragic waste. Instead, the movie seems to outright ignore its own creative idea and instead pads out the run time with needless scenes that add nothing to the already-paper-thin plot. The characters surprisingly have little to no depth which is made even worst by the total lack of chemistry between actors Gallo and Vessey. Besides being dull, the film also raises questions and doesn't bother answering them, leaving the viewer confused and frustrated. I'm all for not having everything spelled out but it's as if the writers and director had no desire in a story at all. In fact, I had watched this film not once, but twice, and I still have no idea what was going on. I will say that actress Béatrice Dalle gives an outstanding performance and her scenes are the only highlights in this entire drab depressing film. Some people seem to dig this film but for my money it's uninteresting and lacks depth in both characters and story.

Wake in Fright (1971)

DIRECTED BY	Ted Kotcheff
WRITTEN BY	Evan Jones, Kenneth Cook (based on novel by)
STARRING	Donald Pleasence, Gary Bond, Chips Rafferty, Jack Thompson, Sylvia Kay, Peter Whittle, Al Thomas
COUNTRY	Australia

Two films released in 1971 really captured the Australian outback like no other; *Walkabout* and Ted Kotcheff's brilliant *Wake in Fright,* based on the Kenneth Cook novel released ten years earlier. John Grant (Gary Bonds) is a teacher who feels trapped in his job and with his overall situation. His only bright spot is his upcoming Christmas vacation where he plans to see his girlfriend in Sydney. Before he gets there he has a stop off in a small dusty town where the locals are strange, to say the least. Through a series of misfortunes Grant is stuck there unable to escape. After watching *Wake in Fright* I felt totally and utterly shaken to my core, which is exactly the kind of impact a film like this should have on its viewers.

Kotcheff presents a brutal portrait of a man who, over a lost beer-soaked weekend loses his humanity and very nearly his sanity. On the surface the film may feel like a not-so-thinly-veiled allegory for vice leading to wreck and ruin and, while that may be the case to a degree, it's also a very ugly examination of a man under a great deal of pressure and frustration swept up in a harsh and unforgiving land. It's a further testament to the outstanding writing that explores his character in very non-glamorous ways and allows for a complete character arch. Kotcheff manages to build enough suspense and quirky characters to keep you firmly invested until ever so slowly you get the carpet ripped out from under you as the film spirals into a nightmarish world of psychological horror. The cast is brilliant and Gary Bond gives a terrific performance and you totally buy his descent into near madness. But, of course, the real scene-stealer is Donald Pleasence who gives one of his finest and rawest performances of his legendary career. Every moment he's on screen is just spellbinding. Screen icon Chip Rafferty is great and, sadly, it was his final screen appearance. *Wake in Fright* is infamous for the kangaroo hunting scene, which is powerful stuff and extremely tough to watch, as it's real footage (not filmed by Ted but rather stock footage, seamlessly integrated), and it gets to me to my very core in its visceral and unflinching matter-of-fact nature. This film ranks up there as one of the finest films to ever be made in Australia, and it's brilliant writing coupled with stark realism takes its audience to some very dark places and the result can be like a punch to the gut. Required viewing.

CHAPTER 5

Drama and strange wouldn't seem like it would go hand in hand, however, while doing my research I found a slew of oddball entries. From Edward D. Wood Jr.'s gender bender *Glen or Glenda* to *Air Doll*, a weirdly human tale about a blow-up doll, these titles cover the psychotropic spectrum. Some of these titles are pretty heavy in theme and subject, and films like *Dogtooth* and *Lost River* are best followed with a comedy chaser. As always, I tried to blend high-brow titles like Fassbinder's *In a Year with 13 Moons* and Samuel Fuller's seminal *Shock Corridor* alongside the wonderfully out-of-its-mind works like *Vampires Kiss* and Peter Jackson's *Heavenly Creatures*. This was a really enjoyable chapter to write as it really opened my eyes to both interesting and heartbreaking themes of life, death, love, and madness with perspectives from all over the globe. Even if drama is not your cup of tea, I feel like the films (for the most part) are all pretty great in their own way and you'd be hard pressed not to find your next favorite among the bunch. Gangster robots, a living love doll, and Bela Lugosi—what more could you ask for?

Drama

3 Women (1977)

DIRECTED BY	Robert Altman
WRITTEN BY	Robert Altman
STARRING	Shelley Duvall, Sissy Spacek, Janice Rule, Ruth Nelson, Robert Fortier, John Cromwell, Craig Richard Nelson
COUNTRY	United States

I don't profess to be a Robert Altman expert but I know I've enjoyed everything of his that I've seen. People may not think weird and Altman in the same breath; however *3 Women* is certainly an off-kilter little masterpiece. The film follows California transplant Pink Rose (Sissy Spacek), a shy and socially inept young woman. She gets a job at a health spa and meets Millie (Shelley Duvall) who takes Pinkie under her wing and they end up being roommates. Like Pinkie, Millie is extremely odd and everyone in her apartment building seems to avoid her like the plague. Things start out great until the strange pair begins to butt heads, leading to a tragic accident leaving Pinkie in a coma. Somber, haunting, and just plain strange only begins to describe the brilliance behind Altman's tour de force. Like his previous films it's totally original, unconventional, and plays by its own set of rules, and it's no wonder it's been compared to Ingmar Bergman's *Persona*. The cast is amazing with Shelley Duvall and Sissy Spacek both giving powerhouse performances. Altman fixes his camera on his subjects but never judges them, yet provides a startlingly honest portrait, showing them as they are stripped down (figuratively), and what we see is oftentimes not glamorous but real. Both actors are quirky which works for the weird melancholy-like vibe. Their roles aren't practically flashy but they totally throw themselves into it and the result is nothing short of spellbinding. I've always felt both Duvall and Spacek were sorely underrated and this film proves that they can carry a film of this magnitude. Further bringing the film together is a stunning and hypnotizing cinematography that captures everything from the beauty and dread of the California desert landscapes to the memorizing and wonderfully eerie murals in a pool. I could go on and on about the various symbolisms and subtext in the film but bottom line is this; it's an amazing and understated work of art by a late great cinematic master.

TRIVIA: Robert Ebert named *3 Women* the best movie of 1977.

CRAZY CONNECTIONS: The cinematographer also was first assistant camera on *Attack of the Giant Leeches* (1959)

Air Doll, aka Kûki ningyô (2009)

DIRECTED BY	Hirokazu Koreeda
WRITTEN BY	Hirokazu Koreeda, Yoshiie Goda (based on Manga by)
STARRING	Doona Bae, Arata Iura, Itsuji Itao, Joe Odagiri, Sumiko Fuji, Ryô Iwamatsu, Mari Hoshino, Miu Naraki
COUNTRY	Japan

Based on a Manga by Yoshiie Goda, *Air Doll* is a shockingly touching story about the meaning of life, love, and ultimately death. A life sized air doll that lives with a lonely man develops conciousness and a soul. As she navigates her new world she falls in love with a young store clerk. Similar to Chan-wook Park's *I'm a Cyborg But That's OK,* writer/director Hirokazu Koreeda takes a premise that could easily go over the top and not only grounds the fantasy elements in a strange kind of reality but also creates deep and, yes, even believable characters and relatable situations. The loneliness of human existence, feminism, and mortality are but a few of the themes explored, but Koreeda never feels like he's preaching. Actor Doona Bea does an amazing job as the title character and she brings a childlike innocence that is perfect for the role. Cinematographer Ping Bin Lee does an outstanding job creating some truly beautiful images, further giving the film a bittersweet poetry. *Air Doll* cleverly explores what it means to be human; something that is truly universal. Instead of a silly comedy it takes a mature yet fantastical look into some very deeply rooted themes. Required viewing.

An American Hippie in Israel, aka Ha-Trempist (1972)

DIRECTED BY	Amos Sefer
WRITTEN BY	Amos Sefer, Baruch Verthaim
STARRING	Asher Tzarfati, Shmuel Wolf, Lily Avidan, Tzila Karney, Suzan Devor, Fran Liberman-Avni
COUNTRY	Israel

Many movies were made in protest to the Vietnam War, a conflict that is still deeply scarred in people's memories. This, however, may possibly be the strangest of those films. Mike (Asher Tzarfati), a young man just coming home from serving in the Vietnam War, flies to Israel as a sort of protest of the United States. What ensues is his quest to find like-minded people while avoiding two robo-humans out to kill him.

No drugs needed to feel tripped out by this far out film by Amos Sefer. *American Hippie in Israel* is a genre-bending film that floats from being a drama to an anti-war art house film filled with unintentional comedy. Its earnest and preachy message comes off more laughable, and that is where the film's camp value comes out in full force. This coupled with heavy-handed speeches, strange robot gangsters with guns, and 'shroom-fueled moments, not to mention a wonderfully downbeat ending makes for a truly stand out film experience. So put down those brownies because this movie will get you buzzed—no munchies included. To quote Mike from the movie, "*Stop pushing buttons . . . fools!*"

Baby Doll (1956)

DIRECTED BY	Elia Zazan
WRITTEN BY	Tennessee Williams
STARRING	Karl Malden, Carroll Baker, Eli Wallach, Mildred Dunnock, Lonny Chapman, Eades Hogue, Noah Williamson
COUNTRY	United States

Before I get into this review I feel a bit of historical context is in order for those new to the film and its legacy. Upon its release *Baby Doll* drew a fire storm of controversy for its brazen and steamy look at sex, and the image of Baker lying suggestively in a baby crib on film posters was enough to set the religious right into a fit. In a sad bit of irony it's not the "sexuality" that is shocking when viewed now but rather the sobering snapshot of the Jim Crowe South with "Whites/Color" signs hanging up in businesses—which was unfortunately the norm for that time. Nobody does steamy Deep South quite like the legendary Tennessee Williams and in *Baby Doll* he serves up a tawdry psycho-sexual drama. The legendary Elia Zazan captures the mood and tension of the time and mines the story for rich character development and drama, much like *East of Eden, On the Waterfront,* etc. This couples with Tennessee Williams' blisteringly clever screenplay filled with depth and psychological tugs of war and, of course, overflowing with overt sexuality, which is incredibly steamy for the time. The scene with Baker and Wallach on the swing is some of the most erotic stuff without ever showing an ounce of nudity—this was still the '50s after all. There is also a level of sleaze and perversion that hangs over the entire thing, and the opening image of Baker in a crib sucking her thumb suggestively is both thrilling and completely unnerving at the same time. *Baby Doll* is anchored by a brilliant cast with the late great Eli Wallach, who is just poured into the role; so much so that you, at times, totally forget it's him. Carroll Baker, a young but already-seasoned actor (having already done *Giant*), gives an incredibly complex performance, and she sways from nasty brat to southern charming, from strong-willed to vulnerable with such ease. Watching Malden, Carroll, and Wallach work together is nothing short of awe-inspiring as all the actors are giving their absolute best. While it may not be as famous as Kazan's other films this is still an amazing feat in filmmaking that is firing on all levels. Required viewing.

GOES WELL WITH: *The Baby*

TRIVIA: A one-sheet poster for *Baby Doll* can be clearly seen in John Waters's *Pink Flamingos*.

First feature film of actor Rip Torn, best known for the *Men in Black* series.

Bug (2006)

DIRECTED BY	William Friedkin
WRITTEN BY	Tracy Letts (based on the screenplay and play by)
STARRING	Ashley Judd, Michael Shannon, Harry Connick Jr., Lynn Collins, Brian F. O'Byrne, Neil Bergeron, Bob Neil
COUNTRY	United States

Playwright Tracy Letts teams up with William Friedkin, legendary director of such master works as *The Exorcist* and *The French Connection,* to bring *Bug,* a brilliant film about love and paranoia in Texas. Agnes White (Ashley Judd) is a poor white trash woman living in a motel in Texas. She works at a redneck bar and is still reeling from the tragedy of losing her son, Lloyd. Her friend introduces her to a shy guy named Peter (Michael Shannon) who sucks her into his paranoid delusions, but are they just that or is something more sinister going on? *Bug* really shows that Friedkin has not lost his touch and can still make a film that is frightening and unnerving on so many levels. He manages to build a thick web of paranoia and claustrophobia that only gets more intense and jarring as the film spirals to a nerve-shattering finale. The really genius thing about this movie is it is purposely vague and is open to the audiences' interpretation, which may be frustrating for viewers who like a neat and tidy explanation, but I personally love a film that challenges its viewers in such a way. The cast is amazing with Ashley Judd giving what I consider her finest performance to date. Far too often it's hard to buy a celebrity as poor white trash and, not at all meant as a slam on Judd, but she really nails it. She is utterly fantastic in the role, which is layered and complex. Michael Shannon is such a vastly underrated actor, and I think he gives an Oscar-worthy turn as the mentally ill Peter Evans and, like Judd, digs deep into the character, not afraid to explore very dark sides. Both plunge head first into the intense and disturbing material and the end result is nothing short of spellbinding. *Bug* is a wonderfully raw psychological thriller that is sure to get under your skin and lay its eggs there. No matter how you personally interpret it, at its core it is an unflinching look at two very broken people who find a warped sort of love from each other. *Bug* is a vastly overlooked film and just further proves that Friedkin can still shock and scare an audience.

Dogtooth (2009)

DIRECTED BY	Yorgos Lanthimos
WRITTEN BY	Yorgos Lanthimos, Efthymis Filippou
STARRING	Christos Stergiolou, Michele Valley, Mary Tsoni, Angeliki Papoulia, Anna Kalaitzidou
COUNTRY	Greece

Bleak, surreal, and at times darkly humorous, *Dogtooth* ranks up there with Marian Dora's *Cannibal* and Jörg Buttgereit's *Nekromantik* as a tour de force in disturbing cinema. Three teenage siblings live totally cut off from the world, which is totally dominated by their strict father (Christos Stergiolou). They are told a whole host of lies, such as cats are man-eating beasts and it's unsafe to leave the house. That is, until their dogtooth falls out. From the very first frame writer/director Lanthimos creates a very eerie, almost otherworldly vibe that contrasts nicely with the seemingly normal family setting. The photography is wonderful and the use of natural lighting and minimalistic camera works greatly in its favor. As you get to actually know the characters it's a slippery slope into a nightmare of dysfunction that makes the family in *Julien Donkey Boy* seem like the Cleavers. In terms of violence the film pulls zero punches and the level of brutality is nerve-shattering in its unflinching depictions. And as jaded as I am I found it chilling and very unsettling. Even with a paper-thin plot there is a certain sideshow quality and things are so messed up its hard to look away, even if you want to at times. This leads me to my one complaint, which is that the characters lack depth and at times the film struggles to find its emotional center. Taboo-breaking and at times difficult to watch, this powerful Greek tragedy is a masterpiece in its own right. I highly recommend it but you might want to follow it up with a comedy.

Glen or Glenda (1953)

DIRECTED BY	Edward D. Wood Jr.
WRITTEN BY	Edward D. Wood Jr.
STARRING	Edward D. Wood Jr., Bela Lugosi, Dolores Fuller, Lyle Talbot, Timothy Farrell, Tommy Haynes, Charles Craft
COUNTRY	United States

Ever wanted to see Bela "Dracula" Lugosi in a bizarre sex change film? Well, my friends, look no further than this '50s classic from the famed cross-dressing director who not only wrote and directed this epic but also starred in it as well. *"Pull the strings!"* shouts Lugosi and ushers in one of the weirdest films ever to creep its way out of the 1950s. Shot in a mere four days, this film follows Glen (Ed Wood) as he goes about his daily double life as, you guessed it, Glenda (also Ed Wood), but keeps his secret from the love of his life, Barbara (Dolores Fuller). Will Glen be able to tell her about his secret? *Glen or Glenda,* an infamous film made even more popular with the Oscar award-winning film *Ed Wood* is certainly a mind-bending film that ranks among my very favorites from the director.

Now, before you call me "pretentious" for looking too deeply into what is at best a trashy train wreck, bare with me, my film-loving friends. Regardless of whether you're a fan of Wood Jr.'s films or not, you can't deny how ahead of its time this film is, as it not only tackles the subject of transvestitism but does it in a way that doesn't mock or demean in any way. And in recent years with the trans rights movement it's much more relevant then when it was made. Wood

also fearlessly makes a personal statement that is extremely meta (before that was even a thing) considering he plays the title character. With Lugosi playing a crazy all-seeing narrator and some really insane and totally random clips of sadism and devils etc., this is most definitely an early form of experimental cinema long before anyone even knew the term. I refuse to admit this is a bad film as it's endlessly entertaining and vastly inflectional with many big name fans. So beware of the big green dragon and give this mind-bending gender bender a try, I think you'll find it fits you as well as a pink angora sweater.

TRIVIA: One of David Lynch's favorite films. In fact he used the howling wind sound effect in his first feature *Eraserhead*.

The film *Seed of Chucky* cleverly pays homage to the cult classic.

Heavenly Creatures (1994)

DIRECTED BY	Peter Jackson
WRITTEN BY	Peter Jackson, Fran Walsh
STARRING	Kate Winslet, Melanie Lynskey, Sarah Peirse, Diane Kent, Clive Merrison, Peter Elliot, Jed Brophy
COUNTRY	New Zealand

Based on a true story that centers on Juliet (Kate Winslet) and Pauline (Melanie Lynskey), who meet and share a common interest in writing and the unusual that helps them form a strong bond. They spend their days in a lush and highly imaginative fantasy world. However, that world comes crashing in and the harsh reality of Juliet being forced to move sets in. In utter desperation the two craft a deadly plan to keep their special friendship alive at any cost. *Heavenly Creatures* marks an interesting turning point for Jackson, and this is his first foray into the more mainstream and something that isn't horror or sci-fi. He still proudly wears his love for the surreal and strange with trademark visuals that are breathtaking and pops with fanciful imagination. Also in full force is his masterful and keen cinematic eye—something he's had going back to his very first feature, *Bad Taste*. Where this film really shines is Jackson's ability to tell a very dark human drama of love and obsession yet blend in the rich and lavish daydream world, giving us a glimpse inside the mind of these two girls.

Thankfully, he never glosses over anything and his examination of their characters are never shallow nor does he cast judgment on them. It allows the viewers to get a fair and objective look. We're not supposed to think they're angels or devils. The cast is amazing—every single person—and there is not a sour performance to be had. Kate Winslet and Melaine Lynskey are stellar and, thankfully, the two have a great chemistry that is paramount to the story. They both reach deep down and give a gutsy and personal performance that is among the best of their career. *Heavenly Creatures* is a film that is heart-wrenching, humorous, dark, and whimsical, and it takes a damn fine screenwriter and director to perfectly balance the tones, but genius Peter Jackson can pull it off beautifully. Critics that say Peter Jackson is all special effects and no story need only see this film to be proven dead wrong. I give this film my highest recommendation.

TRIVIA: Co-writer Fran Walsh would go on to work with Jackson on his *Lord of the Rings/Hobbit* films.

I Will Walk Like a Crazy Horse, aka J'irai comme un cheval fou (1973)

DIRECTED BY	Fernando Arrabal
WRITTEN BY	Fernando Arrabal
STARRING	Emmanuelle Riva, George Shannon, Marco Perrin, Hachemi Marzouk, François Chatelet, Marie-France
COUNTRY	France

On the run from the law, Aden (George Shannon) escapes to the desert where he meets a man named Marvel (Hachemi Marzouk) who is strangely in tuned with his environment. Soon the two forge a bond and Aden decides to take him to the city to show him how regular people live. Much like Arrabal's previous film, *Viva la Muerte*, he takes us into a strange and sometimes off-putting world and holds nothing back in the process, all while providing biting commentary on important issues like religion, politics, etc. Where *Crazy Horse* differs is it dips into the realm of mysticism similar to what Alejandro Jodorowsky did with his epic western *El Topo*. The film interestingly sways from a traditional narrative of police hunting for Aden and the more surreal plot unfolding between the two men. Arrabal weaves his magic with compelling characters and harrowing situations, which gets to the core of its audience and makes the ending all the more powerful. *I Will Walk Like a Crazy Horse* is a spellbinding, trippy, and thought-provoking film and highly recommended.

In a Year with 13 Moons, aka In einem Jahr mit 13 Monden (1978)

DIRECTED BY	Rainer Werner Fassbinder
WRITTEN BY	Rainer Werner Fassbinder
STARRING	Volker Spengler, Ingrid Caven, Gottfried John, Isolde Barth, Lilo Pempeit, Elisabeth Trissenaar, Günther Kaufmann
COUNTRY	Germany

Writer/director Rainer Fassbinder takes the audience on a journey into the heart with his 1978 masterwork *In a Year with 13 Moons*. Erwin (Volker Spengler), a young butcher, confesses his love for his co-worker who innocently replies, "It's too bad you're not a woman," to which he gets a sex change only to be rebuffed. Fast forward years later. Erwin is now Elvira and living with an emotionally and psychically abusive man named Christopher (Karl Scheydt). As a way of picking up the pieces of his life he goes to see the young butcher who is now a successful businessman.

The best way to describe *13 Moons* is like a bittersweet farewell letter to the ghosts of the past, the ones that find a way to haunt us. Like most Fassbinder films it's filled with strange, quirky characters and surreal situations, some of which is played as pitch-black comedy. Actor Volker Spengler gives a brutally raw performance as Erwin/Elvira and he wisely plays the role with a quiet desperation rather than a campy over-the-top one. Your heart truly breaks for him and what he goes through, and you are with him every painful step of his journey. What struck me, outside of the brilliant acting and story, was the amazingly moody lighting and cinematography that really helps set the film's tone. Fassbinder's disturbing, beautiful, and poetic meditation on life, love, and yearning is truly outstanding and moved me in such a profound and earnest way. Required viewing.

Julien Donkey-Boy (1999)

DIRECTED BY	Harmony Korine
WRITTEN BY	Harmony Korine
STARRING	Ewen Bremner, Chloë Sevigny, Werner Herzog, Joyce Korine, Brian Fisk, Evan Neumann, Miriam Martinez
COUNTRY	United States

Harmony once again celebrates the odd and quirky in *Julien Donkey-Boy*, a strange and refreshingly different take on modern home life. A teenage boy with untreated schizophrenia, Julien (Ewen Bremner) struggles in his daily life, living with an extremely dysfunctional family that includes a pregnant sister, a wannabe wrestler brother, and an overbearing and psychotic father (played by Werner Herzog, no less). Like his previous works Korine showcases an interesting range, and *Donkey-Boy* goes from being bleak and disturbing to joyful and downright funny. It really helps to lighten the mood even just a tad. Anyone who is even remotely familiar with the writer/director's films will know this isn't going to be a knee-slapper, and the comic relief is still on the dark side. For example, Herzog has some wonderfully deranged and humorous moments. My one complaint with the film is the stark violence involving Julien at the very start of the film. It's certainly a jolt to the audience but it really makes it hard to feel any kind of compassion towards our hero or anti-hero (however you want to look at it). Heading up an incredible cast is Ewen Bremner, best known for films like *Snatch* and *Trainspotting*. Bremner once again proves what a raw and versatile actor he is, as he delves into this complex character. He purposely walks a razor-edge of real and over-the-top, bringing multiple layers to Julien. It also features an early role for Chloë Sevigny. Like Bremner, she gives a natural and vastly understated performance. And of course, the brilliant director-turned-actor Werner Herzog who virtually steals every scene he is in. His deadpan wry delivery is so perfect for playing the insane gas mask-wearing father. The film features an interesting style, and its low tech, almost homemade look, gives it a gritty documentary feel. Once again, Harmony Korine sucks his audience into an utterly intense, absorbing and blisteringly raw experience that never bores. *Julien* is an outstanding piece of indie cinema and a force to be reckoned with.

Last Year at Marienbad (1961)

DIRECTED BY	Alain Resnais
WRITTEN BY	Alain Robbe-Grillet
STARRING	Delpine Seyrig, Giorgio Albertazzi, Sacha Pitoeff, Françoise Bertin, Héléna Kornel, Françoise Spira
COUNTRY	France, Italy

Director Alain Resnais was a part of what was dubbed the French new wave, a term coined by critics in the late '50s and made famous by filmmakers like Jean-Luc Goddard and Francois Truffaunt just to name a few. In a huge and eerie chateau, a man tries desperately to convince a woman that the two had met exactly one year before. But is there truth in what he says or is it all a strange fantasy, or a mixture of both? Right from the start *Last Year at Marienbad* has a lofty, almost dream-like quality, and looks absolutely stunning in black-and-white. It was photographed by the legendary Sacha Vierny who has worked on such masterpieces as *Belle de Jour* and, later in his career, Peter Greenway's *The Cook, The Thief, His Wife and her Lover.* Vierny adds a stylish and surreal aspect to every single gorgeous frame. A person not used to French new wave may be put off by this film which is very dialogue heavy with very little actual action. However, this is not to suggest in the least that this is a bad film. In fact it's brilliant. The film's narrative and narration is pure poetry and it's not hard to believe that it was nominated for best screenplay by the Academy Awards. While not a horror film outright this film does have a haunting undertone and I'd even go so far as to say it has some roots in Gothic thriller. It features an organ score that could have come straight out of *Carnival of Souls.* Indeed, with a lot of dialogue and similar scenes repeating it's almost as if the hotel is haunted metaphorically by its past, doomed to constantly play on a loop over and over again. The always lovely Delphine Seyrig, best known to horror fans for her outstanding role in *Daughters of Darkness,* really shines in this movie as the mysterious woman. It's also interesting how both this film and *Daughters* take place in a rather large and creepy hotel. Equally good is her costar Giorgio Albertazzi who purrs with his Italian accent and just oozes charm and swagger from every pore. They have an interesting chemistry together and a wonderfully thick sexual tension that grows as the film progresses. While this film is definitely not for the mainstream film buff, those who can appreciate a well-written and complex piece of art will find *Last Year at Marienbad* a wonderful escape from life that you'll want to take over and over again.

TRIVIA: Famous French fashion designer Coco Chanel designed the costumes for this film.

Le Grand Cérémonial, aka The Grand Ceremonial, aka Weird Weirdo (1969)

DIRECTED BY	Pierre-Alain Jolivet
WRITTEN BY	Pierre-Alain Jolivet, Serge Gance, Fernando Arranbal (based on play by)
STARRING	Michel Tureau, Ginette Leclerc, Marcella Saint-Amant, Jean-Daniel Ehrmann, Roger Lumont
COUNTRY	France

Based on the play by Fernando Arranbal this highly uncomfortable film follows a young man named Cavanosa (Michel Tureau) who has a very strange and rich fantasy life in the form of sex dolls. To make things worse he lives with an overbearing and strange mother, and it's strongly implied that there is a sexual relationship between them. He meets a young lady thief that is willing to play his twisted games, which includes whipping and a grand ceremony. *The Grand Ceremonial* is a film that explores numerous taboo subject matters and it at times flirts with the surreal. The biggest flaw with this is that Pierre handles the taboo material with no sharp edges and, sadly, the result is an exercise in restraint rather than true progressive art. Frankly, it baffles me why a clearly interesting director would even bother to tackle such subject matter and be so tame in its execution. Furthermore, the film seems to aimlessly meander from one scene to the next and it sets up plot points that never attempt to be resolved. Even though it never pushes the boundaries it still makes for a weird and sometimes uncomfortable viewing. It also injects some dark humor, interesting symbolism, and over-the-top moments that make it mildly enjoyable. When dealing with themes like sadism, incest, murder, etc., it's always best to not censor yourself and push the limits, and it's a shame because this film feels like it could have been a real nasty and artsy film if only it had tried to be daring. Still it's not altogether horrible and it was just bizarre enough to hold my attention. This film is a mixed bag at best, only for the truly curious but don't expect to be shocked.

Long Live Death, aka Viva La Muerte (1971)

DIRECTED BY	Fernando Arrabal
WRITTEN BY	Fernando Arrabal, Claudine Lagrive
STARRING	Anouk Ferjac, Núria Espert, Mahdi Chaouch, Ivan Henriques, Jazia Klibi, Victor Garcia, Ivan Henriques
COUNTRY	France/Tunisia

After co-founding the Panic Movement with legendary filmmaker Alejandro Jodorowsky in 1962, Spanish playwright Fernando Arrabal directed his first feature film, *Long Live Death* or *Viva La Muerte*, and along with Jodorowsky would usher in the midnight movie. During the end of the Spanish Civil War a boy named Fando's (Mahdi Chaouch) father is taken away and imprisoned as a suspected communist turned in by his mother no less. Fando is told that he is executed; however, he doesn't believe it and goes on a journey to discover the truth. Arrabal's credit sequence for *Viva La Muerte* perfectly sets the tone with children singing a light melody over pictures depicting morbid scenes of brutality and torture. This is rather fitting as the film is about a harrowing and grisly time in Spain's history and the horrors of war all filtered through the eyes of an innocent child. Brilliantly, it sways between reality and the surreal daydreams of Fando, and Arrabal employs a host of interesting visual flare coupled with some outstanding cinematography. Fernando is also not afraid to rattle some cages with his pointed commentary on religion, politics, and war, which is cleverly expressed through Fando. I will say this film is not for everyone, and it's extremely disturbing with images that are not for the squeamish. A scene depicting a cow slaughter is hard to watch and is sure to be burned into your brain. The toxicity of war and its brutal effects on average people, especially families, are examined in painful detail in this powerful and moving work of art, and it's the kind of film that tends to stay with you long after the end credits. An incredible moment in Spanish surreal cinema and something every film buff should see.

Lost River (2014)

DIRECTED BY	Ryan Gosling
WRITTEN BY	Ryan Gosling
STARRING	Christina Hendricks, Iain De Caestecker, Matt Smith, Saoirse Ronan, Barbara Steele, Eva Mendes, Ben Mendelsohn
COUNTRY	United States

A single mother trying to provide for her family is sucked into a dark and horrific underworld, willing to risk her very humanity in the process. Meanwhile, her teenage son is obsessed with finding a secret underwater town. *Lost River* is the directional debut of Ryan Gosling. Critics seemed to have a field day bashing and picking apart this film's carcass—most unfairly. Gosling puts an uncomfortable spotlight on urban decay and the overall theme that the idea of the American dream is nothing more than a rotten illusion—something David Lynch did to great affect in *Blue Velvet*. It's obvious that Gosling has a fondness for not only Lynch but Dario Argento, Mario Bava, etc., and he mashes them all up stylistically and visually into his very own hypnotically twisted fever dream. There are some truly unsettling and unforgettable moments that stuck with me long after the credits have rolled and I escaped its black abyss. *River* has been labeled self indulgent (like that's a bad thing) and confusing, yet it's fueled by a surreal nightmare logic, and people trying to explain everything in a logical way will not fully get it. It's like trying to figure out *Lost Highway;* it's just not going to happen, and it's not fun if you do. I really feel this is an incredibly deep, frightening, and bat-shit-crazy movie, and I hope Gosling doesn't listen to the critics and continues down this path in his career. Forget for a moment a big movie star made this and enjoy it on its own merits.

Man Who Laughs, The (1928)

DIRECTED BY	Paul Leni
WRITTEN BY	J. Grubb Alexander, Victor Hugo (based on novel by)
STARRING	Conrad Veidt, Mary Philbin, Cesare Gravina, Olga Baclanova, Julius Molnar, Brandon Hurst, George Siegmann, Josephine Crowell
COUNTRY	United States

The Man Who Laughs is a silent film, and some of you may be thinking of flipping the page this very moment; however, stick with me here. Films made in the pre-Hollywood code pushed the boundaries of what they could get away with and this film is a good example. I mean, the main drive of the film is a young kid being horribly mutilated before his father is killed—that's some unsettling stuff. Sex, murder, and voyeurism are also explored. Lord Clancharlie offends King James II and, as a horribly cruel act of revenge, before he is killed they carve a permanent smile on his young son Gwynplaine's (Julius Molnar) face. The boy is sent out into the harsh winter and, while looking for a place to stay, he finds a baby (who it turns out is blind) and, as fate would have it, they are both taken in by a kindly man named Ursus (Cesare Gravina). Flash forward: Gwynplaine's (Conrad Veidt) all grown up and working for Ursus in a traveling sideshow billed as the Laughing Man. The girl he rescued, named Dea (Mary Philbin), also works for the show and has feelings for him. He seems to have a pretty good life as a successful clown but future events will lead him into politics and danger. This film is a wonderful example of German Expressionism, and the story is entailing with a sort of grotesque beauty and haunting poetry. The mark of a good storyteller is when we find ourselves invested in the characters and you can't help but root for our hapless hero as he clings to his humanity when others merely mock him. It also continues to resonate with viewers, because on some level we've all been teased, picked on, or made to feel somehow less compared to someone else. The story hangs on its lead and Conrad Veidt gives a stunning and heartbreaking performance as the disfigured hero. It's hard enough to act using no voice, but with a fixed smile Veidt must convey everything with merely his eyes and body language, not to mention enduring the pain the dentures caused him. Knowing all this gives you a new found respect for him in this film. Equally good is Olga Baclanova who plays a similar character to the one she would later play in *Freaks*—another film that pushed the limits of the medium. A well written script, wonderfully detailed costumes and set pieces, coupled with some iconic performances makes this film a classic for the ages. It may very well make a silent film fan out of you if you're not already. I implore those who are not to at least give it a try.

TRIVIA: To achieve the iconic grin actor Conrad Veidt had to wear specially made dentures with hooks, a process that was not only painful but left him unable to speak in them. Good thing it was a silent film!

Does that sinister grin look familiar? Conrad Veidt's chilling makeup is often cited as the inspiration for The Joker in the *Batman* comics.

Maps to the Stars (2014)

DIRECTED BY	David Cronenberg
WRITTEN BY	Bruce Wagner
STARRING	Julianne Moore, John Cusack, Mia Wasikowska, Robert Pattinson, Evan Bird, Olivia Williams, Sarah Gadon, Carrie Fisher
COUNTRY	United States

With such genius films as *Shivers, Scanners,* and *The Brood* under his belt, Cronenberg is the last and final word in body horror. The man single-handedly created the sub-genre. In recent years, however, he has shifted from this to more gritty crime fare. However, he still retained his razor edge weird style that fans have came to love. With his latest he takes a stab at Hollywood . . . Or maybe Hollyweird? A snap hot in the lives of people who live and work in Hollywood, all seemingly have everything, but behind the fame, makeup, and bright lights, they are very damaged people visited by the ghosts of their past. The horrors of Hollywood have never been more fun to watch than in *Maps to the Stars,* a deliciously dark and twisted drama/comedy/satire. Cronenberg takes a sheer delight in peeling back the glittery façade of show business to reveal something sleazy, dark, and repugnant, and rub our noses in it. It's been often compared to Billy Wilder's seminal masterpiece *Sunset Boulevard,* but in reality it's more akin to David Lynch's *Mulholland Drive.* Wagner's screenplay is powerful with compelling characters and great drama blended perfectly with surreal comedy that gets pretty black. The use of the recurring theme of "haunting" as a metaphor for personal demons is another stroke of brilliance. It is weaved into the plot and doesn't feel like it was just random weirdness. The cast of *Maps* is top-notch with Julianne Moore, John Cusack, Mia Wasikowska, and Robert Pattinson along with a fun cameo by Carrie Fisher playing, who else, Carrie Fisher. Moore lately has been making better film choices, and she is fearless in the role of Havana Segrand, a washed up actress whose legacy is mainly built on her mother's cult fame and tragic death. She really lets it all hang out and really gives it her very best. Also, nothing tops seeing the now-Academy Award-winner taking a bathroom break while talking to Agatha Weiss (Mia Wasikowska)—fart noises and all. Funny, sure, but it also takes a lot of guts to do that. Even Cusack, whom I'm not a big fan of, does a very good job as a hack shrink who cares more about the dollars than actually helping people. He and Mia have a scene together; it's a reunion of sorts and he plays it both ice cold and strangely tender. The two worked so well together it makes for a very weird moment. The actor I thought was the weakest was Pattinson whom it seems Cronenberg has found a muse in. Honestly, it's not the fact he was in a tween vampire series that colors my opinion of him, he just simply is not a very good actor. When you are in a movie with so many heavyweights you really need to bring your A-game, and what we get is a very wooden performance. A film that some critics loved and some hated, but if you're like me and love films like *China Town, Valley of the Dolls,* and of course, *Mulholland Drive* you'll be totally entranced with this film like I am.

Men Behind the Sun, aka Hei Tai Yang (1988)

DIRECTED BY	Tun Fei Mou
WRITTEN BY	Mei Liu, Wen Yuan Mou, Dun Jing Teng
STARRING	Jianxin Chen, Hsu Gou, Tie Long Jin, Bolin Li, Zhe Quan, Gang Wang, Jiefu Tian, Jiang Wen
COUNTRY	Hong Kong

Few films have gained the kind of infamy as *Men Behind the Sun,* and I strongly suggest people easily disturbed or offended to stay clear of this film altogether. Okay, for the brave, let's journey on. The film documents the final days of World War II in a Japanese bio-chemical experiment lab called Unit 731. Chinese and Soviet prisoners are unmercifully tortured like lab animals. Anyone expecting a serious war film will be sorely disappointed and, while it does feature some harrowing moments that ring true, most of it is pure film exploitation and a lot of the "facts" were stretched for entertainment value, not unlike *Isla: She Wolf of the SS.* And while this may not be the most historically accurate, it does work as an unflinching piece of splatter-shock cinema. Hardcore gore heads will not be disappointed as the blood guts and gross-out moments fly fast and furious. Many of the moments are genuinely unnerving in not only its subject matter but its detached voyeuristic quality, the effect being

that we feel somehow culpable in the horror taking place. There is a little something to disgust or jar even the most jaded film buffs. Storywise the film is wildly uneven, switching from different perspectives seemingly at will, with no logic in narrative. Also, the film seems to pad out some of the runtime, making it a bit dull in places, and it could have used a little trim. To merely say *Men Behind the Sun* is an unsettlingly movie does it no justice and it's certainly not for everyone. Not something you're likely to want to revisit often but I would say it's important for anyone seriously interested in shock cinema to experience.

TRIVIA: This film is infamous for a scene in which a boy's body is operated on. It's not just unsettling because it's a child but because the body was real, used from a local morgue.

Naked Kiss, The (1964)

DIRECTED BY	Samuel Fuller
WRITTEN BY	Samuel Fuller
STARRING	Constance Tower, Anthony Eisley, Michael Dante, Patsy Kelly, Virginia Grey, Karen Conrad, Marie Devereux
COUNTRY	United States

You know when your opening scene is of a bald Constance Tower wildly trashing a man, you're in for a truly special cult classic film written, produced, and directed by Sam Fuller. Kelly (Constance Tower) is a woman looking to get out of the prostitution business and start fresh with a legit job in a new town. She settles down in a charming little place called Grantsville and finds a charming place to rent and a good job. She also starts seeing Grant, a wealthy man whose family built the town. But her happily

ever after is about to come crashing down when the sins of her past come back to haunt her. Sam Fuller steeps his film in the traditional noir fashion with a decidedly more updated spin that allows him to tackle the subject of prostitution in a very bold and frank way, which would have never been possible in the classical noir era. The film also grapples with other tough subjects such as sexual perversion, violence, and most disturbing of all, pedophilia. Fuller pulls no punches in amping up the creep factor. For example, the harrowing scene when Tower's character discovers her soon-to-be-husband's terrible secret while a recording of the children singing from the local hospital plays in the background makes for a truly chilling juxtaposition. But like noir of the heyday he packs his film with style that harkens back to German Expressionism, and the use of shadows and light are used to craft a haunting mood. But when it boils down to it the film is anchored with a solid story that thankfully never gets too melodramatic or soap opera-like and retains the dirt and grit of the films that inspired it. Constance Towers is fantastic as the tragic heroin doing her best to get straight, and she wisely never goes over the top and we totally buy her heartbreaking plight. It also features some great supporting roles by Anthony Eisley, Patsy Kelly, Michael Dante, and Virginia Grey. Sam Fuller's *The Naked Kiss* is a perfect neo-noir that explores some very dark and harrowing stuff with both maturity and style. Required viewing.

TRIVIA: When Kelly arrives in the town of Grantsville you can plainly see a theater marquee that reads *Shock Corridor,* the previous film directed by Sam Fuller.

According to Constance Tower she did not shave her head for the infamous opening scene, dispelling a rumor to the contrary from director Sam Fuller.

Perth (2004)

DIRECTED BY	Djinn
WRITTEN BY	Djinn
STARRING	Kay Tong Lim, Qiu Lian Liu, A. Panneeirchelvam, Jason Aspes, Boeing, Stefanie Budiman, Stepharn Girodot, Ivy Cheng
COUNTRY	Singapore

Any time you compare a movie with *Taxi Driver,* one of the greatest films of the 20th century, you're really setting yourself up for a failure, as the expectation is nearly impossible to meet. Such is the case with 2004's *Perth* and, to my delight, it actually, for the most part, lives up to its hype. Fifty-one-year-old Harry Lee (Kay Tong Kim) has one desire in life; to live out the rest of his days in Perth. He takes a part-time job driving a taxi in order to pay for his plane ticket. However, things get complicated when he meets a young lady named Mai (Ivy Cheng). Harry's life begins to spiral out of control as he gets closer to leaving for his new home. *Perth* brilliantly doesn't show you all of its cards up front but rather slowly weaves a wonderfully complex character study with underworld crime as a clever MacGuffin. We start out liking Harry Lee and, even as the film progresses and we learn of the horrible things he's done we can't help but still be on his side, which speaks volumes of the great writing and charisma of actor Kay Tong Lim. The film rarely loses its focus and we are forced to watch every moment of Lee's heartbreaking descent into madness and self destruction. It introduces a crime element, but it serves merely as a backdrop and way to introduce Mai's character. Some may find it frustrating that the crime story was not explored; however, I actually liked how the focus was solely on Lee and not weighed down with needless subplot. Wisely, the film is tame on the violence at first and saves it for the incredible ending that really lets the blood fly. Having built up to it makes the impact all the more effective and brutal. Much like *Taxi Driver* the film retains a good deal of mood, which is highlighted by some inventive camera work. I was also pleasantly surprised to see it has a great deal of style and visual flare with shades of Argento in its color palate. I wasn't sure what to expect with this independent Singapore outing; however, I enjoyed its grim, almost poetic, character study, which I found gripping from start to finish. Worthy of being compared to the late '70s masterpiece and should be considered required viewing.

Picnic at Hanging Rock (1975)

DIRECTED BY	Peter Weir
WRITTEN BY	Cliff Green, Joan Lindsay (based on novel by)
STARRING	Rachel Roberts, Jacki Weaver, Vivean Gray, Kirsty Child, Frank Gunnell, Jane Vallis, Jenny Lovell, Margaret Nelson
COUNTRY	Australia

Peter Weir, known for Hollywood classics such as *Witness, The Truman Show,* and *Dead Poets Society,* among others, started making films in his home country of Australia, which at this time was seeing a surge in America. *Picnic at Hanging Rock* was his second feature and helped him gain a foot in the medium for its rich poetic drama and offbeat nature. The story takes place in 1900, on Valentine's Day, and sees a group of school girls taking a trip to Black Rock. What starts out as an idyllic trip goes south when three students and a teacher go missing. Soon everyone is on the hunt but will they be found alive? The film is very interesting since it has no real villain and no real clear-cut answers to the mystery that it sets up. Viewers not used to a more traditional narrative will find this very unsatisfying, and in a certain sense it is, but Weir and Green are aiming for something much higher, and the film is more about mood, subtext, and metaphor that explores the horror of the black unknown. Indeed, the film isn't a horror film per se; however, some have argued that it's horror in its purest form. What really stands out right away is the cinematography, which is beautiful, and certain frames look as if they could be paintings. The use of soft focus gives the film its eerie yet ethereal quality that perfectly sets the mood for this very odd flick. It also takes full advantage of the amazing Australian landscape in which it's set. And finally, some great costumes and production design ties it all together. *Picnic at Hanging Rock* is a wonderfully off-kilter drama that challenges its audience at every turn while sucking you into engaging dark mystery. Highly recommended!

TRIVIA: In achieving the film's dream-like feel, Russell Boyd, the cinematographer put a bridal veil over the lens.

Reflecting Skin, The (1990)

DIRECTED BY	Philip Ridley
WRITTEN BY	Philip Ridley
STARRING	Viggo Mortensen, Lindsay Duncan, Jeremy Cooper, Duncan Fraser, David Longworth, David Bloom, Robert Koons
COUNTRY	Britain/Canada

"...nothing but dreams and decay"; a line uttered by Lindsay Duncan, which I think perfectly sums up this amazingly powerful yet deeply unnerving indie film. A young man named Seth (Jeremy Cooper) has a harsh life in rural Idaho. His father tells him about vampires from the pulp magazine he reads and now he is convinced the widow down the road is an undead bloodsucker. I'm going to say up front that *The Reflecting Skin* is definitely not a film for everyone, and if you are easily disturbed and like something that is warm and fuzzy and uplifting, yeah, this is not like that at all. It's also a slower paced film. Ridley wastes no time in establishing a totally weird and almost suffocating vibe that only increases as the film goes on. It touches upon many deeply rooted themes such as family dysfunction, the afterlife, and of course, the biggest being the danger of being a child. The writing is highly clever with loads of foreshadowing and rich complex characters, but perhaps the most brilliant thing about this is its purposely ambiguous nature. Those of you who like your movies wrapped up neatly in a nice little bow will certainly not like this film, as it deliberately raises questions, and not only doesn't answer them but only raises more. It's interesting how vampires are used as a sly thinly veiled metaphor for how people can emotionally drain you if you let them. Child actor Jeremy Cooper is tasked with carrying the film, as the entire story's point of view is through his eyes, and he does a great job. For such a young actor he is very mature

and seems to grasp the material. Viggo Mortensen makes an early screen appearance and, of course, is eclectic, throwing himself into the role, which is complex and dark. Really the entire cast is just stellar. Cinematographer Dick Pope, whose work ranges from *Dark City* to *The Illusionist,* does an outstanding job capturing the stark beauty and dread of the countryside and really helps to create a surreal and hyper-real feeling. *The Reflecting Skin* is a film about the death of childhood innocence and it's both unrelentingly brutal yet spellbinding with the same strange and unnerving feeling of a David Lynch film. This is a truly great film that will likely stay with you for days after the end credits roll. I highly recommend it and also to have a good comedy to watch afterwards.

River's Edge (1986)

DIRECTED BY	Tim Hunter
WRITTEN BY	Neal Jimenez
STARRING	Keanu Reeves, Crispin Glover, Dennis Hopper, Joshua John Miller, Daniel Roebuck, Ione Skye, Tom Bower
COUNTRY	United States

Flying directly in the face of the John Hughes-style clean-cut teen comedies *River's Edge* is a savage and bleak snapshot of teenage life (and death) in small town America. A high school student named Samson (Daniel Roebuck) brutally kills his girlfriend, but instead of keeping it a secret, the young man brags about it to anyone who will listen. But the reaction through the school is just as cold and shocking as the crime itself. As I mentioned above, the eighties was a time when light teen fare was all the rage, but Tim Hunter boldly explores the darker side of adolescence— something the cult favorite *Heathers* would do two years later, although more as a dark comedy. The writing brilliantly straddles a razor-thin line between startlingly realistic yet totally off-kilter, making the audience feel uneasy at all times. For example, Hopper's character, Feck, and his "girlfriend" are truly something out of a mad dream. The film explores some core themes such as the idea of the nihilism of youth, ineffectual parents, and a warped sense of friendship and loyalty to make up for that lack of parenting. The cast is fantastic with Glover and Hopper giving truly unsettling and unforgettable performances. It is hard not to be in utter awe of these two screen icons who go toe to toe with each other. Daniel Roebuck in an early role is amazingly chilling as Samson. He is so natural in the role, and when you're the scariest person with a cast that includes Crispin Glover and Dennis Hopper,that is really saying something. I also have to mention Joshua Miller who, at such a young age, really brings a frightening maturity to the role. He would go onto do the cult classic horror film *Near Dark* which further showcases his talents. *River's Edge* is a great drama that is both engrossing and disturbing, and executed perfectly by an extremely talented cast of actors. So if you're looking for an '80s teen film but want something "edger" than *Sixteen Candles* than this is the flick for you.

TRIVIA: One for being in character and staying there Crispin Glover went on *The David Letterman Show* as his Layne counterpart (unknown to Letterman) and gave a now infamous and highly strange interview that actually creeped Letterman out. Years later Glover confessed it was all part of a stunt to promote the film.

Stars Keanu Reeves and Dennis Hopper would reunite for the 1994 blockbuster *Speed.*

Shock Corridor (1963)

DIRECTED BY	Samuel Fuller
WRITTEN BY	Samuel Fuller
STARRING	Peter Breck, Constance Towers, Gene Evans, James Best, Hari Rhodes, Larry Tucker, Chuck Roberson
COUNTRY	United States

Maverick director Samuel Fuller never played it safe, both in subject matter and style, and for those unfamiliar with his work, *Shock Corridor* is a good starting point. A journalist with high aspirations of winning a Nobel Prize has himself committed to an insane asylum in order to track down a murderer. This, however, begins to backfire as he desperately clings to his sanity while he searches for the killer. Sam Fuller fearlessly tackles heavy issues such as racism, incest, and madness in very blunt, even shocking, ways. And not only was it daring for its time but it continues to be powerful and thought provoking. He definitely does not use kid gloves while dealing with the overriding theme of bigotry, which reflects the times it was made, and sadly, it remains hauntingly relevant today. As always, he crafts this film noir with a great amount of skill behind the camera as evident by the tight and focused direction coupled with inventive camera work. Also, Fuller is not afraid to dip into his bag of cinematic tricks for dramatic flair. For example, the film is in black and white but, to highlight a certain scene, he uses blazing color to stunning effect. And then there is a scene in which rain is used to highlight a moment and show a characters mental state, and the first time I saw it, it had a profound effect on me. *Shock Corridor* is no doubt a darkly disturbing film, but it also has its camp moments that help keep it from being too unbearable. Harrowing, visually compelling, and not without a dark, witty sense of humor, this a prime example of Fuller's genius. Required viewing.

TRIVIA: A similar plotline is used in *American Horror Story: Asylum.*

Legendary comic artist Daniel Clowes *of Ghost World* fame did artwork for Shock Corridor's re-release.

Tideland (2005)

DIRECTED BY	Terry Gilliam
WRITTEN BY	Terry Gilliam, Terry Grisoni, Mitch Cullin (based on novel by)
STARRING	Jodelle Ferland, Jeff Bridges, Janet McTeer, Jennifer Tilly, Dylan Taylor, Wendy Anderson, Sally Cook
COUNTRY	Canada

Writer, director, and visual maverick Terry Gilliam is certainly known for his strange and compelling storytelling and, really, any of his films could be in this book. But *Tideland* is an experience that is totally unnerving and is criminally underrated. Noah (Jeff Bridges) is an aging rocker junkie whose daughter, Jeliza Rose (Jodelle Ferland), takes care of him, even helping him to shoot up or, as he calls it, going on a vacation. Jeliza's mother, Gunhilda (Jennifer Tilly), overdoses and the two make a hasty retreat to Noah's childhood home; a desolate crumbing home in the middle of nowhere. Rose escapes her harsh reality by totally enveloping herself in a world of wonder and imagination. Gilliam doesn't sugar coat the film and offers an unflinching look at the horrors of drug abuse, but also how the innocence of children can save themselves from their terrible situations. From frame one the audience is thrown head first into a surreal world that is both wondrous and horrifying—all filtered through the eyes of a child. Terry walks a bizarre tight rope of innocent fantasies and stark brutal reality, and one can see this as a grotesque fairy tale of sorts. His trademark surreal images and jaw-dropping set pieces certainly echo this theme. As always, his sets are very well-crafted with incredible attention to detail. Jeff Bridges is terrific as the strung out Noah and he gives one of his finest performances. But the real break-out star is its pint sized star Jodelle Ferland, who had the burden of carrying the film, and she does a brilliant job. It's not hard to see why her career has taken off the way it has. She can certainly hold her own against powerhouses like Bridges, Tilly, and McTeer. Equally good is Brendan Fletcher who plays the mentally impaired and child-like Dickens. *Tideland* is a remarkable film that I could go on and on about but, simple put, it's something that you have to see to believe. Utterly unforgettable and will put you through the emotional ringer. Terry Gilliam is fearless in his vision and is the only director who could pull off such a film in such a masterful way. It may not be a movie you'd want to re-visit often but it's worth the strange journey down the rabbit hole.

Trash (1970)

DIRECTED BY	Paul Morrissey
WRITTEN BY	Paul Morrissey
STARRING	Holly Woodlawn, Joe Dallesandro, Geri Miller, John Putnam, Andrea Feldman, Jane Forth, Bruce Pecheur
COUNTRY	United States

Coming out of Warhol's factory and armed with a camera maverick and a sharp wit writer/ filmmaker Paul Morrissey directs this darkly funny and, at times, downright uncomfortable drama about two drug addicts living in the Big Apple. The film follows Joe (Joe Dallesandro) and his roommate, Holly (Holly Woodlawn), as they bum along New York City looking for their next fix. Along the way they encounter strange people and situations. The film is noteworthy for its groundbreaking and startlingly frank depiction of drug use (which isn't glamorized) and its bold use of nudity. Viewers not used to a freer flowing and less structured narrative may find the film a bit tedious but if you can embrace it you will be well rewarded. Morrissey embraces the film's more inherit camp aspects but it also plays like a timely satirical commentary on the urban plight, but it wisely never gets preachy or heavy-handed. Joe Dallesandro heads up a cast mostly filled with Factory regulars and, even though he isn't the strongest actor, his good looks and undeniable charm help him pull off playing a rough trade heroin addict. Holly Woodlawn, who sadly passed away in 2015, makes her first screen appearance and, like Joe, she has something terribly bold and electric about her. You can't help but be spellbound by her on-screen aura. *Trash* acts like a big middle finger to the flower power movement of the '60s and ushers in a new, more irreverent, and bold viewpoint while also making a wonderful snapshot of a grimy pre-cleaned-up New York. Delightfully over the top and, at times, heroin, I mean harrowing, this is a film not to be missed.

Uncle Boonmee Who Can Recall His Past Lives (2010)

DIRECTED BY	Apichatpong Weerasethakul
WRITTEN BY	Apichatpong Weerasethakul, Phra Sripariyattiweti (based on book by)
STARRING	Thanapat Saisaymar, Jenjira Pongpas, Sakda Kaewbuadee, Wallapa Mongkolprasert, Natthakarn Aphaiwonk
COUNTRY	Thailand

A man dying from a terminal illness encounters the ghost of his late wife and the return of his long lost son one evening, and he recounts his many past lives. Before I get into this review I want to make one thing perfectly clear, I'm someone who loves a good slow paced yet meaningful art house film. And I'm certainly someone who doesn't need a traditionally structured narrative as you may have guessed from previous reviews. However, as much as I wanted to, I just couldn't get into this movie. My major beef is the film moves at a glacier's pace, which again is fine, provided of course, there is something interesting driving everything, and there simply was not. There is a great deal to be said about the filmmakers going for a more slower soulful story, but it just didn't grab me emotionally like I thought it would, especially considering it's about a man facing his mortality. *Uncle Boonmee* isn't my cup of tea, but it seems to have a loyal following, and others seem to have gotten more out of it than I, therefore I still recommend checking it out.

Vampire's Kiss (1988)

DIRECTED BY	Robert Bierman
WRITTEN BY	Joseph Minion
STARRING	Nicolas Cage, Jennifer Beals, Maria Conchita Alonso, Elizabeth Ashley, Kasi Lemmons, Jodie Markell
COUNTRY	United States

Nicolas Cage is certainly known for his, shall we say, less-than-subtle acting style, and here he is at perhaps his most bonkers. But as it turns out it's a damn good film on its own merits; the Cage crazy is just a bonus. Peter Lowe (Nicolas Cage) is an executive at a publishing firm. After a strange tryst with a mysterious woman the already eccentric man begins to think the love bite he received may in fact be a vampire's kiss. Some movies, believe it or not, are actually hard to pin down genre-wise, this film in particular. The film has elements of horror and comedy but really, when you get down to its core, it's a drama. Because once you get passed the moments of hilarity it's a startling look at the how loneliness can have terrible effects on people, even those who seemingly have it all. Bierman constantly plays with the audience's expectations going in a slightly different direction than what you might expect, but at times manages to cleverly tip its hat to standard vampire troupes. *Vampire's Kiss* is also an '80s snapshot of sexism and how the boys club in the work place could get away with pretty much anything when it came to the opposite sex. The social commentaries are very much done on purpose and hold up a mirror to the decade of excess. Many critics then and now seem to lampoon this film because of Cage's over-the-top performance but, honestly, I feel like it works within the context of an already strange and, at times surreal film. And come on, how can you not love seeing Nick Cage wearing plastic vampire fangs chasing pigeons? Wacky star aside Bierman delivers a wonderfully thought-provoking story that is funny, weird, and ultimately heartbreaking. *Vampire's Kiss* is a real gem that needs to be brought out of the coffin and into your living room or crypt.

TRIVIA: During the infamous cockroach scene, Cage being the method actor actually insisted on eating the bug for real.

CRAZY CONNECTIONS: Cult director Larry Cohen's daughter makes a cameo as the female victim in the club.

GOES WELL WITH: *American Psycho, Bad Lieutenant: Port of Call*

Visitor Q (2001)

DIRECTED BY	Takashi Miike
WRITTEN BY	Itaru Era
STARRING	Ken'ichi Endô, Shungiku Uchida, Kazushi Watanabe, Jun Muto, Fujiko, Shôko Nakahara, Ikko Suzuki
COUNTRY	Japan

It has been quite a while since I first laid eyes on *Visitor Q*, and before I re-watched it I reviewed *The Happiness of Katakuris* a decidedly more upbeat but still very weird outing. I thought about how different they were, but after re-watching *Q* I was stunned to realize that they both have a similar message, which is when horrible things happen it brings the family unit closer together. Meet the Yamazakis, the world's most dysfunctional family perhaps of all time. When a stranger starts living with them things spiral deeper into decay, yet surprisingly he helps brings them together. Miike serves up his usual pension for exploring deeply disturbing taboos and absolutely nothing is sacred once he gets his hands on it. But *Visitor Q* isn't just about shocking us and works as a sly comment on not only the ideal traditional family, but its theme of voyeurism also speaks to the reality show craze of the early 2000s, and "the visitor", as he's only known, could be seen as a stand-in for the audience. We get a front row seat into the total freak show that is the Yamazakis and it's surprisingly amusing. Now, it's hard to think of a movie featuring murder, necrophilia, and incest as funny but it is. Of course, it's pitch-black comedy and it helps soften the film's more unsettlingly aspects. Even the violence comes off more cartoonish than actually hard-hitting and only a twisted genius could pull this kind of juxtaposition off seamlessly. Drama and black-as-night comedy has never been as twisted and wonderful as *Visitor Q*. Not for the easily disturbed but highly recommended.

CHAPTER 6

Much like the horror genre, weird and fantasy seem to go pretty much hand in hand. This was definitely a fun chapter to write because of the movies tend to be more stylistically freewheeling and freeform. Fantasy is limited only by the filmmaker's imagination and directors like Jan Svankmajer are boundless in their creativity. You also have to admire the craft, skill, time, and energy that goes into titles like *Greedy Guts* and *Forbidden Zone*. Ranging from the trippy *Black Moon*, the 80s re-telling of *Alice in Wonderland,* to a Mexican Santa flick (with Satanic undertones of course), things are pretty varied in this subcategory, which keeps things interesting. Yes, boys and girls, this is where the rubber truly meets the road in terms of experimental films, and for the adventurous film lover there is a great deal of awesomeness to be found. Just be prepared to chuck all logic out the window and abandon sanity all ye who enter.

Fantasy

Alice (1987)

DIRECTED BY	Jan Svankmajer
WRITTEN BY	Jan Svankmajer, Lewis Carroll (based on the book by)
STARRING	Kristýna Kohoutová, Camilla Power
COUNTRY	Czech Republic

Czech surrealist filmmaker Jan Svankmajer has made a huge impression on cinema with his bold and strange take on the medium, using the art of puppetry and stop motion mixed with live action. *Alice* was a lifelong ambition for the filmmaker and the end result is nothing short of jaw-dropping. Based on Lewis Carroll's *Alice in Wonderland* the film follows a little girl named Alice (Kristýna Kohoutová) as she makes her way through a totally different world where all rules and logic do not apply. In her travels she meets characters such as The Mad Hatter and the White Rabbit.

Alice is a visual feast for the eyes as it seamlessly blends live action and stop motion animation, which is the director's trademark. Considering how long stop motion takes, it's nothing short of an amazing feat and something we seem to take for granted in a CGI-dominated landscape. Right away you'll notice that the world of *Alice* is not bright and happy but rather grimy and grim, which is keeping with Svankmajer's style, and any notion of this being for kids is thrown right out the looking glass. Using strange and, at times, downright macabre-looking puppets the film has a decidedly disturbing nightmare quality wrapped up in the façade of a children's story. It just may be the most interesting interpretation of Carroll ever put to screen, and the painstaking work it must have taken to bring this film to life is impressive. Tim Burton has nothing on Svankmajer who weaves a brilliantly weird and creepy work of art that perfectly realizes the more trippy aspects of the original source material. A must-see.

Apple, The (1980)

DIRECTED BY	Menahem Golan
WRITTEN BY	Menahem Golan, Coby Recht (story), Iris Recht (story)
STARRING	Vladek Sheybal, Catherine Mary Stewart, Joss Ackland, Allan Love, George Glimour, Grace Kennedy, Ray Shell, George S. Clinton
COUNTRY	United States

Stick on your BIM and get ready for the most insane musical to ever slither out of cinema. In an alternate future, the year 1994, to be more specific, a young singing couple is swept up by the satanic musical corporation/government ruled by a man named Boogalow (Vladek Sheybal).

The Apple is an eye-popping lavish camp tour de force and the ultimate good-bad movie you're likely to ever experience. I say experience because you don't merely watch this movie; you go through it, it's that bizarre. Yes it is a bad film filled with terrible songs that are not memorable in the least. The characters are also on the shallow side and of course nothing, and I mean nothing, is subtle. At the heart of the film is a satire on the music industry which was much better realized in Brian De Palma's *Phantom of the Paradise* and never goes any deeper than big bad corporate greed versus innocent youth. Still, I proudly admit I have a special fondness for this bit of celluloid eye candy because it's just so freaking weird it manages to be wildly entertaining. The musical numbers and production designs feel like psychotropic-fueled drag queens and drama school students were given a budget and went wild. The result is a pure unabashedly good time. Even if the songs aren't great, numbers themselves are stuff of legend. Besides the music there are some truly inspired moments thrown in, such as the '60s counter-culture refugees (also known as hippies) that refused to bow to the soulless money hungry Boogalow and his greedy empire. No drugs needed when you watch this wonderfully nutso cult classic. Take a bite, if you dare.

GOES WELL WITH: *Phantom of the Paradise*

Black Moon (1975)

DIRECTED BY	Louis Malle
WRITTEN BY	Louis Malle
STARRING	Cathryn Harrison, Therese Giehse, Alexandra Stewart, Joe Dallesandro
COUNTRY	France/Germany

A young girl named Lily (Cathryn Harrison) escapes a war only to find herself in a bizarre homestead with a spooky old woman, a demented brother and sister, and a unicorn. I'll be blunt; this movie is not for everyone. The casual audience used to quick-edit, music video-like films will no doubt find this tedious and confusing as the narrative does not conform to any sense of logic. However, those like me who are used to and enjoy art house cinema will be treated to something really special. *Black Moon* plays out like a barking mad adult fairy tale similar to *Valarie and her Week of Wonder* with a dash of Terry Gilliam for good measure. Writer/director Louis Malle creates an eerie yet alluring atmosphere due in large part to some stunning cinematography, and he takes wise advantage of the France countryside. As I stated above, *Moon* does not obey any rules of traditional logic, which is perfectly fine if you're willing to embrace the insanity. I've never seen a woman breastfeed an elderly woman before on film and now that's forever burnt into my gray matter. Cult actor Joe Dallesandro gives a wordless performance and, no offense to Little Joe, but it may be one of his better roles. Hauntingly poetic and bat-crap-crazy *Black Moon* is a must-see for anyone into fringe cinema.

Escape from Tomorrow (2013)

DIRECTED BY	Randy Moore
WRITTEN BY	Randy Moore
STARRING	Roy Abramsohn, Elena Schuber, Jack Dalton, Annet Mahendru, Lee Armstrong, Danielle Safady, Katelynn Rodriguez
COUNTRY	United States

If you're like me and have read enough freaky rumors, urban legends, and creepy pastas about Disneyland you start to think maybe there's a darker side to the "happiest place on earth". *Escape from Tomorrow* explores this in a brilliantly dark way. Jim (Roy Abramsohn), a family man on a vacation, wakes up on the final day to a phone call that he has been fired from his job. What ensues is a part reality, part fantasy-based day which sways from fun to downright frightening in the park where dreams and, in this case, nightmares come true. I'd describe Randy Moore's first feature film like home movies directed by David Lynch.

What strikes you right away is the stark black-and-white photography that is not only beautiful to look at but also gives seemingly innocent things a sinister quality. With such a threadbare plot you'd think there would be a lot of padding, but to my delight the film goes at a brisk pace and offers up enough surreal fantasy and dark humor to make the film entertaining. Moore also explores some real drama and, at the  core, the film is a snapshot of a middle aged man who just happens to be hitting his mid-life crisis during his summer vacation with his kid and hateful wife. Jim comes off as likeable enough even if it's mainly due to his overbearing shrew of a wife. Which leads me to the one thing I thought was weak about the film, which is how Jim's wife Emily is portrayed. Sure it makes sense to make her a bitch in order to create conflict, but I thought it turned her into a one-dimensional character, and it would have been nice to see a softer side to her; even just a small amount. *Escape from Tomorrow* is an amazing film, especially from a first time director, and it's evident that this guy has skills behind the camera, and I'm excited for what else he may have in store. Strap in for a delightfully weird ride that won't make you vomit but will leave you wanting more.

Fando and Lis, aka Fando y Lis (1968)

DIRECTED BY	Alejandro Jodorowsky
WRITTEN BY	Alejandro Jodorowsky, Fernando Arrabal
STARRING	Sergio Kleiner, Diana Mariscal, Maria Teresa Rivas, Tamara Garina, Juan Jose Arreola, Rene Rebetez, Adrian Ramos
COUNTRY	Mexico

Why is *Fando and Lis* an extremely important film? Well, it's the first feature by the fore father of underground cinema (and a personal idol) Alejandro Jodorowsky. Loosely based on a 1962 play by Fernando Arrabal the film centers on Fando (Sergio Kleiner), who takes his paralyzed girlfriend, Lis (Diana Mariscal), to the city of Tar, where he hopes to cure her. In their travels they encounter many bizarre people like a blood drinking old beggar. With this film Jodorowsky would set the stage for a brilliant career, and many credit him for single-handedly creating the midnight movie with *El Topo* released two years later. Here he shows off his trademark bold style filled with blisteringly strange surreal images with a sort of mystical poetry to them and, of course, is fused with social and religious commentary. Now, as I said, I'm a huge fan of Jodorowsky's and, even though *Fando and Lis* isn't my favorite, it's still a wholly satisfying mind bender. It's easy to see just how ahead of its time it really was in terms of ballsy experimental storytelling that ditches conventional narrative for a more free-formed style. The photography is just stunning and the striking images look even more haunting and weird in black-and-white. Anyone serious about not only strange underground films but cinema buffs in general need to be familiar with this man's body of work. Required viewing.

Faust, aka Lesson Faust (1994)

DIRECTED BY	Jan Svankmajer
WRITTEN BY	Jan Svankmajer, Christian Dietrich Grabbe (based on the novel by), Christopher Marlowe (based on the play by), Johann Wolfgang von Goethe (based on the play by)
STARRING	Petr Cepek, Jan Kraus, Vladimir Kudla, Antonin Zacpal, Jiri Suchy, Viktorie Knotková, Jana Mézlová
COUNTRY	Czech Republic

Visionary writer/director follows up his dark fairy tale *Alice* with *Faust*, a film that is not only as good as his previous work but, in my opinion, is even better. Taking his own loose inspiration on the play by Johann Wolfgang von Goethe (which is based on an old German folk story) *Faust* tells the tale of a man who sells his very soul to the devil. Svankmajer never ceases to blow my mind to pieces, and once again he dips into his bag of cinematic tricks seamlessly blending live action, claymation, stop motion, and most impressively, puppet theater. The end result is nothing short of pure magic in storytelling with Svankmajer skillfully pulling all the strings. He masterfully bends the very medium to make a twisted dark kind of poetry and, like *Alice,* it is strange but not for strange sake, as everything he does has an exact purpose and meaning. It utterly amazes me when you stop and think about how much time and effort an ambitious project of this kind would take. More impressive than the techniques he utilizes is the film's plot, which interweaves fantasy, real world, and stage play; not an easy task, but he pulls it off effortlessly. Once again this true maverick utilities many techniques to create a spellbinding, creepy, and refreshingly different experience. Highly recommended.

Forbidden Zone (1980)

DIRECTED BY	Richard Elfman
WRITTEN BY	Richard Elfman, Matthew Bright, Nick L. Martinson, Nicolas James
STARRING	Susan Tyrrell, Hervé Villechaize, Gisele Lindley, Jan Stuart Schwartz, Marie-Pascal Elfman, Phil Gordon, Danny Elfman
COUNTRY	United States

I wear my *Mystical Knights of the Oingo Boingo* love proudly on my sleeve and I'm not ashamed of it. Sure, they're long disbanded and Danny has gone on to an award-winning career scoring films and television, but we always have *Forbidden Zone,* an incredible, bizarre, brain-melting film that has gone on to cult infamy. A girl named Frenchy (Marie-Pascal Elfman) accidently slips into a portal in her basement, which leads to the sixth dimension, also known as the forbidden zone. The zone is ruled by the king (Hervé Villechaize) and a wicked queen (Susan Tyrrell). Now it's up to her family to save her before she's trapped there forever. Picture, if you will, an old vaudeville act of the '30s injected with LSD and topped off with a cheeky cartoon-style sense of humor; the result is a mad cap film that is sure to make the jaw drop of even hardened film buffs. The visuals are amazing, owing a lot of its style to German Expressionism and old Hollywood. It's also very creative, utilizing many creative techniques and some well-done animation, further echoing the film's cartoon approach. Hervé Villechaize (yes, Tattoo from the TV show *Fantasy Island)* heads up a brilliant cast, which includes cult superstar Susan Tyrell, best known for her role in *Cry Baby.* She is deliciously evil and wonderful as the wicked queen. Film icon Joel Spinell has a small role and even Danny Elfman himself has a catchy little blues number as the devil himself. The film has been unfairly deemed racist by some critics for the film's stereotypical depiction of African Americans in black face; however, Elfman meant this not as a slam on a race of people but rather as a wry satire of vintage Hollywood, which is a major theme visually in the film. In fact, it's making fun of how the studio system created such terrible caricatures. And honestly, it's hard to take anything in this film seriously. Talking chickens, teachers wielding machine guns, and disembodied floating heads are but a few of the wacky and highly creative things you'll find in the *Forbidden Zone.* Required viewing.

Greedy Guts, aka Little Otik, aka Otesánek (2000)

DIRECTED BY	Jan Svankmajer
WRITTEN BY	Jan Svankmajer, K.J Erben (based on folk tale by)
STARRING	Veronika Zilková, Jaroslava Kretschmerová, Jan Hartl, Pavel Nový, Kristina Adamcová, Dagmar Stríbrná
COUNTRY	Czech Republic

Karl (Jan Hartl) and his wife Bozena (Veronika Zilková), are a couple who want nothing more than to have a baby. In order to help his wife's grief, the husband carves a child out of a stump he finds. To his shock and embarrassment Bozena cares for it as if it were alive. He is even more surprised to find that it comes to life and has an almost unending hunger. Visionary director Jan Svankmajer brings *Little Otik,* based on the folk tale *Otesánek* by K.J Erben, to life, plunging deep into his bag of tricks to blend live action, animation, and stop motion to amazing effect. Those familiar with his previous works will no doubt marvel at his seemingly boundless imagination, which is showcased in his other works. He effortless-

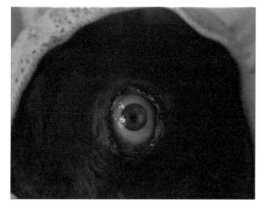

ly fuses reality and the surreal to create a totally altogether different cinematic dreamscape that is a pleasure to lose yourself in, if only for two hours. I love how Erben's fairy tale is not only acted out in the movie but the folk tale itself plays a part in it. Svankmajer drives home the tragedy of infernality but also balances its heavy subject matter with dark humor and, of course, plenty of strangeness. But it manages to be weirdly touching, which I wasn't expecting. For anyone new to Jan Svankmajer, this film might make a good starting point, as its narrative is much more traditional than previous works. My one complaint about this film is that it tends to drag at points, and I feel a good pruning would have served it well. *Little Otik* is a wonderfully fantastical, bizarre, and darkly funny film and one of Svankmajer's finest.

High Rise (2015)

DIRECTED BY	Ben Wheatley
WRITTEN BY	Amy Jump, J. G. Ballard (based on novel by)
STARRING	Tom Hiddleston, Jeremy Irons, Sienna Miller, Luke Evans, Reece Shearsmith, Keeley Hawes, Augustus Prew, Peter Ferdinando
COUNTRY	Britain

Independent maverick Ben Wheatley attempts to take on J.G. Ballard's dark dystopian novel which was largely considered unfilmable. Doctor Robert Laing (Tom Hiddleston) moves into a posh forty-story high rise on the outskirts of London and everything seems normal until he meets the tenants. Tensions boil and mayhem ensures as the upper and lower floors clash. I give Wheatley a lot of credit for having the balls to turn Ballard's vastly important psychological social sci-fi novel into a film. Wheatley boldly abandons a traditional narrative structure for a much looser one and captures the brutal allegory on social class, warfare, and hierarchy with shades of Ken Russell, Stanley Kubrick, and David Lynch for good measure. Wisely, he keeps the audience on rocky ground, constantly subverting expectations and giving you a neverending feeling of unease, which only intensifies as it spirals into savagery and anarchy. From the hypnotic glass elevator to a lush tropical paradise complete with a white horse the visuals are jaw-dropping. This coupled with some brilliant sleek camera work helps propel this film into a pure work of art. While the look and design of the film is flawless there are still some issues. The story tends to lumber in places and feels incomplete like a chunk of footage was removed and, unlike Ben's previous outings, the characters felt like they could have used more depth. It also could have done a better job at exploring its core themes. Despite this I found *High Rise* a wonderful strange, bloody, psychedelic, mind-melting experience which is anchored by top-notch performances from its cast. Ben Wheatley remains one of my favorite indie filmmakers working and, though it's not as good as its source material, it's still a damn fine attempt at bringing the unfilmable novel onto the big screen even with its shortcomings. *High Rise* is certainly worth checking out.

TRIVIA: Bringing J.G. Ballard's novel to the big screen was something long in the making. In fact, the rights were bought upon the book's release and it was originally intended for Nicolas Roeg to direct, but sadly that never happened. It was yet again attempted by Canadian filmmaker Vinenzo Natali of *Cube* fame, but again it fell through.

The release date for *High Rise* is fitting since it marked the forty anniversary of the book's publication.

The ABBA song *SOS* is included in two different versions. The song was released in 1975, the same year as the novel *High Rise*.

Holy Motors (2012)

DIRECTED BY	Leos Carax
WRITTEN BY	Leos Carax
STARRING	Denis Lavant, Edith Scob, Kylie Minogue, Leos Carax, Michel Piccoli, Annabelle Dexter-Jones, Zlata
COUNTRY	France

I'm always up for a good bizarre, surreal film and nobody does that quite like the French. *Holy Motors* follows a typical day of a man named Oscar (Denis Lavant) as he navigates through a series of "appointments", which is various jobs he does switching from one person to another. It's evident that he is losing passion for his work, but through drinking and chain smoking he gets through it. Leos Carax's highly creative film puts a delightfully crazy spin on breaking the fourth wall but, in a way, it doesn't. Throughout we see Oscar riding around a limo meticulously getting into character both by physically transforming himself with makeup but also running lines. In one scene he even thanks his fellow acting partner. But what is so clever is that Carax weaves this into a narrative with its very own mythos, so it's not simply an actor going from one acting job to another. Leos has a great cinematic eye and his attention to detail is simply incredible. For example, the inside of the limo, which acts as a sort of strange work office, is so well-thought-out it's like a character in and of itself. There is also no shortness of surreal imagery that is both disturbing and quite lovely. He also injects some great dark humor, shocking violence, and moments that are just jaw-dropping in their blunt absurdity. Film buffs will also notice the brilliant little nod to *Eyes Without a Face*, a film also known for its dark comedy. Actor Denis Lavant has a tough job not only juggling all these different characters, but he must also endure the hours of prosthetic makeup. He is so natural and at ease with everything that you totally believe he does this every day. It's amazing to see this actor at work. It boils down to whether or not you're someone who can toss logic out the window and watch this purely for its weird and brilliantly abstract ideas. However, *Holy Motors* is not a film weird for weird sake, and it has really interesting ideas and polished directing to back it up. Tired of the same old? Give this film a spin.

Jubilee (1978)

DIRECTED BY	Derek Jarman
WRITTEN BY	Derek Jarman
STARRING	Jenny Runacre, Adam Ant, Neil Campbell, Richard O'Brien, Toyah Willcox, Amy Nitrite, Karl Johnson, Neil Kennedy
COUNTRY	Britain

Grab your leather studded jacket and chuck your boring old history books out the window as *Jubilee* tells the tale of an alternative history of England, and the result is an artistic whirlwind of destruction that is hard to take your eyeballs off of. With the aid of a mysterious angel, Queen Elizabeth I travels to future England and, to her horror, she discovers a burnt out, lifeless land where punks rule and law and order is just a thinly veiled joke. Derek Jarman's early feature film is a blisteringly strange, humorous, and disturbing comment on punk-era society. He dabbles with striking images that are both beautiful and jarring at the same time. For example, the twisted ballet dance done by a burning pile of trash perfectly sums up the film, as it's both poetic and thought-provoking yet still has its middle finger firmly on the chaotic. Furthermore, it uses classical music in a delicious bit of irony. *Jubilee* works as a satire of not only punk culture but of the social and political climate of the time. It also doesn't shy away from the taboo and the uncomfortable. I'm all for a film having a deeper meaning and underlying subtext; however, the message gets too heavy-handed at times and gets in the way of the entertainment. The cast is great with *The Rocky Horror Picture Show* alumni Neil Campbell and Richard O'Brien reuniting and, though they never have a scene together, it's still always a joy to see them in films. Everyone acting-wise is solid, but the real break-out star is Toyah Wilcox as Mad, the delightfully devilish pyromaniac. And while she manages to chew every bit of scenery she gets ahold of she is still utterly spellbinding to watch. Punk rock icon Adam Ant also makes an appearance. *Jubilee* is a blissfully strange world of anarchy and art that challenges the viewer with its shocking and bleak outlook that takes a startling look at the "blank generation" but it's also darkly funny. Highly recommended.

La Belle Captive (1983)

DIRECTED BY	Alan Robbe-Grillet
WRITTEN BY	Alan Robbe-Grillet
STARRING	Daniel Mesguich, Cyrielle Clair, Daniel Emilfork, François Chaumette, Gabrielle Lazure, Gilles Arbona
COUNTRY	France

French director and author Alan Robbe-Grillet made his mark on cinema with his unique blend of off-kilter plots and refreshingly different visual flare. On his way to deliver an important message, Walter (Daniel Mesguich) discovers a beautiful woman lying on the road, the same lovely girl he was interacting with at a nightclub. Things become even weirder when he learns the identity of the woman, and what ensues is a twist-filled mystery. Done in an over-stylized dream-like world conceived inside a crime thriller *La Belle Captive*, like many of Grillet's films, methodically weaves a mystery and employs his usual trademark of repetition and disjointed plot. Indeed this is where the surreal aspect comes into play and viewers not used to this kind of fractured story may find it confusing and off-putting. But, for the audience willing to go with it, the film offers plenty of interesting plot twists that keep everything entertaining enough. While not as haunting or thought-provoking as *Last Year at Marienbad* or *Trans-Europ Express* it still retains his signature sly dark humor and outstanding visual flare, which is heavily influenced by the Surrealist movement in France. For those looking for a strange fantasy neo-noir that may not make a lot of sense but is still a damned enjoyable thrill ride *La Belle Captive* will be right up your alley. It also makes a good introduction to the work of Alan Robbe-Grillet.

Lobster, The (2015)

DIRECTED BY	Yorgos Lanthimos
WRITTEN BY	Yorgos Lanthimos, Efthymis Filippou
STARRING	Colin Farrell, Olivia Colman, Jessica Barden, Roger Ashton-Griffiths, Jacqueline Abrahams, Rosanna Hoult, James Finnegan
COUNTRY	Ireland, United Kingdom, Greece, France, Netherlands

David (Colin Farrell) is taken to The Hotel and is given forty-five days to find a partner or he is turned into an animal (of his choosing) and given a second chance in the wild. Thus is the law in this dystopian future. Lanthimos takes a deliriously mad stab at society's obsession and high expectations of coupledom and boils it down to an insane yet strangely tender and romantic little film that you won't soon forget. What impressed me from the start is that the highly creative and layered screenplay hung on a premise that is easily the most unique to come out in a long time. He really sucks you into this dystopian future and does it with such ease without bogging the audience down in endless exposition. The humor works incredibly well and is definitely of the dark and deadpan kind, which fits the rather quirky and bleak tone. As I stated above, despite being a deeply disturbed film, it is also very much a romance, and it seems like that wouldn't mesh well but surprisingly it does. I was also surprised by how touching the film manages to be at times. Actor Colin Farrell plays brilliantly against type, ditching his usual sexy Irish charm for a bigger waistline and a make under. His performance is impressively low key and he doesn't relie on his signature swag. My biggest problem with the film is that it starts out great, but once we get outside The Hotel the story seems to fall apart and it limps its way to the nearly two-hour mark. Twenty minutes could easily have been trimmed and I think it would serve the story a lot better. *The Lobster* is a dazzling fantasy full of quirky humor as well as thought-provoking commentary and heart. Worth a watch.

Phantom of the Paradise (1974)

DIRECTED BY	Brian De Palma
WRITTEN BY	Brian De Palma
STARRING	William Finley, Paul Williams, Jessica Harper, Gerrit Graham, George Memmoli, Archie Hahn, Jeffery Comanor
COUNTRY	United States

In the '70s and '80s nobody made thrillers quite like Brian De Palma, and films like *Dressed to Kill, Body Double,* and *Blow Out* are considered some of the very best of the genre. However, in 1974, he took a detour from the suspense to take a wonderfully satirical stab at the music industry in this fantasy, horror-comedy. Winslow (William Finley) is a brilliant songwriter who suffers a series of terrible events. First, his music is stolen by the evil music mogul Swan (Paul Williams). Then, Winslow is wrongfully jailed and later disfigured. Now donning a disguise to hide his face, he vows to get revenge on Swan for making him the phantom of the paradise. This wildly entertaining comic book-style film is cleverly written and masterfully blends satirical humor and tongue-in-cheek horror to create something altogether different. But he takes things one step further, playing the film like one big tragic opera, which fits the film's underlying themes like a black leather glove. Like many of De Palma's films he plays with striking images, and the look of the Phantom is pure cinematic gold. Also at play is his trademark style behind the camera and visual techniques like the split screen famously used later in his adaptation of Stephen King's *Carrie*. The cast is also music to the audience's ears, and the brilliantly underrated William Finley does double duty as mild mannered Wilson and his alter ego, The Phantom. Finley clearly understands the material, finding a fine line between seriously and delightfully wacky, and there are times when you really can't help but feel sorry for him. In the female lead is Jessica Harper, who has a natural innocence and charm to her that really serves the character.But stealing the show has to be Gerrit Graham who is deliciously over the top as Beef, a *Rocky Horror*-type performer and, though his role is brief, it's very memorable. Brian De Palma is an amazing filmmaker and, while his suspenseful thrillers are among his best known, he has mastered a number of other genres including this far-out fantasy horror that is both smart and enjoyable.

TRIVIA: According to an interview, Brian De Palma jokingly confronted friend George Lucas for "borrowing" the Phantom's voice box, which is thought to be a direct inspiration.

Like a visit from the Phantom himself the production was hit with several lawsuits including from Universal Studios and King Feature Syndicate, the owners of the *Phantom* comic strip. Thankfully these were all resolved.

Santa Claus (1959)

DIRECTED BY	René Cardona
WRITTEN BY	Adolfo Torres, René Cardona
STARRING	José Elías Moreno, José Luis Aguirre 'Trotsky', Cesáreo Quezadas 'Pulgarcito', Armando Arriola, Antonio Díaz Conde hijo
COUNTRY	Mexico

In general, I have steered clear of kiddie movies for this guide. However, I decided to make an exception for this ultra-wacky Mexican outing. Santa (José Elías Moreno) is minding his merry business when the devil (José Luis Aguirre 'Trotsky') stops by to ruin Christmas. It's up to the jolly fellow, some kids, and the wizard Merlin (for some random reason) to defeat him. I, like many, was first introduced to this movie on an episode of *Mystery Science Theater 3000*. Ever since then it's been a festive tradition. With its crappy dialogue, bottom-of-the-basement production values, and nonsensical plot it's no wonder Mike and the bots had a field day lampooning it, as it's seemingly tailor-made for them. What always struck me, though, was how creepy this is considering it's a "kid's movie", as it's chock full of weird, almost surreal, images, not to mention Satan being a main character. But of course, it's these reasons that make this a total blast to watch on a frosty winters night. Truly Satan Claus, I mean *Santa Claus*, is a gift for the fan of terrible but charming celluloid crapfests. Make this one a yearly tradition.

Shock Treatment (1981)

DIRECTED BY	Jim Sharman
WRITTEN BY	Richard O'Brien, Jim Sharman
STARRING	Jessica Harper, Richard O'Brien, Cliff De Young, Patricia Quinn, Charles Gray, Ruby Wax, Nell Campbell
COUNTRY	United States

Six years after *The Rocky Horror Picture Show* time-warped into theaters with its bold message of "don't dream it, be it" and catchy songs, a sequel tried to fill its rather large high heels. Taking place after the events of the first film, our hapless couple Brad (Cliff De Young) and Janet (Jessica Harper) find themselves on a bizarre game show further testing their love for each other.

I give *Shock Treatment* major props for not simply retreading the plot from the first film, and I love how they took a satirical spin on television, seemingly predicting the public's obsession with reality shows. Also, I love how the entire film has a larger-than-life cartoon-like quality about it. The problem that this film has is it smacks of trying too hard to re-create

the offbeat flavor of its predecessor, and the filmmakers learn the harsh lesson that it's impossible to manufacture the kind of cult classic that *Rocky* embodied so well. And while some of the cast returned, sadly the heart of the movie, Tim Curry did not, leaving a gap for a lot of fans. Probably worst of all are a host of songs that aren't terrible but pale in comparison to the amazingly well-written and catchy songs of the first film. I honestly saw this movie a few times and I can't recall a single song, while on the other hand I have every song from *Rocky Horror* memorized by heart (don't judge me). *The Rocky Horror Picture Show* was a sleeper hit that cast a huge shadow and, while I admire the attempt at a totally surreal strange follow-up, the end result felt like a cynical studio pandering to its audience in hopes of striking gold twice. Even Richard O'Brien has disowned the project. *Shock Treatment* does have its loyal fans and if you're one of them more power to you, but for me it's not a step in the right direction but rather a jump into the uninspired.

TRIVIA: Susan Sarandon declined to reprise the role of Janet due to salary and claims to have never seen the film to this day.

Valerie and Her Week of Wonder (1970)

DIRECTED BY	Jaromil Jires
WRITTEN BY	Jaromil Jires, Ester Krumbachova, Vitezslav Nezval (based on the novel by), Jiri Musil (dialogue)
STARRING	Jaroslava Schallerová, Helena Anýzová, Jirí Prýmek, Petr Kopriva, Libuse Komancová, Alena Stojáková
COUNTRY	Czech Republic

Stringing together elements of *Alice in Wonderland* and folk tales like *Little Red Riding Hood, Valerie and Her Week of Wonder* puts a decidedly more edgy spin on fantasy. Valerie (Jaroslava Schallerová), a young girl of thirteen, explores a rich daydreamy world filled with equal parts beauty and danger, which includes black magic, vampires, and a randy priest. An early scene depicting blood trickling on a flower perfectly sums up the film's underlying theme of our titular character Valerie entering womanhood. This film is

such a stunning and interesting exercise in not only surrealism, but it boldly mixes a fairy tale sensibility to an adult themed film which explores a woman's newly budding sexuality and the fears that come with it. Besides the wonderfully provocative story the filmmakers take full advantage of the rich and lovely exterior, and the result is truly a feast for the eyes and further echoes the dreamy quality. Jaroslava Schallerová, with her natural beauty coupled with an aura of sweet innocence, makes her the perfect choice for the lead. What's even more impressive is the fact that this was her first screen acting job and she carries the role effortlessly. Jaromil Jires' master work is a part dream, part nightmare landscape that melds a childlike tale with much more grown subject matter and the result is nothing short of amazing.

CHAPTER 7

I like to think of myself as a well-rounded film lover, but I've always had a fondness for the horror genre and indeed all things macabre, it seems, going back to a very young age. You might be wondering why this chapter is the only one broken down into countries. Simply put, there was such a wealth of weird horror from all over the world that I decided to go the extra mile and break them down by countries. Prior to writing this book I was exposed to a good deal of world cinema, which I actively seek out. But I have to come clean that in recent years I became less adventurous, tending to stick with my favorites, so this project really forced me to further expand my watching and in doing so re-kindled my love affair for international horror cinema. I discovered trashy treasures like *Absurd,* aka *Horrible,* or delete-bin Mexican monster movies like *The Brainiac.* From Spain I discovered a new guilty pleasure in the films of Rubén Galindo Jr., and I think you should as well. Also it was fun watching some underground French stuff like *Mad Mutilator.* I also found what has to be the strangest slasher ever made. I won't say where it is. You'll have to read on to find it. My brain has never been the same since. Every country has its own interesting brand of horror that is steeped in its unique cultural roots, so you get a different kind of flavor. Hong Kong, for example, has hopping vampires, Italy the sleazy Giallos, America has its budding gore and slashers, and so on. Some great, some bad, some so bad they're great, and everything in between, it was a blast breaking out of my shell and finding these horrific titles and in return helping you find them as well. I implore the casual horror film fan to give these international films a chance because there are so many great strange and crazy delights to uncover.

Horror

Curious Doctor Humpp, The (1969)

DIRECTED BY	Emillio Vieyra, Jerald Intrator
WRITTEN BY	Emillio Vieyra
STARRING	Richardo Bauleo, Gloria Prat, Aldo Barbero, Susana Beltran, Justin Martin, Mary Albano, Alex Klapp
COUNTRY	Argentina

What do you get when you mix *Masters and Johnsons* with *Frankenstein*? You just might get this off-the-deep-end horror skin flick from Argentina. A mad doctor thinks that the key to his longevity is through the sex of others. So naturally he kidnaps men and women with the aid of a cheap-looking monster and pumps them with various libido-inducing drugs and forces his subjects to literally screw until they die. An ultra-retro horror sci-fi with a healthy dose of perversion, softcore mischief, and of course, loads of unintentional camp humor and one seriously cheesy-looking monster seems like a winning combo. However, before you race out to get your very own copy, it's not as awesome as it sounds. Whatever fun might be had from the far-out concept is totally squashed from a severely inept plot that is terribly repetitive and falls back on a series of limp clichés and moves along at a sluggish pace. Worst of all, it strangely plays against its strengths (its camp factor) by going deadly serious, without a hint of humor. It's such an odd choice, and it makes me wonder who this movie was even aimed at? I guess the obvious answer is it was marketed towards the skin flicks of the day and, maybe I'm just horribly jaded, but it's so tame and frankly dull that today's audience would find it more boring than sexy. Still, for trash fans, it does have a certain appeal for its pure bat-crap plot overflowing with spooky black-and-white sexual nightmares and cheap monster movie quality. Truly only recommended for "the curious" but unfortunately this film is all foreplay and no action.

Howling III, aka The Marsupials: The Howling III (1987)

DIRECTED BY	Philippe Mora
WRITTEN BY	Philippe Mora, Gary Brandner (based on novel by)
STARRING	Barry Otto, William Yang, Imogen Annesley, Deby Wightman, Lee Biolos, Max Fairchild, Frank Thring
COUNTRY	Australia

Mora, no stranger to the strange, takes a second bite out of the successful horror franchise, having previously directed the critically panned but, in my mind, wonderfully underrated *Howling II: Your Sister Is a Werewolf*. A race of hybrid human marsupials wolves are living in a remote village of Flow. One such girl leaves and finds herself cast in a B-horror film. There she falls in love with a young man working on the film but she is hiding a deadly and bizarre secret. *Howling III* is a direct result of how unhappy Philippe was with the studio on the previous *Howling* film, and he decided that he would make this an Ozzie comedy rather than a straight up horror film. This is certainly a case where everything *and* the kitchen sink is thrown at the film and, as you might imagine, the end product is a wolf sized mess. The film suffers greatly from a wildly uneven and convoluted plot going as far as throwing in a communism subplot for some weird reason. Early on the film takes a satirical bite out of Hollywood; a device Mora clearly used as a way to vent his frustrations at his earlier experience, but again, it's just another needless subplot and I can't help but think if this was the film's main drive it would have worked much better. Like the plot, the tone is also all over the place, and of course, there are story holes aplenty. *Howling III* is no doubt ridiculous, but it's also a lot of fun if you're in the mood for some mindless over-the-top insanity, which this film has in spades. Philippe is a creative and smart guy, and he was painfully aware the film he made had the stink of wet wolf, but I'd take a film that doesn't play it safe to something predictable any day of the week. Sure it's about as subtle as an axe to the skull but it's just so off-the-wall it's hard not to be entertained, even if it's for all the wrong reasons. True fans of the so-bad-it's-glorious should consider this a must-watch.

TRIVIA: A then relatively unknown Nicole Kidman was considered for the role of Jerboa.

Goodnight Mommy (2014)

DIRECTED BY	Severin Fiala, Veronika Franz
WRITTEN BY	Severin Fiala, Veronika Franz
STARRING	Luka Schwarz, Elias Schwarz, Susanne Wuest, Hans Escher, Karl Purker, Elfriede Schatz, Georg Deliovsky
COUNTRY	Austria

Creepy children in horror films have been a long-standing trope and, whether they're British and want to dominate the world like in *Village of the Damned* or born of Satan and want to, well, dominate the world like *The Omen*, there is just something sinister beyond those seemingly angelic eyes and cute smile. *Goodbye Mommy* takes a different approach to the whole evil kids genre with lots of twists and turns. After a horrible accident a mother undergoes cosmetic surgery and must take care of her identical twins, Lukas (Luka Schwarz) and Elisa (Elias Schwarz) while recovering from the psychical and mental strain. She is also going through a painful separation from her husband. To make matters worse her appearance is rather shocking, as her face is wrapped in bandages. As the children try and cope, their behavior becomes increasingly stranger. Like Takashi Miike's brilliant 1999 film *Audition* this film takes its time exploring and building character development all while amping up the tension until it's almost unbearable. The writing shows great restraint, only giving the audience drips of information at first, leaving you guessing and in a constant state of suspense until its unforgettable ending. This is a nice change of pace from the typical smash-you-over-the-head-with-exposition, which so many films feel the need to do. The film has a lot of symbolism and subtle subtext sprinkled throughout which makes repeat viewings a must. It's evident that the filmmakers have a keen eye, which is reflected in the camera work that perfectly creates a mood that is foreboding yet other times beautiful. A lack of a soundtrack gives the film a more stark reality, and it's a bold choice. Speaking of reality, the film is grounded in it but also playfully sways into the realm of the surreal without going too overboard. While the film isn't the goriest it does offer some very gritty realistic violence that never gets cartoonish, but rather is done in an unflinchingly realistic way that makes it all the more disturbing. This film seems to divide fans, but I think it's a refreshingly moody, suspenseful, and entertaining film that has future classic written all over it.

Daughters of Darkness, aka Les lèvres rouges (1971)

DIRECTED BY	Harry Kümel
WRITTEN BY	Harry Kümel, Pierre Drouot, Jean Ferry
STARRING	Delphine Seyrig, John Karlen, Danielle Ouimet, Andrea Rau, Paul Esser, Joris Collet, George Jamin, Fons Rademakers
COUNTRY	Belgium

When someone asks me what my favorite vampire film is, this elegant and sometimes over-the-top '70s shocker from Belgium automatically pops into my head. A young newlywed couple traveling via train makes an unexpected stop and decides to stay at an isolated resort. Their wedded bliss is about to end, however, when the Countess (Delphine Seyrig) and her lover Ilona (Andrea Rau) check in. Sex, betrayal, and murder are just the tip of what will test their marriage vows. If you go into Harry Kümel's *Daughters of Darkness* expecting a typical Christopher Lee type of Gothic vampire outing you may be disappointed. Unlike most vampire films of the decade Kümel gives things a much needed update and shows off an amazing visual flare that is equal parts eerie and dream-like. Indeed the whole film is like one long waking nightmare of eroticism. *Daughters* also has a wonderfully pitch-black sense of humor and cheeky camp that balances it nicely. It's also not afraid to take potshots at the vampire lore while never crossing into full parody. Delphine Seyrig is absolutely electric as Bathory and her screen presence will have you utterly hypnotized. It's no surprise that she steals every scene she is in. For some, the pacing may be a bit tedious, but those with an attention span willing to hang in there will be rewarded tenfold. More stylish and cerebral than most bloodsucker movies, *Daughters of Darkness* is an erotic, sleazy, and moody little movie and a devilish treat just wanting to be unearthed. Required viewing.

Lucker, aka Lucker the Necrophagous (1986)

DIRECTED BY	Johan Vanderwoestiijne
WRITTEN BY	Johan Vanderwoestiijne, John Kupferschmidt
STARRING	Nick Van Suyt, Helga Vandevelde, Let Jotts, Marie Claes, Martine Scherre, Carry Van Middel
COUNTRY	Belgium

Few movies from the horror video boom are as vile and groundbreaking as *Lucker*. The plot (of what there is) revolves around the titular character, Lucker (Nick Van Suyt), who escapes out of a mental hospital with one goal in mind; to find a female victim that got away. In his wake he leaves a trail of bloody broken bodies, some he likes to play with even after they are dead. Critics like to pan Johan's film for its shortcomings due to its obviously small budget, which I think is both unfair and very narrow-minded. Sure it's not a finely polished work of art; however, this movie is nasty, visceral, and good for some cheap thrills. Its crude camera work actually works in its favor, giving it a raw documentary style that makes the viewers feel as if they are watching a snuff film. Now I'm not saying this is a masterpiece in slasher cinema, because it's not.

With the exception of Nick Van Suyt, the actors are hammy and the plot itself is paper thin with dialogue that is at times cringeworthy. The splatter, while plentiful, is on the primitive side; however, there are a few good gore gags that look halfway decent. It's hard to say what the worst death scene is but certainly John getting his head smashed into a brick wall a dozen time ranks up there. Even with its shortcomings *Lucker* manages to deliver a film that is brutal, fast, loud, and in your face. It's the kind of film that takes you places you never wanted to go and the director makes no apologies for it. Few films reach the level of vile detached level except of course *Nekromantik*. For fans that enjoy the stark reality of *Henry* mixed with the lunacy of Bill Lusting's *Maniac, Lucker* is a film you'll dig.

At Midnight I'll Take Your Soul, aka À Meia Noite Levarei Sua Alma (1964)

DIRECTED BY	José Mojica Marins
WRITTEN BY	José Mojica Marins, Magda Mei
STARRING	José Mojica Marins, Magda Mei, Nivaldo Lima, Ilídio Martins Simões, Valéria Vasquez, Genésio de Carvalho
COUNTRY	Brazil

With piercing dark eyes, long fingernails, and donning a cape and top hat, writer/director and actor José Mojica Marins first played the devilish Zé in À *Meia Noite Levarei Sua Alma* or *At Midnight I'll Take Your Soul*. Not only would the character (known in the states as Coffin Joe) go on to international fame but would inspire other directors, including the legendary Alejandro Jodorowsky. A villainous man named Zé (José Mojica Marins) puts himself above others, mocks religion, and thinks nothing of killing to get what he wants. And what he truly desires is a son to carry on his wicked bloodline. His wife cannot bear children, so he must go out and seek another who will at any cost. With its low production values José Mojica Marins' groundbreaking horror film plays wonderfully like an old-fashioned spook house ride, complete with cheap thrills, skeletons, witches, and hoards of the living dead. Casual film fans may find the film to be slow in places, but those who have an actual attention span and a love for international cinema will find this an unparalleled fright fest which gets better with repeat viewings. For its time, it also pushes the limits in both sexuality and violence which, tame by today's standards, is still pretty nasty. José has a great presence and his suave and maniacal charm is able to cut down on the inherit camp value. *At Midnight I'll Take Your Soul* is a nightmarish black-and-white treat for die hard horror fans.

Awakening of the Beast (1970)

DIRECTED BY	José Mojica Marins
WRITTEN BY	Rubens F. Lucchetti, José Mojica Marins (story by)
STARRING	José Mojica Marins, Ângelo Assunção, João Callegaro, Ronaldo Beibe, Andreia Bryan, Maurice Capovila
COUNTRY	Brazil

When one thinks of meta horror you often think of *Wes Craven's New Nightmare* or later *Scream,* yet (no disrespect to the late great director) *Awakening of the Beast* pre-dates those by more than twenty years. *Beast* is told in a series of increasingly strange vignettes of various depraved acts and psychedelic fueled youth. With the aid of four volunteers, psychiatrists try to investigate what kind of effect José Mojica Marins/Zé do Caixão films have on them. José Mojica Marins trades his spook show trappings of Gothic moonlit nights, full moons, and the undead for an altogether different entry in the popular Brazilian series. The common thread in all of José's films are biting social commentary, and what we get here is an interesting yet still disturbing look into drug culture and heaps full of uncomfortable sleaze. Like *Night* Marins creates an eye-popping, blazing, neon colored scene. Instead of a glimpse into hell this time we get a mindbending LSD trip. Indeed, the whole film feels like one long nightmarish trip. While I do love the dime store horror fun ride of the previous films, I love the fact that he took the series in a different direction and, as always, has something important to say. *Awakening of the Beast*—meta before there was such a thing. Required viewing.

Embodiment of Evil, aka Encarnação do Demônio (2008)

DIRECTED BY	José Mojica Marins
WRITTEN BY	José Mojica Marins, Dennison Ramalho
STARRING	José Mojica Marins, Jece Valadão, José Celso Martinez Corrêa, Helena Ignez, Thais Simi, Cleo de Paris, Cristina Aché
COUNTRY	Brazil

It's been forty long years in a mental asylum but our long-nailed friend is released, being fit to rejoin society. Like the previous films the object of Zé's (José Mojica Marins) desire is simple; find the perfect woman to carry on his legacy by giving him a male child. This time, however, he is not alone, having a small following of loyal cult members to help him carry out his evil dreams. I admit when I went to watch this film I felt some trepidation. This due to the fact I'm a huge fan of the earlier installments in the *Coffin Joe* saga and did not want to see anything less than worthy to be in the cannon of films. Ninety minutes later I was not disappointed but rather insanely entertained. Not only does it work as a standalone horror film but it's a fitting tribute to *At Midnight I'll Take Your Soul* and *This Night I'll Posses Your Corpse.* And as a standalone it doesn't alienate those unfamiliar with the previous films. However, fans of lore are in for a treat, as there are numerous references and inside jokes that make this a lot of fun. The choice of having past victims haunt our anti-hero is great but it takes this idea one step further by filming them in black-and-white like the original films. It's almost as if they're forever trapped in the aged moving picture, a much higher concept then I expected. The look of *Embodiment* is impressive. It really has a nice balance of both macabre and ghastly, yet at the same time striking and beautiful. One could say the best visual of all is that of actor José himself who, even after forty years, still has a presence unmatched by any modern slasher/psychopath in cinema. His evil stare, the long nasty fingernails, and trademark top hat are reasons why he has remained a horror icon. Gore hounds will be very happy, as this film delivers some incredible splatter. In a particularly memorable scene a poor girl literary has her ass handed to her (after being chopped off) and later fed to her. I must say that's a first for me, cinema lovers. Like early Argento, the kills are bloody and plentiful yet with a sense of flare and style, something that is sorely lacking in today's films. The ending is fittingly bizarre and is truly worthy of being the last installment in a legacy that spans over forty years. So if you want a film with guts (plenty of them), style, and shocking cringeworthy horror, this is no old hat. Let's hope this isn't the final nail in Coffin Joe.

This Night I Will Possess Your Corpse (1967)

DIRECTED BY	José Mojica Marins
WRITTEN BY	José Mojica Marin, Aldenora De SA Porto
STARRING	José Mojica Marins, Tina Wohlers, Nadia Freitas, Antonio Fracari, Jose Lobo, Paula Ramos, Tania Mendonca
COUNTRY	Brazil

Grab your top hat and cape for another wild and insane movie by everyone's favorite boogeyman. Taking place directly after the events of *At Midnight,* Zé survives and is brought back to perfect health (and as a plastic surgeon it seems). He is still desperate to find the perfect female to bear his male child. He rounds up a group of women to pick the perfect one. Think of a warped version of *The Bachelor.* But it seems he is being haunted by a former victim who is determined to take him to hell.

On paper this seems like more of the same; however, *Night* does something a good sequel should do, which is expand its story with new characters and situations rather than a simple rehash. But it goes one step further and improves upon its predecessor and, at a longer runtime, is better paced. Thankfully it still retains its classical Gothic spook show vibes. The bankability of *Midnight* ensured a bigger budget and José makes good use of it with a bigger and bolder

nightmare vision. Of course the real stand-out scene is the ten-minute-long neon colored (more striking, as the rest of the film is in black-and-white) psychedelic "trip" into the very depths of hell. It's like a mixture of Bosch and Dali filtered through the crazed mind of José Mojica Marins. And of course there are other nasty little surprises in store. An incredible sequel that is not only as good as the first but in many ways better. Required viewing.

American Gothic (1988)

DIRECTED BY	John Hough
WRITTEN BY	Burt Wetanson, Michael Vine
STARRING	Rod Steiger, Yvonne De Carlo, Sarah Torgov, Caroline Barclay, Michael J. Pollard, Janet Wright, William Hootkins
COUNTRY	Canada

It's Horror Movie 101 that if you're stranded in the woods or on an island, chances are fairly good someone or something is going to kill you. The movie opens with a girl named Cynthia (Sarah Torgov) having been freshly released from a mental hospital. Despite her doctor's wishes her boyfriend Jeff (Mark Erickson) decides to include her in a trip with a group of other young people. Plane troubles force them to land on a remote island that is seemingly uninhabited, but as I mentioned above, we all know that's not true. In search of help they discover a house and a kindly old couple simply known as Ma (Yvonne De Carlo) and Pa (Rod Steiger), who live perpetually in the '20s, with very little to no modern conveniences.

What starts out friendly turns sour, as the couple are deeply religious and "don't take too kindly" to their sinner ways. John Hough has an impressive resume having made the classic Hammer film *Twins of Evil* as well as *Legend of Hell House* and the rip-roaring fun *Dirty Mary Crazy Larry*. His foray into the hillbilly horror genre is truly something to behold.

The film starts out like a museum piece to other slashers, filled with unlikable characters and similar set-ups. However, as the film progresses, it starts a slow yet steep descent into crazy town and surprisingly it only gets weirder and never lets up until its wacky and frenzied finale. The writing is above what you might expect from this kind of outing and it's peppered with some clever foreshadowing, and yes, even some character development. It also has a terrific cast. Veteran actors Yvonne De Carlo, Rod Steiger, and Michael J. Pollard all turn in delightfully strange performances and they leave no inch of set unchewed. What shocked me was how, despite the inherently cheesy nature, the film manages to be downright creepy with moments that might make even jaded fans' skin crawl. *American Gothic* is pure oddball fun that also delivers a refreshingly different spin on the backwoods slasher genre. Criminally underrated and worth seeking out.

TRIVIA: *Star Wars* fans will no doubt recognize the actor who plays Teddy William Hootkins from A New Hope, where he played Porkins (Red Six) and was also in *Raiders of the Lost Ark*.

Actor Rod Steiger had an impressive career, winning an Oscar for *In the Heat of the Night*. But horror fans will best know him in *The Amityville Horror*.

Bite (2015)

DIRECTED BY	Chad Archibald
WRITTEN BY	Jayme Laforest, Chad Archibald (story)
STARRING	Elma Begovic, Annette Wozniak, Denise Yuen, Jordan Gray, Lawrence Denkers, Barry Birnberg, Caroline Parker
COUNTRY	Canada

I'm a huge fan of the "body horror" genre created by master filmmaker David Cronenberg. So I decided to take a chance on *Bite,* a film that seemingly pays homage to films like *The Fly* and *Shivers.* Casey (Elma Begovic), a bride-to-be, goes out with her best gal pals for a Mexican vacation for one final blow out before she gets married. When swimming she is bit by something, but of course shrugs it off. However, when she gets home she develops serious symptoms, yet instead of calling the doctor she lets it go until things go from bad to worse. Now Casey is quickly changing into something deadly. You know you're in for a hard ride when the film opens with some horribly clichéd found footage, which is used to provide its setup. I can suspend disbelief to a degree but the film is littered with huge plot holes and gaps in common sense logic. Worse yet, important plot points are left totally unexplained and unclear, leaving the audience more confused than scared. Drama is injected but it feels phony and forced like a bad soap opera. Further sinking things is the terrible acting. It's hard to really single one person out as they all seem to be all over the place, either overacting or underacting. The only good thing about the film was the decent special effects and wonderful production design. Instead of being a scary body horror in the vein of David Cronenberg the film suffers greatly from a weak and confused script that has moments of unintentional comedy and lackluster acting. *Bite* is utterly forgettable and not worth your time. Avoid.

Brain, The (1988)

DIRECTED BY	Ed Hunt
WRITTEN BY	Barry Pearson
STARRING	David Gale, George Buza, Cynthia Preston, Tom Bresnahan, George Buza, Bret Pearson, Robert King
COUNTRY	Canada

I think deep down there's always a fear that our technology is somehow corrupting people, from the invention of the television to the Internet and beyond. But in 1988's *The Brain* it's our own boob tube that is used to control our minds. Jamie (Tom Bresnahan) is a very bright student but has an appetite for childish mayhem. One day a prank goes too far, and he is given the option of not graduating or seeing Dr. Blake (David Gale), a psychotherapist guru who has a popular cable access show, which is going nationwide soon. It's a no-"brainer" what he chooses, and he goes to see the good doctor. What Jamie soon discovers is that there is a secret plot to control the townspeople and, after that, the world. Now it's up to him and his girlfriend Janet (Cynthia Preston) to save the day. As ultra-cheesy as the film is it does have a few things going for it. The concept of a television shrink that people blindly follow is fortuitous when you look at the glib self help doctors currently on TV today. Now take that and imagine the shrink as a mad scientist straight out of a '50s science fiction film and you really got something different than the typical body count slasher. It also has some well crafted creature effects and the titular Brain monster actually holds up. Sadly, *The Brain* had the makings of a cult classic but never pushed its themes or story far enough to make an effective film. Instead we get a very bland and predictable plot that doesn't challenge or shock the audience. I would have loved it if they would have played up the B-monster aspect while also injecting smart social satire on psychotherapy and television mass consumption. For a low-budget monster movie it takes itself far too seriously, never allowing itself to take a step back and have a laugh. The acting is decent and features the late great David Gale of *Re-Animator* fame. He perfectly embodies a mad doctor and it's very disappointing he didn't have more screen time. Even with its glaring problems it does have camp value and B-grade charm that makes it passable. As a movie lover, it's frustrating to see a film with strong ideas that suffers from a lazy screenplay, uneven tone and worst of all, thinks its above its B-movie status. The end result is certainly a strange little film but a forgettable one. However, I'd say it's worth a look only for those diehard creature feature fans, and I even know some people who enjoy it. For a better movie, Doctor Mike would like to prescribe *TerrorVision* instead.

Curtains (1983)

DIRECTED BY	Richard Ciupka, Richard Simpson (re-shoots)
WRITTEN BY	Robert Guza Jr.
STARRING	John Vernon, Linda Thorson, Samantha Eggar, Annie Ditchburn, Lynne Griffin, Lesleh Donaldson
COUNTRY	Canada

Becoming a huge Hollywood star is hard enough, but staying relevant as an older actor can sometimes be just as brutal as making it. And sometimes it can be downright cutthroat, which is literally the case in this strange 1980s slasher. Veteran director Jonathan Stryker (John Vernon) is in pre-production on *Audra*, a film based on the popular and racy book. Samantha Sherwood (Samantha Eggar), who has worked with the director before (and got him the film rights), feels she was born to play the role. However, Stryker has a reputation for demanding extreme realism from his leading ladies, and to really get into the character's head they cook up a scheme to get her committed to a mental institute so she can see firsthand the suffering and madness that the fictional Audra endures. Her plan backfires when a friend sends her a *Variety* announcing that Jonathan is holding auditions for her part at his mansion. She breaks out and crashes the cozy little casting party Stryker has cooked up. Female fur will fly and blood will be shed in this battle for a role to kill for. Take two films and violently smash them together and that's what you get with *Curtains*. This is due in large part to a horribly troubled production, which included clashing of ideas between its director Richard Ciupka and producer Peter R. Simpson. The result was Ciupka quitting after only shooting forty-five minutes of footage. Simpson had to fill in as director and the film underwent major re-shoots and re-writes. The result is a mangling of different styles, tones, and wildly uneven plotting and pacing. Ciupka obviously brings an Italian flavor in strange lighting and the way he uses the camera, while Simpson takes a more conventional approach. I have to say the writing is above the normal slasher fare, but sadly it seems out of its depths and doesn't provide proper character motivations, introducing people then dropping them quickly from the film, such as Matthew (Michael Wincott) who, after one brief scene, completely exits the film. It's even mentioned by one of the actors and is dropped from the story entirely. This is most likely something that got lost in the re-writes. This film would have worked better with some editing. Certain scenes slow the film down and others stop it dead in its tracks. Despite its glaring flaws *Curtain* is still an enjoyable film. What I respect about this film is it doesn't go the lazy "teen body count" route yet weaves a smart Hollywood satire mixed in with the slasher genre—something that wouldn't be explored in that way until the *Scream* series. Even as jaded as I've become I feel that this film delivers genuinely suspenseful moments and also some classic kill scenes; I'm talking about the famous daytime skating murder. Splatter heads will be pleased with the copious amounts of blood and clever gore gags. The cast of talented actors assembled here is amazing and gives the film a much needed polish. Veteran actor John Vernon is just wonderful playing the villainous film director. He is always on point and never hams it up for the camera. As fine as Vernon is, it's the ladies that shine here. *Avengers* star Linda Thorson and cult favorite Samantha Eggar are eclectic as two seasoned actresses vying for the same role. Scream queens Lynne Griffin (*Black Christmas*) and Lesleh Donaldson (*Happy Birthday to Me, Deadly Eyes*) also do a wonderful job and work so well together. In fact, all the women seem to have chemistry together. Even considering the terrible production problems somehow this film manages to be wildly entertaining and a refreshing break from the same old.

Dead of Night, aka Deathdream (1974)

DIRECTED BY	Bob Clark
WRITTEN BY	Alan Ormsby
STARRING	John Marley, Richard Backus, Lynn Carlin, Jane Daly, Anya Ormsby, Henderson Forsythe, Michael Mazes
COUNTRY	Canada

Films and television rarely dealt head-on with the issue of the Vietnam War, as the country was sharply divided by the conflict. Maverick director Bob Clark, known for comedy classics like *Porky's* and *A Christmas Story,* would tackle the subject head-on wrapped in the guise of a horror film. The Brooks family hasn't received a letter from their son Andy (Richard Backus), and one night their worst fear is realized when they get the news he was killed in combat. That very same night they get another shock when they discover Andy has returned home. Overjoyed, the family can't wait to get back to a normal life, yet something is horribly wrong with the young soldier and things are about to turn deadly. Before *Rolling Thunder* and *First Blood, Dead of Night,* later re-titled *Deathdream,* tackled the issues of a service man coming home changed from war and the conflicts it makes with friends and family. At first I was dismissive of this film until I re-visited it and realized it was a genius and (at the time) timely re-telling of *The Monkey's Paw* folk story about a man who was killed in war and is

wished back to life with terrifying results.
While the metaphor is maybe not so subtle
it's an interesting way to deal with the
frightening changes a person can go through
when they come back from war wrapped
up in a tension-filled horror film. Richard
Backus, who plays Andy, gives a wonderfully
menacing performance that is chilling and
thankfully not hammy, and I must admit

his smile creeped the hell out of me. I also have to give major props to the well-done makeup
effects which, considering the budget, looks just plain scary. My one minor issue with this
film is the message which, while no doubt important, tends to get a bit heavy-handed, leaving
the entertainment value sometimes taking a backseat. Overall though, Clark's horror film
acts as a clever bit of social commentary wonderfully dressed up as a B-horror film. *Dead of
Night* was vastly ahead of its time and worth checking out.

Deranged (1974)

DIRECTED BY	Alan Ormsby and Jeff Gillen
WRITTEN BY	Alan Ormsby
STARRING	Roberts Blossom, Cosette Lee, Leslie Carlson, Robert Warner, Marian Waldman
COUNTRY	Canada

In the 1950s Ed Gein shocked the world with his vile crimes, becoming the most notorious
American psychopath since H. H. Holmes. It's not surprising that films based on his ghastly deeds
would emerge. While *Texas Chainsaw Massacre* (released the same year) is a watershed moment
in horror cinema due in large part to its gritty documentary-style realism *Deranged* has its own
set of grizzly charms. Based (very) loosely on the real-life crimes with names and places changed,
the film follows Ezra (Roberts Blossom), a slow-witted boy that truly loves his mama. Before she
dies she tells him women are evil, diseased creatures, a message she had instilled in him since
childhood. Not accepting her death, he digs up the old gal and places her gingerly in her room,
like any good son would do. He soon starts robbing graves and that quickly escalates to murder.
The more Ezra kills the deeper he goes into his own crazed world of depravity and lust. This is a

film that goes way over the top and takes
itself a bit too seriously, the result is high
camp of the so-bad-it's-good variety.
Mother's death bed scene is strange to the
point of being surreal in its madcap lunacy. Even with her dying breath she gives
Ezra one of the greatest anti-sex speeches
ever. It also has some laughable mistakes.
Like, you also gotta love when a girl is shot
point blank and is totally unharmed moments later and even able to run away

from her chaser. Ezra is played by Roberts Blossom and he is the perfect choice to play the part, his mannerisms and even looks are very close to Gein's and he actually does a great job. It's not surprising that Blossoms would go on to have a pretty good acting career. Though it lacks the documentary-type style of *Texas Chainsaw* it does have some genuinely disturbing moments that stick with the viewer. For example, the insane dinner scene where poor Mary is forced to dine with the "family" of corpses is rather nasty and every bit as good as the similar scene in *Chainsaw*. Another scene that is hard to shake is where Ezra carves up his final victim (inspired by actual crime scene photos); she is hung upside down like a deer and cut from her genitals to her breasts. We don't actually see this, mind you, it's simply implied, which makes it all the more effective and unnerving. Low-budget camp aside, you have to give this director props for being the first film to attempt to tell Gein's story (even if its inaccurate) in a realistic way. Sure it's trashy and not nearly as good as TCM but it's still an entertaining nasty little flick that most definitely deserves its cult following. So unearth this weird little gem and give it a home.

TRIVIA: Actor Roberts Blossom went on to have a great career. Stephen King fans will no doubt remember him in a small but memorable role in *Christine*. He would also have roles in blockbusters like *Home Alone* and *Close Encounters of the Third Kind,* just to name a few.

Dracula: Pages from a Virgin's Diary (2002)

DIRECTED BY	Guy Maddin
WRITTEN BY	Mark Godden (ballet Dracula), Bram Stoker (original source material)
STARRING	Wei-Qiang Zhang, Tara Birtwhistle, David Moroni, CindyMarie Small, Johnny A. Wright, Keir Knight, Stephane Leonard
COUNTRY	Canada

For some horror fans even the idea of a horror ballet will make you shrink away like a vampire to a cross. That's alright. I know it's not for everyone, but *Dracula: Pages from a Virgin's Diary* is such a weird and interesting film I felt like I needed to include it in this book. So for those of you still reading, let's begin. The plot is basically a re-telling of Dracula partly based on the original novel. Besides being staged as a ballet, what also sets this film adaptation apart are the numerous visual techniques Maddin employees, first by framing it entirely like a silent film with no dialogue uttered—a style that has become his trademark. This is used very effectively, and Guy doesn't allow the device to feel stale by using different color filters and various other silent film transitions, etc. It cannot be understated just how truly sublime the dancing is. Every move is filled with grace, and the dancers make it all look flawless. The interpretation flows briskly and manages to hypnotize you with its gothic atmosphere and its transcendent beauty. It also features some impressive set pieces that perfectly capture the mood. Since the birth of cinema filmmakers have captured Bram Stoker's immortal novel with various degrees of success, and with every re-telling the director puts their own unique stamp on it. Through the magic of dance and overwhelming visual style Maddin melds the feverish nightmare world of pure terror with unbridled romance and erotic ecstasy, which is the essence of the source material. Bold choice, yes, and it may not be everyone's cup of blood, but I thought it was an amazing way to tell a story that's already been done to death.

End of the Line (2007)

DIRECTED BY	Maurice Devereaux
WRITTEN BY	Maurice Devereaux
STARRING	Ilona Elkin, Nicolas Wright, Neil Napier, Tim Rozen, Emily Shelton, Nina Fillis, Joan McBride, John Vamvas
COUNTRY	Canada

Far too often a great little gem of a film will come out and get quietly cast aside while other less deserving work gets heaps of press. Such is the case with the film *End of the Line,* a film highly praised by critics but sadly overlooked by fans. Karen (Ilona Elkin), a tired nurse in a psychiatric ward, is taking the last train home but, to her dismay, it stops in the middle of its destination. But a bizarre series of events will make things more disconcerting than just getting home late, because she may not reach her destination at all. The movie starts with an epic jump scare that had me out of my seat, and surprisingly the film has enough nicely paced momentum and frights to live up to its stellar opening. I purposely kept the plot vague because a lot hangs on the film's mystery and various twists and turns. Devereaux takes a low budget and dares to be fiercely original and bold while not shying away from material that might make you uncomfortable but at the same time challenges you. The writing is great with richly drawn and complex characters which, thankfully doesn't rely on clumsy exposition to cloud the waters. One thing is the dialogue at times could have used an over haul, but it's not bad enough to ruin the film. There are also some slight gaps in logic. Wisely, the film is left open to viewer's interpretation, allowing the audience to speculate over it for days afterward. *End of the Line* is not without its flaws, but the good very much outweighs the bad and considering its small budget, what they managed to pull off is incredible. With a well-thought-out and refreshingly different screenplay, talented actors, and keen direction this scary movie actually earns the title and is frightening yet thought-provoking at the same time. Get on board with this nonstop train ride to hell.

Ghostkeeper (1981)

DIRECTED BY	Jim Makichuk
WRITTEN BY	Jim Makichuk
STARRING	Riva Spier, Georgie Collins, Murray Ord, Les Kimber, Bill Grove, Sheri McFadden, John MacMillan
COUNTRY	Canada

The film opens with a text about a Native American lore about the Wendigo, a creature who lives on human flesh. A group of friends go snowmobiling, but in typical horror fashion become stranded, and they stumble upon a creepy and seemingly deserted lodge. The snow is really coming down and it's either risk freezing to death or trying their luck in the building. Of course it is not empty as previously thought and they find a weird old lady who lives there. She tells them she was the former owner but they closed due to bad business. Soon the friends start disappearing and they learn someone else is lurking around the lodge and he just happens to carry a chainsaw. *Ghostkeeper* is a film that baffles me as to how an interesting concept can get so far from itself and end up as an incoherent mess. Before I get into that let's talk about what I liked about this film. The filmmakers wisely used the locations to their advantage and the blistering cold snowy mountains are both beautiful and ominous. Indeed the first part of the movie is very moody and has a strange dreamlike quality, especially when the characters enter the lodge. The biggest problem with this film is its incredibly slow pace, which seems to aimlessly move along while not providing any insight into the Native American lore that it teases at in the opening text. In fact, it's never explored to any degree. It's further hampered by bad acting and clunky exposition. It seems the film was going in a different direction from the slasher craze until it turns out that it's just that. Why go down the human fleshing-eating Wendigo road if you're not going to do anything with it? Now you can see why I was so totally baffled. It's even terribly tame in the splatter department with a couple gags that would be boring even by daytime television standards. Blood and gore don't necessarily make a good film; however, I think in this case it would have improved it greatly. *Ghostkeeper* is a novel concept which tries for a *Shining*-like vibe but falls horribly flat due to a severely underdeveloped confused plot and unlikable characters. Worse yet, it sets up a plot point but never delivers on it all while lumbering at a glacier's pace. The lodging may look promising from the outside but sadly it's rather drab once you explore it. Checking out, please.

Mask, The, aka Eyes from Hell (1961)

DIRECTED BY	Julian Roffman
WRITTEN BY	Frank Taubes, Sandy Haver, Franklin Delessert, Slavko Vorkapich (dream sequence)
STARRING	Paul Stevens, Claudette Nevins, Bill Walker, Anne Collings, Jim Moran, Leo Leyden, Martin Lavut, Ray Lawlor
COUNTRY	Canada

I first heard of *The Mask* from the bible of cult movie guides, *The Psychotronic Video Guide* written by Michael J. Weldon. A young museum professor named Michael (Martin Lavut) discovers an ancient mask while on his latest archeological dig. But he soon learns there is a terrible curse on it. Before he kills himself he mails the damned item to his shrink, Doctor Barnes (Paul Stevens). Will the good doctor suffer the same horrible fate? This movie certainly earns its place in Canadian cult filmdom but sadly its not very good. I can overlook the clunky dialogue, horrible acting, and even its almost nonexistent plot which is riddled with holes. However, at a brisk runtime of seventy-three minutes it's just plain dull. Besides the totally trippy and surreal dream sequences (which make zero sense) the audience is dragged through cliché after cliché, painful melodrama, and underdeveloped story. It feels as if the 3D scenes were done first and the rest of the movie was simply just built around them. Even its build in kitsch can't save it from being a rather dull messy outing.

TRIVIA: *The Mask* holds a special place as the first Canadian horror movie to be widely released in the US.

Pin (1988)

DIRECTED BY	Sander Stern
WRITTEN BY	Sander Stern, Andrew Neiderman (novel)
STARRING	Terry O'Quinn, Cynthia Preston, David Hewlett, Helene Udy, Bronwen Mantal, Patricia Collins
COUNTRY	Canada

The horror movie genre is filled with rage-induced psychopaths that are frothing at the mouth, armed with something deadly like a knife or chainsaw or even a nail gun. 1988's *Pin* happily breaks the mold and offers audiences a very different look at someone who is mentally ill. Leon (David Hewlett) and his younger sister Ursula (Cynthia Preston) live a very sheltered life due largely to their perfection-demanding doctor father and neat-freak OCD mother. Leon seems extremely effected by this and has withdrawn into a world of his own. His only true friend is a medical dummy named Pin (short for Pinocchio) who talks to them, with the aid of the father's skill at ventriloquism. However, Leon believes Pin's real and actually speaks to him. After their parents are killed in a tragic auto accident the children are left the estate and set for life. But now, with their parents gone, Pin is free to move into the house and that's when the terror really begins. Stern weaves a brilliant psychological horror film that examines the effects overbearing parents can have on an already disturbed person. It's also heavily implicd that the parents have mental illnesses themselves. In this regard the film takes a page from *Psycho* where there is mental disease passed down. What makes this the stand-out film is the smart way it tackles Leon and his obvious mental issues, yet doesn't make him a one dimension crazed maniac hacking everything in sight. Instead, we have a layered and complex character and indeed we feel sorry for him like a tragic figure. In fact, one can see this film like a Greek tragedy. We also see the kind of effects someone's illness can have on his loved ones—namely Ursula. There is a great moment when she breaks down and admits to her boyfriend that her brother has schizophrenia. It's a wonderful scene and Preston is genuinely moving in it. Make no mistake though; this film is very unnerving and chilling. Wisely, the scares are not generated by the amount of blood, gore, or shock value but through subtle effective creepiness that builds and builds until its shocking and frenzied finale. Thankfully, *Pin* never gets campy and Stern doesn't debase the material by winking at the audience, and the result is a frightening and strangely human film. It's also boosted by its incredibly talented cast. Terry O'Quinn portrays the father and, as always, gives a solid non-hokey performance. The break-out stars are Cynthia Preston and David Hewlett. Both would go on to have amazing careers, and their acting in this proves it's much deserved. Sadly, because *Pin* wasn't a hack a minute film it bombed at the box office and was dumped quietly on VHS by New World who was heading towards bankruptcy at this point. Luckily, with repeated releases on home video it has found a growing cult following and rightly so. If you're in the mood for something more psychological and downright creepy *Pin* is in, and that's no lie.

Pit, The (1981)

DIRECTED BY	Lew Lehman
WRITTEN BY	Ian A. Stuart
STARRING	Sammy Snyder, Jeannie Elias, John Auten, Paul Grisham, Wendy Schmidt, Laura Press, Paul Grisham
COUNTRY	Canada

I first discovered the brain-numbing goodness of *The Pit* from Anchor Bay Entertainment, a company that was important to my garbage cinema education. This film is a refreshingly different take on the evil kid genre but strangely, is played like a good old-fashioned creature feature. Every town has that one really strange kid everybody avoids, and Jamie (Sammy Snyder) is it. At only twelve he shows signs of deep psychological issues and a severe lack of personal boundaries. His only friend is Teddy, his stuffed bear, who talks to him (in Jamie's voice) and gives him advice. One day Jamie stumbles upon a pit deep in the woods, which is filled with mysterious creatures with an enormous hunger. Meanwhile, his parents are going out of town and leave him with an attractive psych major that specializes in troubled kids. Soon the people in town that have wronged Jamie discover the horrible secret dwelling inside the pit. If I had a weirdness scale, this movie might very well break it. You have the talking teddy bear, the mental kid, and the pit creatures, not to mention some strange sexual perversion and murder thrown in for good measure. The story is all over the place, blending monsters, evil kiddie, psycho drama, and revenge. Whew! It's certainly a mish-mash of a lot of different subgenres and it also suffers from some uneven tone. This is most likely due to a change from Ian A. Stuart's original much darker script, which had Jamie being a lot younger and the trogs being just inside his troubled mind. When Lew signed on to direct he changed his age to twelve, made the trogs real, and added some levity to counter-balance the disturbing facets. Even with the darker stuff toned down it still has skin crawling moments. Like the strongly implied incest happening between Jamie and his overbearing mother. Also, the way Jamie gets his sexual kicks is pretty creepy and psychotic. Anything that might be upsetting about Jamie killing kids and adults is undercut by the intentional tongue-in-cheek creature feature aspects like the cheesy furry suits the monsters wear. Seeing how the character of Jamie is in almost every scene it's important to cast the perfect kid. Luckily, Sammy Snyder is brilliant and really nails the role. He at times seems like a typical troubled teen and other times oozes sinister serial killer. It's a pretty good layered performance. While not spoiling anything I can say the ending has a delightfully bitter irony to it. Even with its uneven tones and various subplots *The Pit* is pure off-its-meds cinema that will keep you entertained while scratching your head. It's something you have to see to believe. Tell'em Teddy sent yah.

Revenge of the Radioactive Reporter, aka Atomic Reporter (1990)

DIRECTED BY	Craig Pryce
WRITTEN BY	Craig Pryce, David Wiechorek
STARRING	David Scammell, Kathryn Boese, Randy Pearlstein, Derrick Strange, Erich Arenson, Mel Asbor, Larry Baker
COUNTRY	Canada

An ambitious young reporter named Michael (David Scammell) is working on a huge story about a toxic chemical plant. Before he is able to go public with his information he is thrown in a boiling sludge vat and left for dead. Of course he does not die, but rather is transformed into a hideous scarred creature out for revenge. Oh boy, where do I start? *Revenge* starts out alright with a solid, albeit painfully predictable, storyline, but it quickly loses its focus and bogs itself down in needless or overly long scenes. The writing is also, for the most part, cringeworthy, as it attempts to mix satirical comedy with horror. The result is terrible jokes that are beyond cornball. It also really dates the movie horribly. The look of our titular radioactive reporter looks a lot like Freddy Krueger, which is most

likely done on purpose (especially since he wears a hat very similar to Freddy's) in order to poke fun at the genre, but I kind of wish they would have come up with something more original. Surprisingly, the makeup itself isn't terrible, considering this looks to be made on a shoe-string budget.

Despite all of this it manages to just squeak by as passable because of its ultra-strange, unabashedly campy quality which it wears proudly on its sleeve. It also features some pretty great death scenes and a random gorilla attack that's never explained or mentioned afterwards. A '90s video oddity that could have been a lot better but still enjoyable if you don't mind wading through a lot of cheese, bad acting, and stinky dialogue. And you know I don't.

GOES WELL WITH: *Things, Freaked*

Shivers, aka They Came from Within (1975)

DIRECTED BY	David Cronenberg
WRITTEN BY	David Cronenberg
STARRING	Paul Hampton, Joe Silver, Lynn Lowry, Barbara Steele, Allan Kolman, Fred Doederlein
COUNTRY	Canada

I'd be shocked if anyone reading this has never seen a David Cronenberg film. He's one of the few filmmakers today that are truly ballsy and risk-taking. *Shivers* marks his first feature film and, simply put, it's a delightfully nasty taste of his work to come. Residents of an upscale apartment complex, Starliner Towers, are being plagued with a rash of sexually based attacks after a Doctor Emil Hobbs (Fred Doederlein) savagely strangles a young girl and cuts his own throat. It seems the good doctor unwillingly unleashed a nightmare on everyone in the building and possibly the world. It's up to the surviving residents of the building to fight against this deadly, slimy foe and the crazed tenants infected by it. Cronenberg's first feature lays out the blueprint for what will be an amazing body of work and, speaking of body, he would single-handedly create the horror subgenre, body horror. *Shivers* explores important social issues such as sex, violence, and illness in a smart way but wraps it up in a gooey monster movie. Another theme he explores in this and later works is the idea of our own systems fighting against us and the deep rooted fear we all share, which is the reality that someday this well-oiled machine we call a body will ultimately fail us. It's a story device that is amazingly effective and unsettling as hell. Cronenberg doesn't soften the blow in terms of violence and right off the bat the audience is forced to watch a brutal and slow strangulation and later dissection of a pretty young girl, all filmed in a very cold and detached way. It's very disturbing and sets the tone for the rest of the film. It's all the creepier when you realize how much Dr. Hobbs looks like the BTK killer. The concept of a man-made parasite that is sexually transmitted is a really interesting one and he knows how far to push it to the extreme without getting into high camp. Thankfully Cronenberg's smart writing and skilled directing allows him to play everything dead pan. Yes there is a small amount of levity injected into the film but make no mistake, this is not a goofy monster film. Also impressive is the wonderful cast, which includes cult actress Lynn Lowry as Nurse Forsythe and the dark goodness herself Barbara Steele as Betts. She adds a touch of class to this very weird outing. *Shivers* takes you down a deep dark spiral of eroticism and fevered nightmares that climaxes in sheer delirium and terror that is rarely ever matched.

Things (1989)

DIRECTED BY	Andrew Jordon
WRITTEN BY	Andrew Jordon, Barry J.Gillis
STARRING	Barry J.Gillis, Bruce Roach, Doug Bunston, Amber Lynn, Gordon Lucas, Daryn Gillis, Jeff Payne, Glenn Orr
COUNTRY	Canada

This movie is brought to you by beer, lots and lots of it. And that's what you will need before viewing this infamous Canadian horror epic. A man wanting to have a child makes his wife undergo a risky procedure, which results in her giving birth to a mutant creature. Now alone with the "thing" in a remote cabin, three friends must fight to stay alive. Shot on Super 8 and fueled by bad mullets, a dime budget, and love for horror films, Andrew Jordon and Barry Gillis create the perfect storm of bad cinema. It has it all; terrible, almost surreal dialogue, crappy lighting, bad editing, and a story that doesn't seem to follow any logic whatsoever. To Jordon and Gillis' credit they have an obvious love for the genre, with some references sprinkled throughout. And of course there is the gore, which is plentiful and covers every square each of the celluloid. The practical effects are, as you might have guessed, pretty bad but surprisingly the creatures are decent looking. Over the years *Things* has gained a small but loyal cult following, and like a glorious train wreck it's hard not to stare. Your brain may never be the same again. Recommended for anyone seriously interested in the weird, surreal, and the so-bad-it's-amazing.

GOES WELL WITH: *Gut Pile*

Sinful Dwarf, The (1973)

DIRECTED BY	Vidal Raski
WRITTEN BY	Harlan Asquith and William Mayo
STARRING	Torban Bille, Clara Keller, Tony Eades, Anna Sparrow, Gerda Madsen
COUNTRY	Denmark

When looking for a skin crawling film that spews filth from every celluloid pore, one only has to pick up this vile little film.

The Sinful Dwarf is truly an insane workout trash art, and truly one of a kind. A young couple named Peter (Tony Eades) and Mary (Anna Sparrow) is desperately looking for a place to stay and, more importantly, one they can afford. They stop at a very sordid-looking place owned by Lilah Lash (Clara Keller), a former vaudeville star (not to mention the greatest

character name), and her deformed and deranged son Olaf (Torban Bille). It would seem renting rooms doesn't pay the bills so they have a side business. They kidnap girls and force them into sexual slavery and smuggle drugs in toys. They also feed the girls the drugs to keep them dependant and unable to leave. Needing fresh meat, they decide Mary would be a much needed addition to the stable. Mother and son cook up a plan to get Peter out of the picture and make it look like Mary left him. He doesn't buy this, and he soon sets out to look for her, but he just might discover the seedy secrets that lurk above him. The casting of Torban Bille is a stroke of pure genius and is a key factor is why this film works so well. Having not seen him before or since I must only assume he only exists in the deepest darkest parts of cinema hell. Yes, he's hammy but his looks and mannerisms just ooze twisted perversion. I'd even go so far as to say he's one of the few screen villains who actually give me the creeps. Playing the mother is Clara Keller, and she delightfully camps it up as a former night club singer and now aging relic. She joyfully chews scenery, the highlights of which are her over-the-top musical numbers. The young Brit couple, Pete and Mary, played by Tony Eades and Anne Sparrow, has zero chemistry together and also very little acting talent. But hey, this is not some Hollywood epic, and bad acting can be forgiven as long as the film delivers the depraved goods, and boy, does it. While it's not very plot heavy it does do its job in always having some nasty little surprise to keep the audience entranced. This movie has something for everyone; sex, violence, strange musical numbers, and of course a very sadist angry "dwarf". I'd also like to take a moment and point out the amazingly grimy sets used, which look so disgusting you feel like you might catch something just looking at them. I also enjoy the little details like old show posters that Lilah Lash hangs around the house, further echoing her need to stay stuck in the past. *Blood Sucking Freaks,* made a few years after this, is the only other film to match its over-the-top, sick, vile, and delightfully chaotic style. Simply put, *The Sinful Dwarf* is a must-see for anyone serious about exploring far-out nasty cinema.

Alleluia (2014)

DIRECTED BY	Fabrice Du Welz
WRITTEN BY	Fabrice Du Welz, Vincent Tavier (story by)
STARRING	Laurent Lucus, Lola Dueñas, Héléna Noguerra, Stéphane Bissot, Pili Groyner, David Murgia, Sorenza Mollica
COUNTRY	France/Belgium

Loosely based on the real-life killer duo dubbed The Lonely Hearts Killers, *Alleluia* is the story of Gloria (Lola Dueñas), a divorced woman looking for her true love. With a friend's push she meets Michel (Laurent Lucus) on a blind date. Sparks fly and Gloria is head over heels, but little does she know that her love will set off a chain reaction of madness and murder. From the director of the brilliant and sorely overlooked *Calvaire* comes another outstanding film, this time exploring the depths of depravity and obsession all in the name of love. As always, Welz pulls no punches and isn't afraid to take his audience (sometimes by force) into some very bleak and haunting places. Like his previous films, he showcases a defiant flare with some wonderful inventive camera work while also using a naturalist style in lighting, giving scenes an eerie ethereal look. A stand-out scene is a frenzied sexually charged dance done at night by a roaring bonfire which is lit only by the fire's light. Another Welz trademark is his jarring and brutally frank use of violence, and what's most disturbing is not that it's ultra-gory but rather done in a cold clinical way. The gritty non-cartoon style gives it a far more unnerving quality that tends to stick with you long after the film's end. It's a lesson a lot of up-and-coming filmmakers should heed. Laurent Lucus and Lola Dueñas are perfectly cast as the killer duo and each bring an intense yet nicely understated performance. Fabrice Du Welz once again boldly takes his viewers into an unsettling and twisted world of the depraved lows people can go to in the name of love and devotion. This nasty little horror thriller is both stylish and well-acted and totally grips its audience by the throat and doesn't let up until the final moments. *Alleluia* is a must-see.

Amer (2009)

DIRECTED BY	Hélène Cattet and Bruno Forzani
WRITTEN BY	Hélène Cattet and Bruno Forzani
STARRING	Bianca Maria D'Amato, Charlotte Eugène Guibeaud, Delphine Brual
COUNTRY	France

A good Italian Gallio should be a part of any horror film buff's balanced diet. Lately, the genre is enjoying a resurgence of interest, and naturally, this lead to films paying tribute to them. Without a doubt this is one of the best love letters to the films of Dario Argento, Mario Bava, etc. Before I go any further in this review, I should note this film will not be for everyone. This is tailored toward the hardcore Italian horror/Gallio fan, and casual horror film viewers might get frustrated by the lack of plot. Like classic Argento films it's about the visual journey that he takes you on, not the actual plot, and fans of these types of films get that. This Gallio is broken up into three parts, all of which tell the story of a girl's journey from childhood, teen years, and full grown adulthood. Don't worry, it's not as boring or sappy as it sounds. The look of *Amer* is very much the stand-out thing. Forzani and Cattet employ a number of breathtaking visual techniques and a very hyper color palette that is as bold as the film itself. This coupled with slick and well-thought-out editing and sound design that can only be described as masterful; the end result is nothing short of brilliant filmmaking. Seldom has a movie gripped me in such a hypnotic state and not let up till the end credits. It can turn something as normal and mundane as a car ride and turn it into a sexually charged feast for the senses. Fans will no doubt recognize the score

from Italian masters Bruno Nicolia, Stevio Cipriani, and the legendary Oscar award-winning Ennio Morricone. Wisely, the exquisite filming locations such as the French Riviera and Belgium are taken full advantage of and give the low-budget film a lot of production value on a budget. Equally beautiful are Charlotte Eugène Guibeaud and Bianca Maria D'Amato, who can say a lot with very little dialogue. *Amer* is an experience that will blow the back of your mind out and harkens back to the good old days of films like *Bird with the Crystal Plumage*, Sergio Martino's *All the Colors of the Dark*, etc. The use of colors and mind-bending effects creates a beautiful and sinister world that is soaking wet with dark desire and dripping with equal amounts of eroticism and nightmare logic. I give this my highest recommendation.

Calvaire, aka The Ordeal (2004)

DIRECTED BY	Fabrice Du Welz
WRITTEN BY	Fabrice Du Welz, Romain Protat
STARRING	Laurent Lucas, Jackie Berroyer, Brigitte Lahaie, Gigi Coursigny, Phillip Nahon, Jean-Luc Couchard, Mac Lefebvre
COUNTRY	France/Belgium

Coming out bare knuckled and swinging, *Calvaire* is an early example of the new wave of French horror that would go on to include such modern classics as *Inside, High Tension Frontier(s)*, etc. Marc Stevens (Laurent Lucas) is a low-rent performer who is traveling south to a Christmas Gala to sing and hopefully catch the attention of some producers. He has some troubles when his van breaks down and he is forced to spend the night in an Inn run by a man named Bartel (Jackie Berroyer) who offers to get him help in the morning. It seems Marc is stuck at the inn when he finds out that a mechanic is not possible right away. Marc is frustrated but tries to make the best of his situation. Bartel warns him not to wander too far and to not go down to the village. From the very start Du Welz crafts a very strange and uncomfortable tone; something that slowly grows and grows until its hard left turn. Building upon its tone is Welz's use of camera work, which is wonderfully expressive and helps tell the story. This coupled with quirky and downright unnerving characters helps weave a brilliantly simple yet effective way to create a tremendous amount of tension which never lets up until the film's end. The filmmakers never show their hand and, like a good magic show, it's all about purposeful misdirection, and this little pot boiler offers many twists and turns, and you're not quite sure where it's going until it blindsides you like a sucker punch to the face. And those who are patient are rewarded by an amazingly brutal and bizarre ride in a nightmarish hell. All the actors are great but I have to say Jackie Berroyer was stand-out, giving a layered performance, and takes it just far enough without going into high camp. Director Fabrice is obviously a fan of the *Texas Chainsaw Massacre* as he does his own take on the infamous dinner scene in a clever little homage. Critics unfairly panned the film, but over the years it's finally starting to get the respect and praise it deserves. *Calvaire* is a total assault on the viewer and is disturbing in not the amount of bloodshed but the psychological attack, which in my opinion is more effective. My advice: Try and go in totally fresh if you can, because it makes the shocks all that more potent and, as you can see, I went to pains to tiptoe around major plot points. Bravo to Fabrice Du Welz for truly impressing this sometimes jaded film lover. Required viewing.

Eyes Without a Face (1960)

DIRECTED BY	George Franju
WRITTEN BY	Pierre Boileau, Thomas Naracejac, Claude Sautet, Jean Redon (based on novel by)
STARRING	Pierre Brasseur, Edith Scob, Alida Valil, Juliette Mayniel, Alexandre Rignault, Charles Blavette, François Guérin
COUNTRY	France

It's hard to say what exactly is my favorite French horror film, but *Eyes Without a Face* would most certainly rank right up there. It's a wonderful example of how a film with a low budget and a minimal plot can not only transcend those limitations but be an outstanding example of how, a lot of times, less really is more. After his daughter suffered a terrible auto accident world-famous doctor Génessier (Pierre Brasseur) vows to give his little girl her beauty back by any means necessary. And by any means, we mean kidnapping young women to experiment on. What really struck me right off the bat with this film is its dark humor, which is hinted at its playfully morbid credit theme, which perfectly prepares you for the wild ride you're about to take. But it's really the film's visual style, which is nothing short of breathtaking. German born cinematographer Eugen Schüfftan lights and frames the film in such a methodical way, bringing out its dark and poetic beauty. The whole thing has a hauntingly surreal, almost dreamlike quality. Similar to first gazing at the monster in 1931's *Frankenstein*, the moment we first see Christiane's character in her mask is such a visceral moment and terror washes over the audience. Even now, looking it at still gives me the creeps. We really take for granted a lot in terms of violence, so it's hard to imagine just how shocking a film like this was back in 1960. While obviously not gory by any means the film does boldly show things like a skinless face, the scalpel as it removes said face and other moments that again may seem tame to our jaded eyes, but it's something that definitely could not have been produced in America at the time. The film's legacy is vast and has inspired such filmmakers as Jesse Franco, Pedro Almodóvar, John Woo, and even John Carpenter has said to have drawn inspiration for Michael Myers iconic blank white mask on the one that character Christina wears. It's no wonder the film continues to inspire generations of filmmakers and film buffs alike. I highly recommend this film for anyone not only serious about the horror genre but films in general.

TRIVIA: The world's first full facial transplant was completed in Spain in 2010. Prior to this the first partial face transplant was done five years earlier in, fittingly enough, France.

Billy Idol has gone on to say that, yes indeed, his song *Eyes Without a Face* was inspired by the film.

CRAZY CONNECTIONS: Cinematographer Eugen Schüfftan won an Oscar for 1962's *The Hustler*.

Grapes of Death, The, aka Les Raisins de la Mort (1978)

DIRECTED BY	Jean Rollin
WRITTEN BY	Jean Rollin, Christian Meunier
STARRING	Marie-George Pascal, Felix Marten, Serge Marquand, Brigitte Lahaie, Patricia Cartier, Oliver Rollin
COUNTRY	France

Grab a seat and let's crack open a vintage Jean Rollin sleaze fest. This time he's taking a page from George A. Romero, which just so happened to come out the very same year as the original *Dawn of the Dead*. But how well has this film aged? Elizabeth (Marie-George Pascal) boards a train with a friend, off to soak up the local culture and ultimately end up at a winery. However, due to deadly pesticides that are carelessly sprayed on the grapes anyone who drinks the wine is infected with a virus that first gives you hideous sores and then insanity and a murderous rage. It just so happens that the local wine festival has taken place and now, instead of the villagers having a nice hangover, they have a hankering for murder. Elizabeth must fight her way to the winery where Michael, her fiancé, works. I've been told the films of Jean Rollin are an acquired taste, and what few of his films I've seen, I have to agree with that. The film starts out promising enough with some great moody set pieces and some nicely paced action scenes which literally waste no time kicking into gear. Plus the concept of a French wine-soaked *Night of the Living Dead* seems pretty darn interesting. Sadly though, due to a lackluster screenplay the film quickly runs out of steam and is hampered by drama that falls flat and character motivations that are sketchy at best. Poor editing and laughably cheesy and dated practical effects further sink this film down to Z-grade level. Also it's just plain boring in parts. Rollin tries to shoehorn some pointed political and social commentary but it just doesn't work. I think I could have forgiven all this had this film tried to up the scares or at least inject some tongue-in-cheek humor. Maybe it sounds like sour grapes on my part but this ill conceived film isn't the flavorful horror film I had hoped and methinks it stayed on the vines just a bit too long. Still if it's just a cheap ultra-trashy sleaze fest and you don't mind some dull moments than I think you could do worse, and even hardcore lovers of his work have to admit that his output is highly suspect to begin with. As I stated above, his films are something you have to have a taste for, and for the most part I don't. But I'm far from a film snob and I don't look down on those who do. Open this bottle at your own risk, just wipe off the oozing pus.

Horsehead (2014)

DIRECTED BY	Romain Basset
WRITTEN BY	Romain Basset, Karim Chériguène
STARRING	Lily-Fleur Pointeaux, Catrionia MacColl, Murray Head, Gala Besson, Vernon Dobtcheff, Phillip Nahon
COUNTRY	France

Jessica (Lily-Fleur Pointeaux) is studying in the field of lucid dreaming in hopes to understand a recurring nightmare she's had since she was little. With the passing of her grandmother she returns to the family estate. But what should be a happy homecoming is anything but, as her relationship with her mother (Catrionia MacColl) is strained at best. Making matters weirder is the fact that dead grandma is lying in bed next-door to where Jessica is staying, as they are having a traditional wake in the deceased bedroom. While staying there she begins to have vivid dreams that turn nightmarish, and she soon learns to use her lucid dreaming skills to unlock a dark family secret.

Right out of the gate Basset proves to a re-freshingly different voice in the world of horror, and *Horsehead* is an utterly amazing piece of transgressive art. The screenplay is tightly focused and brilliantly straddles the lines between reali-ty and dream in a way that seems totally new despite it being done before. Masterfully, the lines between reality and fantasy blur and, as the film progresses, a wonderfully complex mystery unfolds. It's clear from the very start that Romain has a firm grasp on creating a distinctive and evocative nightmare-like imagery that ranges from the erotic and beautiful to the dark and twisted, and you can no doubt see shades of Argento Bava and even Ken Russell. Helping bring these images to life is FX wiz David Scherer, who at such a young age has already worked with heavy hitters like Richard Stanley and Gaspe Noes and, as always, his work is brilliant. Across the board the cast is wonderful, but it's newcomer Lily-Fleur Pointeaux who really shines. She has the task of carrying the majority of the film and she is more than up to the challenge, bringing a strong female pres-ence, yet isn't afraid to show a vulnerable side. Cult actress Catrionia MacColl, best-known for such films as *The Beyond* and *City of the Living Dead,* proves she's still got it and is abso-lutely electric, giving a layered performance. *Horsehead* is a nonstop, tension-filled, surreal nightmare that throws enough clever twists and turns and is also dripping with psycho-sex-ual eroticism. A stunning feature film debt and, mark my words, you'll see more great things from this director.

In My Skin (2002)

DIRECTED BY	Marina de Van
WRITTEN BY	Marina de Van
STARRING	Marina de Van, Laurent Lucas, Léa Drucker, Marc Rioufol, Adrien de Van, Alain Rimoux, Bernard Alane, Dominique Reymond, François Lamotte
COUNTRY	France

Whew! Want to watch a movie to make your skin crawl or even leave your body? Watch Marina de Van's *In My Skin*. A woman named Esther (Mariana de Van) has a great boyfriend, friends, and is quickly climbing the ladder in her job. While at a party one night she hurts herself pretty badly and requires medical attention. What starts as a healthy curiosity with her wound quickly spirals into an obsession that leads to self-mutilation. Marina de Van takes us into the bleak void of mental illness and cutting. The film itself is a slow burn, but once it gets going it's an unflinchingly disturbing portrait of a woman driven over the edge. What exactly sets her off is not made clear and frankly it's not important, as we get just enough information. Besides a clever and layered script, what really sells this is, of course, the stand-out performances by Marina de Van and Laurent Lucas. Both play off each other extremely well and bring something intense yet understated to the film. Marina de Van puts a mirror up to mental disease and forces the viewers to watch every painful second. It is the kind of movie that stays with you long after the finale. To call this movie simply unsettling wouldn't begin to describe this entry in the body horror genre. Bravo. Required viewing, but you might want to watch something funny afterwards.

Mad Mutilator, aka Orgroff: The Mad Mutilator (1983)

DIRECTED BY	N. G. Mount
WRITTEN BY	N. G. Mount
STARRING	Robert Alaux, Françoise Deniel, Pierre Pattin, Alain Petit, Michel Pratt, Jean-Pierre Putters, Alain Cayol
COUNTRY	France

Orgroff: The Mad Mutilator is an obscure film (or at least obscure as I'm writing this) that I had often heard of, and thankfully, I was able to track a copy down with subtitles. The plot, of what there is, consists of the titular character going about his daily activities of killing hapless people who venture into the woods. Oh, and there are zombies over halfway through, because why not? Right off the bat, the film wastes no time in showing the audience a disturbing and violent murder of child in somewhat graphic detail. This is just a taste of the nasty little surprises in store.

It's evident that the director is a horror fan and takes cues from stuff like *The Texas Chainsaw Massacre*, which is clearly the idea behind the villain's pad, filled with hanging bones and other twisted items. While the film no doubt has an amateur quality, it also adds to the grimy documentary style. The problem with *Orgroff* is that it has no actual plot to speak of and almost an hour into the film zombies start popping up. Why? Because they just do, apparently. It's as if the filmmakers were like, "Ok, I'm bored with the serial killer bit, hey zombies, perfect, film it." As you might expect the zombie makeups and the strange doll-like masks they wear are just as cheap and awesome as you might expect, further enhancing its bizarre surreal quality. I won't spoil it, but at the end yet another random unexplained creature pops up. Despite the lack of a real narrative and its laughably low-budget randomness, it's wildly entertaining if you're in the mood for a slice of international Grindhouse

cheese. This film is loads of fun and best to watch with a crowd of like-minded horror fiends with plenty of cold suds and greasy junk food.

Maleficia (1998)

DIRECTED BY	Antonie Pellissier
WRITTEN BY	Antonie Pellissier
STARRING	Nelly Astaud, Guy Cicorelli, Brigitte Garrigue, Claude Gatumel, Nicolas Pellissier
COUNTRY	France

Anyone who knows me knows how much I love French cinema of all genres, but especially their horror, which is often brutal and complex with an artsy flare. However, there are always exceptions to that rule—point in case, *Maleficia*. The Karlson family is headed to a castle they have inherited east of Transylvania. Much to their horror they discover themselves smack dab in the middle of a Satanic cult and freshly resurrected zombies, and of course, vampires who seem perfectly fine in the daytime. Director/writer, and most likely producer Antonie Pellissier makes a common but fatal mistake with new filmmakers by throwing in as many ideas as possible but forgetting that a lot of times less really is more. This shot-on-video horror outing is ambitious in that it's a period film that mixes Satanists, zombies, and vampires but forgets to actually have a plot, and the film seems way more interested in all

the blood and gore it can throw at you, which is perfectly okay but I like to have a story to go with my brutality. Worse yet, its attempt at melodrama is laughable, like the scene where the grandmother apparently can't tell a zombie from her own grandson and beats his ever-loving brains in with a rock. Later, after stabbing him (repeatedly) with a stick she FINALLY notices who it is, and of course, some wonderful overacting ensues. I will say some of the special effects were decent as are the period costumes, which I'm guess-

THE ULTIMATE GUIDE TO STRANGE CINEMA

ing is where the entire budget went. With a more polished script I could actually see this director doing something pretty good; however, this film suffers greatly from a threadbare plot and a general sense of ineptitude across the board.

Malefique (2002)

DIRECTED BY	Eric Valette
WRITTEN BY	Alexander Charlot, Franck Magnier
STARRING	Gerald Laroche, Philippe Laudenbach, Clovis Cornillac, Dimitri Rataud
COUNTRY	France

They say that prison is its own horror, which I guess is why few horror movies are set in one. Eric Valette's first feature film, however, is. Carrere (Gerald Laroche) is a powerful CEO that is used to the good life. Fancy cars, beautiful houses, and the finest cigars, nothing but the best for him. However, that lavish lifestyle comes crashing down as he is caught ripping off his company and sent to jail. He suddenly has to adjust to a much simpler life while sharing a cell with three other inmates. There's Marcus (Clovis Cornillac), a tough brute who just so happens to want to become female, and his sidekick Paquerette (Dimitri Rataud), a mentally disabled young man who will virtually eat anything in sight, and lastly, there is Lassalle, a soft spoken and highly intelligent older man who's in for murder. They discover a book written by a former prisoner and find out it contains black magic rituals that just might help them escape. But will the book be their salvation or damnation? I admire the bold decision to meld supernatural horror and a prison break film. It seems like a combination that would be criminal but, thanks to inventive directing and a smart screenplay, it pulls it off wonderfully. The pacing is surprisingly brisk for a movie that takes place mainly in one cell and it never lets itself get boring. Unlike a lot of horror, Valette attempts at exploring the characters and gives us brief glimpses into their past while not judging them. They are not exactly likable but you still feel invested in them, which is a tricky thing to pull off. Visually the film is bleak with muted colors in keeping with the overall tone. This is coupled with some amazing production designs that are wonderfully detailed. For example, the cell that ninety-nine percent of the film takes place in, looks like a medieval dungeon, further giving the audience a Gothic horror vibe. On a small budget this film has a lot of great practical special effects as well as CGI. One flaw is that the film feels very stagey at times, and I thought the ending, while interesting, could have been more thought out as it feels a bit rushed. *Malefique,* often cited as a mixture of *Hellraiser* and *Cube,* is a refreshing change from the pile of unoriginal horror reboots and retreads that dominate the landscape. Lock yourself in for the evening and give this film a watch.

Marquis (1989)

DIRECTED BY	Henri Xhonneux
WRITTEN BY	Henri Xhonneux, Roland Topor, Marquis DeSade (source material)
STARRING	François Marthouret, Valérie Kling, Michel Robin, Isabelle Wolfe, Vicky Messica, Bob Morel, Roger Crouzet
COUNTRY	France

Ever wonder what the Marquis DeSade would be like done by Jim Hensen and dipped in LSD? Wonder no longer, as 1989's French surrealist film *Marquis* answers that very question, and you're not likely to ever sleep again! Seldom does a movie render me totally speechless as the credits roll, and of course this is one of them. *Marquis* is set in a pre-French Revolution in the infamous Bastille where political prisoners are being held and horribly mistreated. One of them is the Marquis, a poet who spends his time writing and yearning for the sweet air of freedom. Oh, and did I mention he's a dog/human hybrid who regularly talks to his member, who in turn also talks and interacts with everyone in the film? Meanwhile, a woman named Justine is raped by the king and she is now with child, which obviously creates quite the stir among the powers that be. The solution is to have Marquis have sex with the woman in order to claim it was his child and not the king's. The plan backfires and the prisoners plan to rise up against the king. What makes this film so stand-out is that the entire cast of actors are in mechanical anthropomorphized costumes. In terms of expressions they are quite detailed even if they are grotesque in appearance. There is simply nothing like it, and even something like Peter Jackson's *Meet the Feebles* only comes close to the design quality. *Marquis* is not for the easily upset, as the filmmakers don't just push the envelope they gleefully rip it to shreds, and sadly it can be quickly dismissed for that. However, even if it's at times over the top and offensive it does tell a story rooted in historical fact and executed with jaw-dropping visual flare. Stop-motion animation is at times blended in and further gives the film an avant-garde feeling. The subject matter also is rift with political and social satire that elevates it from just merely jokes done in poor taste. Non history buffs may find some of the film dry, but I think there is enough weirdness to keep you entertained. Truly something one-of-a-kind, and even if you find the story a bit on the dull side you can't help but be in total awe over just how insane this film is. For the adventurous, this is worth checking out.

Burning Moon, The (1992)

DIRECTED BY	Olaf Ittenbach
WRITTEN BY	Olaf Ittenbach
STARRING	Beate Neumeyer, Bernd Muggenthaler, Ellen Fischer, Alfons Sigllechner, Thomas Deby, Andrea Arbter
COUNTRY	Germany

Shot on video, splatter film *The Burning Moon* has gained some infamy for its violence and was even outright banned in Germany for two decades. Sure it's gory, but how does it stack up otherwise? A troubled man involved in gangs and drugs is left in charge of babysitting his younger sister, which of course makes a lot of sense. He decides to tell her some bedtime stories which are the two segments in this horror anthology. Hey, I just thought of an alternative title: *Tales from the Junkie*. It's clear that Olaf is a diehard splatter/horror fan and it shows from his high-energy early outing. The first segment is about an escaped serial killer who is just looking for that special someone. Easily the weaker of the two, this tepid slasher is filled with tired clichés and a weak story with a plot hole so big I could hardly believe it. There are some moments of twisted genius though, in particular the eyeball P.O.V. The second segment is about a man of God who is on a quest for purity. Better in terms of a more compelling story with some genuinely disturbing moments; however, again this suffers from a confused plot which is fairly predictable. I will say that the gore is extremely well-done with some gags that are pretty impressive especially considering what I'm sure was an ultra-low budget. It's also clear that Ittenbach has some skill behind the camera, which is evident by decent camera work and editing, and he even gets into the realm of the surreal which is very ambitious. Sadly, the subpar writing sinks *Burning Moon* like a stone. Still, if you want just a good ol' splatter fest and don't mind some corny and plodding plot you could do a lot worse. *The Burning Moon* is not great but fun, and if you're a gore hound you will most likely enjoy it.

Cannibal (2006)

DIRECTED BY	Marian Dora
WRITTEN BY	Marian Dora
STARRING	Carsten Frank, Victor Brandl
COUNTRY	Germany

Taking inspiration from a real-life 2003 case of "consensual" cannibalism, few films are as bleak, haunting, stylish, and oppressive as Marin Dora's *Cannibal*. A character simply credited as Man (Carsten Frank) takes to the Internet to find that special someone in his life. However, his idea of the perfect mate is someone he can eat. After many tries he meets a man simply credited as The Flesh (Victor Brandl), who wants to willingly be eaten. What sets this film apart from the other imitators is that not only does Dora fearlessly explore every aspect of the relationship between Man and Flesh but pulls no punches in showing you their journey into savagery and cannibalism. Dora takes a sadist delight in bringing the audience (kicking and screaming at times) into the mind of two very sick and twisted characters. Surprisingly though, it's done with a lot of style and carefully crafted scenes. Dora does this first by choosing a very unnatural color palette. Even in daytime scenes there is something off about the color—things are slightly out of focus, giving it a strange otherworldly feeling. As the film progresses and things get nasty he switches to darker tones. Second is his choice of classical music in certain spots and later a very strange soundscape style of music when things get really hardcore. However, it's really the great special effects and sound design that pull this film together and make it a believable and unsettlingly experience. At times it's almost like you're watching a snuff film. Perhaps the best and most brutal example is when Man is slowly gutting his willing victim. It also doesn't shy away from showing you everything and ranks up there as some of the sickest images captured on film. After re-watching this for review purposes it dawned on me that this out-disturbs even the infamous *Nekromantik*, which is really saying a lot. While it may not be everyone's "taste" it's a master work in unflinching and disturbing art and in my book is choice cut. I do suggest a comedy palate-cleanser though. *Cannibal* is truly dangerous art and required viewing if you have the stomach for it.

Death King, The, aka Der Todesking (1990)

DIRECTED BY	Jörg Buttgereit
WRITTEN BY	Jörg Buttgereit and Franz Rodenkirchen
STARRING	Hermann Kopp, Heinrich Ebber, Eva-Maria Kurz, Hille Saul, Mark Reeder, Angelika Hoch, Nicolas Petche Frank, Victor Brandl
COUNTRY	Germany

Jörg Buttgereit certainly embraces the darkest corridors of the human experience and doesn't mind taking his audience to some extremely unsettling places. *Der Todesking (The Death King)* explores suicide and death in a seven part anthology—one for each day of the week. For those of you who have not seen a Buttgereit film, they are quite depressing but also very powerful. This film is very different than his others, as it doesn't deal with any exploitation the way *Nekromantik* or *Schramm* do. His lack of narrative and polish gives it a gritty documentary feel which enhances the unsettling effect. What I find most interesting is how Buttgereit plays with the idea of violence on films causing violence, and the irony of course is he does this within his own film. Take, for example, Tuesday: A man walks into a video store, picks out a movie, a Nazisploitation film. He's enjoying his film when his girlfriend walks in and nags him and he calmly shoots her, splattering her brain matter all over the white wall. He then takes an empty picture frame and puts it over the blood and brain matter. It's a great way of showing violence as an art form, meant no doubt as a commentary on his own films. This point is further driven home when the camera pans back to reveal that entire segment was a film and the person watching it hung themselves. Touches like these make this film feel more personal to Jörg then his other works. Also, as I stated above, he strips away anything sensational, leaving the viewer with a very bleak and haunting film about pain and human suffering. Thursday is simply a sweeping camera going over a motorway bridge with names and ages and occupations of actual people who have jumped over the years. Gore hounds looking for gory bits may find this boring, but in my book it's the second most disturbing segment, very moving and sobering. The first would certainly go to Sunday (no spoilers of course) which is raw, savage, and painful to watch. Wisely, he doesn't glamorize the acts depicted, yet presents it in a very matter-of-fact way. Newcomers to Jörg Buttgereit's films might want to start here and decide if you can handle something more hardcore, like say *Nekromantik*. Some segments work better than others but all together it makes for a very powerful piece of cinema. A must-see for fans of his previous films or those who are just discovering them.

Fan, The, aka Der Fan, aka Trance (1982)

DIRECTED BY	Eckhart Schmidt
WRITTEN BY	Eckhart Schmidt
STARRING	Désirée Nosbusch, Simone Brahmann, Bodo Steiger, Helga Tölle, Klaus Münster, Jonas Vischer
COUNTRY	Germany

I think we've all had a crush on a film star or musician as a teenager. After all, the media system builds them up as mythic, almost God-like creatures, something us mortals don't dare touch. And like the rest of us, we move on and maybe we still admire them but in a healthy way. In Eckhart Schmidt's dark thriller we examine a teenage girl's obsession that turns deadly. Simone (Désirée Nosbusch) worships a pop star known as R (Simone Brahmann). She writes to him, and when he doesn't write back she assumes it must be a plot against her, blaming various people including the postal workers (who she attacks at one point), and after numerous attempts she decides to track him down in person, because after all, they were meant to be together. But how far will this innocent crush go? Schmidt's film is an uncompromising portrait of a young girl's blind devotion to a rock star and how it totally consumes every aspect of her life. The world he crafts is totally detached and nondescript, similar to how the object of Simone's attention is simply called R. He is unflinching in how he documents her descent and it makes for a terribly uncomfortable experience. Further highlighting this is the style of shooting, which gives everything a very cold and clinical feeling. Even the film's one sex scene is devoid of any passion or warmth. It certainly ranks up there as one of the unsexiest erotic scenes ever. I only wish the screenplay had been more fleshed out, giving us a little more insight into the character and more of her home life. The Fan isn't a big gory splatter fest but for the patient viewer the film builds to a wonderful fever pitch finale which is just plain nuts. While the film's concept isn't exactly new it is engaging nonetheless and is chock full of style and a cool '80s soundtrack. And of course, it's also an unnerving little bundle of weird that reaches an incredible end. The Fan plays all the right notes and should become your next obsession.

Schramm: Into the Mind of a Serial Killer, aka Schramm (1993)

DIRECTED BY	Jörg Buttgereit
WRITTEN BY	Jörg Buttgereit, Franz Rodenkirchen
STARRING	Florian Koerner von Gustorf, Monika M., Micha Brendel, Carolina Harnisch, Xaver Schwarzenberger
COUNTRY	Germany

If it's a Jörg Buttgereit film you know it's going to be a blisteringly uncomfortable and disturbing celluloid trip through hell. The narrative is told in a nonlinear fashion and the film actually starts at the end, and through the character's last dying breaths we see various memories and the events leading up to the lonely death of the lipstick killer, Loather Schramm (Florian Koerner von Gustorf). Very few films shift the point of view totally on the serial killer, while at the same time not glamorizing what they do. Buttgereit strips the Hollywood polish bare and we are left with something raw and uncompromising. As with his other films, Buttgereit takes us sometimes kicking and screaming into the world of the deeply disturbed and depraved, and we go through his various fetishes and perversions.

The casting of the titular character is a stroke of brilliance, and Florian Koerner von Gustorf can switch from mild mannered and even likable to maniac, yet never gets into theater style theatrics. His attack on the couple at the beginning is one of the most frightening frenzied kills caught on camera and it sticks with you even after the film ends. Fans of films like *Nekromantik* looking for extreme gore might be disappointed that the splatter is relatively tame, but to the film's credit it's more rooted in psychological horror, which is much more effective and unsettling in my opinion. *Schramm* features Jörg Buttgereit's usual art house sensibilities and utilizes some amazing camera work, and you can clearly see how he's grown as a filmmaker since his early work. What makes Loather so terrifying is that he doesn't hide behind a hockey mask; he's someone you might work with, live next to, or bump into on the streets. He's a very real flesh-and-blood monster that really exists in the world we live in. Not since the brilliant *Henry: Portrait of a Serial Killer* has a filmmaker captured the pure savagery and disturbing nature of a killer without adding the safe polish and clichés of Hollywood. *Schramm* forces the audience to inhabit the mind of a serial killer in a very cold and clinical way, and the experience is jarring and unforgettable. I'm a huge fan of Jörg Buttgereit's films and this is definitely a movie worth checking out. It's not for the easily disturbed and I would recommend a comedy chaser.

Island of Death, aka Ta paidia tou Diavolou (1976)

DIRECTED BY	Nico Mastorakis
WRITTEN BY	Nico Mastorakis
STARRING	Robert Behling, Jane Lyle, Jessica Dublin, Gerard Gonalons, Ray Richardson, Efi Bani, Marios Tartas
COUNTRY	Greece

Grab your sunscreen and hide your goats, get ready for a trip to the *Island of Death*. Christopher (Robert Behling) and Celia (Jane Lyle) arrive in the sun-drenched paradise of Mykonos, a Greek island. This seemingly innocent couple, as it turns out, is a pair of bloodthirsty psychopaths on a religious-based killing spree. *Island of Death* seems to split a lot of fellow horror/exploitation fans. One camp hails it as a masterpiece of the genre while another considers it a lackluster and uninspired entry. Even writer/director Nico Mastorakis has stated that the driving force for the film was simply money. Well, my feelings lay somewhere in between. This is one of those movies that feels like it goes out of its way to offend, and this grimy gonzo film certainly does its job. *Island* is pretty light on actual story, and its religious killers are a tired horror chestnut. Despite this there are some truly awe-inspiring moments of nasty that really spun my head around. Its gold lies in its utterly shameless exploitation, which as I stated above, does everything in its power to get its audience to react. For these reasons it's hard for me to outright hate this movie even if it's at times hum drum. And it scores bonus points for the totally insane ending which is burnt into my gray matter. Not one of my favorites but still a noteworthy entry in the horror shock genre.

Singapore Sling (1990)

DIRECTED BY	Nikos Nikolaidis
WRITTEN BY	Nikos Nikolaidis
STARRING	Panos Thanassoulis, Meredyth Herold, Michele Valley
COUNTRY	Greece

One critic boldly claimed this to be the most disturbing film of all time, and ironically the late avant-garde director considered it a comedy in the vein of a Greek tragedy. Well, no disrespect, but this film is far from a chuckle fest even though it has moments that are amusing, albeit in a wicked way. A mysterious man is looking for a lost love named Laura and comes upon a twisted mother/daughter duo. The pair kidnaps the man and ties him up. Later they force him to play a series of perverse sexual games for their amusement. As the film progresses he thinks he may have discovered the terrifying truth behind the missing girl, or is it just another game? Few films can compare to Nikolaidis' uncompromising and resplendent tale of dark obsession, murder, and bizarre sexual fetish. He feverishly and seamlessly blends the Neo-noir and Gothic noir genres into one and the resulting mood he creates is drenched in a psycho-sexual fevered nightmare that is unrelenting and surreal. The ambiance he creates is so thick you can swear you can smell stale perfume wafting throughout the sinister broken-down mansion. Nikos does not shy away from exploring some very troubling taboo issues such as incest and sadism, and does so in a very causal matter-of-fact way. As I stated above, the film is far from what I'd call an actual comedy, but it does have a pitch-black sense of wicked humor. Definitely not for those who are sensitive or easily disturbed, as the film is a pure assault on the audience, testing their limits at every corner. *Singapore Sling* continues to find a new audience and Peter Strickland pays a clever homage to it in his film *The Duke of Burgundy*, which also explores similar themes and tones.

Black Magic (1975)

DIRECTED BY	Ho Meng-Hua
WRITTEN BY	Kuang Ni
STARRING	Lung Ti, Lieh Lo, Ni Tien, Lily Li, Feng Ku, Ping Chang, Chun Chin
COUNTRY	Hong Kong

Picture if you will a soap opera made in the '70s and involving the dark arts: sounds awesome, right? Well, I think so, and that is what you get with this ultra-strange slice of eastern horror. Deep in the dark forest an evil magician that casts various spells, including ones to make people fall in love and others that cause only sickness, madness, and death. Meanwhile, a love triangle brews between a rich widow and a construction worker who's set to marry another woman. Things get worse when magic and betrayal take center stage in this hyper-nutso horror outing. The film wastes no time in ramping up the ultra-weird magic rituals in a nicely done credit sequence that perfectly sets the mood. Sadly however, this is the rare case of the sequel being better than the original, and it's mild when stacked together. It doesn't exactly have a lot of depth and suffers from plot holes and conveniences. Still, *Black Magic* has its very own set of "charms" and there is plenty of twists and turns, and of course lots of fantastic '70s cheese. Rituals used in the movie are not as hokey as you might think and it does a decent job at adding an air of creepiness that surprised me. You also can't help but love an epic battle of good versus evil, complete with wonderfully dated special effects. Its problems aside, I still found myself glued to the film, and it offers some genuinely good off-putting moments blended with unintentional hilarity. Get in the groove with this trashy black magic epic.

Black Magic 2, aka Revenge of the Zombies (1976)

DIRECTED BY	Meng Hua Ho
WRITTEN BY	Kuang Ni
STARRING	Lung Ti, Ni Tien, Lieh Lo, Terry Liu, Wei Tu Lin, Lily Li, Kwok Kuen Chan, Chok Chow Cheung
COUNTRY	Hong Kong

It seems that audiences were ready for another heaping helping of weird black magic rituals and ultra seventies cheese fest by the legendary Shaw Brothers. A group of scientists are baffled by illnesses in a remote area. The locals, however, know it was caused by a wicked magician who has a band of zombies that do his evil bidding. Now the skeptics are going to get a crash course in good old-fashioned black magic havoc. Even though it's a sequel in name only to the first *Black Magic* it still is a sort of companion piece and they both have similar themes. Like the first film you're in for lots of strange magic spells, liberal use of violence, and a really weird fixation on what they call human milk, which is a nice way of saying breast milk. Seriously, it's a major plot point in both films. But one thing is certain, the second film really amps up the pure insanity that is only skimmed in the first one. Most notable, the sexual perversion is really laid on thick and never lets up. While both plots aren't brilliant, I honestly prefer the first one, which I feel was more tightly structured with a classic good versus evil arch. It also seems like this one is more needlessly complicated and aimlessly goes from one set piece to another. Still, if it's straight up weird kicks you're after this definitely is the better film with lots of nicely done gross-out moments and stuff you just have to see to believe. Zombies, octogenarian love-making, and monster births are just some of the things in store in this gonzo horror film.

Corpse Mania (1981)

DIRECTED BY	Chih-Hung Kuei
WRITTEN BY	Chih-Hung Kuei, On Szeto
STARRING	Ni Tien, Yung Wang, Tsui Ling Yu, Siu-Kwan Lau, Erik Chan Ka Kei, Chok Chow Cheung, Ping Fong
COUNTRY	Hong Kong

Another highly weird film produced by the legendary Shaw Brothers. This one delves into some fairly dark areas and for the time it was pretty bold. From the director of the off-the-rails *Boxer's Omen* comes *Corpse Mania*. A killer is on the prowl and having intercourse with recently dead victims. He seems to have a grudge against the girls at Madam Lan's (Ni Tien) brothel. And soon the police are closing in on the psycho but not before a lot of people meet a horrible end. This is a really interesting film that feels a lot like a standard giallo popular in Italy. All the trappings are there, a lurid sleazy killer with a sexual fixation, outrageous gore, and of course the killer's look fits the giallo mold. It also follows some American slasher motifs such as killer P.O.V., etc. The plot is a cut above what you might expect and, at a scant eighty-one minute runtime, the film moves briskly with lots of action. The violence and gore is wonderfully excessive and, as I stated above, the added necrophilia gives the film a whole other level of ick factor. Without ruining anything, I'll say that whatever the director paid the poor actresses it wasn't enough. So many directors set up a provocative premise yet fail to truly be bold enough to realize it, and I applaud Kuei for actually delivering the goods he promises. I was also pleasantly surprised to notice how beautifully the film was shot, with some wonderfully moody lighting. It is something you'd hardly expect from a film of this kind and adds much needed polish. With a brisk and interesting story, perversion, and gore galore, topped off with a decent little twist at the end, this Hong Kong/giallo hybrid is a must-see. Impress your hardcore splatter friends with this weird and wild gem.

Devil Fetus, aka Mo tai (1983)

DIRECTED BY	Hung-Chuen Lau
WRITTEN BY	Wen-Hua-Cheng, Ging-Jiu-Lo
STARRING	Eddie Chan, Yung-Chang Chin, Pak Kwong Ho, Dan Lau, Meng-Kuang-Hsu, Sha-Fei Ouyang, Hsiu Ling Lu, Pui-pui Liu
COUNTRY	Hong Kong

A cheesy '80s Casio score, hilarious special effects, and a demon fetus: What more could you ask for in a movie? A woman buys an antique jade vase which, unbeknownst to her, contains an evil spirit. It promptly possesses its new owner and later kills both her and her husband. Fast forward twelve years and the ancient evil is woken up, taking control of the family dog and later, the owner's nephew. Now it's up to the grandmother to stop the demonic monster before it kills the entire family. *Devil Fetus* certainly lived up to my expectations as an ultra-low-budget, wacky, and eye-popping bit of insanity the way only Hong Kong can. The plot is at times wildly incoherent but contains enough action and craziness to keep things interesting, and there is hardly a dull moment to be had. For example, the baby fetus making its grand appearance is a rather fun and unforgettable moment. It also wisely caters to the splatter fans, and there are enough goopy surprises to keep every gore hound sated. The special and practical effects range from decent to downright laughable; however, even at its worst it only adds to its campy Grindhouse charms. By no means a masterpiece; however, what it lacks in polish it more than makes up for in sheer goofy gonzo fun. Highly recommended for fans of low-rent trash cinema.

Doctor Lamb, aka Dr. Lamb (1992)

DIRECTED BY	Danny Lee, Billy Tang
WRITTEN BY	Kam-Fai Law
STARRING	Danny Lee, Simon Yam, Kent Cheng, Siu-Ming Lau, Dave Lam Jing, Julie Lee, Parkman Wong, Yin-Ting Tsang
COUNTRY	Hong Kong

Doctor Lamb is based on the real-life serial killer, Lam Kor-wan, who savagely killed four women before he was caught in 1982. A Taxi driver is compelled to kill women when it rains. It seems Lam-Gor (Simon Yam) has a love for amateur surgery and likes to remove body parts from his unlucky victims. After he is caught he recounts his depraved deeds to the horror of detectives. The story and the action are sadly more on the conventional side, spending far too much time on the cliché detective interogation stuff, and while they attempt to explore the inner workings of Lam Gor-Yu, it seems terribly shallow.

Maybe I've become jaded, but for a Category III, this film is relatively tame on volience, especially when you stack it up with films like *Ebola Syndrome* and *The Untold Story,* which is literally coated in blood and entrails. There are some nasty bits but nowhere near the level you might think. Of course the depravity is ever present with taboo subjects like necrophilia and pedophilia making the film very disturbing and uncomfortable. But even still, it seems low-key compared to the other films I mentioned. I will give the film props for being visually interesting, which I did not expect for a film of this type, with great uses of lighting that give it an eerie and almost ethereal look. *Doctor Lamb* is somewhat entertaining with some undeniably unnerving subject matter; however, a weak screenplay bogs itself down and only scratches the surface of the inner mind of a psychopath. Worse yet, it is rather dull in its contrived police subplot, never fully realizing its true nasty potential. If you want a second opinion I'd say watch *The Untold Story* and call me in the morning.

GOES WELL WITH: *Taxi Hunter, The Untold Story*

Ebola Syndrome (1996)

DIRECTED BY	Herman Yau
WRITTEN BY	Ting Chau
STARRING	Anthony Wong, Yeung-Ming Wan, Fui-On Shing, Tsui-Ling Wong, Miu-Ying Chan, Meng Lo, Edward Corbett
COUNTRY	Hong Kong

More than two decades before the ebola scare was all too real the film *Ebola Syndrome* was unleashed on a ticket-buying public. Directed by Herman Yau, who previously made the disturbing and funny *The Untold Story,* not only does this film manage to be as weird, but I can safely say it out-does it in that department. A misfit restaurant worker (Anthony Wong) with an already deadly past contracts the virus after he rapes a South African woman. Now he's infected, and a ticking timebomb of insanity and hatred. While I enjoyed *Untold Story,* this film is a step above

in terms of direction and writing. The film still tends to gloss over character development; however, not as much as his previous effort. But to be fair, these films aren't meant to be in-depth studies of human behavior. It also packs more insanity in the first five minutes than most films do in their entire runtime. And shockingly, it keeps up the momentum with hardly a dull moment in the film, and it takes depravity to a whole other level. Once again, Anthony Wong stars, playing yet another sleazy psycho killer, and once again he throws himself into the role, this time giving a *slightly* more subtle performance. Herman Yau's trademark dark humor is in full force, and unlike *Untold* it doesn't have the forced "comic relief" to bog itself down. The on-screen violence and gore is off the charts, and once again, Herman doesn't hold a single thing back, and the experience is pure gore hound gold, with enough blood soaked gags to make Herschell Gordon Lewis himself smile. Best described as pure nihilism on film with its tongue firmly inserted in cheek, *Ebola Syndrome* is a much more polished film in terms of writing, with a more coherent sense of direction and it also ups the depravity to new heights. Fans of ultra-violence and dark comedy will find this trashy little film to be infectious in a good way. A Category III that is in a category all its own.

Gu, aka Bewitched (1981)

DIRECTED BY	Chih- Hung Kuei
WRITTEN BY	On Szeto
STARRING	Melvin Wong, Fei Ai, Fanny Fen-Ni, Lily Chan, Wei Tu Lin, Jenny Liang, Hussin Bin Abu Hassan, Chun Chin
COUNTRY	Hong Kong

From the director of ultra-crazy *The Boxer's Omen* comes another head-spinning foray into the supernatural. A man named Stephen Lam Wai (Fei Ai) murders his five-year-old daughter in a cold and brutal manner. He claims he was under a spell and didn't know what he was doing. Lead cop Bobby Wong (Melvin Wong) travels to southern China (Nan Yang, to be more specific) where the man claims it happened. It turns out Stephen had met a young woman there, used her, and stood her up. As an act of revenge the woman had him put under a spell. In seeking the aid of a monk, Bobby is put into grave danger and soon he starts to experience strange and horrible things. It seems he too has been placed under an evil control.

I've seen my share of black magic movies and I have to say this is by far one of the better ones. Director Chih-Hung Kuei unfolds a nicely paced horror ride that has less cheese than other similar entries such as *Black Magic* and its sequel. The violence and splatter are plentiful with some truly disturbing moments. The *worm spell* scene, for example, is really quite nasty and altogether different. The effects themselves are at times hokey (it is low-budget after all), but for the most part are well-done.

Like *Boxer's Omen,* there are plenty of psychotropic, mind-bending moments that make you feel like you've been secretly dosed. If you're someone looking to get into Hong Kong magic movies this is definitely a good one to start with. It has plenty of exciting action, nightmarish visuals, and trippy weirdness, pretty much everything you could ask for in a movie. Recommended.

Killer Snakes, The, aka She sha shou (1974)

DIRECTED BY	Chih-Hung Kuei
WRITTEN BY	Kuang Ni
STARRING	Kwok-Leung Gan, Lin Lin Li, Chun Chen, Hao Chen, Shao-Lin Chen, Chi Chou, Li Jen Ho
COUNTRY	Hong Kong

Snakes? Not a huge fan. And while I'm told they're good for the environment, etc., I'm perfectly all right with staying away from them. Now snakes in horror films on the other hand are something I can get on board with. A shy young guy seems to have the world beating him down, as he is constantly bullied, robbed, and just outright rejected. His only friends are a pack of injured snakes, which he nurses back to health and, grateful for this, his scaly brothers help the boy get revenge of those who have wronged him. When watching this film I thought it might be your run-of-the-mill nature-run-amok outing; however, to my delight it has more going for it than you might think. *The Killer Snakes* wastes no time in snaking in the kinky sex and ultra-sleaze, which slithers throughout the entire film. Plot-wise it brings nothing new to the table and plays like a bizarre remake of *Willard*, replacing the rats with snakes. I was, however, struck by the totally weird sense of morals (or lack thereof) the film has and our hero, as it turns out, is just as bad, if not worse than, the people he seeks revenge from. Visually the film has an interesting flare and put me in mind of a live-action comic book with its bold colors and interesting camera tricks. While it doesn't offer up anything new in the way of story it does have enough action, perversion, and trauma-inducing snake attacks to make it worth a watch.

Robo Vampire (1988)

DIRECTED BY	Godfrey Ho
WRITTEN BY	William Palmer
STARRING	Robin Mackay, Nian Watts, Harry Myles, David Borg, Joe Browne, Nick Norman, George Tripos, Diane Byrne
COUNTRY	Hong Kong

Ah yes, another wonderful unofficial remake of an American film. This time the classic *RoboCop* is given an Eastern twist "cleverly" re-titled *Robo Vampire*. Because when you think Cyborg fighting crime you of course think of the bloodsucking dead. Tom Wilde, a narcotics agent, is brutally gunned down and is given a flashy new upgrade and a new lease on life.

He is given a mission to rescue the lovely Sophie, an undercover agent who is being held by the drug lords. The leader of the underworld, Mr. Young, just so happens to have a small army of vampires at his command and a lovesick female ghost, because why not? Now it's Robo Warrior to the rescue in his genre-bending film. First off, when your vampire minions hop around like bunnies it tends to severely undercut their scariness. *Robo Vampire* is a delightfully bat-crap-crazy film that seems to throw every single thing at the audiences, hoping something sticks. Kung Fu actions, check; vampires, check; low-rent science fiction, double check; throw in a flimsy romance subplot, why not. Sure it's laughably low-budget and the villains are anything but scary but what the film lacks in polish it makes up for in pure high-flying insanity, and damn if I wasn't entertained by it, even if it was for all the wrong reasons. Sadly, the film is relatively tame on the splatter, with the exception of a few nasty bits, and while gore doesn't make a movie better it certainly helps when you're working with a dime store outing like this. So if you want to see your favorite Cyborg cop dipped in LSD look no further. For die hard trash fans, and makes the perfect film for a movie night with friends.

Seeding of a Ghost, aka Zhong gui (1983)

DIRECTED BY	Chang Yang
WRITTEN BY	Yee-Hung Lam, Kamber Huang (story)
STARRING	Norman Chu, Philip Ko, Maria Jo, Yung Wang, Mi Tien, Kar-Man Wai, Ling-Chi Fu
COUNTRY	Hong Kong

Similar to *Black Magic* and *Black Magic 2*, the main drive is revenge and magic with a heavy dose of insanity thrown in for good measure. *Seeding of a Ghost* somehow manages to out-crazy those two by a mile and a half. A mild mannered taxi driver has the misfortune of hitting a man who was fleeing some rather angry people. It just so happens that the man he struck was someone who practices the black arts. The driver helps him escape, and for his troubles he is warned that since he interpreted a black magic ritual he would have grave misfortune fall upon him. Soon after this his wife cheats on him and it leads to her being raped and murdered by two thugs. Now, in order to avenge himself and his wife, he seeks the sorcerer's help, and soon everyone will pay with blood. *Seeding* is a movie that may not have the most well-thought-out screenplay but what it lacks in a coherent narrative it makes up for in pure trashy entertainment and some of the most off-the-wall sequences that will leave you wondering what the hell you've been watching. And like *Black Magic*, it has an interesting visual flare which results in a wonderfully strange, even surreal atmosphere. The splatter and grisly gore fly fast and furious and the crude look of the practical effects only adds to the grimy Grindhouse charms. The practical effects themselves are actually decent. For example, the wife's rotting corpse is damn eerie looking which is further enhanced by air bladders added to her cheeks whenever she's possessed. Typically, good versus evil films of this kind wrap everything up nicely; however, I have to give filmmakers props for going with a bleak ending, which I find far more interesting, and I honestly didn't see it going that way. *Seeding of a Ghost* ranks up there as one of the weirdest horror/gore fests to come out of Hong Kong, and despite its lackluster story it was oh-so-enjoyable and endlessly watchable.

GOES WELL WITH: *Black Magic 2, Boxer's Omen*

Untold Story, The (1993)

DIRECTED BY	Danny Lee, Herman Yau
WRITTEN BY	Wing-Kin Lau, Kam-Fai Law
STARRING	Anthony Wong, Danny Lee, Emily Kwan, Eric Kei, Fui-On Shing, King-Kong Lam, Parkman Wong, Julie Lee
COUNTRY	Hong Kong

The problem with wanting to see a movie for so long is that it often creates certain hype in your own mind that often doesn't meet expectations. So needless to say, when I finally obtained a copy of *The Untold Story* I was pretty stoked to see it. Wong Chi-hang (Anthony Wong) fled from his dark past and bought a restaurant known for their meat buns. But Wong seems a little too familiar with chopping meat, and after some limbs are found the cops start to investigate him for possible murder. This film did indeed live up to the high hopes that I had for it. Wisely, the filmmakers don't hit the audience over the head with Wong's back story or dig too deep into motivations; he's almost a blank canvas, which allows us to project onto him what we will. A large part of the film's notoriety stems from its on-screen violence with a rape scene that is very hard to watch. The gore is truly outrageous and comes fast and loud, never holding a single thing back, even breaking the firmly-held horror film taboo of harming children. I also liked the fact that characters didn't just die easily like in more slick Hollywood type films. For example, when a character is given an eyeful by our villain he doesn't just merely drop dead, and it's quite jarring to watch. The film does a solid job at being both horrifying and darkly comical. The scene where our anti-hero feeds the cops ground up body parts in food he prepared is revolting, yet very humorous at the same time, even Hannibal the cannibal himself would have been proud of that. Ironically, it's the more standard comic relief (various banter between cops) that falls flat and feels forced upon the audience. Actor Anthony Wong just oozes creepy psycho killer and it's not hard to see why his career took off the way it did. His performance goes a little bit over the top, but he still does a great job at throwing himself into the role. *The Untold Story* really lived up to its reputation and was everything I had hoped it'd be and more. Strap yourself in for a twisted gore-soaked ride that is both jarring and wickedly funny. It is worth checking out but not for the easily offended or the faint of heart. So belly up to this sick little stew, if you dare. You'll never look at chop sticks quite the same way.

Absurd, aka Anthropophagous 2, aka Horrible (1981)

DIRECTED BY	Joe D'Amato
WRITTEN BY	George Eastman
STARRING	George Eastman, Annie Belle, Charles Borromel, Katya Berger, Ian Danby, Hanja Kochansky, Ted Rusoff
COUNTRY	Italy

Take John Carpenter's seminal classic *Halloween* and run it through an insane Euro filter, and presto, you have the aptly titled *Absurd,* starring the Lon Chaney of sleaze, George Eastman. A mysterious man tries to break into a house in the middle of the day and is accidently hurt on the homeowner's gates. The man identified as Miko Stenopolis (George Eastman) is rushed to the hospital. To everyone's amazement they discover that Miko has an almost super-human ability to heal himself, making him virtually unstoppable. After a priest comes to see him in the hospital we learn that the man is a thing of evil and can only be stopped by a shot directly to the head. Of course the fiend escapes and returns to the house he had visited earlier, which just so happened to have two children that are being babysat. *Absurd* is one of those rare trashy treasures that has a lot of problems but still manages to be wildly enjoyable. The story is not what you'd call coherent at times with gaps in logic and plot holes that leave you scratching your head. Also, you might guess from the plot summary that the film gets convoluted, and of course features the wacky dialogue you come to expect in an Italian horror film. At the center of this very weird film is a great villain played to the hilt by George Eastman. He has an unparalleled menacing presence and he's really the glue that holds this wonderful mess together. Thankfully, splatter-wise the film is definitely on-point and features some really well-done gore gags, sure to slate the thirst of any horror fan. What I love about this film is its over-the-top nature and unintentional camp hilarity; for example, a major plot point is everyone in town is watching "the big game". But it's funny to see how Italians imagine Americans watching football. I can tell you it's certainly not in formal wear while eating pasta. It also features perhaps the worst babysitter in cinema history (the temp babysitter) who tells the young boy the Boogeyman is going to kill him—yeah, that's really nice. Surprisingly, there are some nice moments of suspense and I have to admit the way they use the bedridden sister actually pays off nicely. And of course, who could forget the amazingly wacky ending? *Absurd* is a movie that really lives up to its title, but it has loads of fun cheese, gore, and humor to make this really entertaining.

Baba Yaga, aka The Devil Witch, aka Kiss Me Kill Me (1973)

DIRECTED BY	Corrado Farina
WRITTEN BY	Corrado Farina
STARRING	Carroll Baker, George Eastman, Isabelle De Funès, Ely Galleani, Sergio Masieri, Angela Covello, Cesarina Amendola
COUNTRY	Italy

The popular erotic Italian comic *Valentina* by Guido Crepax was given a big screen adaptation with *Baba Yaga*. Valentina (Isabelle De Funès) is a top photographer with a penchant for pushing the boundaries. Her hunky boyfriend Arno (George Eastman) works as a freelance filmmaker, doing everything from political pieces to commercials, which pay the bills. Valentina's carefree swinging world comes crashing down when she meets Baba Yaga (Carroll Baker), a strange old woman who casts a spell on her. Soon her life is set into a tailspin of horror and sexual sadism, but is it really Baba doing all this or is it all in Valentina's waking dreams? I have to say I've seen a lot of Italian films, but this managed to be a refreshingly different experience. Wisely, the filmmakers tried to stay true to the original source material, which is reflected not only in the title sequence but is echoed cleverly throughout the film. Farina has a wonderfully bold visual flare which works very well for a comic book adaptation. He crafts an amazingly funky, trippy, swinging '60s horror film that is overflowing with bizarre sensuality. One can look at Baba Yaga as a metaphor for the nightmare of repressed, unchecked sexuality that Valentina is desperate to let out. Of course the twist ending also seems to support this interpretation. The cast is solid with the beautiful Isabelle De Funès as the heroin and Carroll Baker playing the "tit"ular character, Baba Yaga. One might say Baker is miscast, because she's a stunning woman playing a much older character, with some not-so-subtle makeup; however, I'm okay with suspending disbelief. Both play off each other well. Cult stars George Eastman and Ely Galleani are also wildly entertaining. Fans not used to Italian films that are more style over plot substance may find this film a bit confusing or tedious, but if you're willing to dive right in it's quite an amazing psychedelic trip. *Baba Yaga* is a surreal waking dream with some wild imagery paying homage to its source material with great use of camera and still photography. It's a horror film about dark erotic desires but it is also intentionally tongue-in-cheek, making for a nice balance. For being a jaded film buff I truly felt like this was a very interesting and weird little film that I definitely recommend.

TRIVIA: Cult fans may remember Ely Galleani from such hits as *Five Dolls for an August Moon* and *Lizard in a Woman's Skin,* just to name a few.

Bay of Blood, aka Twitch of the Death Nerve (1971)

DIRECTED BY	Mario Bava
WRITTEN BY	Mario Bava, Filippo Ottoni, Giuseppe Zaccariello, Franco Barberi (story), Dardano Sacchetti (story)
STARRING	Claudine Auger, Luigi Pistilli, Claudio Camaso, Anna Maria Rosati, Chris Avram, Laura Betti, Isa Miranda
COUNTRY	Italy

Before *Black Christmas* and the seminal *Halloween* introduced audiences to the concept of teenagers lined up for a slaughter, Italian master Mario Bava blazed a bloody trail and laid the blueprint for what would become the slasher film. And while the true origins of the subgenre are debatable, one thing is certain, *Bay of Blood* is a milestone in the genre. An elderly heiress

 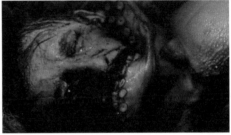

is brutally killed for control of her estate. Soon the relatives are bumping each other off for the inheritance. It just so happens a group of carefree young people decide to camp nearby and what ensues is an epic blood bath. The opening of this film is just incredible, and the double murder that creeps up on the viewer really sets the stage for what's to come. All of the director's trademarks are in full force, from his outstanding visuals utilizing bold colors and inventive camera work, to his wicked sense of dark humor. Bava breaks with horror convention having the bulk of the murders take place during the daytime. In fact, in a stroke of brilliant irony he stages the killings in very beautiful locations. The murder scenes themselves are very effective and the fact that they are done in an almost sexualized fetishistic manner makes them all the more unsettling. Highlighting this is the infamous scene (borrowed for *Friday the 13th, Part 2*) where a spear goes into a pair of lovers mid-intercourse. While the film is most famous for its excessive violence it manages to be entertaining outside of that, featuring plenty of juicy twists and turns and a mystery that keeps its viewers engaged. Unrelentingly brutal, *Bay of Blood* is Bava's most influential film, which holds you in its icy grip and never lets go till the end credits. A must-see for anyone serious about the horror genre.

Beyond the Darkness, aka Buio Omega, aka The Final Darkness (1979)

DIRECTED BY	Joe D'Amato
WRITTEN BY	Ottavio Fabbri and Giacomo Guerrini
STARRING	Kieran Canter, Cinzia Monreale, Franca Stoppi, Sam Modsto, Anna Cardini, Mario Pezzin, Klaus Rainer
COUNTRY	Italy

When thinking of films for this book a few titles instantly sprang to mind: *Buio Omega, aka Beyond the Darkness* was one of those. Frank (Kieran Canter) is a spoiled young man who lives in a sprawling estate that he inherited when his parents died in a car crash. He lives alone expect for his housekeeper Iris (Franca Stoppi) who takes care of his every desire, which includes playing mother. His girlfriend is very ill and before she passes away he vows to her that death itself cannot keep them apart. She dies, and Frank, being true to his word, digs her corpse up and, using his skills in taxidermy, preserves her and places her in bed. Of course Iris is just as sick he as he is and helps him make her look pretty and even chops up and disposes of his various victims. That's loyalty you just do not get these days. But a nosey detective is closing in on Frank.

Director Joe D' Amato is hit or miss for me but I can't deny he was one warped guy and delivered his own brand of Italian horror trash. Few films ratchet up the level of pure sleaze and perversion that *Beyond the Darkness* achieves. For example, the scene where Frank essen-

tially makes his girlfriend into a doll is stuff of nightmares. He films a lot of the scenes in a very cold and clinical way, which makes the material all the more unnerving. It also breaks several taboos including cannibalism, mother/son incest role-play, and implied necrophilia. It's not without its flaws, however, and its rather loose plot sometimes loses its focus on the main thread. Still, one can't help but be entertained by the pure grotesque and over-the-top spectacle D'Amato lays before you. This film is also notorious for having there soundtracks done by progressive rock band *Goblin*. It's not their best score but it still has their trademark sound that fits the film's haunting and strange vibes like a bloody glove. Like most Italian films they wisely take advantage of the lush and beautiful landscapes and it gives the film a lot of added production value. Splatter punks will enjoy the gore which comes fast and furious, and considering its low budget is well done. *Beyond the Darkness* is somewhat incoherent but is a nonstop descent into buckets of gore, depravity, and cheesy '70s goodness.

Beyond the Door, aka The Devil Within Her (UK title) (1974)

DIRECTED BY	Ovidio G. Assonitis, Robert Barrett
WRITTEN BY	Ovidio G. Assonitis, Antonio Troiso, Robert Barrett
STARRING	Juliet Mills, Richard Johnson, Gabriele Lavia, Nino Segurini, Elizabeth Turner, Carla Mancini, Barbara Fiorni
COUNTRY	Italy

I know I've said this before, but damned if I don't dearly love when other countries do odd unofficial remakes of popular films. The horror classic *The Exorcist* spawned many, including *Abby* and a personal favorite, *Mausoleum*. This time the seminal film was put through the extremely crazy Italian filter and what we get is something quite interesting. Jessica Barrett (Juliet Mills) has two children and a wonderful husband, a very normal and even dull life. Her happy life is about to be turned upside down when she unexpectedly becomes pregnant. It's a joyous time until she finds out it's the spawn of Satan. Now it's not only a battle for her soul but for the future of mankind. Obviously the filmmakers had no shame in there *Exorcist* homage as there are many not-so-subtle possession scenes and various other references (the kid obsessively drinking pea soup is my favorite) that seem like they were just begging to be sued. And indeed they were sued by Warner Brothers but unsuccessfully. Sadly, the film gets bogged down in some needless padding with scenes that bring the film to a standstill as well as holes in the plot. Still, fans can easily forgive its shortcomings because it has its very own set of charm. Fans of delightfully trashy Italian fare can expect the usual wacky dialogue, which at times makes very little to no sense, and of course is hilarious.

But *Beyond* actually manages to have some genuine creepiness which is created with visuals that perfectly set a mood that evokes a feeling of lingering dread and foreboding. For example, the scene with the kids and their toys is especially well done. *Beyond the Door* will forever live in *The Exorcist's* large shadow but it does stand on its own, with scenes that manage to be eerie and visually compelling. But of course, it's ultra-cheesy, trashy, and  unabashed in its unoriginal plot and makes for the perfect guilty horror pleasure.

Bloody Pit of Horror (1965)

DIRECTED BY	Massimo Pupillo
WRITTEN BY	Romano Migliorini, Roberto Natale, Marquis De Sade (loosely based on writings)
STARRING	Mickey Hargitay, Walter Brandi, Ralph Zucker, Alfredo Rizzo, Nando Angelini, Albert Gordon, Gino Turini
COUNTRY	Italy

Many films have been loosely based on the writings of everyone's favorite sadist (the terms even based on his name), French writer Marquis De Sade. *Bloody Pit of Horror* is certainly a weird euro-trashy update on his work made in the swinging '60s. A writer, photographer, and a group of playmates find a castle to shoot some photos for possible novel covers. It just so happened that they picked the former home of a madman who took it upon himself to execute many innocent people and was in turn killed for his terrible crimes. The owner, a rather odd and insanely private man, begrudgingly allows them to stay and take some pictures. But as people start to disappear they begin to wonder if the bloodstained slayer is among them and out for revenge on anyone who dares disturb him. Say you took the campy kitsch of *The Addams Family* or *The Munster's* and mixed in scantily clad Italian babes and some torture and you have this wonderfully absurd and entertaining little gem. The "horror" of *Bloody Horror* is of course not that scary and the dialogue and character motivations are at best laughable, but the overall low-budget charm, sadistic grime, and eye candy make this a so-bad-it's-glorious. It also features a really rad and slightly surferish score mostly gone on an organ, complete with a woman wailing, which perfectly sets the mood for spooky and cheesy fun. The on-screen violence is tame by today's standards but when you consider the landmark American gore film *Blood Feast* was released a mere two years before this you can see that the film landscape was still conservative on the blood front. And while I would have liked them to have pushed the boundaries in the gore department it does make the dark subject matter more tongue-in-cheek and thus more approachable. Even the nudity is implied, further giving the film a kind of innocence despite its sleazy and sadistic roots. For those of you who dig titillating torture set to a groovy organ jam and insane set pieces (including the legendary spider web), wacky dialogue, and head scratching motivations, then this film is for you.

Burial Ground, aka Burial Ground: The Nights of Terror (1981)

DIRECTED BY	Andrea Bianchi
WRITTEN BY	Piero Regnoli
STARRING	Peter Bark, Claudio Zucchet, Anna Valente, Antonella Antinori, Roberto Caporali, Mariangela Giordano
COUNTRY	Italy

Leave it to the good folks in Italy to make one of the craziest and profoundly twisted zombie films. The best way to describe Andrea Bianchi's *Burial Ground* is it's like they took George A. Romero's classic *Night of the Living Dead* and ran it through an extreme Euro sleaze filter. A

scientist working in an ancient crypt unwillingly unleashes a curse that brings the dead back to life. For his troubles he is quickly and painfully dispatched. Meanwhile, three randy couples and a very creepy boy named Michael (Peter Bark) arrive at a sprawling mansion at the request of the scientist. Soon their weekend of pleasure turns into a blood frenzied nightmare when the undead awakens hungry and looking for their main course. Fans of Italian zombie films are in for a real treat as Bianchi taps into what his audience wants, which is sex and violence and no filler. It takes very little time for the zombies to get to the mansion and when they do it's nonstop action until the gut-chomping end. Let's talk about the zombies. In terms of makeup they range from laughably terrible to just plain awful. It also doesn't help matters when the bulk of the zombie attacks take place in bright daylight, which hides nothing. With that being said some of the zombies are very well done. And even with the limited money the gore effects are actually better than one would expect, using the tried-and-true methods of zombies pulling out and munching on guts—well, animal guts, more like it. Cheap, yes, but very effective nonetheless and even on par with bigger budget films. Another nasty little touch is the nice stream of thick yellow pus that flows out of the wounded flesh eaters. *Burial Ground* tips the deeply disturbing scale due to the incest subplot that runs through it. There is one very twisted breastfeeding scene that is something you won't soon forget. The cast is great with Italian beauties and hunks, yet Peter Bark seems to outshine everyone. Casting Mr. Bark was a stroke of pure genius. Bark was a little person playing a child; which is obvious from age lines. One can assume that they cast an adult in the role due to the sexual scenes between him and Mariangela Giordano, who plays his mother. His strangely dubbed "child" voice adds an extra layer of bizarre. *Burial Ground* may not be the most polished or well-made film but it is a high-impact, blood-soaked celluloid nirvana that will be sure to delight fans of ultra-cheese and sleaze. So unearth this rotten little gem.

Cannibal Apocalypse, aka Invasion of the Flesh Eaters (1980)

DIRECTED BY	Antonio Margheriti
WRITTEN BY	Antonio Margheriti, Dardano Sacchetti
STARRING	John Saxton, Giovanni Lombardo Radice, Elizabeth Turner, Tony King, Cinzia De Carolis, Wallace Wilkinson
COUNTRY	Italy

What do you get when you mix the unbalanced vet of *Rolling Thunder* with a sprinkle of gory *Dawn of the Dead* and a generous helping of flesh-chewing *Cannibal Ferox*? Why, the in-your-face ultra-trashy splendor that is *Cannibal Apocalypse*. Norman Hopper (John Saxton) is a battle-scarred Vietnam veteran who is just trying to get on with his life and raise a family with his lovely wife Jane (Elizabeth Turner). His chance for a happy life, however, comes crashing down when a former vet named Charlie (Giovanni Lombardo Radice) phones him up; the very same one who he caught committing cannibalism with another vet while in the jungle. Charlie wants to meet up but Norm, seemingly unable to face him, passes. It seems that the call was a cry for help and Charlie goes nuts biting a woman and fleeing, trapping himself in a store. It's later learned that the craving for human flesh may be a strange virus and now Norman is getting the hunger.

Can he find a cure before he starts eating random people? *Cannibal Apocalypse* is interesting for a couple of reasons. One, it's a very pointed social commentary on the Vietnam War, which few horror films brought to the forefront. It also takes the cannibal subgenre out

of the jungle and into an urban environment, the urban jungle if you will. Lastly, it subtly blurs the line between cannibals and zombies, having the flesh-eaters suffering from a mysterious virus not unlike zombies who also crave human meat. The message and commentary on war thankfully does not become too heavyhanded and serves merely as the film's set-up and common thread. And once it kicks off into high gear it rarely lets up on the action, which includes motor-cycle stunts, flamethrowing mayhem, and an amazing gore gag in an awesome finale. The filmmakers wisely cast John Saxton as the male lead. He perfectly anchors the absurd plot and, come on, who doesn't love John Saxton? I'd watch him read the phone book and still be entertained. Giving an equally great performance is sleaze cinema treasure Giovanni Lombardo Radice who just oozes creepy from every pore of his body. He is just wonderful in the role and is always a blast to watch at work. The splatter is on the tame side but it's still ample enough to keep any gore junkie fully satisfied. Sure the plot is ridiculous and the drama is on the flimsy side but it's a pure in-your-face thrill ride that wears its trash status proudly on its blood-soaked sleeves. Also, amazingly, it did the crazy veteran plot a whole two years before *First Blood* ripped through theaters. Other titles may be better, but if you're after cheap kicks and down-and-dirty thrills look no further.

Cross of the Seven Jewels, aka La croce dalle sette pietre (1987)

DIRECTED BY	Marco Antonio Andolfi
WRITTEN BY	Marco Antonio Andolfi
STARRING	Marco Antonio Andolfi, Gordon Mitchell, Annie Bell, Paolo Fiorino, George Ardisson, Zaira Zoccheddu
COUNTRY	Italy

You know you've seen a weird yet horrible movie when your brain feels numb. Such is the feeling after experiencing *Cross of the Seven Jewels*, a movie I risked my very sanity just to bring you back the full wookie. This may not be the weirdest Italian film but so far it ranks high on the list. A man loses a cross with seven jewels (hence the title), which he goes to great lengths to get back. It seems that the cross keeps him from turning into a werewolf but without it he goes on a rampage. In the history of werewolf movies this has  to be the strangest with one of the worst-looking makeup jobs ever. The plot is all over the place and to simply say it's confusing and incoherent is putting it mildly with major story holes just completely glossed over. Seriously, you'll hurt yourself trying to figure this thing out. Sloppy writing aside, the film is paced horribly and you need saint-like patience to get through the plodding material. The only up-side is the hilarious werewolf who is buck naked (not covered in fur, except a small patch on the private parts), and as I said above has to be the lamest werewolf makeup in the history of film. I mean it doesn't even cover all of his face. Oh, and have I mentioned the satanic subplot with yet another monster that is so cheap-looking it would make the beast in *Trog* look positively Rick Baker-worthy? The moment that will go down in horror camp history has to be when the random Chewbacca-like creature makes love to a woman. Why? Because who knows, stuff just happens in this movie. I reluctantly recommend this film if only for the brain-melting strangeness and unintentional comedy. *Cross of the Seven Jewels* is for true gutter trash horror fans only.

Don't Torture a Duckling, aka Non si sevizia un paperino (1972)

DIRECTED BY	Lucio Fulci
WRITTEN BY	Giafranco Clerici, Lucio Fulci, and Roberto Gianviti
STARRING	Marc Porel, Barbara Bouchet, Tomas Milian, Irene Papas, Florinda Bolkan
COUNTRY	Italy

Mario Bava and Sergio Martino might have crafted better giallos but no director had made them sleazier or stranger than Lucio Fulci. His 1972 film *Don't Torture a Duckling* is among his most disturbing films only outdone by *New York Ripper,* and without a doubt the grimmest giallo to come out of Italy, period. In a small Italian village someone is killing off innocent children and violent hysteria from the townsfolk ensues. As the body pile grows it's up to journalist Andrea Martelli (Tomas Milian) to find the killer. As far as giallos go, it follows the usual formula; death happens at the hand of a mysterious killer, a town is in panic, and an outsider plays amateur sleuth because of the ineffectual police. There are also a slew of suspects, and this one has some really interesting ones such as La Magiara (Florinda Bolkan), a local outcast who is known to practice witchcraft.

Fulci breaks a taboo of the genre with children being the victims, an unwritten law that is still hardly broken. He doesn't go soft or pull any punches just because they're children which makes it hard to watch at times. Also, while it's never outright explored, there is a

creepy pedophilia vibe that is lurking. Unlike the numerous films in this sub-genre it actual has a lot to say and it explores some themes that are very deeply rooted in the human experience. Community, religion, innocence, guilt, and sin are all explored and cleverly weaved into the plot. I would go deeper into this but it's hard to do without re-maining spoiler free. Fulci is known for his brutality and *Duckling* certainly ranks high on the list of his most bloody. The scene where the villagers seek revenge on a local murder suspect is haunting, unflinching, and something you won't soon forget. Aside from the gore the film is boosted by some fine camera work and wonderful music by Riz Ortolani; horror fans will no doubt remember his haunting score from *Cannibal Holocaust. Duckling* is filled with twists and turns, and spirals towards a heart-stopping climax that is oh-so-satisfying. A must-watch for any fan of Italian horror.

Flesh for Frankenstein, aka Andy Warhol's Frankenstein (1973)

DIRECTED BY	Paul Morrissey
WRITTEN BY	Paul Morrissey
STARRING	Udo Kier, Joe Dallesandro, Monique van Vooren, Arno Juerging, Srdjan Zelenovic, Dalila Di Lazzaro, Nicoletta Elmi
COUNTRY	Italy

Looking for an awesome grimy double feature? Look no further than the Warhol-produced *Blood for Dracula* and *Flesh for Frankenstein*. Baron Frankenstein (Udo Kier) has an insane desire to create a new race of perfect men. He has the perfect pieced-together female; now all he needs is her mate. Through a series of twists of fate he gets an asexual young man who's not interested. Writer/director Paul Morrissey stitches together a wildly horrific and darkly humorous tale. Much like *Blood for Dracula,* he wonderfully plays with the motifs of the original source material (with a few winks thrown in for good measure) while injecting a healthy dose of over-the-top sex, sleaze, and lots of blood. He also cleverly takes real-life horrors and blends them seamlessly into the Mary Shelley lore. For example, Baron Frankenstein wants to create a master race much like Hitler did. Everything is played very much over-the-top with lots of intentional tongue-in-cheek, which is the perfect way to go when you're doing a film of this type. Fans of the ultra-splatter will also find a lot of deranged gore that is gleefully strewn all over the set. The infamous gut sex scene is something truly nasty and forever burned into my brain. Morrissey and his cinematographer take full advantage of their shooting location in the Italy countryside. It really gives the film a bigger scope and a much more expensive look. The cast is incredible with Warhol hunky mainstay Joe Dallesandro and an aging sex pot Monique van Vooren turning in memorable performance. But of course, character actor Udo Kier really steals the show. He is just amazing as always. *Flesh for Frankenstein* is a devilishly campy, twisted, and brilliant re-telling of *Frankenstein* which breathes new life into a sometimes lifeless tale. Required viewing.

Frankenstein's Castle of Freaks, aka Terror! Il castello delle donne maledette (1974)

DIRECTED BY	Dick Randall
WRITTEN BY	Mark Smith, William Rose, Roberto Spano
STARRING	Rossano Brazzi, Gordon Mitchell, Michael Dunn, Loren Ewing, Eric Mann, Robert Marx, Margaret Oliver
COUNTRY	Italy

I'm sure Mary Shelley is spinning around in her grave after this ultra-weird Italian horror romp, but for the trashy film fan it's certainly an entertaining but terrible little flick. Count Frankenstein (Rossano Brazzi) wants to make a scientific contribution to society and with the help of a twisted little person named Genz (Michael Dunn) and Igor (Gordon Mitchell) they help in the doctor's mad experiments. Meanwhile, a romance is brewing between Frankenstein and his daughter's friend. Oh, and a savage cave man is roaming the countryside,

because why not? But it seems when Genz is let go from employment he sets off for revenge against Frankenstein and teams up with the prehistoric pal. Take the classic Universal horror tropes, stitch together perverse sexploitation, a random cave man, and fuse it with pure '70s Italian insanity and you have *Frankenstein's Castle of Freaks*. Now enjoying this movie is really up to how much of a junk horror fan you happen to be. Going in I was expecting low-budget strange, and I was definitely not disappointed, as the film has loads of broken down charm and is heavy on the dime store atmosphere. Admittedly the plot is nonexistent and languishes in its own filth all while going nowhere, seemingly unable to really further the story. Also, as you might expect, the dubbing is horrible. Your personal mileage may vary but for me it somehow all works in a z-grade way and, say what you will about the actual quality, it's never dull with tons of weirdness to keep you entertained. This is the perfect movie if you want something with tons of so-bad-it's-good variety.

GOES WELL WITH: *Count Dracula's Great Love, Something Weird*

House of Clocks, The (1989)

DIRECTED BY	Lucio Fulci
WRITTEN BY	Gianfranco Clerici, Daniele Stroppa, Lucio Fulci (story)
STARRING	Al Cliver, Carla Cassola, Keith Van Hoven, Paolo Paoloni, Peter Hintz, Bettine Milne
COUNTRY	Italy

When you think of the films of Lucio Fulci many fans automatically think of his classics like *The Beyond* and his legendary *Living Dead* trilogy. All great masterworks; however, surprisingly it's a made-for-TV movie that remains one of the finest works of his later career. Three criminals decide to break into an upscale house where an elderly couple live. Their seemingly simple plan quickly goes south and they discover that their hosts hold a sinister secret in the form of their clocks. The couple accidently gets shot and the thugs continue with ransacking the place. Little do they know their time is about to run out as hunters become the prey.

Made-for-TV horror tends to get a bad rap and it's hard to think of Italian gore master Lucio Fulci making one; however, in my opinion, it's one of his stronger efforts in the twilight of his career. While not his most visual film it does manage to create a great deal of spooky atmosphere and sets the mood perfectly; furthermore, the use of a soft focus lens gives the whole thing a dream-like quality. Its high production values also give the low-budget film a more polished look. The concept itself is pretty lofty and takes a totally new spin on the living dead genre, something that Fulci did extremely well in his younger days. His trademark twisted sense of humor and obsession with cats are also present here. Fans of the director's penchant for gore galore will not be disappointed, as this film has enough splatter moments to keep even jaded viewers happy, especially considering this was made for television. The film is of course not without flaws and it tends to negate its own premise at times; also, some of the rules of the time-reverse aren't altogether clear. Despite its shortcomings *House of Clocks* earns huge points for being not just another zombie film, with plenty of action, gore, and creepy moments to satisfy diehard fans of Fulci or someone who is new to his body of work. Sure it's not as good as his earlier films, but considering this was a late entry it doesn't feel like a director at the end of his career, and its high-energy spirit makes up for its sometimes convoluted plot. It's "about time" *House of Clocks* gets dusted off and rediscovered for the minor classic in the director's catalog.

Inferno (1980)

DIRECTED BY	Dario Argento
WRITTEN BY	Dario Argento
STARRING	Leigh McCloskey, Irene Miracle, Alida Valli, Daria Nicolodi, Eleonora Giorgi, Sacha Pitoëff, Veronica Lazar, Feodor Chalipan Jr
COUNTRY	Italy

Inferno is the second entry in Dario Argento's unofficial *Three Mothers* trilogy, which was started with the watershed *Suspiria* and finished with *The Mother of Tears*. A young lady named Rose Elliot (Irene McCloskey) living in New York City discovers an old book in a shop and becomes convinced that the witches inside the text are not fiction but horrifying fact. She is savagely killed but not before writing her brother in Rome who picks up the investigation. Argento is at his very peak in terms of high art in the theater of pain, and *Inferno* certainly encapsulates his masterful touch in the horror/gore genre. Similar to his previous films, he chucks out conventional logic for a more freeform nightmare like reasoning. Some critics have wagged their fingers stating that the film is style over substance and, while that is true to a degree, it doesn't make it a bad film, and Argento keeps its audience constantly on its toes with shifting central characters and a twisting and turning plot. He also knows just how to create a great deal of suspense and terror without the aid of gimmicks. Most fans and newcomers alike can agree that the look of this is simply stunning, juxtaposing style and beauty with a dark fairy tale-like vibe. Like *Suspiria*, he brilliantly dips into his bold color palette to make this truly standout, and his style has been often copied but never fully matched. Like the visuals, the murders themselves are done with a great deal of flare, and in terms of violence it ranks among his most over-the-top. *Inferno* was made during a time when Dario ruled the Italian horror genre and what he crafted here is a visually stunning, beautifully disjointed, nonstop psychedelic terror ride that never gets old, as many times as I've revisited it. Required viewing.

TRIVIA: Although not officially credited, the legendary Mario Bava had worked on the film and even co-directed the famous underwater scene.

Kill Baby, Kill, aka Operazione paura, aka Curse of the Dead (UK re-issue) (1966)

DIRECTED BY	Mario Bava
WRITTEN BY	Mario Bava, Romano Migliorini, Roberto Natale
STARRING	Erika Blanc, Giacomo Rossi Stuart, Piero Lulli, Giovanna Galletti, Micaela Esdra, Franca Dominci, Giuseppe Addobbati
COUNTRY	Italy

While not as famous as Bava's *Black Sunday* or as gory as *Bay of Blood, Kill Baby, Kill* is nonetheless a landmark film by the Italian master. In a small village in the Carpathians a series of grisly murders are taking place; each victim has a coin placed inside their heart. Dr. Paul Eswai (Giacomo Rossi Stuart), an outsider, is called in to do an autopsy on a woman's corpse. When he arrives he finds nothing but closed doors from the highly suspicious townfolk. Aided by a female doctor, Monica (Erika Blanc), they soon discover the horrifying secrets that lurk deep in the black heart of the Villa Graps. Few people in the horror genre could match Mario Bava in his heyday and *Kill Baby, Kill* is among his greatest achievements. He takes material that easily could be hokey and transforms it into a live wire of tension and walking dread by utilizing his flair behind the camera. With evocative camera work, moody set pieces, and eye-popping colors he creates a sinister neo-Gothic that is both mature and wildly entertaining. It would be very hard to understate just how gorgeous this film is. Furthermore, the use of rich landscapes and decaying buildings give it a haunting feeling and indeed, the entire film has a hazy nightmare-like ambience. Like many Italian films on a budget the filmmakers make great use of their practical locations, giving the film more polish and production value. This coupled with an engaging and twist-filled story makes this a true gem of the genre. It's a symphony of unrelenting horror and poetic beauty that makes it a nearly perfect Italian horror film.

Killer Must Kill Again, The, aka L'assassino e costretto ad uccidere ancora (1975)

DIRECTED BY	Luigi Cozzi
WRITTEN BY	Luigi Cozzi, Daniele Del Giudice
STARRING	George Hilton, Antoine Saint-John, Eduardo Fajardo, Tere Velazquez, Alessio Orano
COUNTRY	Italy

Luigi Cozzi might not be as well-known or as prolific as say Argento or Bava but he is an interesting Italian filmmaker nonetheless. His entry into the giallo is nasty and surprisingly well-written but is sadly not that well-known. Giorgio (George Hilton) is a ruthless man who cheats on his wife and uses her for her family's fortune. He sees his lavish lifestyle go up in smokes when his wife threatens to cut him off. As fate would have it he catches a man with a freshly killed body and makes him a deal: I'll keep quiet and pay you twenty grand to kill my wife. It's an offer he just can't refuse, and he kills Giorgio's wife. He puts her body in the trunk and goes back inside to clean up, but when he goes outside he realizes a couple, Luca

(Alessio Orano) and his girlfriend, have stolen the car, with the body still inside. Now it's a deadly game of cat and mouse as the killer must kill again. Similar in tone to Sergio Martino's *Torso Killer* is a bleak and unrelenting thriller that would make Hitchcock himself proud. Cozzi tells a well-crafted story that is filled with many twists and turns while also subverting the audience's expectations. It's also interesting that this giallo is not a standard whodunit since we know who it is from the start. The cast is great and features genre fan favorite George Hilton, who easily fits the part of the wonderfully sleazy womanizer. But the real stroke of casting Antoine Saint-John, who is one of the most menacing looking villains in Italian film history. His skeletal face and hollow-looking dark eyes make him unbelievably unnerving. Cozzi shows he has a dark sense of irony in the way he edits certain scenes. For example, the way two sequences are put together, one showing Luca cheating on his girlfriend with a dizzy blonde and the other showing that same girlfriend being savagely raped by the killer who also happened to be a virgin. The love-making and rape scenes make for a disturbing juxtaposition, made even more bitter by the fact that said boyfriend isn't there to protect her. *Killer Must Kill Again* is a nonstop sadist perverse thrill ride and has enough nasty thrills to keep it interesting. Viewers must watch this, again and again.

Last House on the Beach, aka La settima donna (1978)

DIRECTED BY	Franco Prosperi
WRITTEN BY	Gianbattista Mussetto, Romano Migliorini, Ettore Sanzo (story by)
STARRING	Florinda Bolkan, Ray Lovelock, Flavia Andreini, Sherry Buchanan, Stefano Cedrati, Laura Trotter, Karina Verlier
COUNTRY	Italy

I have to say, very few movies actually turn my stomach, yet leave it to the Italians to make a movie that really got me right in the gut. Three criminals on the run from the law break into a remote villa, but it turns out they are not alone, as Sister Cristina (Florinda Bolkan) and a group of teenage girls are staying there to study for exams. Things go from tense to bloody as the men take full advantage of the girls in this bleak Italian horror thriller.

Last House on the Beach is not what you would call plot heavy and it goes through the motions to get the audience from one nasty scene to the next as it increases the violence and depravity to all time highs or lows, however you look at it. It's fair to say the film leans far too much on its shocking aspects rather than providing a more polished story with a fairly predictable plot. But however you might feel about its shock value *Last House* is undeniably

filthy work of Italian art, and it makes no apologies for itself, and something about that makes it enjoyable to watch despite its flaws. I also have to give the director props for offering its audience zero comic relief, and he spares no indignity brought on upon the innocent girls. And in my opinion, it features one of the most unnerving death

scenes in film history, which I won't spoil, but I will say it involves a piece of wood in a very sensitive area. I'd even go as far as to say it may top even the infamous *New York Ripper* in terms of savagery and sadism. What it lacks in a skilled screenplay it makes up for in sheer over-the-top carnage and ends with a frenzied finale you won't soon forget. Recommended.

Macabre, aka Frozen Scream (1980)

DIRECTED BY	Lamberto Bava
WRITTEN BY	Antonio Avati, Pupi Avati, Lamberto Bava, Roberto Gandu
STARRING	Bernice Stegers, Stanko Molnar, Veronica Zinny, Roberto Posse, Ferdinando Orlandi
COUNTRY	Italy

Lamberto Bava, son of famed director Mario Bava, came onto the scene with *Macabre,* his very first movie. This is one of those films that really shocked me with its ending. So for the love of cinema don't let anyone ruin it for you. In fact, it's best to go in as cold as possible. Jane Baker (Bernice Stegers) has a wonderful husband, two children, and a lover on the side. She secretly rents a room from Mrs. Duval (Elisa Kadigia Bove) and her blind son Robert (Stanko Molnar) to take her lover Fred (Roberto Posse) to bed. While away on one of their hot flings Jane's daughter drowns her little brother just for the fun of it, it seems. She gets a frantic call and is told to come right away. Her and her lover rush over but get into a horrible auto accident that claims the life of Fred.

With the shock of both her son and lover dying and feeling guilty about both she suffers a breakdown and is put into a mental institute. One year later she is released and returns to the rented room where she spent her happiest times. Mrs. Duval is now dead and Robert owns the house. Jane isn't over her great love and will stop at nothing to make sure they keep their passionate flame alive. What I find interesting about Lamberto's first feature is that it's not big and splashy and full of tons of gore, but rather it's a slow burning creeper that relies heavily on its story and odd characters, building to one of the best horror finales. Taboo and sexual perversion is the driving force of the film, and Bava is not afraid of taking his time developing characters and showing there ugly sides. The main character of Robert is introduced in a rather weird way. We first see him in the bath tub and later his mother washing him. Another example is daughter Lucy (Veronica Zinny), who for no reason brutally drowns her brother and, not only is she never charged with her crime (ruled an accident), but she taunts her mother by sneaking a picture of him up to her room. It's so unsettling. Jane is really no better as she takes a sick delight in sexually teasing poor Robert only to later ignore his advances. There is a scene where she insists he stay and talk to her while she takes a bath. As the film progresses it amps up the weird until it reaches a level that few films achieve. As I stated above, this isn't a bloody, wild, fast-paced romp like his other movies; however, it's got a great story that keeps you interested until the very end. Bava would later go on to do *Demons,* a film that would firmly place him alongside his father as a master of the genre. Sadly, this film never gained the kind of cult status as his later works, but it's still a great pot boiler filled with truly unsettling and twisted moments without using ultra-gore as a crutch. It's not my favorite of his body of work but it certainly is a film that should get more attention.

Manhattan Baby (1982)

DIRECTED BY	Lucio Fulci
WRITTEN BY	Elisa Briganti, Dardano Sacchetti (story)
STARRING	Christopher Connelly, Laura Lenzi, Brigitta Boccoli, Giovanni Frezza, Carlo De Mejo
COUNTRY	Italy

It's basic horror movie 101 that when a creepy old hag gives you a weird looking charm you DO NOT take it, ever! Well, sadly that advice was not taken in Fulci's 1982 effort *Manhattan Baby*. Professor George Hacker (Christopher Connelly), an archaeologist, takes his daughter Susie (Brigitta Boccoli) with him on a dig in Egypt. Hacker disturbs a tomb and loses his sight for his troubles. Meanwhile, a mysterious woman gives an unaccompanied Susie an Egyptian charm. When the pair return to New York they quickly discover that Hacker awoke an accidental evil and brought it back with them. For some, *Manhattan Baby* is an acquired taste and certain fans of Fulci's films will make the case that it's a good (but admittedly lesser) film. And as much as I love Lucio's body of work I just can't agree. First let me say that what I've always admired about Lucio Fulci is how he took risks and tried different things. The early '80s were dominated by slashers in America and giallo in Italy but he went in a totally different direction for this film, and it's really interesting to set your horror film partly in Egypt. I think what hurts this film the most is that it has no clear narrative to the story. Characters drift in and out, random spooky things happen for no discernible reason and to make matters worse it's terribly contrived and at times dull. I can't help but think this might have worked a lot more successfully as a segment in a horror anthology rather than a feature length film. Even by Italian horror standards the acting is just terrible and it seems as if the actors simply can't muster up the energy to give even a passable performance. Fans expecting the director's trademark gore will also be in for a huge disappointment, as this is very tame compared to previous horror outings. There is one gore scene involving stuffed birds and it's so laughably bad because the strings are clearly visible. It's hard to believe that just a year before this he made *The Beyond,* which many, including myself, consider to be his greatest film. Yet he seemed to forget that what made that movie great was partially its simple yet effectively creepy plot, which has visual flare and much better acting. I'm someone who really enjoys Lucio's films but don't consider everything he did to be gold, and this certainly was a huge misstep in his career. I'd say watch it only if you are a hardcore Italian/Fulci fan but be prepared to be underwhelmed.

THE ULTIMATE GUIDE TO STRANGE CINEMA

My Lovely Burnt Brother with the Squashed Brain (1988)

DIRECTED BY	Giovanni Arduino, Andrea Lioy
WRITTEN BY	Giovanni Arduino, Andrea Lioy, Andrew Giulietti
STARRING	Burnt Bernie, Giovanni Arduino, Paul Delos, Anne Tzakol, Mefi, Nick Tortone, John J.Bridge
COUNTRY	Italy

I found it! Yes, found it. The strangest slasher ever made. Something so weird it makes films like *The Redeemer* and *Absurd* seem positively coherent and well constructed. And of course it is brought to us from the good folks in Italy, who always find new ways of ramping up the weird. A girl who works at a dentist office is tired of the abuse she takes on a daily basis. What's a girl to do? Well, apparently you get your horribly disfigured brother (who wears a Klan hood) to be your zombie-like slave by injecting him with your urine. Wow . . . Meanwhile, an ex-punk rocker with a score to settle trades in her guitar for a badge and is on the track of the hooded killer. The film's opening, which suggests the audience enhance their viewing experience after drinking a whooping thirty-five cans of beer, is a clear indication that the whole film is going to have its bloody tongue jammed tightly in its cheek, and it certainly does for better or worse as the case may be. The film has some jaw-dropping weird, even surreal, set pieces that reminded me of early John Waters (minus the polished writing) in its raw, over-the-top nature. Some of the film's humor serves the film well with some genuinely brilliant bits that you can't help but laugh at. Sadly though, most of the attempts at comedy fall flat and smack of trying too hard. Worst yet, even at a scant seventy minutes the film drags, and even the more absurd moments of the film can't mask the director's aimless direction with scenes that grind the film to a halt. One such scene is simply a bad music video for the film's band, The Sick Roses, bringing things to a dead stop. Gore hounds will enjoy some nasty gags in the vein of H. G. Lewis, and considering the budget, it's not too badly done. I only wish they would have pushed the splatter just a tad bit further. Even with its glaring flaws *My Lovely Burnt Brother* is enjoyable on a so-weird-it's-entertaining level, and like a train wreck it's kind of hard to look away. Drinking a few beers would most likely enhance your viewing experience, just don't try it with thirty-five. Gross-out, offensive, and at times brilliantly funny, this totally whacked film needs to be seen to be believed.

New York Ripper (1982)

DIRECTED BY	Lucio Fulci
WRITTEN BY	Dardano Sacchetti, Gene Luotto (English version uncredited)
STARRING	Jack Hedley, Howard Ross, Alexandra Delli Colli, Andrea Occhipinti, Paolo Malco
COUNTRY	Italy

If one were to make the case that Italian horror maestro Lucio Fulci and his films were misogynistic *New York Ripper* would be exhibit A. This film has a well-deserved reputation for being his most brutal and unmercifully savage, all directed towards females. Women are being slaughtered in the Big Apple by a mysterious killer who sounds like a duck. Yes, you read right. It's up to Lt. Williams (Jack Hedley) to solve the crime before more bodies pile up. At a loss, he turns to an expert in psychotherapy, Dr. Paul Davis (Paolo Malco), and they begin to close in on the duck-sounding killer. The gallio genre was anything but tame; however, Fulci took the already outrageous genre to new heights in sleaze and butchery. Indeed, the driving force of this film is its unrelenting violence. What sets this film apart from the piles of other bloody films is not the amount of red kroovy it sheds but the painfully intimate way the girls die. He isn't happy with merely a throat slash or a knife to the chest; oh no, he has something else in mind. The attacks are done with such blind rage it makes it very uncomfortable to watch. Besides the attacks themselves there is an overall theme of women leading perverse lives, which is echoed by the characters that inhabit the film. Take, for example, Jane Lodge (Alexandra Delli Colli), a smartly dressed woman who trolls live sex shows, or the prostitute who Lt. Williams sees from time to time. But I'd have to say the degrading toe scene involving Alexandra Delli Colli is possibly one of the strangest in all of gallio history and the sleaziest. It almost seems like the film is a twisted morality play. Fulci ups the crazy factor, having the killer talk like Donald Duck, a nod to *Don't Torture a Duckling*, perhaps? Whatever the intention, it's extremely menacing and is weaved cleverly into the finale. Even with its unsettling moments and gore it's far from a perfectly crafted gallio. What hurts the film is the unbalanced story, which introduces an important character more than halfway through the film. Also, it spends too much time on red herrings and not enough on giving clues to the real killer's identity. Then there's the issue of misogyny. Now, do I believe Fulci actually hated women? No, I do not. I think that as an artist he wanted to up the stakes and, of course, that meant breaking taboos and playing by a new set of rules. Many of these movies come off as misogynistic, but that was the movie culture for better or worse. To paraphrase a favorite show of mine, repeat to yourself it's just a movie, you should really just relax. Even with some story problems this film boldly pushes the limits of taste and doesn't shy away from anything. Fulci somehow manages to create a nightmare world of sexual perversion and blood-soaked ecstasy that will leave you wondering what the hell you just experienced. Not for the squeamish, but for fans that are serious about the horror genre, it's a must-see.

Other Hell, The, aka Guardians of Hell (1981)

DIRECTED BY	Brunio Mattei
WRITTEN BY	Claudio Fragasso
STARRING	Carlo De Mejo, Franca Stoppi, Susan Forget, Francesca Carmeno, Paola Montenero, Sandy Samuel
COUNTRY	Italy

From the writer of *Troll 2* and the director of *Buio Omega* (what a combo!) comes this wildly weird and campy horror/nunsploitation flick that is sure to leave you questioning your very sanity by the end. A series of savage murders take place in a quiet little convent, and it's believed that the very devil himself is to blame. A young skeptical priest is brought in and he is sure that he is dealing with a flesh-and-blood killer and not of the cloven

hooved variety. Can the priest discover who is behind the slayings, or is it really the beast himself that's bringing down all this hell? I must admit I'm a bit jaded when it comes to shocking cinema but even I have to admit I was impressed with Brunio Mattei's *The Other Hell,* which is a nonstop kaleidoscope of sleaze and psycho-sexual perversion that only gets stranger as the film progresses. This isn't what you'd call plot heavy (as you might expect) and teeters on the convoluted, but it's by no means a bad film and is helped greatly by a brisk pace that has little to no padding and a new shocking twist around every turn. It's also chock full of creepy and outrageously bizarre set pieces that make the audience feel like they are trapped in a blood-soaked nightmare of repression and debauchery. Further helping the film is its ear-pulsing score by Italian progressive rock band *Goblin,* which adds to its already atmospheric tone. Its low budget only adds to the dirty, trashy Grindhouse vibe that carries this film so well. Not for the easily offended or the faint of heart, but lovers of Italian insanity will find this a grimy little gem just begging to be unleashed.

GOES WELL WITH: *Buio Omega, Alucarda*

Phenomena, aka Creepers (1985)

DIRECTED BY	Dario Argento
WRITTEN BY	Dario Argento, Franco Ferrini
STARRING	Jennifer Connelly, Daria Nicolodi, Donald Pleasence, Fiore Argento, Patrick Bauchau, Mario Donatone
COUNTRY	Italy

Despite some recent bombs, Dario Argento still ranks among my favorite horror directors because he takes risks and, for better or worse, you have to give him credit for blazing a trail different than his peers. *Phenomena,* also re-titled *Creepers* for some video releases, is among his most bizarre, hence why it's in this book. Jennifer Corvino (Jennifer Connelly), the daughter of a famous actor, is just starting at an upscale, all-female boarding school, but to her dismay a murderer is stalking young women. To make matters worse, she sleepwalks at night which gets her labeled as weird. Oh, and she also has the ability to communicate with insects telepathically, a gift that will help her as she faces the savage killer, stalking co-eds and tourists alike. Argento deliriously mixes together fantasy, horror, giallo, and supernatural in a totally strange mish-mash of different genres. Convoluted, you bet, with all logic thrown right out the window. Sadly, the film features some subplots that feel under-done, like they could have been developed better. But the glue that really holds this incredibly all-over-the-place plot is the two lead actors; future Oscar winner Jennifer Connelly and screen icon Donald Pleasence. Connelly gives a solid performance and brings a certain depth to the role, showing both a maturity yet a sweet innocence and her range is rare in a child star. And of course, the always-on-point Pleasence wisely plays everything quite seriously, never hamming it up or winking at the audience. While not as stylish as say *Suspria* or *Inferno* the film does feature some very nice atmospheric and dream-like set pieces, which echoes the film's fairy tale-like feeling. And of course, splatter fans that have come to expect the gore from an Argento film will not be disappointed, as it features some very creative and pretty gruesome gags. Despite the totally off-the-wall, genre-defying, and somewhat confusing plot the film never gets dull, with a constant array of twists and turns, and for the viewer willing to suspend a lot of belief, will be treated with a wild thrill ride. It also features a jump scare that I admit still gets me to this day. Highly recommended.

Ring of Darkness, aka Satan's Wife, aka Un'ombra nell'ombra (1979)

DIRECTED BY	Pier Carpi
WRITTEN BY	Pier Carpi
STARRING	Anne Heywood, Valentina Cortese, Frank Finlay, John Philip Law, Irene Papas, Marisa Mell, Ian Bannen, Ezio Miani, Lara Wendel
COUNTRY	Italy

Riding the wave of successful films such as *The Exorcist* and *The Omen* Italian filmmakers were quick to cash in with such titles as *Beyond the Door* and *House of Exorcism*, just to name a few. The trend also gave us this strange little toxic sludge. Four women in a satanic coven begin to notice odd goings-on when one of the women's daughters, Daria (Lara Wendel), begins to show signs of great power well beyond her years. Now as members start dying they have to wonder if she has made her own pact with the devil, an even stronger one. Right off the bat, the film sets the tone with a gloriously whacked-out, fog-filled dance sequence complete with scantily clad women and men in skin tight red spandex, because why the hell not? Lovers of Italian trash will not be disappointed, as the film provides plenty of strange dialogue, sex, and nudity, and of course a nice eerie vibe further enhanced by a great score by Stelvio Cipriani, best-known for scoring Mario Bava's seminal *A Bay of Blood*, amongst others. His music is great and perfectly captures that grimy '70s *Goblin* feel. The film manages to be entertaining despite a disjointed and convoluted plot, which at times feels repetitive; however, it features enough Grindhouse cheese and sleaze to keep fans coming back for more. I also loved the totally bleak and wonderfully absurd ending. For the hardcore Italian horror fans this is a sinfully delicious guilty pleasure even with a lack of splatter.

TRIVIA: Italian horror fans will no doubt recall Lara Wendel from *Ghosthouse* as well as Dario Argento's *Tenebre*.

Shock, aka Beyond the Door II (1977)

DIRECTED BY	Mario Bava
WRITTEN BY	Lamberto Bava, Francesco Barbieri, Paolo Brigenti, Dardano Sacchetti
STARRING	Daria Nicolodi, John Steiner, David Colin Jr., Ivan Rassimov, Paul Costello
COUNTRY	Italy

To simply say Mario Bava was a huge force in Italian cinema is an understatement, and *Shock*, Aka *Beyond the Door II*, was his final feature film. I love films about ghosts and the paranormal, and when Italians do it they always seem to add some taboo and perversion to the party. Hoping to start anew, Dora Baldini (Daria Nicolodi) and her second husband Bruno (John Steiner), along with their son Marco (David Colin Jr.), move back to her former house. Dora lost her first husband to an accident out at sea and she's hoping to bury the past. Well it seems the past refuses to stay at rest and she notices her son is acting strange. She soon realizes the lengths her former husband will go to be reunited with the family. Fans of Bava's body of work will find his final film a mixed bag. Sorely missing is his signature flare for interesting color and lighting schemes. In fact the real "shock" is how drab-looking it is; it has a feeling of something made for television. Even the camera work isn't very inventive. What Bava does get right is some interesting ideas; for example, the concept of a former lover/husband possessing your child is certainly different and profoundly unnerving. He also throws in hints of underlying incest. There is a brilliant moment when the mother and son are playing outside and he pins her to the ground, holding her arms down with a strange sadist, almost sexual, look on his face. Another thing that helps the film is the terrific cast. Fan favorite Daria Nicolodi plays Dora and brings grace, class, and sex appeal to the character. Danny Colin Jr. plays the boy, and he has a great weird presence to him and comes off unsettling even when he's not possessed. Bava implores the less-is-more approach, slowly giving the audience drips of terror. The problem with this is the gaps between the scary moments are at times painfully dull. Some scenes could have been shortened and others just stop the movie dead. While you watch the film you get a sense that Bava is tired and did not want to push himself to the level of his previous works. What made a movie like *Kill Baby, Kill* so effective were the subtle and artful methods that were used. *Shock* is far less subtle, using very cheap William Castle-style gimmicks, as evident in the laughable ghostly box cutter scene. The final twists also feel weak and contrived. Even though *Shock* has some creepiness and at times surreal moments it's hampered by uninspired style and a plot that is terribly predictable and at times slow. It doesn't even feel like a Mario Bava film, which I think disappoints fans the most. Sadly, this film closes a brilliant career that spanned decades. In my mind he will always be a master of not only horror but cinema in general; it's just a shame this was his swan song. *Shock* is for hardcore Italian and Bava fans only.

Troll 3, aka Crawlers, aka Creepers, aka Contamination 7 (1993)

DIRECTED BY	Joe D'Amato, Fabrizio Laurenti
WRITTEN BY	Fabrizio Laurenti, Albert Lawrence, Rossella Drudi, Daniele Stroppa
STARRING	Mary Sellers, Jason Saucier, Vince O'Neil, Bubba Reeve, Billy Buttler, Lord Chester, Eddy Eby, Carol Kroft
COUNTRY	Italy

Leave it to the king of Euro-sleaze, Joe D'Amato, to make a film called *Troll 3* that has zero to do with the film series or even trolls at all. This most likely explains the multiple alternative titles. In a small town the forest is not only positively radiant but it turns out it's actually radioactive. This of course, causes the plant life to become self-aware killing machines, causing anyone or anything in its path to die a horrible death. It turns out the cause is a nearby power plant dumping toxic sludge, and it's up to a group of townspeople to fight back before they all become plant food. *Troll 3*, or *Creepers*, or whatever you know this as, is pretty much as bad as you might imagine and then some. The acting is at the level of adult entertainment with dialogue that is just so baffling and unintentionally funny. Plot-wise, it's everything you've already seen from a hundred other films of this sort, and there's not a spot of originality in its radioactive roots. And while, yes this is a steaming pile of celluloid, it also has enough z-grade charm and campy comedy to make it so bad it's good. It also manages to have some decent gore, though, even that looks horribly dated. I think to really enjoy this film you have to have a love for films like *Troll 2* (oddly enough) and pretty much anything ever shown on *Mystery Science Theater 3000*.

Audition, aka Ôdishon (1999)

DIRECTED BY	Takashi Miike
WRITTEN BY	Takashi Miike
STARRING	Ryo Ishibshi, Eihi Shiina, Tetsu Sawaki, Jun Kunimura, Renji Ishibshi, Miyuki Matsuda, Toshie Negishi
COUNTRY	Japan

Audition will always hold a special place for me, because not only is it an unbelievably effective film but it also turned me on to the amazing body of work of writer/director Takashi Miike, a sick love affair which still continues to this day. A widower named Shigeharu (Ryo Ishibshi) lets a co-worker talk him into holding a special film audition, which is a ruse to find a suitable wife. After interviewing many women he meets a shy girl named Asami (Eihi Shiina) who seems to be a perfect match for him. But behind that soft voice and innocent look is something deadly. What makes this film work so well is the way Miike employs a wonderfully subtle approach and methodically allows the film to slowly simmer and ever so slowly turns up the heat until this little pot boiler overflows with tension and savagery that might make even hardened hardcore fans squirm in their seats. But the film is not shock for shock's sake and has a lot to say, including a comment on the traditional female gender rules in Japanese culture and how men typically hold the upper hand. It also makes you examine your moral conscience, making you feel torn between the actions of Shigeharu. Yes, ultimately what he is doing is sleazy, underhanded, and deceptive, yet on the other hand we can understand his reasons, being a lonely man still hurting from the loss of his wife, which adds an extra layer to the character. The film is wonderfully shot and it's clear that Miike has a laser focused cinematic eye. He carefully and deliberately fills the frame, and the camera is as much a part of the storytelling as the screenplay. Also, he knows how to slyly misdirect the audience and I don't mind admitting the bag scene still gets me. *Audition* doesn't rely on jump scares and cheap gimmicks but rather is supported by a well plotted story, visually stunning camera work, and incredible tension that reaches epic levels. It may be a slow burn but for the patient horror fan the end result is oh-so-satisfying. *Audition* is darkly hypnotic and yet grotesquely beautiful at the same time, and for me it ranks up there as one of the greatest J-horror films ever made. Creepy as hell and something you will find yourself thinking about long after the credits have rolled.

Entrails of a Virgin, aka Shojo no harawata (1986)

DIRECTED BY	Kazuo "Gaira" Komizu
WRITTEN BY	Kazuo "Gaira" Komizu
STARRING	Saeko Kizuki, Naomi Hagio, Megumi Kawashima, Osamu Tsuruoka, Daiki Kato
COUNTRY	Japan

Oh Japan, land of crazy, violent cartoon porn and films that defy any rash explanation. Such is the case with *Shojo no harawata*, aka *Entrails of a Virgin*. Three sleazy men who work in the fashion industry take three of their models out for a good time. However, the good time they have in mind is using these models solely for their pleasure and they'll stop at nothing to get it. On the road they encounter car troubles and must spend the night at an empty house in the middle of nowhere. Little do they know a demon is lurking in the fog. *Entrails* is a prime example of the title and the cover art being way better than the actual film. It's interesting that the film's setup is very similar to an American horror film. You have a group of potential victims on a foggy road at night, and of course there is car trouble, which forces them to spend the night in a creepy house. That is where the similarities end for sure. While it doesn't have a ton of visual perk it does manage some nice creepy atmosphere. The biggest issue with this film is its terrible pacing, and at a scant seventy-one minute runtime the bulk of the film is soft corn and probably the unsexiest stuff ever committed to celluloid. It takes a whopping hour before the true horror happens and when it gets weird, it really goes full gonzo. I will give this film props for featuring some truly outrageous moments that are pure bat-crap-insane. The gore effects themselves are fairly decent for what I'm sure was a shoestring budget. What's frustrating is *Entrails* has the makings of a good little splatter film; however, the filmmakers clog up an entire hour with non-plot and unsexy "action" that leave everyone bored to tears. *Entrails of a Virgin* is only recommended for the final twelve minutes of an otherwise wholly forgettable outing.

Exte: Hair Extensions (2007)

DIRECTED BY	Sion Sono
WRITTEN BY	Sion Sono
STARRING	Chiaki Kuriyama, Megumi Sato, Ren Osugi, Tsugumi, Eri Machimoto, Yuna Natsuo, Ken Mitsuishi
COUNTRY	Japan

Fun but morbid fact, even when you're dead your hair continues to grow. *Exte* takes this strange tidbit of information and builds an entire film plot around it. Fun times! The body of a young woman is found in a storage container full of hair. She is brought to the morgue and when she's all alone the worker there, Yamazaki (Ren Osugi), goes to work on his side job, which is cutting off dead women's hair and selling them as, you guessed it, extensions. Yamazaki is amazed to see that after he shaves her head it miraculously grows back and soon he becomes obsessed with the girl and her hair. Soon the hair extensions are wreaking havoc on whoever wears them. *Exte* has an interesting concept that plays on the standard J-horror tropes. But as you know, a strong concept doesn't make a good movie and sadly, a few key things stand in its way. The film makes the bold choice of playing this totally straight which isn't a bad thing per se, but if you're going to go this route you better make sure you bring some legit scares. And it does have some very creepy and disturbing visuals. Problem is it suffers from some wildly uneven tones; the main examples are the over-the-top moments with the character of Yamazaki. For a movie that is playing everything deadpanned his outrageous scenes feel completely out of place; it also doesn't help that he's annoying. Audiences also have to wade through a ton of unwanted melodrama that only serves to undercut the horror and stop the film in its tracks. It's also not above dipping into horrible clichés like the standard detective that feels clumsily jammed for some reason. It's really a shame because the idea is an interesting one and the scenes when the hair actually attacks is not as cheesy as you'd think; in fact, they arc quite effective. Once again a film that has nuggets of greatness bogs itself down in needless padding and quickly loses sight of its own story. Worse yet, it takes itself far too seriously for its own good. The result is a tangled mess.

Hausu, aka House (1977)

DIRECTED BY	Nobuhiko Ôbayashi
WRITTEN BY	Chiho Katsura, Chigumi Ôbayashi
STARRING	Kimiko Ikegami, Miki Jinbo, Kumiko Ohba, Ai Matsubara, Friko Tanaka, Mieko Satô, Masayo Miyako
COUNTRY	Japan

It would be unthinkable to write a film guide to the weird and not include Ôbayashi's classic 1977 film *Hausu*, or *House* as it's known in America. A school girl invites six of her friends to a summer getaway to her aunt's house in the country. All is fun and happy until one by one the girls vanish, and it's clear that an evil force has possessed everything in the seemingly normal house. Now it's a fight to stay alive in this wicked and wacky horror outing. Ever feel like someone secretly dosed you during a film and you begin to question your own sanity by the end? Well that's exactly what you can expect with this mind-bending epic. Sure the plot is all over the place but really it's not the story that has cemented this film in cult infamy but its highly creative visual flare. The director uses just about every technical trick in the filmmaker's arsenal and the end result is an eye-popping, mind-erasing assault on the audience and something you're not likely to forget. Even before the girls get to the titular house it's clear that the film has a dreamy quality by use of a soft focus lens and purposely artificial-looking set pieces (Oshare's house in particular). But when we get into the house it's like Alice falling down the rabbit hole and all rules of logic and reality are chucked right out the window. What always fascinates me about this movie is how it straddles a strange line between an innocent fairy tale and more adult horror with nudity and delightfully macabre imagery. It may not be gory, but there are some very gruesome nasty bits that really make you sit up and pay attention. A psychedelic horror funhouse of spooky thrills and chills that will be sure to make even the most jaded horror buffs rub their eyes in disbelief. Truly a film that needs to be seen to be believed and is highly recommended.

GOES WELL WITH: *Evil Dead 2, Suspiria*

Horrors of a Malformed Man (1969)

DIRECTED BY	Teruo Ishii
WRITTEN BY	Teruo Ishii, Masahiro Kakefuda, Rampo Edogawa (based on novel by)
STARRING	Teruo Yoshida, Yukie Kagawa, Teruko Yumi, Mitsuko Aoi, Michiko Katayama, Kei Kiyama, Reiko Mikasa
COUNTRY	Japan

Horrors of a Malformed Man was a seminal Japanese horror film and was so upsetting it was outright banned shortly after its release. Many also consider it a precursor to the Pinky violent subgenre. Hirosuke (Teruo Yoshida), a young medical student, escapes from a mental institution after killing a mysterious bald man in self-defense. In an ironic twist of fate he takes on the identity of a dead man in order to discover his own. His journey takes an even darker turn when he discovers an island that belongs to the dead man's father. Nothing could prepare him for the walking horrors that await him. The film plays like a metaphor for the deep, dark resentment of the aftermath of the atomic bombs that destroyed two cities, leaving many dead and others horribly deformed and subsequently deformed children born in its wake. It's a theme that is at the very forefront; without ever uttering a word about the a-bomb, it's all in the rich subtext. Teruo purposely keeps you in the dark while he weaves a strange mystery giving just drips of information while continuing to ratchet up the tension. Some viewers may find this tedious with some gaps in logic but, trust me, it's worth the buildup. Once on the island the film spirals into a nonstop descent into a grotesque nightmare with images that are unforgettable, and Ishii isn't afraid to explore uncomfortable, even taboo topics. *Horrors of a Malformed Man* was said to make people literally run out of theaters screaming, not unlike *The Exorcist* in America. It still has the power to shock, horrify, and be rediscovered as the masterpiece that it is. Anyone seriously interested in great horror from Japan should make this classic film a must-see.

Long Dream (2000)

DIRECTED BY	Higuchinsky
WRITTEN BY	Higuchinsky, Kyoichi Nanatsuki, Junji Ito (based on Manga by)
STARRING	Ken Arai, Kaei Asano, Shima Ashizawa, Eriko Hatsune, Masami Horiuchi, Mika Ooshima, Shûji Kashiwabara
COUNTRY	Japan

Dreams and horror films seem to go hand in hand, or hand in razor glove if you ask a certain burnt faced serial killer. However, Freddy has to sit this one out, as we're talking about *Long Dream*, an extremely strange film from director Higuchinsky. A patient named Mukoda Tetsurou (Shûji Kashiwabara) is suffering from a strange illness that makes him believe his simple night's sleep lasts days, later months and years, and even decades. This drives the young man insane and this leads to a horrible psychical transformation. *Long Dream*, a made-for-TV movie, has an interesting premise that explores some heavy and deep-rooted themes, something J-horror is known for. And while I certainly applaud the effort I can't help but feel that the screenplay was just a little under-done, glossing over a lot of important points. Now some of this issue no doubt stems from the time allotment for the small screen and I'd love to see a remake of this. The other thing is the film's makeup effects were really poorly done and even laughable. Higuchinsky does try, and for the most part effectively captures the manage feel (of which the original source stems from) with some wonderfully eerie set pieces and creepy dread-filled atmosphere by way of lighting and visual flare. *Long Dream* isn't a terrible film, and its creative premise helps keep it entertaining enough, but sadly the screenplay feels a tad bit underdeveloped and the makeup could have used a more skillful hand. It's no sweet dream of a film but not a nightmare either, and one thing is certain, it's damn weird.

Red Room (1999)

DIRECTED BY	Daisuke Yamanouchi
WRITTEN BY	Daisuke Yamanouchi
STARRING	Yuki Tsukamoto, Mayumi Okawa, Hiroshi Kitasenju, Sheena Nagamori
COUNTRY	Japan

If reality TV has proved anything it's how people are all too happy to debase themselves for some cold card cash. *Red Room* takes this to new depraved lows. A husband and wife and a pair of sisters are brought to a mysterious building to play a game for ten million yen. The game, King Card, is simple: Players draw a card, and whoever has the king card gets to make two players do whatever they want. The object of the game is to make the players quit; last player left wins. Things start out with harmless dares but quickly

escalate into more deadly games with only the strongest surviving. *Red Room* is a movie that is rifted with social commentary and satire; however, sadly it never attempts to exploit these. Things are also a bit confusing. For example, we assume what we are watching a hit reality game show but surprisingly it never makes that crystal clear, and as I stated it's a missed chance by the filmmakers to make a pointed and humorous statement about the nature of game show greed. Worse yet, the rules of the game are also not laid out, which seems like they don't even care about their own premise. At the black heart of the film is a director more interested in shocking its audience than actually giving them something creative, thought-provoking, and chilling. Despite its lackluster screenplay the film manages to be mildly amusing, and thankfully it bows out at a scant running time. I'm not someone big on remakes; however, I would love to see this film overhauled with a more polished script that actually explores its own concepts in a smart way rather than just merely trying to get a rise out of its audience. Worth a rental but sadly this game is played out due to its lazy writing.

Strange Circus (2005)

DIRECTED BY	Sion Sono
WRITTEN BY	Sion Sono
STARRING	Masumi Miyazaki, Issei Ishida, Rie Kuwana, Mai Takashai, Mame Yamada, Erika Mine, Keiko Yokomachi
COUNTRY	Japan

After having viewed Sion Sono's *Strange Circus,* I feel icky and I want a good shower and a comedy, stat. A writer named Taeko (Masumi Miyazaki) is exploring the dark saga of a family in her latest book, but when a young editor comes to help her, fiction starts to bleed into reality, and soon it's hard to tell one apart from the other. Sono, known for delving into the darkest corners of the human experience, delivers something thought-provoking yet intensely disturbing. What struck me from frame one is this film has a lot of style (similar to his other films) and he utilizes everything in his frame to its fullest effect. He also has a keen understanding of how to use his color palette and he creates some truly stunning visuals. *Circus* explores abuse and incest in painfully graphic ways and is hard to watch at times in its harsh matter-of-fact violence and taboo subject matter, and those easily disturbed by such material may want to steer clear of this movie altogether. The film also strikes a weird kind of balance, blending the reality and the dream state and the beautiful and the grotesque, making for an unsettling and totally different viewing experience. Much to my surprise Sono actually seems to find the depth in his characters that are sorely lacking in some of his other efforts. *Strange Circus* is not for the casual viewer, or the easily offended, but I found it had a dark poetry to it and a narrative that kept me interested even if I was getting sick to my stomach. Recommended.

Tetsuo: The Iron Man (1989)

DIRECTED BY	Shin'ya Tsukamoto
WRITTEN BY	Shin'ya Tsukamoto
STARRING	Tomorowo Taguchi, Kei Fujiwara, Nobu Kanaoka, Shin'ya Tsukamoto, Naomasa Musaka
COUNTRY	Japan

Like *964 Pinocchio,* this is yet another Cyberpunk film from Japan. And I can hardly believe this but it manages to out-weird it by miles. A man is driven to insanity by the maggots inside his brain; he runs outside and gets struck by a car being driven by a businessman and his wife. The couple decides not to report it and go on their merry way. It seems the driver got away scot free until he starts a horrible and painful transformation into half-man/half-machine. What unseen force is doing this and how can it be stopped? *Tetsuo* is a film with style over substance and that's not a bad thing when it's this brilliantly executed. Tsukamoto's groundbreaking film is a fast-paced hyper-kinetic plunge into a surreal nightmare world of steel fused with flesh and blood. You can easily see the influences of early David Lynch and even Jörg Buttgereit and, like those filmmakers, he is not afraid to take this super-weird and creative premise and milk it for all its worth. It's pure artistic expression and it boldly pushes the boundaries of the medium while also infusing some interesting concepts. The amount of detail is staggering and it makes me wonder just how long some of these set pieces took to complete, with many intricate gears, wires, etc. This is taken a step further with some jaw-dropping stop-motion animation. Some not used to this kind of cinema may be confused by the lack of plot, but as I said above this film is more about the visual storytelling and less about a tightly structured narrative that most viewers are used to. Wading in a pool of dark eroticism and pitch-black grotesque oddity this film takes its viewers into some very haunting places, and the whole film feels like one long surreal dream. By the end, you'll swear your brain has turned to jelly and is seeping out of your ears and you'll enjoy every second of it. *Tetsuo* is a totally refreshing and different film that is worth your time.

GOES WELL WITH: *964 Pinocchio, Long Dream*

Wild Zero (1999)

DIRECTED BY	Tetsuro Takeuchi
WRITTEN BY	Tetsuro Takeuchi, Satoshi Takagi
STARRING	Guitar Wolf, Drum Wolf, Bass Wolf, Masashi Endô, Shirô Namiki, Kwancharu Shitichai, Makoto Inamiya
COUNTRY	Japan

A rock band fronted by Guitar Wolf must defend the human race after aliens cause the undead to come to life and make the living a walking buffet. *Wild Zero* smacks of a film that tries too hard to be hip and cool and the result is a story that lacks any real focus or direction. I like to say at least there is an interesting concept behind this but there isn't. Just merely a poorly thrown-together jigsaw of other better films. On the plus side it does have a nice high energy with decent action and plenty of gore-splattered zombies to keep the hardcore horror fans sated. The gore effects themselves are not bad but sadly they opt for CGI at times instead of practical effects. This wouldn't be bad per se but the computer graphics totally take you out of the film. Probably the worst thing, though, is the zombie makeup, which is really hokey. I know they were working on a budget but when you make a zombie film you better make sure they look good. On a very basic level this movie is servable as a horror, rock-and-roll movie; however, those expecting *Burst City* meets *Dawn of the Dead* will be very disappointed. Poor writing, laughable zombie makeup, and at a lack of direction makes this a film hard to want to re-visit, despite some fun moments.

Bloody Reunion, aka To Sir with Love (2006)

DIRECTED BY	Dae-wung Lim
WRITTEN BY	Se-yeol Park
STARRING	Seong-won Jang, Eung-soo Kim, Yeong-Seon-Kim, Mi hee Oh, Yeong-hie Seo, Hyo-jun Park, Ji-hyeon Lee
COUNTRY	Korea

For most of us just the idea of going to a class reunion can fill one with a kind of creeping dread, and in 2006's *To Sir with Love,* later re-titled *Bloody Reunion,* that premise is taken quite literally. Teacher Ms. Parks (Mi hee Oh) is very ill, and a former student/current caregiver decides it would be nice for her to have a reunion of a group of her former students. As the film goes on we learn that the students are anything but fond of their former educator and that she had a deformed child that she hid in the basement. Dae-wung Lim executes a solid film using simple but effective storytelling but also delivers the goods in terms of pure twisted brutality. As the audience slowly learns the true nature of the teacher the tension between her and the students builds and builds and does not let up into the finale. Lim also peppers the film with great nightmarish imagery that sets the tone of constant dread. It wisely tackles some deeply human issues such as self image, resentment, and how the ghosts of one's past can come back to bite you when you least expect it. As great as it is, it's still beset with some minor gaps in logic and plot holes. You might have guessed from the title that plenty of blood and gore would be showcased and this movie does not disappoint. It's extreme and in your face just the way fans like it. The effects themselves are extremely well-done and clearly a lot of talent went into crafting the on-screen carnage. I won't sugar coat it, the ending may upset some people. I personally liked it but felt it may have worked stronger another way, but I think I let it slide because it really throws you for an unexpected loop, which is better than being boring and predictable. However you feel about the twist at the end, it can't be denied that *Bloody Reunion* is a unique whodunit that is not only a smart and tense little film but coats the screen with gore. School may be out but this movie is a master class in suspense and terror.

Alucarda (1977)

DIRECTED BY	Juan Lopez
WRITTEN BY	Alex Arroyo, Juan Lopez, Tita Arroyo (story by), Yolanda Lopez (story by), Sheridan Le Fanu (based on novel by)
STARRING	Tina Romero, Susana Kamini, David Silva, Lili Garza, Tina French, Birgitta Segerskog, Adriana Roel
COUNTRY	Mexico

Satan has been a device for cinema since the very birth of the medium, and over the years the horned one has taken many shapes, sizes, and forms but none has captured the kind of spirit quite like *Alucarda.* Justine (Susana Kamini) is a new student in a convent where she meets Alucarda (Tina Romero), a weird but passionate young girl who has a very active fantasy life. The pair goes exploring and discovers an eerie old crypt. Despite Justine's fear, they decide to open a coffin and moments later become possessed by a demon that dwells inside. Now it's a battle for the very souls of two young girls, and a full force of Satan's wrath is let loose inside the convent. People seem to expect Mexican horror to be hokey but nothing could be further from the truth as evident by this '70s shocker. Lopez crafts a film that has a wonderful Gothic poetry, and its use of lush landscapes and bizarre set pieces give it a morbid fairy tale feeling. *Alucarda* is a fevered walking nightmare that boils over with eroticism and bloody vengeance that is rarely matched. The film ramps up its frenzied orgy of destruction until a blisteringly chaotic finale that is oh-so-satisfying. Fans of bloodshed will be absolutely bowled over by the sheer gallons of the red stuff sprayed, which coats every grimy frame. However, the film is not just about pure violence and acts as a very clever satiric look at the hypocrisy of religions and its customs with over-the-top self flagellations and the nuns wearing strange mummy-like garbs stained in blood. Its message of abuses in the church is a powerful and timely one. I also love the references from *Dracula*, like the tomb belonging to a Lucy Western, and the overall theme of science versus superstition is similar in both. Thankfully its message isn't too heavy-handed and doesn't get in the way of the entertainment value. Unfortunately for cinema lovers, Lopez gave us only five feature films before passing away at the age of sixty-three. But he still managed to leave behind an amazing legacy in Mexican cinema proving oftentimes its quality not quantity. And this film easily makes my top five devil/demon possession movies. It's an easy-to-find film and so worth checking out.

Brainiac, The (1962)

DIRECTED BY	Chano Urueta
WRITTEN BY	Federico Curiel, Adolfo López Portillo, Antonio Orellana
STARRING	Abel Salazar, Ariadna Welter, David Silva, Germán Robles, Luis Aragón, Mauricio Garcés, Ofelia Guilmáin
COUNTRY	Mexico

In the world of cheap Mexican monster movies one name stands out among the pack, and that is, of course, the legendary *The Brainiac*, which offers so much dime store trash it makes an Ed Wood movie look positively Michael Bay-like in comparison. The year is 1661, and the Holy Inquisition has sentenced Baron Vitelius d'Estera (Abel Salazar) to be burnt alive for his wicked crimes, which include witchcraft and necromancy among others. And like most witches, or in this case warlocks, he makes a last second threat to his tormenters, swearing revenge beyond the grave. Flash forward three hundred years: A comet passes by, bringing with it the late Baron in the form of a hideous beast who plans to get his vengeance on the descendants of those who wronged him. The film blends supernatural horror, science fiction, and z-grade monster movie in one totally bonkers outing that is beyond low-budget. With a silly plot that makes very little sense and a horrible makeup job on the monster this is one of those so-bad-it's-amazing films that just begs to be watched with a group of friends over some good suds and greasy pizza. It's painfully clear that the actors are not thrilled with the project and you can't help but wonder how they got through a take without laughing. But their misfortune is our pleasure, and for those you who, like me, enjoy totally far-out, unintentionally z-grade hilarity this is a total treat. And come on, how can you not love a brain-slurping, ultra-cheesy Mexican monster that looks like an even cheaper version of *Pod People*'s Trumpy? *The Brainiac* is recommended if only for its camp value and gut-busting so-bad-it's-funny humor.

Cemetery of Terror (1985)

DIRECTED BY	Rubén Galindo Jr.
WRITTEN BY	Rubén Galindo Jr.
STARRING	Hugo Stiglitz, Bety Robles, José Gómez Parcero, Leo Villanueva, Maria Rebeca, Raúl Meraz, Servando Manzetti
COUNTRY	Mexico

Mexican filmmaker Rubén Galindo Jr. melds a *Halloween*-like knock-off with a supernatural spin on it. The result is pure Grindhouse magic. It's Halloween night and the former doctor of a recently dead mass murderer is convinced that someone could use a demonic book to bring him back to life and orders a judge to cremate his body at once. Meanwhile, a group of bored med students try and scare their dates by going to the morgue and stealing a body.

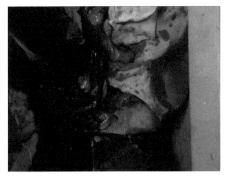 

They just so happen to get ahold of said book and perform a ritual that brings back the killer from the dead and with him a host of zombies, because why not? Now it's a fight to stay alive on the evilest night of the year. It's clear from frame one that *Cemetery of Terror* is a spooky little film filled with lots of atmosphere and plenty of cheesy cheap thrills. The plot is not as awful as I expected and I was perfectly okay with suspending some major disbelief and glossing over a few plot holes in order to enjoy the film for its entertainment value. The story has a major shift, going from the medical students, which is the main focus of the first act and second act, to children who are out for a night of trick-or-treating and get caught up in the mayhem. It's just an odd switch but considering the whole film is a bit out of its head you kind of just go with it. Besides the gaps in logic and the weird focal-point change the film is briskly paced with never a dull moment to be had. Rubén also throws plenty of splatter and gore which, considering the budget, looks decent. If you're looking for a fun alternative slasher film for the Halloween season consider this far-out, spooky, Satanic, slasher zombie flick brought to you by the good folks in Mexico. No tricks and all treats here.

GOES WELL WITH: *Absurd, Grave Robbers*

Curse of the Crying Woman, aka La maldición de la llorona (1963)

DIRECTED BY	Rafael Baledon
WRITTEN BY	Rafael Baledon, Fernando Galiana
STARRING	Rosita Arenas, Abel Salazar, Rita Macedo, Carlos López Moctezuma, Enrique Lucero, Mario Sevilla
COUNTRY	Mexico

Curse of the Crying Woman is based on an old Mexican folk lore often told by roaring campfires. Ever since the '30s the legend has graced the silver screen but still remains largely unknown to Western audiences. Amelia (Rosita Arenas) and her husband, Jaime (Abel Salazar), are invited to stay with her Aunt Selma (Rita Macedo) under highly mysterious circumstances. The young newlyweds soon learn there is an evil curse that looms inside Aunt Selma's decaying mansion.

It's clear from frame one that the film has a wonderfully atmospheric flavor that reminded me a lot of Mario Bava's classic *Black Sunday*. It features some wonderful cinematography using the black-and-white medium to its utmost effectiveness. Similar to early Hammer, the film takes the reins where Universal horror films left off and it features many familiar tropes. In fact there is a bit where Selma walks through a spider web almost exactly like 1931's *Dracula*. And even if the plot plays like greatest hits of other classic horror it also sets itself apart by its properly weird monsters and nightmare logic-like style. Admittedly, the makeup effects are horribly dated and on the hokey side but it didn't derail this chiller for me, and in fact only heightened its spooky horror funhouse-like vibes. Certainly a treasure in the vault of Mexican horror cinema that has a lyrical Gothic poetry to it, and of course it has plenty of bizarre goings-on. If you're looking for a great film to watch around the Halloween season this will make a nice international alternative. So dry those tears and seek out this sorely underrated Gothic thriller.

Grave Robbers (1990)

DIRECTED BY	Rubén Galindo Jr.
WRITTEN BY	Rubén Galindo Jr.
STARRING	Fernando Almada, Edna Bolkan, Maria Rebeca, Ernesto Laguardia, Erika Buenfill, María Rebeca, Toño Infante
COUNTRY	Mexico

Mexican horror filmmaker Rubén Galindo Jr. once again explores Satanism and the unholy undead in another wild and wildly entertaining blood-soaked outing. A group of teenage thugs decide to plunder a grave for anything of value. After digging up a grave one of them falls through a tunnel leading to a secret chamber filled with jewels and gold. The gang thinks they struck it rich, and as they gather up there loot they find a skeleton with an axe embodied in it. Stupidly, they decide they want the axe, so they remove it and by doing so unleash an ancient evil bent on a bloody rampage. Not far from where this is taking place four college students are camping in the worst case of wrong place wrong time. Like *Cemetery of Terror* the theme of Satanism is explored, but this time the film has a slightly more polished look with some decent period costumes and sets at the beginning. *Grave Robbers* has a more coherent and focused screenplay, but sadly it still suffers from some holes in the plot and stretches in logic. It also could have done a better job at exploring its own mythology. Still, the film is excellently paced with thrills a minute and hardly a dry moment.

Rubén's trademark blood and guts are in full force as well with some well done gore gags, the highlight being a hand ripping out of a guy's chest a la *Alien*. When a film is this fun and ultra cheese-tastic it's easy to forgive some flaws in the screenplay. *Grave Robbers* is just a wonderfully enjoyable piece of Grindhouse grime that satisfies on so many levels.

Black Sheep (2006)

DIRECTED BY	Jonathan King
WRITTEN BY	Jonathan King
STARRING	Nathan Meister, Peter Feeney, Tammy Davis, Danielle Mason, Oliver Driver, Tandi Wright, Nick Blake
COUNTRY	New Zealand

Henry Oldfield (Nathan Meister) is returning to the homestead after years away. But it's not a happy homecoming, as he suffered a traumatic episode involving, you guessed it, sheep. His brother Angus (Peter Feeney) is now in charge of the farm and is going in a bigger, bolder direction than his late father. This means funding strange science experiments that of course go horribly array. Now the sheep are transformed into man-eaters on the hunt. *Black Sheep* harkens back to outrageous horror splatter comedies in the vein of early Peter Jackson films such as *Dead Alive* and *Bad Taste*. Similar to *Shaun of the Dead* King strikes a nearly perfect balance between over-the-top gore, horror, drama, and of course comedy. It's not easy to blend those all together yet King's skill at writing manages this well. King would go on to pen *The Tattooist,* an incredibly underrated horror-noir which in my opinion was more thrilling than *Seven*. It takes the mad scientist/animal revenge subgenres both sadly under-utilized and fuses them seamlessly, while also sneaking in commentary about genetically enhanced food without being preachy. I also love the little touches like the mint jelly being used like holy water. Wisely, King takes great care in fleshing out characters.

What also keeps this from being a hokey mess is the incredible effects pro-vided by none other than Peter Jackson's WETA workshop. 'Nuff said. I am baffled why this film hasn't earned the kind of cult status it deserves, because it's across-the-board brilliant. *Black Sheep* is a fun, fast-paced, horror comedy that really delivers. Required viewing.

Beast of the Yellow Night (1971)

DIRECTED BY	Eddie Romero
WRITTEN BY	Eddie Romero
STARRING	John Ashley, Mary Charlotte Wilcox, Eddie Garcia, Leopoldo Salcedo, Ken Metalfe, Vic Diaz, Don Lipman
COUNTRY	Philippines/United States

If it's weird and it's from the Philippines chances are it's written and directed by schlock master Eddie Romero, known for his infamous Vacation Blood Series. In the jungle a killer on the run makes a bargain with the devil when it's clear he is dying. But of course Satan has the better part of the deal using him as a vessel for evil, transforming him into a hideous

beast creature. I just know there is a totally awesome Eddie Romero film out there; I just have yet to find it. The problem with this and his other films is not the ultra-low budget, which looked like it cost maybe a hundred bucks, but it's the slapped together story that is needlessly convoluted, wildly incoherent, and skims over what you'd think were major plot points. Worst of all, a tepid melodrama is shoe-horned into the film and, come on, it's a hokey monster movie; nobody wants to see a couple with relationship problems. Even fans of hardcore cheese and dumpster bin Z-grade horror epics may have a hard time not reaching for the fast forward button. Eddie Romero no doubt worked hard to bring his wacky horror opuses to life but sadly he seemed to never be in on the low-budget joke, which is partly why fans find them so endearing, but maybe a little more tongue-in-cheek may have saved this film. This is hard to recommend even to fans of the so-bad-it's-good.

Brides of Blood (1968)

DIRECTED BY	Eddie Romero, Gerardo de Leon
WRITTEN BY	Cesar Amigo
STARRING	Kent Taylor, Beverly Powers, John Ashley, Eva Darren, Oscar Keesee, Bruno Punzalan, Pedro Navarro
COUNTRY	Philippines

"A Brutal Orgy of ghastly terror," screams the tagline for this far-off Pilipino shocker. American scientists Dr. Paul Henderson (Kent Taylor), his wife Carla (Beverly Powers), and Jim Farrel (John Ashley) go on to an isolated island in order to discover the effects of nuclear fallout there and also help the people build a care center, etc. However, a god-like monster roams the island looking for native virgins in this low-budget schlock fest. Eddie Romero,

the king of Z-grade monster flicks, brings what is the first of the unofficial Blood Island Trilogy.

The film tromps through the usual dumpster-grade monster trappings yet it's decidedly weirder and more adult oriented than what you'd expect. It languishes in a world of deeply bizarre sexual perversion, where things are not overtly graphic (as we never actually see the monster mating) and are merely left up to the viewer's imagination, which somehow makes it all the more unnerving.

Romero does his very best to stretch the already bare bones premise to the breaking point and the result is scenes that are either outright needless or simply go on way too long. For example, I could have done with the weak attempt at melodrama between husband and wife. The acting (and I'm using that term loosely here) is pretty much what you'd expect, and while Beverly Powers is certainly not hard to look at her acting is interesting, to say the very least. *Bride of the Blood*'s B-movie oddity charms only slightly outweigh this underwhelming effort. What holds this film back is not that it's low-budget but it's the rather plodding plot and boring melodrama. If you see only one deeply strange jungle outing where trees attack, mutant butterflies buzz around, and a randy monster is looking for a date, than this is it. *Bride of Blood* is recommended for true trash fans.

Green Elephant, The, aka Green Elephant Calf (1999)

DIRECTED BY	Svetlana Baskova
STARRING	Sergey Pakhomv, Vladimir Epifantsev, Aleksandr Maslaev, Anatoliy Osmolovskiy
COUNTRY	Russia

This film has gained a lot of infamy over the years, and after finally seeing it I can see why. Two men who we assume are officers are imprisoned in a dirty dank cell with a pipe that constantly leaks. The one man is obviously slow-witted and talks endlessly and tries to pass the time by telling racy stories, doing push-ups, etc. Things quickly escalate, however, when the other prisoner gets fed up with his cellmate's constant talking. Things only get worse from there, spiraling into a nightmare world of pure rage and brutality. This is certainly an unpleasant film experience but something worth seeing, if only once. Part of the film's disturbing nature stems from its amateur-style camera work and it being shot on video, giving it a gritty and realistic documentary quality. While the men are in their cell, the director uses mostly medium and close-up shots, giving an unbearable sense of claustrophobia and tension; something that builds as the film goes on. The first thirty to forty minutes are relatively slow with the two men just talking and fighting, but if you hang in there it starts getting progressively more disturbing. Towards the end things descend into a brutal assault on the audience, and the level of pure animalistic savagery is something seen in few films. On such a low budget the gore is very well done, and I'm guessing they used some sort of animal guts; whatever they did it's very effective. It's tough to say if I'd recommend this. It is certainly something worth seeing but most people, including myself, will find one viewing more than enough. Raw, violent, and totally unforgettable, it is not for the easily offended or those with a weak stomach, and it's definitely a good idea to have a comedy to cash this down with. Get the strongest vodka ready—you're going to need it.

Black Candles (1982)

DIRECTED BY	Jose Larraz
WRITTEN BY	Jose Larraz
STARRING	Helga Line, Vanessa Hidalgo, Christopher Bright, John McGrat, Betty Webster, Alfred Lucchetti, Tito Valverde
COUNTRY	Spain

Nobody loves a good cheese-tasic devil movie more than your humble author, and sometimes you have to root around outside of *The Omen* and *Rosemary's Baby* to find the really great grimy little gems. After the sudden death of her brother, Carol (Vanessa Hidalgo) and her boyfriend travel to England to settle his estate, and she is greeted by brother's wife Fiona (Helga Line). Right away she senses something is horribly wrong and her paranoia turns to be founded as she stumbles upon a coven of witches among them. From the very start it's clear this film pushes the boundaries in its eroticism—a theme that would play heavily in the film. It also has a great mood and its use of a soft focus lens lends to the dream-like atmosphere. For a devil movie it's surprisingly not hokey, with some genuinely shocking moments, and you can see how the filmmakers tried to go against the grain; however, sadly it still falls into some old clichés. All of that could be forgiven but the film's ideas and concepts seem flimsy at best, and at a scant eighty-two minutes it tends to drag a bit with a lot of needless scenes that do nothing to move the plot forward. It also doesn't help that our heroin Carol is as dull as dishwater, and Larraz doesn't give her anything to do expect complain. Surprisingly. the on-screen violence is extremely tame except for one nasty bit with a sword that is sure to make even jaded fans flitch even just a little bit. *Black Candles* was a novel attempt at breaking away from the usual satanic movie fare, and in a way it seemed almost ahead of its time with darker, grittier vibes similar to *The Lords of Salem*. But as provocative as it was it still fell into the same trappings as more conventional films coming in the wake of *The Exorcist*, suffering from an underdone screenplay that is at times dull. Ultimately a good try but it's just too uneven to be truly memorable. Still if you're looking for an ultra-sexy, trashy, and utterly bizarre devil outing you could do worse—just keep your expectations in check. And you can always say the devil made you do it.

Blood Splattered Bride, The, aka La novia Ensangrentada (1972)

DIRECTED BY	Vicente Aranda
WRITTEN BY	Vicente Aranda, Matthew Lewis (story by), Sheridan Le Fanu (based on novel by)
STARRING	Simón Andreu, Maribel Martin, Alexandra Bastedo, Dean Selmier, Angel Lombartre, Montserrat Julió
COUNTRY	Spain

Loosely based on the legend of *Carmilla* and the novel by Sheridan Le Fanu, *The Blood Splattered Bride* is a film that I came late to, having watched this for this review. It truly lived up to the hype and its repetition. A newly married couple returns to the husband's creepy mansion location on a lovely sprawling estate. However, the honeymoon is soon over when a strange specter from the past comes out of the grave to ensnare the lovely bride. For an artful and spicy Spanish horror film you can't go wrong with this film. *Bride* tackles the theme of gender roles and sexuality in a major way, and right off the bat the film lays on a thick and uncomfortable air of misogyny which cleverly will be flipped on its head. It also explores the subject of fetishes, and while

it's not explored in depth, it does play as background subtext, which was pretty progressive considering the time it was made. It also throws some ingenious foreshadowing like the hunted fox, which will be echoed towards the highly intense finale, and indeed the idea of predator/ prey motif is cleverly used throughout. Now I will say, this is not a fast paced movie but for the patient viewer you'll be rewarded many times over. I honestly didn't find it dull in the least, but it's certainly not as brisk as its modern counterparts. If you're like me and are a fan of stylish art house this will certainly please, as the film has great Gothic set pieces coupled with some wonderful cinematography that takes full advantage of its exterior locations. Playing like an erotic fever dream wrapped up in gory '70s horror, it is endlessly entertaining and constantly keeps you both guessing and glued to the screen. Highly recommended.

TRIVIA: Quentin Tarantino is a huge fan of this film, and in fact a chapter in *Kill Bill* is titled *The Blood Splattered Bride*.

GOES WELL WITH: *Symptoms, Daughters of Darkness*

Cannibal Man, The, aka La semana del asesino (1973)

DIRECTED BY	Eloy de la Iglesia
WRITTEN BY	Eloy de la Iglesia, Antonio Fos
STARRING	Vincent Parra, Emma Cohen, Eusebio Poncela, Charly Bravo, Goyo Lebrero, Vicky Lagos, Rafael Hernández
COUNTRY	Spain

Here is another prime example of a film's title being misleading, as the film is not quite the little cannibal fest you are led to believe. Still it's a film that works on many different levels. Marcus (Vincent Parra), a working class man, accidently kills a cab driver while out with his girlfriend. This sends off a domino effect of killing. Now Marcus is flung into a world of murder and madness with no way out. *Cannibal Man* is a sociopolitical commentary on the Franco regime cleverly masquerading in the guise of a horror film. Its comment on Spanish life and its corruption that shows favoritism towards the rich is both timely and sadly still relevant in the world. Thankfully the message is present but doesn't get preachy and simply plays as an extra layer. It also works as a grimy, gritty little

psychological film and shows the very bleak and harrowing spiral into insanity much in the vein of *Repulsion*. It's wonderfully understated with a very oppressive, strange vibe that puts you in the psychopath's frame of mind. Further adding to this uneasy feeling is the addition of some sexual tension between Marcus and his upper-class neighbor. The deaths are also savage and many are done up-close and personal, giving it a more disturbing aspect. *Cannibal Man* may not be quite the throat-chomping film you might guess from the title; however, it actually achieves so much more on a small budget. *Cannibal Man* is an under-loved little nasty gem that deserves to be the main course in your next movie night.

Count Dracula's Great Love, aka Cemetery Girls (1973)

DIRECTED BY	Javier Aguirre
WRITTEN BY	Javier Aguirre, Alberto S. Insúa, Paul Naschy (as Jacinto Molina)
STARRING	Paul Naschy, Rosanna Yanni, Mirta Miller, Haydée Politoff, Víctor Alcázar, Ingrid Garbo, Susana Latour
COUNTRY	Spain

Paul Naschy was a legend in Spanish horror cinema. Not only did he act in more than one hundred films he also directed them and wrote more than forty screenplays. Talk about a triple threat. Now I don't claim to be a Naschy expert but I've seen enough of his films to really dig the man's work, good or bad. He has played many different creature roles, and in *Count Dracula's Great Love* he "undertakes" the undying bloodsucker in this Spanish shocker. Four beautiful women and a gentleman friend are traveling when their carriage loses a wheel; worse yet, the poor driver gets kicked to death by his own horse, leaving them stranded. It just so happens there's an infamous sanitarium in walking distance (of course), and so naturally they seek shelter. Dr. Wendell Marlow (Paul Naschy) answers and offers them a place to stay until they can get them on their way again. The good doctor is actually . . . you guessed it, Count Dracula. It was foretold in a diary written by vampire hunter Dr. Van Helsing that a virgin would come to Dracula of her own free will and give herself to him—could it be one of the girls now staying with him? Yes, but you already guessed that. The film starts off with a rather nicely done kill delivered by an axe to the skull. The poor fellow falls down the stairs in slow motion, which is repeated during the entire credit sequence. When I showed this to a group of friends everyone was howling with laughter. It sets the mood for what the rest of the film has to offer, which is cheap thrills and campy humor. This time around Javier Aguirre takes a page from the Universal/ Hammer Horror formula and adds a wonderful Spanish flavor. You

have the usual set-up: the wrecked carriage, pretty young girls in peril, and of course it's set in a Gothic castle, or in this case a Spanish villa. It's also filled with great atmosphere that is on par with its American and British counterparts. What makes this different is the way they push the envelope on both the gore and nudity front, both of which are exploited whenever possible. From a splatter perspective it's not on the level of say an H. G. Lewis film but still there are plenty of nice gore gags and lots of blood dripping down bare bosoms. Speaking of which, the film attempts to blend the horror genre with eroticism, something very few films were doing at the time. Fans will go batty for this high-camp, horror cheese fest, chock full of unintentional humor, cheap sets, horrible dubbing, and dialogue that never ceases to perplex. If you're looking for a nice, cute, nudie alternative to a Universal or Hammer vampire film with a spicy Spanish edge this one is a must-see, fangs, I mean, flaws and all.

Erotic Rites of Frankenstein, aka La maldición de Frankenstein (1973)

DIRECTED BY	Jesús Franco
WRITTEN BY	Jesús Franco, Mary Shelley (based on characters created by)
STARRING	Dennis Price, Howard Vernon, Beatriz Savon, Anne Libert, Alberto Dalbes, Luis Barboo, Daniel White
COUNTRY	Spain, France

Let's delve into the sex-crazed imagination of Jesús Franco with this bat-crap-crazy re-telling of everyone's favorite stitched-together anti-hero. Dr. Frankenstein (Dennis Price) has achieved success in creating a living, breathing creature. But before the good doctor can celebrate he is killed by his rival, Cagliostro (Howard Vernon), and his monster is taken to his castle. With the aid of his bird woman he creates a perfect mate for his newly acquired man.

Frankenstein's daughter, Vera (Beatriz Savon) gets wind of this and vows to get her revenge. My head was spinning from the first ten minutes of this delightfully cheesy slice of horror from master director Jesús Franco. Wow . . . Take a deep breath because you're in for a deliriously depraved and totally wacked-out vision of Mary Shelley's  immortal classic. From a silver-painted Frankenstein's monster to a fully nude cannibal bird girl (in bluish green feathers) there is so much strangeness to behold. As the title suggests there is plenty of bare flesh on screen, and being Franco there is plenty of perversion and fetishisms thrown in for good measure. A completely nude man and woman being whipped (by Frankenstein's monster no less) on a spiked floor is just so twisted. The plot isn't brilliant and it struggles to make sense at times, and more baffling is the fact that the titular monster almost seems to takes a backseat. Despite this it still manages to be entertaining and oh-so-hypnotically bizarre with nasty little touches only Franco could pull off. *Erotic Rites of Frankenstein* is a kaleidoscope of sexual sadism and trashy Euro horror.

Horror Rises from the Tomb, aka El espanto surge de la tumba (1973)

DIRECTED BY	Carlos Aured
WRITTEN BY	Paul Naschy
STARRING	Paul Naschy, Emma Cohen, Víctor Alcázar, Helga Liné, Betsabé Ruiz, Cristina Suriani, Luis Ciges, Juan Cazalilla
COUNTRY	Spain

In fifteenth-century France, an evil warlock named Alaric de Marnac (Paul Naschy) along with his lovely partner in crime Mabille De Lancré (Helga Liné) are to be put to death for their horrible crimes, which include vampirism, witchcraft, etc. Before they're executed they  vow to get revenge from beyond the grave, your standard pre-death threat. Flash forward to present day: Hugo de Marnac (Paul Naschy) and a group of friends hold a séance where they get in contact with the spirit of the long-dead warlock. This peaks their curiosity and the group decides to go to Hugo's family estate, which is rumored to hold treasure. Instead of riches they only find terrible horrors including the severed head of Alaric de Marnac. Like many of these types of films the plot is incoherent and all over the place, with parts of the story that could have used more explanation. However, it has more things going for it than against it. This is possibly one of the best examples of Euro-Gothic, which is thick with atmosphere that takes it cues from classic horror motifs of Universal and later Hammer, yet makes it its own, giving the entire film a nightmare-like quality. It also surprisingly has a stylish edge not unlike early Mario Bava using pink and purple hues to highlight its weird and creepy vibes. Fans of tons of splatter and gore will not be disappointed, as this film deals it out in great amounts. What I found most interesting though is how the violence is almost always sexualized, which adds an extra unnerving aspect. The score is also shockingly good and helps re-enforce the mood it creates. Even with its problems this is one of the better Paul Naschy vehicles, and while it never strays far from familiar Gothic horror tropes its approach is bold enough to make it feel fresh, unlike the rotting dead in this film.

GOES WELL WITH: *Panic Beats, Vengeance of the Zombies*

Last Circus, The (2010)

DIRECTED BY	Álex de la Iglesia
WRITTEN BY	Álex de la Iglesia
STARRING	Carlos Areces, Antonio de la Torre, Carolina Bang, Enrique Villen, Manuel Tejada, Alejandro Tejerias, Manuel Tallafe
COUNTRY	Spain

I certainly admire when a film can have political overtones yet wrap itself in a genre like horror. Because in many ways a lot of classic genre films have come out of real-life horrors. *The Last Circus* is an overt commentary on fascist Spain. The film opens in 1937, in Spain during the brutal Spanish Civil War. A happy clown is interrupted during a performance for a group of children, including his son, and forced to fight in the militia still wearing his clown makeup and clothes. His father is captured and imprisoned; when his son expresses interest in being a happy clown he advises him against it. He says his life is too tragic and he should play the sad clown and that revenge is a way to ease his pain. He tried to save his father by breaking him out; however, it backfires and while others were freed his father was killed. Years go by and now Javier (Carlos Areces), all grown up, joins a circus as the sad clown but quickly learns that he is playing sidekick to a psychopath named Sergio (Antonio de la Torre), the happy clown. Things become worse as the foolish clown falls for Natalia (Caroline Bang), a trapeze artist who just happens to be seeing the insanely vicious and jealous Sergio. Soon the meek young man spirals into a dark and disturbing black hole and everyone who's laughed at him will pay. The film starts off strong with plenty of action, intrigue, and delightfully dark comedy. Director Iglesias employees his signature brand of style and inventive camera work, which works beautifully to tell this story that is both bleak at times and garish and grotesque. The story plays with many themes, including the absurdity of war, how it makes clowns of people, stripping their humanity away. It also plays on an interesting duality between the clowns and how they start out as polar opposites, but over time Javier becomes just as bad, if not worse than Sergio. This is brilliantly echoed when both clowns showdown in full makeup. As strong as the film is it suffers from wildly uneven tone and a third act that isn't quite as strong as the first and second, with subplots with pay-offs not as big as you'd like them to be. It also could have used a trim, with some scenes that either go on too long or are needless altogether. I also think Javier's character could have been just a bit more likable or sympathetic. *The Last Circus* is, despite its flaws, a wonderfully strange and heartfelt horror and sociopolitical film that plays like one big macabre operatic tragedy with shades of classics like *The Man Who Laughed* and *Phantom of the Opera*. Álex de la Iglesia remains one of Spain's most interesting and brave directors working today.

Loreley's Grasp, The, aka When the Screaming Stops (1974)

DIRECTED BY	Amando de Ossorio
WRITTEN BY	Amando de Ossorio
STARRING	Helga Liné, Tony Kendall, Silvia Tortosa, Josefina Jartin, Loreta Tovar, José Thelman, Betsabé Ruiz
COUNTRY	Spain

From the director of the infamous *Blind Dead* series comes this extremely odd little monster flick very loosely based on folklore. A horrific lizard-like creature is savagely murdering young girls and ripping out their hearts in the process. A hunter named Sigurd (Tony Kendall) is hired to protect the scantily clad girls of a nearby school. But is he up to the task or will the body count keep rising?

The Loreley's Grasp is a highly interesting yet deeply flawed Spanish creature feature. On the one scaly hand it plays on many classical horror tropes and even features the standard torch-baring villagers right out of *Frankenstein,* but it also plays like a '50s B-monster film with an obvious '70s update filled with nudity and violence. Unfortunately, the plot is wildly uneven and it tends to lose its focus, with scenes that just simply fizzle out rather than actually move the story forward. Also, it's just plain incoherent, with the audience needing to suspend a lot of disbelief and other times just totally chuck logic out the window. Believe it or not, I actually enjoyed this film because, despite its problems, there is never a dull moment. What the audience is in store for is a cheese-tasic monster movie filled to the brim with lots of decent gore and overflowing with nudie cuties and painfully retro fashions. It plays almost like a greatest hits of H. G Lewis meets Eddie Romero with a decidedly spicy Spanish flavor. I would highly recommend for hardcore trash fans that love their monsters in the so-bad-they're-good category.

Night of the Werewolf, The, aka El retorno del Hombre Lobo (1981)

DIRECTED BY	Paul Naschy
WRITTEN BY	Paul Naschy
STARRING	Paul Naschy, Julia Saly, Silvia Aguilar, Azucena Hernandez, Pepe Ruiz, Tito Garcia, David Rocha, Charly Bravo
COUNTRY	Spain

Paul Naschy, the Mexican Lon Chaney Jr., stars in this werewolf vampire battle royale. Elizabeth Bathory (Julia Saly), the famed scarlet countess (based on the real-life person), and her followers are executed for their ghastly crimes. Before she dies she vows that she will rise from the ashes and seek revenge, your standard pre-death curse. Years later an evil woman schemes to bring Bathory back from the dead. It just so happens that Waldemar Daninsky (Paul Naschy), aka the Werewolf, is also dug up and brought back to life to join the fun. Soon it's bloodsucker versus throat-biter in a strange match-up. Naschy again does triple duty in one of his werewolf films and what fans get is a mixed bag. There is no doubt that this film plays like a greatest hits of classic horror: You have it all; an evil woman laying down a curse before she is executed, castles, moonlit nights, and cemeteries; it's a cornucopia of staples that fans have grown to love. Some may see this as clichéd, and you'd be right, but I personally like this aspect and I'm more than okay with that. It is also rich in Gothic expressionism and its set pieces are wonderfully moody, as you'd expect from an ultra-cheesy Naschy outing. Like many of these films they also wisely take advantage of the wonderful practical shooting locations. So here is where the film loses its audience. Despite a wonderful opening with a lot of great action, at some point the film tends to drag with shoe-horned melodrama that doesn't serve the story and only bring things to a dead stop. It's also needlessly complicated and terribly contrived at times with lots of stretching of logic. Sadly, even the big showdown between Bathory and the Werewolf is a bit of a letdown. The violence is mostly tame but does contain a few nice nasty bits like our favorite countess bathing in her favorite iron-based substance. *The Night of the Werewolf* may be hit or miss but if you're a fan of silly, trashy, Spanish monster outings chock full of familiar horror trappings then this is the one to sink your teeth into.

Panic Beats (1983)

DIRECTED BY	Paul Naschy
WRITTEN BY	Paul Naschy
STARRING	Paul Naschy, Julia Saly, Lola Gaos, Silvia Miro, Manuel Zarzo, Jose Vivo, Frances Ondivela
COUNTRY	Spain

More Gothic nasty fun from everyone's favorite Spanish maestro, Paul does triple duty in this far-out Spanish revenge horror thriller. A wicked man dressed in knight armor brutally slays his unfaithful wife and his own children. Flash forward one hundred years later and his descendant, Paul (Paul Naschy), who bears a striking resemblance to the mad killer, takes his ill wife to his family's estate to give her some much needed rest and relaxation.

But is the mad knight really resting in peace? Or will everyone end up in pieces? *Panic Beats* is an interesting and odd film, as it constantly defies viewers' expectations for better or worse. And while the plot is not terribly original it does manage to keep the audience guessing with its various twists and turns. The setup, while a bit on the slow side, does sprinkle

clues and foreshadowing and is the kind of film that really builds to its ending, which for me packed a nice punch. It also has a lot of visual style that harkens back to the days of Hammer, with cemeteries, foggy moonlit nights, and lots of gothic overtones to perfectly set the creepy atmosphere. Indeed, there is a nightmare-like quality that permeates the entire film. This is also notably one of Naschy's goriest efforts and, while it's not the messiest film by far, it does deliver some delightfully over-the-top carnage, which will have even jaded splatter heads screaming for more. Let's just say axe meets human and it's as disgusting as you hope it'll be. Though the effects themselves are somewhat crude for the time and, I'm sure, budget the gore gags are rather nicely done and the practical makeup in the finale is so effective and unnerving. *Panic Beats* may not be the most brilliantly conceived idea with a sometimes lumbering pace and a few plot holes, but it's still a great little film that has everything a good horror/thriller should have; plenty of suspense that leaves us guessing at every turn. And how can you resist the Spanish charms of Paul Naschy, one of the horror cinema's most prolific writer/actor/directors? This makes for the perfect movie *knight*.

Sleep Tight, aka Mientras duermes (2011)

DIRECTED BY	Jaume Balaguero
WRITTEN BY	Alberto Marini
STARRING	Luis Tosar, Marta Etura, Alberto San Juan, Iris Almeida, Carlos Lasarte, Roger Morilla, Pep Tosar, Tony Corvillo
COUNTRY	Spain

In 2007, Balaguero made a huge splash with fright lovers with his masterpiece of horror *[REC]* and its two sequels. Flash forward to 2011, when he brings us *Sleep Tight*, and folks, you'll sleep anything but after seeing this flick. The film follows the life of Cesar (Luis Tosar), a desk manager at an upscale apartment building, who always has a smile on his face. Turns out he is anything but the happy person that residents think he is; in fact, he can't feel happiness at all. That is until he found a hobby that brought meaning to his life, namely bringing misery to the happy-go-lucky tenant, Clare (Marta Etura). With access to all the keys, Cesar begins a campaign to make her life a living hell. It starts out innocently enough, but soon escalates to more disturbing things. But when Clara remains happy even with Cesar's torment, he decides to step up his game, with deadly consequences. *Sleep Tight* is a film that totally blew me away. Like *[REC]*, Jaume Balaguero has weaved a masterful story of terror and suspense, and he brilliantly uses the moment when we are most vulnerable, namely alone and sleeping, and creates a walking night of dread and sexual perversion. I love how Jaume plays with the old childhood fear of the boogeyman under the bed, which takes on a whole new dimension in this film. Major credit goes out to Alberto Marini for writing a skin-crawling screenplay that is both believable and well balanced. He knows how to just go far enough without getting silly or too over-the-top, with characters that are fleshed out and believable. Not to mention a story that is gripping from beginning to the pulse-pounding ending. The material also hangs largely on the villain, and Cesar is the ultimate sociopath; he takes the power and the trust he is given and perverts it to his own sick ends. The most disturbing thing is, he's not a snarling, raving maniac; he could be anyone. Like Travis Bickle in *Taxi Driver* Cesar is an alienated loner who we watch spiral into a void of blackness of his own creation. Jaume is wise in not making him sympathetic; he is a monster, plain and simple. Jaume Balaguero already proved himself to be a force to be reckoned with in the genre, and with *Sleep Tight* he firmly cements himself as a master of terror. It just goes to show you that to make a disturbing film you don't need gimmicks or gallons of blood and guts, just a smart, suspenseful script filled with well-rounded, complex characters. This film not only gets under the covers but it'll crawl under your skin and stay there for days. So "sleep tight!" Don't let the creepy bald guy bite!!

Vengeance of the Zombies, aka La rebelión de las muertas (1973)

DIRECTED BY	León Klimovsky
WRITTEN BY	Paul Naschy
STARRING	Paul Naschy, Romy, Mirta Miller, Maria Kosty, Antonio Pica, Luis Ciges, Aurora de Alba, Ramon Lillo
COUNTRY	Spain

Paul Naschy, the master of horror, plays not one but three characters in this highly weird Spanish outing. A sadist Indian mystic named Kantaka (Paul Naschy) brings back the dead in bizarre voodoo rituals. The zombies obey his every deadly demand and he collects an ever growing undead army to exact his revenge. Swinging '70s Euro-trash doesn't get better or weirder than *Vengeance of the Zombies,* which was said to be inspired by a nightmare Naschy had. This seems rather fitting as the whole film feels like one long surreal fever dream, filled with grotesque images like a butcher's meat locker right out of a Francis Bacon painting. It switches effortlessly from retro pop art to Gothic horror, and the result is a highly sensual psychedelic trip into hell with a groovy jazz soundtrack to boot. If there was one major issue it would have to be the admittedly laughably cheese-tasic zombie makeup, which consists of garish dark circles under their eyes and an ashy complexion. On the flip side of this, however, Naschy's devil makeup is impressive considering what I'm sure was a small budget. It's genuinely off-putting and a great understated devil makeup. Paul Naschy is pretty entertaining to watch as he plays three characters, which consist of the Yogi Krisna, the evil brother Kantaka, and the very devil himself. The film has a decent pace with enough action and mystery to keep the audience glued. For splatter fans the film features some great gags and, while the violence isn't extreme, it is plentiful. Thankfully, the film doesn't go the *Scooby Doo* route like I thought it might and you can even forgive the sometimes clichéd detective stuff. Trashy and ultra-sleazy Spanish chiller written and starring the horror guru himself, and highly recommended for a fun film night with friends. It's three times the Naschy for the price of admission, what could be better?

Who Can Kill a Child?, aka Island of the Damned (1976)

DIRECTED BY	Narciso Ibáñez Serrador
WRITTEN BY	Narciso Ibáñez Serrador, Juan José Plans (based on novel by)
STARRING	Lewis Fiander, Prunella Ransome, Antonio Iranzo, Miguel Narros, Luis Ciges, Juan Cazalila, Antonio Canal
COUNTRY	Spain

Who Can Kill a Child? kicks off a different sort of children-based horror subgenre in which adults have to break a moral taboo and defend themselves against what is largely considered the most innocent—children. This theme would be further echoed by later films like *Children of the Corn, Beware: Children at Play,* etc. English tourists Tom (Lewis Fiander) and Evelyn (Prunella Ransome) visit a remote island, which is said to be both beautiful and not over crowded with other tourists. When they arrive they are shocked to find that the entire island seems to be deserted. Tom, thinking everyone is at a fiesta on the other side of the island, doesn't panic, and the two explore, looking for any signs of life. It just so happens that there are people amongst them; children who are thirsty for murder. The film opens with a credit sequence featuring real footage of atrocities that took place during the Holocaust and the Korean War. I find this in the poorest taste, cheapening a tragedy like this for the sake of shocking an audience. It's one thing to see footage of this kind in a documentary but to carelessly splash footage of dead bodies around in a horror film just reeks of attention-seeking in order to prod its viewers. Indeed, for a long time this footage was deleted from the film altogether until Dark Sky Films re-released it on home video. After sitting through the pointlessly depressing credits the film is padded out with needless vacation footage, which doesn't do much in the way of establishing characters and seemed more like watching someone's home movies. The film, however, does manage to pick up with some decent amount of tension and a few delightfully twisted moments, but it's clear that the writing is under-developed and skims over a lot of important plot points. Keeping the kids murder spree a mystery would have been a good way to go but the film lazily makes a case for . . . wait for it . . . evolution. Because that makes a lot of sense, how? Furthermore, the weird plot device of the kids having psychic powers to convert the other children only serves to completely diminish the disturbing aspects of the film, giving a clear reason for the mayhem instead of a more unnerving randomness to the crimes. *Who Can Kill a Child?* has its moments but sadly, like the credit sequence, it only serves to try and jolt its audience rather than giving them something really disturbing.

Evil Ed (1995)

DIRECTED BY	Anders Jacobsson
WRITTEN BY	Anders Jacobsson, Goran Lundstrom, Christer Ohlsson
STARRING	Per Lofberg, Johan Rudebeck, Olof Rhodin, Camela Leierth, Gert Fylking, Cecilia Ljung
COUNTRY	Sweden

It's always a great thing when past horror films can inspire a crop of new talent to forge ahead with their own careers, and sometimes it's nice when you can tip your hat to your cinematic heroes in your own film. However, *Evil Ed* comes off like a fan boy given a budget, but lacks genuine talent of his own. Ed (Johan Rudebeck) is a soft spoken film editor who, much to his dismay, gets reassigned to cut a horror film series called *Loose Limbs*. He must spend time watching the violence and snipping them. This quickly drives him into full-blown mania in no time flat. Timid Eddie is now a bloodthirsty butcher who wants final cut, with his knife. I've always felt like the title and cover art for this film were far better than the actual product. Jacobsson makes it painfully clear he has a major love for classic horror films, more specifically *Evil Dead* and *Evil Dead 2* (you lose count of how many times you see the poster for it), and even a character is a not-so-subtly named Sam Campbell. While homages are not bad a thing per se, it should be able to stand on its own merit. *Evil Ed* does have a promising premise but it lacks an interesting script with compelling characters, and worse yet it's horrible contrived and too far over the top. Worst of all, it takes its already thin plot and stretches it to the limit. The film is said to be a comment against Swedish's censorship but it seems to completely contradict its own commentary. Ed is a normal, seemingly well-adjusted person until he is driven mad by splatter films. If it's meant to be ironic it didn't get the point across. Think of this movie like a five-year-old child. It can be loud, obnoxious, and desperate for attention. It screams in your face and begs to be looked at. I will say the film sports some decent effects and has a few moments where the humor is spot-on. It never ceases to amaze me that this film has found its own small but loyal cult following, and if you enjoy it, more power to you. I'm not condemning this film for paying tribute to other horror films, but if you're going to do that you need to balance it with a smart script that doesn't smack of an over-the-top plea for approval. It took a promising concept with lots of room for social satire and condensed itself down to what feels like a poorly written *Tales from the Crypt* episode spread out to a feature length film.

Bloodlust, aka Mosquito Rapist, aka Mosquito der Schänder (1977)

DIRECTED BY	Marijan Vajda
WRITTEN BY	Mario d'Alcala
STARRING	Werner Pochath, Ellen Umlauf, Birgit Zamulo, Gerhard Ruhnke, Charly Hiltl, Hary Olsbauer, Marion Messner
COUNTRY	Switzerland

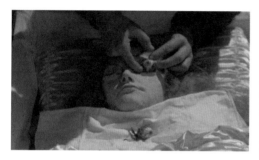

"...will haunt the darkest corners of your mind" screams the tagline to this late '70s sleaze feast. It may not have haunted my mind but it is a truly unique horror outing. A deaf and dumb man who has suffered physical and mental abuse in the past acts out in disturbing ways. He has a fetish for breaking into mortuaries to dismember and play with the dead and drink their blood. The press dubs him The Mosquito. When a girl dies (who he is secretly in love with) he takes his rage a step further and begins to kill. Wow, *Bloodlust* is a seriously mentally ill experience. Director Marijan Vajda wastes zero time in creating an uncomfortable icky feeling which only gets worse as things progress. The plot and characters suffer from being paper thin, yet it's hard to not be mesmerized by its grimy and disturbing nature, with scenes that have to be seen to be believed. It really takes twisted perversion to new heights, and lovers of films like *Nekromantik* and *Beyond the Darkness* will find this an unexpected nasty little treat.

GOES WELL WITH: *Beyond the Darkness, Bloodsucking Freaks*

Ghost of Guts Eater, aka Krasue Sao (1973)

DIRECTED BY	S. Naowaratch
STARRING	Sombat Metanee, Metta Rungrat, Sulaleewan Suwanatat, Pisamai Wilaisak
COUNTRY	Thailand

A young woman's grandmother dies but not before giving her a mystical ring. Later, as often tends to happen, dear old Granny re-appears in the ring from beyond the grave demanding her granddaughter feed her. And her food of choice is guts of course. Now with a popped-off

floating head, the poor girl must need-lessly search for human blood and guts. If you are familiar with *Mystics in Bali* (and if you're not, you really should be) you will no doubt see that the setup is similar. But sadly, *Guts* isn't as entertain-ing. With a title like *Ghost of Guts Eater*, there is no excuse for this to be a boring and utterly forgettable film. Yes, it has the broken-down charms of *Bali,* but it's bogged way down by painfully dull melodramatic subplot when all we really want is crazy, head-floating, blood-sucking action. Part of the charm of these films is that they are completely unaware of the crap they were making, yet this film would have been helped greatly by some fun, over-the-top moments to keep things at least interesting. Not worth tracking down.

Asphyx, The (1972)

DIRECTED BY	Peter Newbrook
WRITTEN BY	Brian Comport, Christina Beers (story by), Laurence Beers (story by)
STARRING	Robert Stephens, Robert Powell, Jane Lapotaire, Alex Scott, Terry Scully, David Grey, Tony Caunter
COUNTRY	United Kingdom

The Asphyx is proof that not all period horror/sci-fi movies were made by Hammer. Sir Hugo Cunningham (Robert Stephens) is interested in paranormal studies and finds a curious black smudge on photographs of the dying or recently deceased. This leads him to a breakthrough in finding a physical embodiment of the spirit called the Asphyx, and that if you can contain it, it somehow means you'll live forever. This is a film that seems to divide fans, with some calling it an underrated masterpiece and others writing it off as a silly and under-developed effort. Well, my feelings lay somewhere in the middle. First, what I liked about the film. The concept is refreshingly different; especially when you consider British horror at this time was starting to dip its toes into more proto-slashers and psycho-thrillers rather than period horror. I also have to give it serious props for it taking a more philosophical bend, and it isn't afraid to lay the drama on a bit thick. What sinks this film is, even with a strong and interesting concept, it's never fleshed out enough, leaving the audience with more questions than answers. I'm all for suspending some disbelief but the film takes that to new heights, and there are some confusing and sometimes laughable holes in the story. The acting is also uneven at best and even the usually solid Robert Powell does a tepid job as the uncharismatic stepson of Robert Stephens's character. I can certainly see why some viewers like this film for its more cerebral attempt at some heavy issues. Sadly, though, the message gets a bit too heavy-handed and the entertainment value takes a backseat to a very talky chamber piece. This coupled with some glaring story problems and uneven acting makes this a novel effort that unfortunately never quite got off the ground. I actually think this would have worked a lot better as a short anthology segment. Not terrible and worth seeking out if only for something totally different but not altogether good.

Beast in the Cellar, The (1970)

DIRECTED BY	James Kelley
WRITTEN BY	James Kelley
STARRING	Beryl Reid, Flora Robson, T.P McKenna, John Kelland, Vernon Dobtcheff, Merlyn Ward, Peter Craze, Dafydd Havard
COUNTRY	United Kingdom

Forget gems like *Blood on Satan's Claws, Curse of Frankenstein,* etc. We're scraping the bottom of the Brit barrel with this low-budget horror outing. A series of brutal murders rocks an English town. At first it is thought to be simply a wild animal, but it is something far worse. Two elderly sisters living in a charming house hold the key to the vicious slayings. "*A chill-filled horror festival,*" screams the tagline. Well, I hate to burst the filmmaker's bubble but it's neither chill-filled nor horrific. Kelley, unfortunately, does not create any actual scares nor is he able to build any suspense. The plot isn't exactly new and it struggles to come up with anything exciting and original. But all is not lost, however. The film's daffy old biddy spinsters, provide its real strength, being unintentional camp value and hilarity; because the plot is just too ridiculous to actually take even a little bit seriously even with a bit of "drama" injected. You also have to love the laughable "beast". It's like they weren't even really trying to make him scary. The other highlight is the acting of its two leads, Beryl Reid and Flora Robson. Both have a long history in the film industry and they add a bit of class and polish to the z-grade material. *Beast* is by no means a good movie but it's just weird and funny enough to justify a viewing. It may not be a shining example of British horror but it's certainly entertaining, even if for all the wrong reasons.

TRIVIA: One of only two films directed by James Kelley. The other being *What the Pepper Saw.*

Blood on Satan's Claw (1971)

DIRECTED BY	Piers Haggard
WRITTEN BY	Robert Wynne-Simmons
STARRING	Patrick Wymark, Linda Hayden, Michele Dotrice, Wendy Padbury, Anthony Ainley, Barry Andrews, Simon Williams
COUNTRY	United Kingdom

Blood on Satan's Claw ranks up there as one of the best and often neglected British horror films of all time. No cheesy monsters or psycho killers, the film deals with a much darker subject and is done in a semi-realistic manner. The peace of a country village is rocked when a farmer accidently digs up remains that are humanoid in nature. Ever since its unearthing, strange events begin to occur, seemingly bewitching the children into doing some very wicked things and converting them into a devil-worshiping cult. The film is not what you'd call heavy on plot but what it lacks in that department it more than makes up for in heavy atmospheric and dreamy, surreal quality. A little like blending *Village of the Damned* and *Rosemary's Baby,* the film has an off-kilter nightmare logic to it and a general sense of unease and dread and a dark eroticism that is unexpected in a British film, especially for the time. Indeed, this film relies less on the splatter and more on the pure horror it creates, using simple and effective storytelling and its palpable mood. I'm not saying the film is perfect, and sadly they seem to gloss over some important story elements and the results are holes in plot. Also, our hero is not the most appealing chap. Like a lot of British horror they take advantage of the beautiful exterior locations, and the interiors are also rich in design, providing a lot of small details. It helps really to suck you into the story and buy its loony plot. The period costumes are also quite well done especially considering what I assume was a lower budget production. Its wonderfully eerie dream-like quality, polished production values, and some genuinely disturbing moments helps *Blood on Satan's Claw* rise above its sometimes confusing, convoluted plot and remains a prime example of Gothic Noir cinema. An instant horror classic and should be considered required viewing by any horror fan serious about the genre.

Corruption (1968)

DIRECTED BY	Robert Hartford-Davis
WRITTEN BY	Donald Ford, Derek Ford
STARRING	Peter Cushing, Sue Lloyd, Kate O'Mara, Bill Murray, Noel Trevarthen, Vanessa Howard, Wendy Varnals
COUNTRY	United Kingdom

"*Corruption is NOT a woman's picture, therefore no woman will be admitted alone to see this super shock film.*" Thus screams the poster and trailer ads and possibly the winner of the most sexist movie gimmick in history. An upstanding doctor, Sir John Rowan (Peter Cushing) and his model fiancée Lynn (Sue Lloyd), attend a super '60s house party thrown by her sleazy photographer friend. After a jealous fight between John and the photographer breaks out a hot light burns Lynn, disfiguring one side of her face. Feeling guilty, Sir John does anything he can to restore her face, including murder. In the annals of ultra-grimy Brit films, *Corruption* reigns supreme. Like a mad scientist, Davis takes a standard nasty slasher and fuses it with Gothic horror undertones of vampirism (finding victims for everlasting beauty could have came straight out of *Countless Dracula*) and Jack the Ripper-style butchery in a swinging '60s setting and even a little MacBeth insanity thrown in for good measure. And shockingly, for the most part it works. The legendary Peter Cushing was vocal about not liking this film; however, you would never know it because he is at the top of his game. His touch of English class and respectability somewhat help keep balance to this off-the-rails horror film. I say somewhat because it succumbs to uneven tone and story, and the admittedly dodgy makeup effects don't help matters either. However, I've grown to love this film, and where it may stumble in some departments, it makes up for by its high-energy, almost hypnotic insanity. For example, the whole final act would really be a whole other movie on its own, even introducing new highly strange characters to the mix. And let's not forget the violence, which is unrelentingly brutal and filmed in a very cold, matter-of-fact way. The infamous train kill is still chilling in its execution. Wildly all over the place, sure, but *Corruption* is refreshingly different, grimy, and has the magic touch of Peter Cushing in a rare non-period film. It is truly a film everyone should see.

Creeping Flesh, The (1973)

DIRECTED BY	Freddie Francis
WRITTEN BY	Peter Spencely, Jonathan Rumbold
STARRING	Peter Cushing, Christopher Lee, Lorna Heilbron, George Benson, Kenneth J. Warren, Harry Locke, Duncan Lamont
COUNTRY	United Kingdom

I'm a firm believer in Amicus being just as good as Hammer, but admittedly this was a huge misstep for the company and the normally brilliant Freddie Francis, a director who all horror fans should be familiar with. Dr. Hildern (Peter Cushing) returns from his trip to Papau New Guinea with a possibly earth-shaking discovery; the skeletal remains of what he believes is some prehistoric embodiment of evil. A curious thing happens one day when cleaning it—it seems applying water to it makes it grow muscle and flesh. Can he contain the evil or will it walk freely in Victorian London? I really wanted to enjoy *The Creeping Flesh* because not only does it star two of the greatest horror icons in British cinema, Peter Cushing and Christopher Lee, it also tries to do something outside of the typical Gothic thriller. But sadly, some key factors really hold this film back from being memorable. First, let me say the real highlight is, of course, watching the new masters, Lee and Cushing, at work, and even with so-so material they add a lot of class and charm like no other. It also explores some interesting ideas such as nature versus nurture and combines evolutionary theories with a biblical-like evil. It also acts as a sly commentary on sexually repressed Victorian London. The problem is *The Creeping Flesh* takes an already flimsy at best premise and stretches it to its very limit, and sadly a lot of the film feels like a horribly padded-out anthology segment. It also suffers from uneven tone and a convoluted story with some glaring holes. Making matters worse is the melodrama, which is laid on extra thick, and let's face it, it's not like this is Shakespeare or a Bergman production. They seem to forget what makes films like *Countless Dracula* so much fun is the tongue-in-cheek quality that helps you get away with a lot more in terms of quality.

And while some of the practical effects are well done like the limbs in Lee's Dr. Frankenstein-like lab, others are downright laughable. For example, it's hard not to snicker at the horribly phallic-like finger, which is cut off the skeletal remains and apparently grows skin and veins. The cheap effect looks even worse (and more hilarious) magnified when suspended in liquid. *The Creeping Flesh* is a novel effort with some clever ideas; however, it bogs itself down in uninteresting story and contrived plot. With some trimming and a stronger concept this could have been a really great little film, but sadly its star power and unintentional camp hilarity just doesn't make up for the overall inept and frankly dull outing.

Death Line, aka Raw Meat (US title) (1972)

DIRECTED BY	Gary Sherman
WRITTEN BY	Ceri Jones, Gary Sherman (story by)
STARRING	Donald Pleasence, David Ladd, Clive Swift, Sharon Gurney, June Turner, Hugh Armstrong, Christopher Lee
COUNTRY	United Kingdom

Before CHUDs roamed the NYC subways seeking human flesh there was this weird little British film, *Death Line*, better known in America as *Raw Meat*. Alex Campbell (David Ladd) and his girlfriend Patricia (Sharon Gurney) are on the London tubes at night and discover a man lying on the steps. Alex says he is just a drunk and to leave him be, but Patricia, having something called human compassion, is worried about him and talks him into getting help, but when the police arrive they discover he is gone. This wouldn't be a huge deal for the police but it turns out the man in question has top secret military secrets and they don't like that he is missing. Little do they know something is lurking in the dark, something hungry and wanting human flesh.

Death Line is sadly not as fun or horror-inducing as it may appear from the lurid posters that show a herd of cannibal monsters, while in reality there is just one—well two until one dies early on. My biggest problem with this movie isn't the laughably misleading advertising, but that it's mostly filler with scenes that don't advance an already paper thin plot, and it seems like everything could have been wrapped up in half an hour. It's another case of an interesting idea that gets lost in its own plot and gets bogged down in excessive padding. The real bright spot is of course Donald Pleasence, and he is delightfully mad cap. Sure he chews every bit of scenery he can get ahold of and, whether he is totally drunk at the pub or constantly screaming for tea, he's a lot of fun to watch. And you gotta love his brief scene with another screen legend, Christopher Lee. It's a shame the scene didn't go on longer or hadn't been more memorable, because having two brilliant character actors together is not something you want to waste. The other highlight is the decent spattering of splatter throughout and some nice grisly scenes with the cannibal known only as "Man," played by Hugh Armstrong. But even this is tame and, considering the time this was made, it really did push the envelope when the film does finally get to the "meat" of the story. It's a real shame that the screenplay wasn't more polished because I think it had a lot of untapped potential. Even still, fans of grimy cheese from the '70s may find this amusing, but honestly the only reason to watch this is for Pleasence. May not be my cup of tea but depending on your trash mileage it might be yours.

TRIVIA: This film features both Donald Pleasence and Christopher Lee. Lee turned down the role of Dr. Loomis in *Halloween* (1978), which went to Pleasence—the film became a monster hit. Lee has said in interviews he often regretted the decision, but looking at Lee's resume, it obviously didn't hurt him one bit.

Demons of the Mind (1972)

DIRECTED BY	Peter Sykes
WRITTEN BY	Christopher Wicking, Frank Godwin (original story by)
STARRING	Robert Hardy, Shane Briant, Gillian Hills, Paul Jones, Michael Horden, Patrick Magee, Yvonne Mitchell, Robert Brown
COUNTRY	United Kingdom

Hammer returns to its Gothic roots in *Demons of the Mind,* another in its psychological thriller series after it had retired its monsters back to their crypts. Emil (Shane Briant) and his sister Elizabeth (Gillian Hills) are prisoners of their own house by order of their father Zorn (Robert Hardy). Zorn is a man obsessed with the notion that his children have inherited the same madness as there late mother. A shrink by the name of Falkenberg (Patrick Magee) is brought in to help the family but is it already too late? Peter Sykes and writer Christopher Wicking craft a wonderfully eerie and highly provocative little thriller that has more going for it than your run-of-the-mill psycho-chiller. Like all of Hammer's period films there is a great amount of details in the production design as well as some marvelous costume work that helps the audience lose themselves in the haunting story.

They wisely take advantage of practical exterior locations, and the rural setting helps give it a *Wicker Man* type of vibe. Sykes delightfully plays with the concepts of incest, fear, and madness, which can utterly consume a person's life. However, the problem is these ideas

and themes are never taken far enough to be cutting-edge, and the screenplay feels a tad bit underdeveloped. It also suffers from uneven tone, like it's hard to take the film seriously, with over-the-top moments like the villagers with flaming torches straight out of *Franken-stein.* The love subplot also feels shoe-horned in and not organic to the story. Furthermore, hammy over-acting also throws the film off balance and takes it down a notch Despite its shortcomings *Demons of the Mind* does manage to have a lot of unsettling moments and a thick sense of dread that permeates the entire film, due in part to some nice production values. Sadly, it doesn't go out on a limb with its own subject matter, but it's an entertaining enough return to the Gothic form which made the studio legendary and will be loved by hardcore Hammer fans.

Frightmare, aka Cover Up (1974)

DIRECTED BY	Pete Walker
WRITTEN BY	David McGillivray, Pete Walker (story by)
STARRING	Shelia Keith, Rupert Davis, Deborah Fairfax, Paul Greenwood, Kim Butcher, June Yule, Fiona Curzon, Edward Kalinski
COUNTRY	United Kingdom

What's in a name? Just as we try not to judge a book by its cover I implore fans to not judge this movie but its cheesy title. *Frightmare* is a sleazy, gore-soaked little gem from British cult icon Pete Walker. As usual, he doesn't merely push the envelope ,he gleefully sets it on fire while flipping us the bird. After spending fifteen years in jail for cannibalism Edmund (Rupert Davis) and Dorothy (Shelia Keith) Yates are free to return back into society. Dorothy's stepdaughter Jackie (Deborah Fairfax) tries to help sate her stepmother's desire for flesh by giving her raw meat from the butcher shop. However, it's not enough to keep the old gal from going on the hunt again for real human victims. Writing-wise this outing is a more complete and polished vision compared to the trashy and fun yet less-realized *The Flesh and Blood Show*. Characters are more fleshed out and the focus is more concentrated. Walker's trademark British domestic melodrama even serves the film and greatly enhances the utterly brilliant shock ending. It also includes the dead pan wit and wonderfully grim social commentary and satire that he is well known for. Thankfully, his message is not as pointed or heavy-handed as say *House of Whipcord* or *The Confessional,* allowing the film's entertainment to shine. Actress Shelia Keith, a bit player in Walker's other films, wisely gets a much meatier role, and *Frightmare* is the perfect vehicle for her. She is a cinematic force of nature and her uncommon looks and strange acting style make her oh-so-right for the role. It's no wonder her face was used on various promotional items. Classically trained actor Rupert Davies does a great job, and he and Keith have a strange but perfect chemistry together. Davis plays it totally serious, never winking at the audience, and it helps to anchor some of the madness. *Frightmare* is of course not perfect, and while it may never think outside of its own mad concept, it still manages to be a gritty, grimy piece of cinematic anarchy, and we can even forgive its more over-the-top aspects. Every frame is coated in an eerie walking dread, which builds and builds until a frenzied finale. In the world of weird British films Pete Walker is an unsung hero and this is certainly his best film. So if it's a bloody good cannibal flick you're hungry for, *Frightmare* will surely please.

Girly, aka Mumsy, Nanny, Sonny, and Girly (1970)

DIRECTED BY	Freddie Francis
WRITTEN BY	Brian Comport, Maise Mosco (based on play by)
STARRING	Michael Bryant, Vanessa Howard, Ursula Howells, Pat Heywood, Howard Trevor, Robert Swann, Michael Ripper, Imogen Hassall
COUNTRY	United Kingdom

Like offbeat Brit dark humor? Looking for something totally different? *Girly* might just be the flick for you. Living on a giant estate in a big house isn't all fun and games for Girly (Vanessa Howard) and her brother Sonny (Howard Trevor). Mumsy (Ursula Howells) and Nanny (Pat Heywood) dote on them but they also have set rules, because afterall, "were would we be without rules?" But their games are far more sinister then just hide-and-seek. The kids kidnap various men to be their "play mates" and force them to participate in various activities or else they'll have a trial and "get sent to the angels". The household is divided after "New Friend #2" enters the picture, and soon the kids aren't the only people playing dangerous games. The biggest problem with *Girly* is its wildly uneven tone. Seemingly, it's first and foremost a horror film; however, it also has overt comedy camp with elements of psychological thriller. This isn't a problem per se but the screenplay isn't strong enough to juggle all these themes successfully. Perhaps if the horror or psychological threads had been stronger it may have helped even out everything else. Also you have to gloss over a lot of plot holes and gaps in logic and sketchy character motivations. Part of the problem may lie in it being adapted from a stage play, because frankly some plays are very difficult to make a successful translation on to the big screen. Still, it's hard for me to actually hate this film despite its flaws. The sheer ridiculousness and the obvious tongue-in-cheek humor along with loads of sleaze and horror make it enjoyable. One thing you have to give Francis credit for, he certainly goes for it, for better or worse, and I find its no-shame, over-the-top lunacy endearing for the most part. *Girly* is a case of source material and concepts that get lost in the translation, with an underdeveloped screenplay filled with problems in logic and a rather dull leading man who doesn't quite carry the premise. Still, the film isn't terrible and for fans of over-the-top camp lunacy it's not a bad way to spend a hungover Sunday morning.

GOES WELL WITH: *The Anniversary, The Pit*

LOOK FAMILIAR?: The large castle-like house has been used in many Hammer Horror films; however, it's most famously featured in the original *The Rocky Horror Picture Show*.

Gothic (1986)

DIRECTED BY	Ken Russell
WRITTEN BY	Stephen Volk, Lord Byron (based on story), Percy Bysshe Shelley (based on story)
STARRING	Gabriel Byrne, Julian Sands, Natasha Richardson, Myriam Cyr, Dexter Fletcher, Timothy Spall, Alec Mango, Pascal King
COUNTRY	United Kingdom

When fans question if women can cut it in horror I merely have to point out that Mary Shelley, at the tender age of nineteen (published at twenty), wrote one of the greatest and long-enduring tales of terror ever put onto paper. Its legacy is unquestionable, and like the monster itself it remains immortal. And it all came about from an amusing writing contest between friends Lord Bryon and Mary and Percy Shelley. The result was *Frankenstein, or The Modern Prometheus.* Ken Russell, a filmmaker seemingly as misunderstood as the creature himself, sews together a film that is nothing short of genius. *Gothic* recounts the legendary visit of Mary and Percy Shelley and Mary's half-sister Claire Clairmont (Myriam Cyr), which produced the epic horror story. The trio spends a brutally stormy night consuming drinks laced with hallucinogens, and boundless madness and imagination ensues. High-energy and over-the-top, the film plays like one long nightmare that was ripped right out of our deepest, darkest subconscious. Visually the film is stunning, and Russell masterfully recreates the time period with painstaking details in both the lavish interiors and costumes. He perfectly captures the unrestrained decadence that overflowed with sex and drugs using his signature inventive camera work and gorgeous cinematography. The end result is a film equally horrific and beautiful and a feat of pure surreal expressionism madness. It also boasts a rather impressive cast, and Julian Sands and Gabriel Byrne turn in Oscar-worthy performances. Future *Harry Potter* villain Timothy Spall is also stellar and shows he can handle some intense scenes. Myriam Cyr is equally great and her part is as demanding as her male counterparts. On paper the story of a group of people stuck in a house one stormy night seems like a rather dull affair, but with a top-notch screenplay and unparalleled direction they capture a lightning storm of eroticism and psychological horror that culminated in the creation of one of the greatest horror stories ever written. Just amazing in every respect, this film is a must-see and I give it my highest recommendation.

Hands of the Ripper (1971)

DIRECTED BY	Peter Sasdy
WRITTEN BY	Lewis Davidson, Edward Spencer Shew (story by)
STARRING	Eric Porter, Jane Merrow, Angharad Rees, Dora Bryan, Lynda Baron, Keith Bell, Derek Godfrey, Norman Bird
COUNTRY	United Kingdom

After Hammer studio exhausted every monster and creature under the moon they decided to dip into a very British real-life horror, the murderer Jack the Ripper. It seems poor Anna (Angharad Rees) just can't catch a break. At a young age she suffers a very traumatic event involving, you guessed it, Jack the Ripper. Flash-forward to her adult life: We find she has been taken in by a Mrs. Golding (Dora Bryan), a rather loathsome woman who cons people for a living. She also pimps Anna out. When one gentleman gets too rough it ends badly with a bloody murder taking place. Of course, they place the blame on the girl and lock her up. Dr. John Pritchard (Eric Porter), a student of the Freudian form of psychiatry, springs her. His plan is to cure the poor girl, so now the doctor must unravel the web of darkness; a darkness which leads back to Jack! Peter Sasdy's *Hands of the Ripper* thankfully breaks the mold of other Ripper-based movies, as it doesn't focus on the original White Chapel murders but rather goes in a totally new direction. It manages to mix the traditional Gothic horror costume period (which put the studio on the map) with the emerging gore/slasher genre, spliced with the psycho thrillers made popular after *Peeping Tom* and Alfred Hitchcock's *Psycho*. And for the most part it all fits together well. The film hangs together because of a solid screenplay with a compelling story and engaging and developed characters. And while we're on the subject, it also does something horror movies of the time rarely did, which is showcase strong female characters. What sours the film, however, is a clunky romance subplot between Michael (Keith Bell) and Laura (Jane Merrow), which serves only to bring the main story to a grinding halt. While both actors do a fine job they have zero chemistry together. Though it can be a little slow at times *Hands of the Ripper* is a well-acted and directed film, which blends a host of subgenres together and surprisingly it meshes well. This coupled with some solid performances and genuinely nasty carnage, a bit of dark humor makes this an unsung Hammer gem that will make you think twice about booking a flight to England.

TRIVIA: Surprisingly, *Hands of the Ripper* is one of only two films the studio produced about Jack the Ripper. The other is *Room to Let* (1951)

Horror on Snape Island, aka Tower of Evil, aka Beyond the Fog (1972)

DIRECTED BY	Jim O'Connolly
WRITTEN BY	Jim O'Connolly, George Baxt (story by)
STARRING	Bryant Haliday, Anna Palk, Derek Fowlds, Jill Haworth, Anthony Valentine, Dennis Price, George Coulouris
COUNTRY	United Kingdom

Horror on Snape Island, better known in the US as *Tower of Evil,* is a sorely overlooked British horror film that is progressive in not only being a proto-slasher, it also may just be the first film to show male nudity—something that is a rarity even today. A group of American teens are savagely killed on a remote isolated island leaving one girl alive who is presumably the one who did it. The girl's family hired a private detective named Evan (Bryant Haliday) to find the real murderer and he joins a team of archaeologists that just happens to be going on the island looking for valuable artifacts. However, the group soon learns they are not alone and that the murders may have something to do with a treasured idol. The best way to describe the film is a sexy psychotropic little gore-soaked gem that has high concept on a low budget. The hazy, fog-drenched island and moonlit nights project an atmosphere that is more akin to Gothic horror rather than a standard dice-'em-up flick. It's not without its problems, and suffers from rather sizable plot holes and tends to get a little convoluted at times. Also, I wish they would have explored certain aspects of the mystical god in more depth. And while some of the practical effects are decent some are just downright laughable. Speaking of the effects, the splatter and gore are plentiful and nasty in places. And while it's not particularly inventive in that department it does feature a nice decapitation and numerous hacks with sharp objects. Surprisingly the film boasts an impressive list of actors including Dennis Price, cult favorite Bryant Holiday, and even George Coulouris, best-known for his role in *Citizen Kane,* has a small but memorable role. Most of the main cast is filled with hot hunks and beautiful babes known for their looks more than their acting skills, but it's not like we're watching a production of Shakespeare so it's perfectly servable. *Horror on Snape Island* is a deliciously macabre and refreshingly different film that offers a heaping helping of sex, blood, and some unintentional camp hilarity. But it's also a pre-cursor to the kinds of films that came in the wake of *Halloween,* and indeed you can even see this as an early example of the "mutant/hillbilly" subgenre which became popular after *Hills Have Eyes.* Criminally under-loved bloody good flick that gets a recommendation despite some of its shortcomings.

House on Straw Hill, aka Exposé, aka Trauma (1976)

DIRECTED BY	James Kenelm Clarke
WRITTEN BY	James Kenelm Clarke
STARRING	Udo Keir, Linda Hayden, Fiona Richmond, Patsy Smart, Karl Howman, Vic Armstrong
COUNTRY	United Kingdom

Sometimes a film can pleasantly surprise you, especially one that seems to be sadly ignored. *House on Straw Hill* is a trashy, sleazy, and wonderful little gem. Paul Martin (Udo Keir) is a very successful but quirky and paranoid writer who is working on his next big hit. He is working on an isolated farmhouse dubbed Straw Hill, which is only staffed with an elderly housekeeper. He decides to bring in a pretty young girl named Linda (Linda Hayden) to be his secretary. But the strange writer gets more than he bargains for as a weird mind game of cat-and-mouse ensues with bloody consequences. *House on Straw Hill* is a film that really sneaks up on you, and when you're not looking sucker punches you in the mouth. Clarke perfectly creates a strange vibe that is palpable, and it only gets more intense as the film goes along. He further teases the audience with clues to the big reveal all while ratcheting up the tension and an overwhelming feeling of claustrophobia. It is also overflowing with overt sexuality that adds a spicy element to an already tasty dish. The cast is small but really great, with Udo Keir perfectly cast as the neurotic writer (aren't we all?), and this film just reinforces why he is such a brilliant character actor. Legendary Hammer actress Linda Hayden also shines, and she and Kier have an interesting chemistry together. The violence is tame compared to today, but it does feature some nasty carnage with some decent effects work. Even when you think you have the ending pegged you don't, and there is a double twist ending, which admittedly forces the viewers to suspend a great deal of disbelief, but I still found it thoroughly satisfying. Clarke, a director with small filmography, comes out swinging in this erotic and blisteringly violent horror thriller that is hypnotically strange and wildly entertaining. An overlooked film that deserves your attention.

TRIVIA: This film made the infamous Video Nasties list in the UK for its violence and unsettling nature.

Killer's Moon (1978)

DIRECTED BY	Alan Birkinshaw
WRITTEN BY	Alan Birkinshaw, Fay Weldon (uncredited)
STARRING	Anthony Forrest, Tom Marshall, Georgina Kean, Jane Hayden, Pete Spraggon, Nigel Gregory, David Jackson
COUNTRY	United Kingdom

After Hammer and Amicus slowly went out of vogue, British horror began getting into the slasher market emerging in America. In fact one can even make the claim that they were ahead of the game with films like *Peeping Tom* and *Bay of Blood* as pre-*Halloween* proto-body count films. One thing you can say about Brit-slashers, even with various degrees of success they usually have an element of the bizarre. Four mental patients, who believe they are in an LSD-fueled dream as part of some radical therapy, are loose and on a killing spree in a sleepy rural countryside. As bad luck would have it a bus full of young female singers breaks down and they are taken in by a kind woman who owns an inn, which is closed for the season. And of course the crazies find their way to the innocent girls and mayhem ensues. *Killer's Moon* manages to build a decent and strange vibe right off the bat, highlighted by wacky dialogue and the infamous three-legged dog, which is wonderfully random, but does have a point in the story. Its rural setting, hazy drenched moonlit night, and the castle-like look of the inn also help to give it a classic Hammer Horror feeling. My main problem with the film is, while it has some entertaining moments, it also seems to be the same one note played to death and goes through the motions of a tepid game of cat-and-mouse all while playing its convoluted "dream" plot for everything it's worth. Still it's hard to outright hate this film, as it offers enough weirdness, nasty violence, and some splatter to make it passable despite its mostly stilted plot. Not the greatest example of British slashers but in a pinch you could do a lot worse.

Lair of the White Worm (1988)

DIRECTED BY	Ken Russell
WRITTEN BY	Ken Russell, Bram Stoker (story based on the book by)
STARRING	Hugh Grant, Amanda Donohoe, Catherine Oxenberg, Peter Capaldi, Sammi Davis, Paul Brooke, Stratford Johns
COUNTRY	United Kingdom

Ken Russell boldly took Bram Stoker's *Lair of the White Worm*, a critically panned book, and turned it into a critically praised film that is still highly regarded in the world of cult cinema. Angus Flint (Peter Capaldi), a young Scottish archaeologist, digs up an amazingly weird skull on what he later discovers is the accident ruins of a convent. Flint tells Lord James D'Ampton (Huge Grant), who recently inherited the title and the land, about his find, and James tells him the tale of a giant white worm that was slain by his family. It seems that the colorful story may be true and Flint may have found the worm's remains. Meanwhile, the very glamorous Lady Sylvia Marsh (Amanda Donohoe) slithers into her mansion after a nice hibernation. The large skull attracts her attention, and soon nothing will stop her from her quest for delicious virgins and to make the ultimate sacrifice to her god. Ken Russell has created some amazingly strange yet thought-provoking works of art and *Lair of the White Worm* is a prime example of his talent. The film acts as an updated grim fairy tale with Lord D'Ampton as a modern day Prince Charming off to slay dragons. This is further echoed by the beautiful use of Gothic interiors and lush exterior locations that really give it an off-"kilt"tered, once-upon-a-time feeling. Not only does Russell build a rich tapestry of folklore he of course throws in his trademark overt Catholic themes of sexual repression and the idea of original sin. There is even a bit where Lady Sylvia and a character aptly named Eve almost reenact the forbidden fruit story in the Bible. This also has a clever double meaning as Marsh is a serpent-like creature. He also injects a lot of dry British wit and dark humor that helps balance the more serious and trippy moments in the film. The cast is great, with Hugh Grant in an early film role. He has just the right amount of sardonic wit, semi-smug but at the same time awkwardly charming. Playing a duel role is Amanda Donohoe, who is both seductress and monster, and she pulls both off beautifully, never winking at the audience or playing it campy. Above I mentioned the wonderful look of the film, which is largely due to legendary Hammer DP Dick Bush (*Twins of Evil, Blood on Satan's Claw*), which gives the film an odd beauty yet hyper-psychotropic quality in equal amounts. Ken Russell does the horror writer Bram Stoker justice with his fresh interpretation of the material. Run, crawl, or slither your way to this bold and insane mind-binder of a master work.

Mum and Dad (2008)

DIRECTED BY	Steve Sheil
WRITTEN BY	Steve Sheil
STARRING	Perry Benson, Dido Miles, Olga Fedori, Ainsley Howard, Tobey Alexander, Mark Devenport
COUNTRY	United Kingdom

Lena (Olga Fedori) starts working at an airport where she meets Birdie (Ainsley Howard) and her adopted brother Elbie (Tobey Alexander). Circumstances lead to Lena missing her bus home and Birdie offers to put her up for the night. Little does she know that once at home she is drugged and held captive and forced to be "part of the family," which includes Mum (Dido) and stern Dad (Perry Benson). Director Steve Sheil's first feature is at best a mixed bag.

The biggest problem with *Mum and Dad* is once the novelty of the weird family wears off it's just another girl-held-captive movie. The film stretches its premise to the very breaking point with many scenes only serving to slow the film down. Now this is not to suggest this is totally horrible, and it has some good things going for it. The film is delightfully in-your-face brutal with some great over-the-top nasty bits that are just

strange enough to be memorable. Sheil also injects a lot of wicked humor, which helps soften the blow and keep it entertaining and not an endurance test. For example, the porn playing at the breakfast table while a (mostly) typical chatter is going on is a humorous juxtaposition and maybe even sly commentary on the family unit. The cast is solid, with actor Perry Benson playing the psycho patriarchy, and as always is brilliant and he throws himself head first into the role and walks a fine line, never getting too campy or carried away. Newcomer Olga Fedori is equally great and she really nails the role, giving a subtle yet believable performance. Ainsley Howard and Tobey Alexander are also quite good. When you consider the fact that this was Steve Sheil's first feature film it's impressive. He certainly has the director part down, getting stellar performances from his cast and creating some amazingly odd set pieces, the Christmas decorations being especially nice and grisly. However, where the film fails is a screenplay that could have done with more focus and development. If you're looking for a great alterative Christmas film to gross out your family, this nasty little Brit film may just do the trick.

Nanny, The (1965)

DIRECTED BY	Seth Holt
WRITTEN BY	Jimmy Sangster, Marryam Modell (based on novel by)
STARRING	Bette Davis, Wendy Craig, Jill Bennett, William Dix, Pamela Franklin, Jack Watling, Harry Fowler, Alfred Burke, James Villiers
COUNTRY	United Kingdom

Not to be confused with the '90s television comedy of the same name, this wickedly disturbing and darkly humorous film is a wonderful yet criminally overlooked gem in Hammer's fright catalogue. Master Joey (William Dix) has just returned home from a two-year stay at a hospital for mentally ill children after a horrible incident left his young sister dead. He seems to have a pure hatred for Nanny (Bette Davis), who looks after his ill and high-strung mother, Virginia (Wendy Craig) but is Joey's mistrust and hate for Nanny founded or is it all in his sick mind? Seth Holt's painfully overlooked psychological thriller, based on the novel by Marryam Modell, is a sheer macabre delight and wisely takes its time in unraveling a bleak story with some dark humor thrown in. Viewers used to Hammer's more traditional films like *Dracula: Prince of Darkness* may find it at times dull, as it's a film that really builds to its ending. Holt and Sangster (who previously worked together on *Scream of Fear*) weave a psychological game of cat-and-mouse and purposely keep the audience in the dark about key plot points, creating a degree of mystery leading up to a disturbing ending. It's also strange in very understated ways from the childlike neurotic

mother to the sexually curious Bobbie (Pamela Franklin), and the almost matter-of-fact way it handles the death of a very young child. Speaking of children, the film boldly switches the film's perspective almost totally on Joey's point of view and to a smaller degree to Bobbie's. The performances are surprisingly very good. Powerhouse star Bette Davis gives a wonderfully subtle and subdued performance as the titular character. Wisely, she is not as over-the-top as her second (and final) film for Hammer, *The Anniversary*, as the role calls for a more somber and creepy approach, which she nails perfectly. She almost projects a blank detached quality that is unnerving. William Dix and Pamela Franklin are stellar and turn in performances that are every bit as good as there grown-up counterparts. If you ever wanted to see a twisted version of *Mary Poppins* done as only Hammer could do during their psychological horror period, this is the film for you. *The Nanny* is a wonderfully dark and understated horror gem that deserves more recognition.

Peeping Tom (1960)

DIRECTED BY	Michael Powell
WRITTEN BY	Leo Marks
STARRING	Karlheinz Böhm, Anna Massey, Moira Shearer, Maxine Audley, Brenda Bruce, Miles Malleson, Martha Miller
COUNTRY	United Kingdom

Peeping Tom was released to an unsuspecting British public and was met with harsh criticisms and an outcry for its shocking subject matter. It was so bad that it virtually destroyed director Michael Powell's film career. Thankfully though, it has found a new life and critics now hail the film as a landmark in psycho-sexual horror. Mark Lewis (Karlheinz Böhm) is a man who loves making films; in fact it's an obsession. A young children's writer named Helen (Anna Massey) starts a friendship with him, but the more she learns about Mark's disturbed childhood the closer she gets to discovering his terrifying secret. Nowadays it's easy to take a film like this for granted, but when you view *Peeping Tom* you can't help but see how ahead of its time it was, tackling some really unnerving and twisted subject matter and not sugar-coating it for the audience. Indeed, this is why the film was hated at the time of its release, yet also why it's now widely praised by both critics and fans alike. And as much as I love *Psycho*, released the very same year, I have to admit, for me Powell slightly edges it out, and when you stack the two together *Tom* is far more intense and delves into darker places. In fact, in terms of the plot one could almost see this as a pre-cursor to the *Saw* films, with Powell introducing us to his twisted kill device. The film is also interesting how it blurs the line with its character of Mark and, yes, he's a monster, but you also see him as a victim himself, and it's jolting, especially since he's our viewpoint character. It's clear that Powell has a keen eye and his use of camera tricks and editing serves to heighten the storytelling and the suspense. Tense, twisted, and cleverly plotted this psycho-sexual thriller blazed a trail, and in doing so Michael Powell wrecked what was a bright career. If you want to see the true proto-slasher you need to go no further than *Peeping Tom*. Highly recommended.

TRIVIA: It's long been said that *Peeping Tom* was the first film to use the killer POV, a standard slasher device.

Scream . . . and Die, aka The House that Vanished (1974)

DIRECTED BY	José Ramón Larraz
WRITTEN BY	Derek Ford
STARRING	Andrea Allan, Karl Lanchbury, Maggie Walker, Judy Matheson, Annabella Wood, Alex Leppard, Edmund Pegge
COUNTRY	United Kingdom

If you're looking for weird Brit thrillers with healthy amounts of perversion and sex you can't go wrong with the films of José Ramón Larraz, who is just now finally getting some attention but still not nearly as much as he deserves. I'd even go as far as to say he and Pete Walker rank among my favorite British genre directors. A young model named Valerie (Andrea Allan) is talked into breaking into a house by her sleazy photographer boyfriend, and once inside the creepy house she witnesses a murder. Making matters worse her friend is nowhere to be found. Later, when she goes to look for the house, it's vanished. Valerie is soon flung into a strange psycho-sexual world of madness and horror. With Larraz's background in art, it's no surprise that his work has an interesting aesthetic that just drips with Gothic atmosphere lending to its surreal dreamlike quality. What really keeps things from getting tedious is the many twists and turns, and Larraz knows just how to racket up the tension while adding a layer of dread and mystery. Add to this plenty of quirky characters, weird randomness, like a pet monkey, and of course heaps of sex, and you really got something different and entertaining. He was never someone to shy away from the taboo, and a creepy incest subplot is explored, which only adds an extra layer of madness to an already nutty plot. The one problem with this and most of José's films is he doesn't write women very well, and our heroin sometimes comes off bubble-headed instead of strong and proactive. Also, while the plot is highly interesting it does get plodding at times and suffers from some holes in the story. Problems aside, I very much enjoyed the weird and perverse ride that Larraz takes us on, and even when he's slightly off he is still more interesting than most horror/thriller directors of his time. Fans of off-kilter British horror will have a blast with *Scream . . . And Die*, which I highly recommend.

Shout, The (1978)

DIRECTED BY	Jerzy Skolimowski
WRITTEN BY	Jerzy Skolimowski, Michael Austin, Robert Graves (story by)
STARRING	Alan Bates, Susannah York, Tim Curry, John Hurt, Julian Hough, Carol Drinkwater, John Rees, Susan Woodbridge
COUNTRY	United Kingdom

Fans of the less-is-more school of horror are bound to enjoy this little-known Brit gem from the late '70s. Anthony Fielding (John Hurt) is a musician living a rather humdrum life with his wife Rachel (Susannah York), until a weird man named Charles (Alan Bates) worms his way into their lives and turns everything upside down. What deadly secret does Charles possesses and what exactly is the shout? Rather than have a gore-soaked, slice-'em, *The Shout*

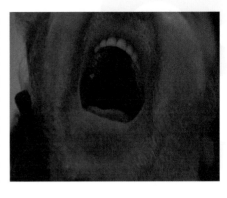

defies the horror genre norms of the time with a refreshingly bold and different story that keeps you guessing at every twisted turn. And while it has an interesting concept, it feels as if the story and its mythos could have used a great deal of expanding, and I was left wanting more. There are also some gaps in logic and plot holes, which again could have been taken care of had the story been more opened up. Where the film really redeems itself is its purposely slower pace, which builds a great deal of strange tension and a dreamlike, almost poetic quality.

The cast is great, with Alan Bates, John Hurt, and a young Tim Curry all giving great performances. Sadly though, Tim Curry is horribly under-used and, as much as I love Alan Bates in this, I actually think he would have been better in the role instead. Granted, at the time he was not the huge star he would later become, it is still just a shame to see a great talent like Curry wasted on the sidelines. Even with the film's issues it's really hard to outright hate this film because of its hauntingly weird and wonderfully different plot, which is carried by some excellent actors. I'm not huge on remakes but it may be interesting to see what a great filmmaker could do with this one. *The Shout* is worth seeking out.

Straight on Till Morning (1972)

DIRECTED BY	Peter Collinson
WRITTEN BY	John Peacock
STARRING	Shane Briant, Rita Tushingham, James Bolam, Annie Ross, Tom Bell, Harold Berens, John Clive, and Tinker as himself
COUNTRY	United Kingdom

Hammer slowly retired their stable of monsters for the ever popular psycho-thrillers that kicked off with *Peeping Tom* in the UK and *Psycho* in the US (both coming out the same year), and while I adored their Universal-style monster outings I am equally fond of their psychological horror.

Brenda (Rita Tushingham) lives in a world of fantasy, writing child's tales while wishing she would find her very own Prince Charming to take her away from her drab existence. Problem is she's not what you'd call attractive, and men seem to be put off by not only her looks but also her odd behavior. Fate and dog-napping lead her to meet Peter (Shane Briant), a handsome young man who is independently wealthy and proudly boasts that he never works, or do anything in fact. Like Brenda, he also lives in his own imagination and has a fixation on the tale of *Peter Pan*. Brenda tearfully confesses to him that she wants a child from him badly and he agrees, as long as she lives with him and takes care of the housework, etc. All seems to be going well, but cracks in Peter's mask begin to appear and soon she will learn the terrifying secret he keeps. Peter Collinson crafts an interesting little thriller using the less-is-more approach and creates a good amount of tension and a very weird vibe that never lets up until the finale. Another interesting move was to opt for a less bloody outing, further keeping with his more subtle approach to the material. This may disappoint splatter fans but in my opinion it works, giving it a more old school Hammer feeling. Thankfully, it does still manage to have some unnerving scenes; for example, the one involving Peter and his dog Tinker I found hard to watch. *Straight on Till Morning* isn't perfect by any meansl and its writing seems to suffer from some gaps in logic and a few contrived plot points. I also found the whole Peter Pan metaphor to be labored, and it is not clearly explained or explored. And while I find it refreshing that they strived for a more psychological angle it doesn't go quite deep or dark enough to be truly effective. *Straight on Till Morning* is something of a mixed bag; on the one hand, you have a barking mad and entertaining enough story that harkens to Hammer's glory days, but it doesn't go nearly far enough to really stand out among the other similar thrillers being made. Things are made worse by a sometimes underwhelming plot. Not a terrible Hammer outing but not brilliant either.

Symptoms (1974)

DIRECTED BY	José Ramón Larraz
WRITTEN BY	José Ramón Larraz, Stanley Miller, Thomas Owens
STARRING	Angela Pleasance, Peter Vaughan, Lorna Heilbron, Nancy Nevinson, Ronald O' Neil, Mike Grady, Raymond Huntley
COUNTRY	United Kingdom

It baffles me how a film that was praised so highly at Cannes the year it was entered could fade so quickly into obscurity. Thanks in large part to a rescued re-release with the help of the British Film Institute it has been preserved and given a new life. A young woman named Helen (Angela Pleasance) invites her friend Ann (Lorna Heilbron) to her home in an isolated yet beautiful part of the English countryside. But right away Ann notices that her friend seems to be acting very odd but dismisses it at first. However, as time goes on it's clear that Helen is hiding a dark secret that revolves around a missing girl named Cora (Marie-Paule Mailleux). But the deeper Ann digs to uncover the truth the more sinister things in the house become. For me, Larraz is a director who is always uneven in terms of hits and misses but one thing is clear, the man did have a strong visual language to his work, something that stemmed from his background in art. Indeed, some frames of the film look as if they could be gorgeous paintings. The look of *Symptoms* is an incredible mixture of lush beauty, yet at the same time hypnotically haunting. A thick layer of dread and foreboding hangs on every frame, and it's very much akin to a romantic era Gothic. Horror fans looking for a fast-paced kill fest will be sorely disappointed, but for the patient viewer the rewards are a slow burning unnerving film full of enough mystery to keep the film from becoming dull. I liked that care was taken to develop characters and establish a palpable mood, which very much serves the film well. It also takes a refreshingly different look at a person who suffers from mental illness, which isn't at all cheesy or ham-handed. The result is something startling, honest, and frightening. Bringing Helen to life is Angela Pleasance, who does an amazing job in the role, which is both natural and layered. Thankfully, the BFI helped to rescue this sublime psycho-sexual thriller from obscurity and it very much deserves to been seen. *Symptoms* is darkly poetic, brutal, and mesmerizing, even managing to be on par with such classics as Roman Polanski's *Repulsion*. I give this film my highest recommendation.

Torture Garden (1967)

DIRECTED BY	Freddie Francis
WRITTEN BY	Robert Bloch
STARRING	Jack Palance, Burgess Meredith, Beverly Adams, Peter Cushing, John Standing, Bernard Kay, Michael Bryant
COUNTRY	United Kingdom

Ah yes, Amicus. The less successful, but at times more interesting, little brother to Hammer Horror. One thing you have to give the studio, they did have some stellar output and their anthologies were pretty darn strange. At a carnival, the creepy and charismatic Dr. Diablo (Burgess Meredith) talks a group of strangers into taking an extra-special tour; not just any old spook show walkthrough but rather a look deep into their dark souls. Each one is instructed to look into the sheers of Atropos, a female deity of fate. And it's said that this fate could be changed if the viewer heeds its grave warning. *Enoch:* The first segment centers on Collin (Michael Bryant), a man obsessed with money. He visits his sick uncle Roger (Maurice Denham) and demands he tell him where he has hidden his fortune, and when he doesn't he denies him his medicine causing him to die. After the coroner takes the body away he begins a frantic search and unearths a coffin, and inside he finds not treasure but a black cat that jumps out. The cat it seems can psychically link with Collin, and in exchange for the gold he must bring the hungry cat victims. Certainly one of the more interesting segments; the problem is it seems far too ambitious for merely a short story and the rush is evident in its lackluster ending. Still it's just different enough to be entertaining, but I would have loved to see it as its own feature. *Terror Over Hollywood:* The second segment tells the story of Carla (Beverly Adams), a Hollywood wannabe that will do anything to be in the pictures, even if it means hurting people to get there. She soon discovers a terrifying secret behind the powerful men and women behind Tinsel Town. This is probably the weakest of the stories and, while the premise was interesting, the story was on the weak side and again it felt confided to its limited time slot. Even its decent twist ending felt like it could have been better had time allowed for a stronger build-up. *Mr. Steinway:* The third segment is about a lonely but world-renowned pianist named Leo (John Standing), who meets a young lady and falls in love with her. However, his piano, named Euterpe, is seemingly possessed and is jealous of his new love. Mr. Steinway is, in my opinion, the best segment, and its simple yet eerie plot doesn't suffer due to its runtime, and the ending is nicely done. Maybe not as ambitious in story as the rest but it's better realized and executed. *The Man who Collected Poe:* The final story focuses on a diehard Poe collector named Ronald (Jack Palance), who meets another collector named Lancelot (Peter Cushing). Ronald visits the collector and makes a shocking discovery, for Lancelot may just possess the ultimate rare item and it may just end of possessing him in the process. While not as good as the previous story the sheer presence of Cushing and Palance make this a lot of fun to watch. Story-wise it's decent, with some clever twists, but again the ending felt forced and underdeveloped. Overall, despite its problems, this anthology has things going for it, one of which is a wonderful cast, including the always-fun-to-watch Burgess Meredith. He is delightfully over the top and I wouldn't have it any other way. And of course Jack Palance and the legendary Peter Cushing and, as I mentioned above, seeing them work together is worth the price of admission. The writing, while deeply flawed, is a cut above most, and each story was interesting in its own way. Maybe not as gory or shocking as other horror anthologies made at the time, this little fright fest is enjoyable, and if you're sick of the same old Dr. Diablo has the cure.

Urge to Kill, The (1989)

DIRECTED BY	Derek Ford
WRITTEN BY	Derek Ford
STARRING	Peter Gordeno, Sarah Hope Walker, Jeremy Mark, Tiga Adams, Sally Ann Balaam, Maria Harper
COUNTRY	United Kingdom

Computers have certainly come a long way since the '80s and it's only a matter of time before we all bow down to our high tech overlords. But until that day comes sit back, relax, and take in this ridiculous slice of cheese stored under the "so-bad-it's-good" file. Bono (Peter Gordeno), a rich record producer is a tech junkie, wiring his entire house with a computer program he subtly named S E X Y. If there is anything he loves more than his lavish high-tech lifestyle it's women, lots and lots of them. But it seems his computer system has become self-aware and quickly becomes insanely jealous of the various girlfriends in Bono's life. Of course this jealousy turns deadly and the computer kills anyone that gets in her artificial way. Anyone searching this film's hard drive for an actual plot, with things like character development, logic, or really any sense of coherent filmmaking will almost surely come up error 404. The film meanders from one scene to the next, going through the motions only to provide plenty of moments of nudity sprinkled with violence and some tepid action. Needless to say the film is pretty awful, but if you're in the mood for mindless cheap thrills that are filled to the brim with ultra-sleaze and lots of unintentional comedy, this is the movie for you. It is also totally out of its mind, to the point of almost being surreal. *The Urge to Kill* is a movie for the midnight crowd looking for some worthless mind junk and camp value galore.

GOES WELL WITH: *Death Spa, Hardware*

Alice Sweet Alice, aka Communion, aka Holy Terror (1976)

DIRECTED BY	Alfred Sole
WRITTEN BY	Rosemary Ritvo, Alfred Sole
STARRING	Linda Miller, Paula E. Sheppard, Brooke Shields, Jane Lowry, Gary Allen, Niles McMaster, Rudolph Willrich
COUNTRY	United States

Sadly, some horror films from the '70s just don't age well, and for every amazing film like *Halloween* it seems like you have a dozen that just don't hold up. *Alice Sweet Alice*, however, is a rare example of a film only getting better with age. Karen (a very young Brooke Shields) is going to receive her first communion, a milestone in her young life. Her sister, Alice (Paula E. Sheppard), however, seems to be jealous of all the attention and gifts lavished on her. Tragedy strikes as Karen is senselessly murdered, and the last person to see her was Alice. Could this child have really committed murder or could someone else have reason to do the unthinkable? Alfred Sole's seminal masterpiece is an exercise in a director crafting a tension-filled movie that is plenty strange yet doesn't succumb to the pitfalls of most American horror films at the time. Right off the bat there is a thick layer of dread and perversion that only tightens like a noose as the film progresses.

Its unseen killer, quirky characters, and sometimes over-the-top performances very much give it an Italian Giallo feel. Bravely, the film breaks taboos such as killing a child and boldly uses the Catholic church as a backdrop for the story. Sole also injects some sly commentary as well as dark humor to help undercut some of the more unsettling aspects of the film. He also cleverly uses scene juxtaposition to further illustrate his wicked comedy. For example, the scene where uber-creepy landlord Alfonso calls Alice a bitch is quickly followed by a woman singing at mass. The film may go slightly into camp but since the film acts as one weird hyper dream it actually works in its favor. Even after more than four decades the film still remains disturbing and absolutely mesmerizing. Guilty pleasures don't come as sweet as *Alice Sweet Alice*.

TRIVIA: Ranked #89 *Bravo's The 100 Scariest Movie Moments.*

CRAZY CONNECTIONS: The film's composer, Stephen Lawrence, has won three Emmys for composing music for *Sesame Street.*

Attack of the Beast Creatures, aka Hell Island (1985)

DIRECTED BY	Michael Stanley
WRITTEN BY	Robert A. Hutton
STARRING	Robert Nolfi, Julia Rust, Lisa Pak, Robert Lengyel, Frank Murgalo, John Vichiola, Kay Bailey, Frans Kal
COUNTRY	United States

Have you ever seen a still from a movie that looked so far-out and wonderfully weird that you make it your life's mission to find out exactly what film it is so you can stuff it into your warped eye sockets? Such is the case with the terribly inept yet fun *Attack of the Beast Creatures*. Imagine, if you will, an island filled with poorly done Zuni fetish dolls (from *Trilogy of Terror*) and lots of bad melodrama thrown in. A group of men and women are shipwrecked on an island and must survive with little food and water. To make matters worse doll-like creatures inhabit the island, and they don't take kindly to strangers; they greet them not as friends but rather with murderous intent. Like *Black Devil Doll from Hell* this is a film that gained obscure cult infamy but seems to be relegated to the bottom of the cinematic barrel hardly seeing the light of day. A huge flaw with this film isn't its ultra-low budget or even its uninspired plot, but its deadly serious approach to the material and the ham-fisted "drama" only comes off as laughable. Worse yet even at a scant eighty-one minutes the film drags and stretches its threadbare plot to the very breaking point. The highlights, of course, are the attacks from the beast creatures that are so horribly done you can't help but find them endearing. Considering the material, the acting is not too terrible and everyone plays it without a single wink to the camera. I had a blast chatting with actor Frank Murgalo, who played Philip, and he confirmed that everyone, including director Michael Stanley, did not see the humor in the film. I have to say, hats off to the cast for even getting though a take with those puppets hanging off them. I'm really torn here because while I love the deliriously weird beast creatures and wonderfully random stuff like the lake of acid, the film just takes itself far too earnest for its own good and even fans of the so-bad-it's-good variety will no doubt find the pacing tedious. Had the filmmakers played up the inherent camp value and had some fun with it while also giving the plot more action this could easily have been a more enjoyable experience. Z-grade horror fans that don't mind wading through some padding will no doubt find this a trashy treasure waiting to be unearthed.

TRIVIA: The film was shot in chronological order due to budgetary reasons.

In an exclusive interview with actor Frank Murgalo he revealed that there was only one set of clothes for each actor and they were not washed for the entire two-week shooting period.

According to Frank Murgalo the effect of the boat sinking was achieved using a glass painting with the actors in the lifeboat in the foreground.

Interview with Actor Frank Murgalo (Paul)

MV: How long was the shoot? Do you recall?

FM: It was a two-week shoot on this island. We ate nothing but berries. I weighed ten pounds heavier at the end of two weeks then I did at the beginning of the shoot because we partied all the time, drinking and eating well.

MV: Where did they shoot this?

FM: It was shot in South Port and Fairfield. South Port was right on the beach overlooking multimillion-dollar mansions, and there was a golf course, and we had to try and get away from that.

MV: What's the one thing that really stuck out about the production?

FM: The thing was, nobody broke character; you thought you were dealing with Orson Welles. Nobody laughed at anything, there was no laughing on the set. One of the actresses spoke to me on the side and said, "Don't you think this is crap?" And I said, "Absolutely not. I guess you don't understand film." [laugh]

MV: [Laugh] That's awesome.

FM: [Laugh] I know, because the filmmakers were so serious and I don't know if they were trained in filmmaking. I wasn't sure. They came from money, I know that. It was their dream and they were serious and we were basically serious about it. Nobody saw the humor in it.

MV: That's interesting, because in my review of the film, the one major drawback was the fact that the material was taken so deadly seriously, but on the other hand you had these little puppet things.

FM: [Puppet chant]

MV/FM: [Laugh]

Axe, aka Lisa, Lisa (1974)

DIRECTED BY	Frederick R. Friedel
WRITTEN BY	Frederick R. Friedel
STARRING	Leslie Lee, Jack Canon, Ray Green, Frederick R. Friedel, Frank Jones, Carol Miller, Smith Hart
COUNTRY	United States

Axe may not be the strangest film in this chapter but it certainly has a weird, almost hypnotic, vibe that makes it a perfect fit in my opinion. Three criminal thugs go to rough up a guy (for some reason) and end up killing him. Now they are on the run and find a farm house in the middle of nowhere, seemingly the perfect place to hide out till the heat dies down. Living there is a girl and her paralyzed grandfather, which seems ideal for the outlaws. Little do they know, one of them is hiding a deadly secret and this will be anything but a peaceful stay in the country. The film opens with overt homophobia in the form of a wildly stereotypical gay guy who, of course, cross-dresses and is quickly and savagely beaten to death. It's regrettable, but I overlooked it, taking into consideration the time it was made. The film has an interesting setup but is beset by weak character motivations and plot holes that leave the audience scratching their head. Also, the acting, and I'm using that term rather loosely, is pretty much what you'd expect. But despite its shortcomings it is an entertaining and nasty little flick. *Axe* coasts a lot on its dime store Grindhouse charms, and Friedel is always ramping up the pervasion and grime factor until you feel like you want a shower afterwards. I love the fact that we know virtually nothing about any of the characters and it doesn't waste any time with clunky back stories. The filmmakers wisely take advantage of their shooting location and it helps give the film a feeling of isolated dread that gets tenser as the film goes on. With a name like *Axe* you'd think the film would be a splatter punk's dream yet the film is relatively tame on the gore front; however, this actually works in its favor. For the most part, we don't see the dismemberments but rather hear them off-camera and, considering its shoestring budget, is a more creepy and effective route to go. The murders are also filmed in a very cold matter-of-fact way that adds to its disturbing nature. This is required viewing for horror fans that love pure '70s chop'em up fare. *Axe* may not be the sharpest tool in the shed but what it lacks in polish it more than makes up for in trashy subversive fun.

Baby, The (1973)

DIRECTED BY	Ted Post
WRITTEN BY	Abe Polsky
STARRING	Ruth Roman, Anjanette Comer, David Mooney, Marianna Hill, Suzanne Zenor, Michael Pataki, Beatrice Manley
COUNTRY	United States

I discovered *The Baby* purely based on the cover at my local video shop. Prior to this I knew nothing about the film and its cult status. I saw the film and, one blown mind later, I was a lifelong fan. Ann Gentry (Anjanette Comer) is a plucky social worker whose life tragically comes apart when her husband is in a horrible auto accident. She takes an interest in a very strange case of Baby (David Mooney), an adult man who is dressed like and acts like, you guessed it, a baby. Living with Baby is Mrs. Wadsworth (Ruth Roman) and her two daughters, Germaine (Marianna Hill) and Alba (Suzanne Zenor). It's clear from the start that the family is furiously protective of Baby. But, as the social worker tries to do her job, things spinal out of control and Baby's diapers aren't the only thing that will get messy in the end. It's hard to find a weirder film made by a legit director using actors who have been in Oscar-winning films. *The Baby* is pure '70s oddball that will have even the most jaded of film buffs rubbing their eyes in disbelief. The strength of this film is that Ted Post and the actors play it totally straight without a single wink to the audience, which services to heighten the film's surreal aspects. A great cast is worth mentioning, and this film has some very interesting actors. The leader of the psycho clan, Mrs. Wadsworth, is played by the wonderful Ruth Roman. She is a pure cinematic treasure and, with her gravelly voice, no-nonsense attitude, and at times viciousness, it seems like she is channeling the great Joan Crawford. Not to be outdone is the amazing Scream Queen Marianna Hill (Blood Beach, Schizoid), whose hair seems to get bigger as the film progresses. Like Roman, she gives it her all and plays the character in such an odd wooden way that works for the film. Playing the younger of the two daughters is Suzanne Zenor. She, like the others, takes delight in chewing every bit of scenery, and that's alright in my book. Pacing is brisk with only a few scenes that could have used a tighter trim; however, it's really hard not to become bored with the pure level of insanity spread out before you. Gore hounds looking for a lot of the red stuff might be disappointed, but fear not, as there are plenty of nasty little surprises and some moments that are downright disturbing. Without any spoilers, this film has one of the best WTF endings that even left my fellow horror head friend in disbelief. *The Baby* is something that oozed out of the Grindhouse era and it still has the power to both grip its audience and even shock them. With loads of sleaze, some decent twists, and lots of camp, this film is endlessly entertaining for lovers of over-the-top '70s trash. It should be considered required viewing and truly needs to be seen to be believed.

GOES WELL WITH: *The Redeemer, Whatever Happened to Baby Jane?*

Bad Biology (2008)

DIRECTED BY	Frank Henenlotter
WRITTEN BY	Frank Henenlotter, R.A. The Rugged Man
STARRING	Anthony Sneed, Charlee Danielson, Tina Krause, James Glickenhaus, Krista Ayne, R.A. The Rugged Man, Mark Wilson, Beverly Bonner
COUNTRY	United States

After more than a decade away, exploitation master Frank Henenlotter makes an incredible return with *Bad Biology*. Fans of Henenlotter rejoice as it's very clear he has not lost his flare for the wonderfully bizarre and gripping storytelling. All of the trademarks that make his films so damned entertaining are front and center. They include twisted sex and nudity, over-the-top violence, and of course, a biting dark sense of humor. The story is clever and, thankfully, it doesn't have the feel of a museum piece of his gory days, I mean glory days, as the writing is fresh with a gritty urban flavor. It's really interesting that a religious theme runs throughout (something not seen in his previous work) and it surprisingly meshes well. Wisely, he plays up the more campy elements and the comedy balances everything quite well. Plus, it features a penis monster, so yeah . . . Actors Anthony Sneed and Charlee Danielson both do outstanding jobs and their earnest performances help anchor the wacky plot. *Bad Biology* is a witty, dark splatter fest with a wonderfully cerebral plot that is sure to please old fans and new alike. Required viewing.

Basket Case 2 (1990)

DIRECTED BY	Frank Henenlotter
WRITTEN BY	Frank Henenlotter
STARRING	Kevin Van Hentenryck, Annie Ross, Judy Grafe, Heather Rattray, Beverly Bonner, Chad Brown, Leonard Jackson
COUNTRY	United States

The first *Basket Case* could easily fit this book like a pus-filled glove; however, in terms of sheer insanity, the prize really has to go to the first sequel. The film starts right where part one left off with our hapless hero Duane (Kevin Van Hentenryck) dangling from the Hotel Broslin. After falling, he and his twisted conjoined brother, Belial, are taken to a nearby hospital. A kindly old woman named Granny Ruth (Annie Ross) owns a safe haven for human oddities and takes them both in. There they meet a host of outrageous freaks that welcome them into their new home. But just as they are getting settled in, a nosy journalist working for a trashy news rag will stop at nothing to get the story of the "freak brothers." Wisely, Frank Henenlotter

chose not to simply remake the first film like so many directors do in sequels, but rather take the mythos he created in the first and expand the universe with exciting new characters, locations, etc. Thankfully, what does stay the same is his penchant for dark comedy that zings, and the film is littered with clever inside references. FX wizard Gabe Bartel gives Belial an upgrade and does an outstanding job breathing new life into the monster. He also takes great pains to craft the numerous freaks that inhabit the film, and each is deliriously weird and incredibly well-done. The cast is great with Kevin Van Hentenryck returning as Duane, and it's a blast watching his character get more insane as the film progresses. Jazz legend Annie Ross is an absolute treat to watch as Granny Ruth and she brings a nice warmth to the role. Also making a cameo is Beverly Bonner who reprises her role as Casey from the first film. *Basket Case 2* plays to its delightfully absurd strength, and it's one of the reasons why it's my favorite of the trilogy.

CRAZY CAMEO: Jason Evers, who starred in the cult classic *The Brain that Wouldn't Die,* plays the editor. This was his last feature film.

Writer/Director Frank Henenlotter on Casting Annie Ross (Granny Ruth)

I just cast her. I had another actress in mind originally. When I wrote the script I really saw Granny Ruth as a very old woman. And I was really thinking of this other woman, and they told me we could never get insurance for her, also she probably couldn't take the strain of making the film. So with that in mind, totally new mindset, I started looking at headshots of people available, and when I saw Annie Ross I'm thinking, "Oh my God, she would be perfect." I mean, Jesus, I knew her from her jazz music and knew her from films like Throw Momma from the Train. I invited her in to meet me, she was such a lovely person, and one of the funniest people I have ever met. I immediately couldn't see anyone else in the part.

Originally printed in *Scream Magazine,* Issue# 5. Questions and interview conducted by Michael Vaughn

Begotten (1990)

DIRECTED BY	E. Elias Merhige
WRITTEN BY	E. Elias Merhige
STARRING	Brian Salzberg, Donna Dempsey, Stephen Charles Barry, James Gandia, Daniel Harkins, Michael Philips
COUNTRY	United States

Begotten tells the surreal and bleak story of the death and rebirth of gods. Even as a fan of transgressive cinema I really wanted to like this gory chunk of '90s indie cinema. Sadly though, I found the overall effect boring rather than exciting. I feel like this would have made an amazing short film but it really loses something stretched out to feature length. It's a shame, because Merhige obviously has a bold and interesting style and he creates some truly nightmare-inducing imagery. This unique vision would carry over to his feature *Shadow of the Vampire,* a wonderful and underrated film. Some hints of greatness that get bogged down in its own creativity. Worth a look at only but not something you'll likely revisit again.

Black Devil Doll from Hell (1984)

DIRECTED BY	Chester Novell Turner
WRITTEN BY	Chester Novell Turner
STARRING	Shirley L. Jones, Keefe L. Turner, Chester Tankersley, Marie Sainvilvs, Ricky Roach, Willie Kinerman
COUNTRY	United States

Some movies tend to claw themselves up from out of the toxic ooze that languishes at the bottom of the cinematic barrel, refusing to fade into obscurity. Such is the case with *Black Devil Doll from Hell*, a film that I've often heard about but finally prepared myself mentally to actually watch. The plot centers around a good Christian woman who finds a puppet at a local thrift store. She is given a very ominous (and hard to hear because of the Casio [but more about that later]) warning that the doll has a weird power and it always returns to the store. She, of course, ignores this and takes him home only to find out it's alive —it then proceeds to rape her. Now with a taste for lust, she turns in her Bible for the pleasures of men. Well, I certainly wasn't disappointed in the weird department, but anyone expecting a killer doll movie a la the *Child's Play* series might feel cheated. So, let's get this out of the way right now, this movie is terrible, from its ear-piercing and ridiculous use of a Casio keyboard to laughable "acting," a horrible screenplay, lighting, and generally no sense of what actually makes a film. However, its unintentional humor and overall ineptitude make it worth its weight in camp gold, and even though it tends to meander from one scene to another, it's hard to take your eyes off this cinema train wreck. I also love how this movie has absolutely zero morals and the "message" of the film is basically that a night of forced intercourse led the main character to promiscuity, overpowering her previous piety. The titular doll is a cross between Chucky and Dave Chappelle's Rick James character, and you can't help but laugh when he curses a blue streak. Also, I've never seen a human-puppet sex scene and thankfully it wasn't a film trend that caught on. Only for the truly brave who are looking for some sheer insanity and hilariously bad filmmaking in equal doses. Gather up your friends, get the cold beverages flowing, and get ready to watch one of the greatest (and only) evil doll Christian films ever.

TRIVIA: A comedy remake simply called *Black Devil Doll* was released in 2007.

Blood Feast (1963)

DIRECTED BY	Herschell Gordon Lewis
WRITTEN BY	Allison Louise Downe, David F. Friedman (story), Herschell Gordon Lewis (story)
STARRING	William Kerwin, Mal Arnold, Connie Mason, Lyn Bolton, Scott H. Hall, Christy Fourshee, Astrid Olson, Gene Courtier
COUNTRY	United States

What was the first "gore" or splatter film? Well just like the origins of the slasher sub-genre it's a subject that is hotly debated. However, if we were looking for a smoking gun, *Blood Feast* would definitely rank high on the list. A series of bizarre murders take place, baffling police. It seems that a man named Fuad Ramses (Mal Arnold) is cooking up a blood feast for a 5,000-year-old goddess. The idea of basing a horror movie on Egyptian lore is pretty clever, but sadly the film takes its interesting plot and stretches it painfully thin with needless padding. The really interesting material involving Ramses takes a back seat to a tepid clichéd detective story featuring maybe the worst police force in cinema history. Many of the scenes merely show the two officers talking about the case rather than investigating, finding clues, and moving the story forward. Oh, and one of them has the bright idea to question every single old male in the area; yeah, let that sink in. And the acting is so amateur and over the top it's hard not to burst into uncontrollable laughter. The infamous gore that the film built its success on is also horribly dated and isn't helped by its high definition re-master which showcases every flaw. Even though the film has its share of problems it's still very much worth checking out with its built-in kitschy camp value, deliriously weird plot, hammy acting, and intentional and unintentional humor. While it may not hold up as well by today's standards it's still a vastly important film in the horror genre and therefore should be respected for its trailblazing carnage that many filmmakers still use today. So get a bloody eyeball full of this wonderfully weird and wild piece of early '60s drive-in cinema.

TRIVIA: As a publicity stunt vomit bags were given out to theater-goers.

The film was remade in 2016.

Blood Freak (1972)

DIRECTED BY	Brad F. Ginter
WRITTEN BY	Brad F. Ginter, Steve Hawkes
STARRING	Steve Hawkes, Dana Cullivan, Heather Hughes, Bob Currier
COUNTRY	United States

Some films defy any kind of logic and sanity. Such is the case with this eye-popping early-'70s monster movie that will make you think twice about turkeys. Biker Herschell (Steve Hawkes) offers road assistance to Anne (Dana Cullivan), a pretty religious girl, and she takes him back to her place to pray their brains out. There he meets Anne's wilder sister, Angel (Heather Hughes), who seduces him and talks him into smoking pot, and he instantly becomes an addict. Herschell gets a job at a local turkey farm where he meets two scientists that offer him extra money to test out chemicals in turkey meat. Um yeah . . . So Herschell being the bright lug that he is sees no down side in this.

To his horror and the audience's bemusement, the tainted turkey meat turns him into a killer most "fowl", sporting a cheaply made turkey head that has a bloodlust, preferably the blood of drug addicts, of course. This movie puzzles me in what its point was. Its heavy-handed anti-drug message and religious overtones seem out of place in a bloody monster flick. It's never quite clear if this was meant to have a serious message or not as the movie is played dead pan serious with zero sense of irony or humor. Whatever the intention is the camp value is extremely "high" Let's talk turkey (I mean cast). Playing the motorcycle simpleton-turned-blood-gobbler Herschell is Steve Hawkes who also co-wrote the film. Honestly, I've seen better acting in porn films, and he looks as if he's half asleep in every scene he's in. I'd say stick to the writing but it's very evident he shouldn't do that either. Dana Cullivans and Heather Hughes are also not going to win any awards with their wooden acting. And then we have director Brad F. Ginter who also plays the narrator; basically he just sits at a table while chain smoking and spouts pointless philosophical nonsense. It's just strange to the max. Towards the end he talks about the dangers of weed and seconds later nearly coughs up a lung from his cigarette. Again, is this supposed to be ironic? Who knows? Certainly not the filmmakers. Despite the film's many issues I have a soft spot for this overcooked bird, and fans of brain-melting, z-grade cinema will agree it's worth flocking to see. I, like others I know, make this a yearly tradition on Thanksgiving. Your mileage may vary, but if you enjoy the so-bad-it's-glorious you will dig this crazy train wreck. And that's no jive turkey.

GOES WELL WITH: *Blood Rage, The Baby*

Blood Harvest (1987)

DIRECTED BY	Bill Rebane
WRITTEN BY	Ben Benson, Emil Joseph, Chris Vaalar (story), William Arthur (story)
STARRING	Tiny Tim, Dean West, Itonia Salcheck, Peter Krause, Lori Minnetti, Frank Benson, William Dexter, Albert Jaggard
COUNTRY	United States

Bill Rebane, the Wisconsin schlock master, tried his hands at the slasher genre and used possibly the greatest bit of stunt casting of the decade. Tiny Tim was already a cult icon with his odd looks and crazy high singing voice so casting him as a psycho clown seems like a stroke of mad genius. Jill (Itonia Salcheck) is a college student returning to her hometown, which is tense, because she is the daughter of a hated bank owner who is currently foreclosing on a lot of farms in the area. Meanwhile, someone is preying upon the people of the small town. Could it be Mervo (Tiny Tim), a deranged man that dresses like a clown? As I stated above Tiny Tim was well-known for his offbeat looks and different voice so putting him in creepy clown makeup is a smart idea and likely to cause a few sleepless nights. But does this film transcend its novelty casting? Sadly, it does not. First of all, this film is terribly misleading from its promo art, and fans hoping for a killer clown movie in the vein of *100 Tears* or *KillJoy* will be sorely disappointed. Also, this film bogs itself down in a confused and contrived plot which further suffers from horrible padding and pointless melodrama. It feels like Tiny Tim's character was shoe-horned into the plot, like he was written in as an afterthought. Speaking of which, Tim is surprisingly good and with his naturally weird charms manages to be genuinely off-putting. With a better script this would have been a perfect vehicle for him. The rest of the actors turn in performances that are pretty much what you'd expect from a low-budget outing such as this. Rebane's *Blood Harvest* feels like just a hollow attempt to cash in on the already dying horror subgenre which is tame in the splatter department but, worst of all, plays like a soap opera with thriller/mystery elements haphazardly jammed in. A promising concept and some great casting of Tiny Tim just couldn't save this clichéd and severely underdeveloped outing. Worth checking out if only for its strange star but don't expect much in any real horror.

TRIVIA: Peter Krause, actor of such hits as *Six Feet Under* and *Parenthood,* made his acting debut in this film, though I'm sure he's loathe to admit it.

Blood Rage, aka Nightmare at Shadow Valley (theatrical re-cut [1987])

DIRECTED BY	John Grissmer
WRITTEN BY	Bruce Rubin
STARRING	Louis Lasser, Mark Soper, Julie Gordon, Marianne Kanter, James Farrell, Lisa Randall, Douglas Weiser
COUNTRY	United States

As I'm writing this it's the day after Thanksgiving, it's cold outside, and I couldn't think of a more perfect thing to do than to eat leftovers and watch a totally off-its-meds slasher film. The year is 1974, and Maddy (Louise Lasser) is getting hot and heavy at the drive-in. Problem is, her twin sons Todd and Terry are peacefully snoozing in the back. The little buggers sneak out, however, and Terry brutally murders a fellow drive-in patron. He quickly frames his brother, Todd, who spends ten years in an asylum. On Thanksgiving Day, he escapes and he's coming home. Maddy's new romance triggers the real killer to wreak his revenge. You may have noticed I haven't included a lot of slasher films in this book because many simply aren't really that strange. But I felt like I needed to include *Blood Rage,* which is bonkers. I admit I came late to this film but now I'm hooked. John Grissmer plays this film like a love letter to other slashers, most notably *Halloween* (the opening in the drive-in is a prime example), yet it has its very own grisly charms to make it stand on its own. One element that makes this movie so nuts is Lasser;s character, Maddy. First off, they make her up to look like a little girl (her clothes and her hairstyle) which makes it both off-putting and humorous. Taking this a step further is some of the bizarre things she does that range from binge eating in front of the refrigerator spread-eagle, maniacally cleaning the house while drinking, or being passed out also spread-eagle. This brings me to what makes this movie so magical—its wicked sense of humor. The film nicely juxtaposes horror and tongue-in-cheek comedy which works in the film's favor. It walks a fine line of taking itself just seriously enough but still let's itself have some fun. Is the film brilliant? No, not really. It's over the top, the acting is bordering on camp, and the plot is nothing you haven't already seen before. But what makes this film special is its dark humor, great kills, and off-beat charm. I only wish they would have played up the Thanksgiving Day theme more. Along with *Blood Freak, Blood Rage* makes a great Turkey Day movie! It's just a lot of fun.

TRIVIA: Horror fans will no doubt notice the cameo by Ted Raimi, brother of Sam Raimi. He plays the condom salesman at the drive-in.

Special effects legend Ed French has a small acting role.

Bloodsucking Freaks, aka The Incredible Torture Show (1976)

DIRECTED BY	Joel M.Reed
WRITTEN BY	Joel M.Reed
STARRING	Seamus O'Brien, Luis De Jesus, Allan Dellay, Niles McMaster, Viju Krem
COUNTRY	United States

Few Grindhouse movies have achieved the kind of infamy as Joel M. Reed's deliriously wonderful film *Bloodsucking Freaks,* and after all these years it still both shocks and repulses some and delights others. Whatever your views may be, it certainly is a film that has stayed in pop culture. Master Sardu (Seamus O' Brien), along with his pint sized assistant Ralphus (Luis De Jesus), operates a very grimy Grand Guignol-style show, featuring various tortures and acts of sadism. Certainly it's all just a show, right? Sardu also operates a white slavery ring to make extra money. The audience is filled with the normal shocked viewers but this particular night, theater critic Creasy Silo (Alan Dellay) is in attendance and is less impressed with what he sees. In fact, he lets it be well-known that he thinks the show is a piece of trash. Also in the audience are ballerina Natasha DeNatalie (Viju Krem) and her football star boyfriend Tom Maverick (Niles McMaster). Inspiration strikes and Sardu must have Natasha dance in his show and get his revenge on the critic all at the same time, while achieving legit status for his show. *Bloodsucking Freaks* is a gleefully mad cap gross-out film and one could see it as satire of the gory films of the decade. Reed's use of the theater critic is an obvious and very clever stab at film critics that love to dig there poison pens in films that they don't deem "high art". Also, the notion that Sardu can make this "show" more legit with a star could easily also be said about a film. Also, listen to what Sardu says before introducing himself to the crowd: "This is just a theatrical presentation, a show which offers no reality, not a fraction, and just allows us you and me to delve into or grossest fantasies far beyond eroticism." And when the critic is kidnapped he calls the situation, "trite and theatrical," another wink at the film audience. Before you think I'm pretentious for trying to find deeper meaning in this film, I am merely pointing out that this film is more than just mindless violence, but injects some sly commentary. But rest assured, this movie is about entertainment first and foremost, but it does sprinkle in great inside jokes that are brilliant. The cast is above average, with the wonderful Seamus O'Brien delightfully chewing scenery. His comedic timing and dry wit play perfectly with the character. The true scene-stealer, however, is Luis De Jesus who plays Ralphus. You can't help but be creeped out and at the same time charmed by him. And sure, I've been known to do the Ralphus happy dance in private. Like O'Brien, he has good comedic timing and both have odd but wonderful chemistry together. Joel Reed manages to fill his movie with just about every torture and crazy taboo with much mirth and merry that will be sure to please even the most jaded of gore fans. Ironically, like in the film, critics have taken this film far too seriously, failing to see its comedy and satire. They are just being a Silo stick in the blood, I mean mud. After all, like Sardu says, it's just a way to explore our grossest fantasies. Gutter Punk Grime at its finest! A must-see.

Blue Sunshine (1978)

DIRECTED BY	Jeff Lieberman
WRITTEN BY	Jeff Lieberman
STARRING	Zalman King, Deborah Winters, Mark Goddard, Robert Walden, Charles Siebert, Ann Cooper
COUNTRY	United States

Jeff Lieberman taps into the drug culture scene in this highly strange Grindhouse film. It's just your typical party with drinking, music, and you just know someone is going to make a fool out of themselves. Suddenly someone at the party freaks out and kills a bunch of people after someone rips off his wig. A fellow partier, Jerry Zipkin (Zalman King), is falsely accused of the crime and must solve the mystery of blue sunshine before it's too late! *Blue Sunshine* has an interesting concept and I think that's where the film is at its strongest. I just wish that he would have explored that deeper, but instead what we end up getting is a glossed-over "Wrong man accused" film with LSD-freaked-out bald people. It also could have also played more with the drug culture and added some much needed levity. Some unintentional humor comes from the overacting and the over-the-top camp aspect of the maniacs. The film does do a capable job of building the mystery while also providing enough action to not be boring. Also, I liked the political humor that was injected throughout the film. Even though this movie is not very visual it can't be understated how genuinely striking and weird the people look completely bald, especially the actress Ann Cooper (wisely featured in promotional material). It is quite a sight to see her in a bathrobe, bald, and chasing children with a huge knife. It's both comical and disturbing. Jeff Lieberman will always have my respect for his original ideas, I just wish his films had stronger screenplays that would allow those strong concepts to really flourish. *Blue Sunshine* is a great idea but with a lackluster screenplay that pigeon-holes itself, it's hard to say this is a great film. However, it's "wigged out" psychos and over-the-top acting gives it a camp quality and makes it a must-see for the midnight crowd. So, if you're in the mood for a psychedelic freak-out this is sure to be a fun "trippy" film experience.

Brain Damage (1988)

DIRECTED BY	Frank Henenlotter
WRITTEN BY	Frank Henenlotter
STARRING	Rick Hearst, Gordon MacDonald, Jennifer Lowry, Theo Barnes, Vicki Darnell, Lucille Saint-Peter, John Zacherle as Aylmer
COUNTRY	United States

Deranged genius Frank Henenlotter's answer to Nancy Reagan's "Just Say No" program, this deliciously mad cap horror film has chewed up brains as well as horror. Brian (Rick Hearst) is just a typical guy until he finds a mysterious phallic-like creature named Aylmer (voiced by John Zacherle) who, by drilling into his brain stem via his tongue, gives him a mind-blowing trip filled with color and excitement. But like any junkie he wants more, which is just fine with his new pal, as long as he supplies him with fresh brains to eat. Henenlotter always makes interesting films, and instead of just simply doing a typical slasher or supernatural horror, *Brain Damage* is a pitch-black horror comedy that also acts as a not-so-thinly-veiled metaphor for drug addiction and its effects on people's friends and family. But thankfully, the film's message takes a backseat to the entertainment, and it never gets self-righteous or preachy. The story is highly creative and takes enough care to give Aylmer a rich mythos instead of just taking the lazy route. Everything moves at a very brisk pace with no padding and never a dull moment in sight. As always, the film features Henenlotter's delightfully warped sense of humor, which is always on point and never feels forced or glib. Gore fans will not be disappointed, as the film has plenty of splatter and outrageous brain-munching carnage. The acting is much better than you might expect, and leading man Rick Hearst gives a good, albeit zany, performance as our hapless hero. At its bloody core *Brain Damage* is a loving homage to B-monster films of the '50s and '60s with a decidedly more edgy twist. Highly recommended

CAMEO: Kevin Van Hentenryck makes an appearance as Duane from *Basket Case*. He can be seen on the subway holding, of course, his brother.

TRIVIA: Legendary horror host Zacherle the Cool Ghoul lends his voice to Aylmer.

Bride of Frank (1996)

DIRECTED BY	Steve Ballot
WRITTEN BY	Steve Ballot, Allan Galperin, Billy Morgan, Alley Ninestein
STARRING	Frank Meyer, Johnny Horizon, Victor Delvalle, Bruce Frankel, Morgan Tara, Rena Ballot, Arnell Dowret
COUNTRY	United States

Somewhere deep down in the bubbling, oozing toxic waste of forgotten cinema lies *Bride of Frank*, a late '90s film that certainly went for something totally nuts, and its vision is uncompromising. Frank (Frank Meyer) is an elderly man with a steady job, lots of crazy friends, and several stray cats he calls his babies. It seems like he has it all, but Frank has an obsession with large breasts, and he goes on a quest (aided by his co-workers) to find that special lady. However, his hunt seems to end up bloody, but can this lonely guy find true love or will he keep leaving his dates in pieces? Well, I wanted to find the weirdest that cinema had to offer and I got all that and more with this totally out-of-its mind comedy horror about the misadventures of a factory worker and his large sexual appetites. The humor is pretty raunchy and, while I'm all for comedy pushing the limits of good taste, some of its jokes are just lame (unless you're a teenage guy) and feels ham-handed. The other problem is it gets a bit repetitive and the result is the edgy material loses its sting. Like many first-time filmmakers, Steve Ballot throws a lot of ideas at the screen to see what sticks and what you have is a messy and aimless plot that suffers from uneven tone and needless padding. Even though the film has problems keeping its focus, *Bride of Frank* is still a mind-bender of a film that doesn't just push the envelope, it tears it to shreds and shoves it down the audience's throat. With touches of John Waters and David Lynch the pitch-black humor works well at times, and I loved the wildly gross-out moments and the hint of surrealism thrown in for good measure. Yes, it has its share of problems, but I have to give this filmmaker props for not playing it safe and delivering a film that is altogether different and, at the end of the day, it did (for the most part) entertain me. It's sad that Steve Ballot never made another film because I could see raw talent through its rough edges. Not for those easily offended but deliriously mad cap and refreshingly different.

Bucket of Blood, A (1959)

DIRECTED BY	Roger Corman
WRITTEN BY	Charles B. Griffith
STARRING	Dick Miller, Barboura Morris, Ed Nelson, Julian Burton, John Brinkley, Anthony Carbone, Judy Bamber
COUNTRY	United States

I mentioned in my introduction how much Roger Corman's film *Little Shop of Horrors* changed my cinematic world. Ever since then I've been a big fan of his work, the good, the bad, and the ugly. I even had the extreme pleasure of meeting him. *A Bucket of Blood* is a fun camp film along the lines of *Little Shop* and is just as weird. Walter Paisley (Dick Miller) is a hardworking meek busboy at a local beatnik joint. But he has aspirations to be an artist and, after a bizarre twist of fate, makes a clay cat out of a real cat that he accidently kills. All of a sudden Walter is the toast of the art scene and is hailed by the beatniks as a modern genius. Through another accident Paisley kills a man and decides the best thing to do is to cover him up with clay, like the cat. His art cred grows along with his ego and soon he has money, fame, friends, and maybe even Carol (Barboura Morris), a girl he likes. Can Walter keep his diehard fans from discovering his vile secret to his success? Fans will have a howling good time with Corman's outrageous low-budget horror comedy take on not only beatnik culture but the art world. What makes this film work is how relatable and likeable Walter is, and you can't help but root for him. Bringing him to life is the great character actor Dick Miller (*Gremlins, Terminator*). Miller is typically a bit player but this is a rare time when he carries a film. He brings a real sweetness and almost childlike innocence to the role, which is endearing. Legendary screenwriter and long-time Corman colleague Charles B. Griffith pens a clever and briskly paced film. Admittedly, it's not very plot-heavy and it's predictable, but it takes an absurd concept and runs with it, even if it is ridiculous and kind of silly. It also lampoons beat culture and the hypocrisy of the art world in a very clever and funny way. Lots of talent went into a film that is rightly considered one of Roger's best. Like most of his films, it suffers from a painfully low budget, but what it lacks in funds it more than makes up for in fun and has loads of offbeat retro charm. Corman and crew have a gleefully macabre time taking pot shots at the beatnik scene in this wildly weird low-budget outing. A film that should be seen by everyone!

TRIVIA: Horror legend H.G. Lewis has credited this film with inspiring *Color Me Blood Red,* the final film in his Bloody trilogy.

Blood belongs to that rare horror sub-genre of bodies or blood in art.

Bunny Game, The (2012)

DIRECTED BY	Adam Rehmeier
WRITTEN BY	Adam Rehmeier
STARRING	Rodleen Getsic, Jeff Renfro, Gregg Gilmore, Coriander Womack
COUNTRY	United States

I've always found that the scariest monsters are people, and the depths of depravity they are capable of. Nothing could be truer than *The Bunny Game.* Bunny (Rodleen Getsic) is your typical strung-out junkie, who turns tricks to feed her habit. One day she picks up a trucker credited as Hog (Jeff Renfro) thinking it'll be easy money. It turns out to be a deadly mistake when she learns the mysterious stranger has some extremely sadist games in mind. Unlike *American Psycho* Adam Rehmeier never glorifies the actions of his villain. There is nothing glamorous about what the trucker does. Plain and simple, he is a cancer destroying everything in sight. He's not satisfied with quickly killing his victims but mentally destroying them first, which is far worse.

The actors are amazing and at times you forget you're watching a fictional movie but rather a filthy snuff film. Rodleen Getsic, who plays Bunny, is so good that it's frightening, giving a performance that is award worthy. She not only has to be completely nude but also be degraded and have her head totally shaved. Jeff Renfro, a real-life trucker, plays the driver that picks Bunny up and turns her world into decay. His level of intensity is brutal and frightening and never gets hammy. He doesn't say much in the film and, really he doesn't have too. You'd be hard pressed to find a more convincing on-screen serial killer. Both Rodleen and Renfro push themselves as actors and plunge deep down into a pitch-black spiral that at times is difficult to watch. Visually this film takes a minimal approach using black and white which enhances the dread and terror a thousand percent. It's harder to work in black and white, but it's masterfully done and starkly beautiful. Rehmeier has an impressive eye for style and his fifteen-plus years of working in film really shows. I rarely comment on this aspect but the editing is very well-done, creating a psychotic and kinetic energy. But what I find most impressive is that there is little to no blood shed, and it relies solely on the characters and the audiences' imagination. Young filmmakers can learn something from this. It's not about the gallons of blood you pour on your victim, because any hack can do that, it's how you make the audience feel emotion for the character. *The Bunny*

Game forces us to take a look at the most depraved and ugly aspect of the human condition and leaves you with a very bleak outlook. And while it's not a movie you're likely to re-watch often it is an exercise in outstanding and ballsy filmmaking.

TRIVIA: Currently banned in the UK.

Loosely based on an actual event that happened to actress Rodleen Getsic.

Writer/Director Adam Rehmeir on *Bunny Games*

....

Its a polarizing film for sure. I don't really like working any other way, and I don't have much respect for filmmakers that aren't working in that headspace. I am very proud of Rodleen and Renfro's work in the film, and the experience of making it was unique and fresh for me. Since this wasn't a scripted project, I was really just relying on what happened on the day, the film simply is what it is.

On negative reviews:

I'm ok with that because it had nothing to do with my motivation for making the film, working so closely with my friend, and going on this bizarre, incredible journey. For me it was a gift. And I can't stress how important that is for a filmmaker, because if you're just painting by numbers, phoning it in, you're not growing as an artist. You're just prepping for puppetry.

Carnival of Souls (1962)

DIRECTED BY	Herk Harvey
WRITTEN BY	Herk Harvey, John Clifford
STARRING	Candice Hilligoss, Frances Feist, Sidney Berger, Art Ellison, Stan Levitt
COUNTRY	United States

There are a handful of films from the '60s that had a major impact on the horror genre and *Carnival of Souls* might be one of the most important, beaten only by *Psycho* and George A. Romero's seminal classic *Night of the Living Dead* (which is said to have been a huge influence). Mary (Candice Hilligoss) and a few other girls are riding in a car when the driver is challenged to a drag race. Accepting his challenge, he puts the pedal to the metal, but loses control on a bridge, plunging the car and everyone in it into the river. After three long hours of dragging the murky

depths, Mary, the solo survivor emerges seemingly unharmed but in a daze. She needs a change and takes a job in Utah as an organist at a church. We learn she is a strong independent woman that doesn't believe in God or in wanting to be with men, or anyone for that matter. After settling down in her new town and job she begins to notice strange ghostly images that haunt her whenever she goes.

Carnival of Souls is a master class in the subtle, less-is-more way of filmmaking. By today's standards it might be considered slow, but it wisely takes its time in setting mood and developing characters while building to an amazing hypnotic and nightmarish ending. What I admire about it the most is the fact that it doesn't use blood as a substitute for storytelling, and its use of surreal imagery and haunting atmosphere is the stuff of film legend. Interesting camera work coupled with the black-and-white photography gives it a dreamlike quality, and using basic lighting tricks gives faces a profoundly unsettling appearance. And speaking of dreamlike, the film's shooting locations give an off a grave-like feeling of isolation and dread which further enhances the eerie otherworldly mood. Topping everything off is its unnerving and creepy score that fits the film perfectly, using simple yet effective organ music. Sadly, director Herk Harvey had such a bad experience making this film he would never make another, leaving many fans to wonder what other great films he could have made. Truly, he went out with a bang making a classic work of feverish nightmares and untapped sexuality that has survived the test of time and continues to have a large loyal cult following. I make it a Halloween tradition in my household. *Carnival of Souls* is a must-see for anyone serious about films.

TRIVIA: Rob Zombie's solo band was originally going to be called *Carnival of Souls,* after the film, but went with *White Zombie* instead, a film which starred Bela Lugosi.

Candice Hilligoss's agent refused to represent her after seeing the film.

Chopping Mall, The, aka Killbot (1986)

DIRECTED BY	Jim Wynorski
WRITTEN BY	Jim Wynorski, Steve Mitchell
STARRING	Kelli Maroney, Tony O'Dell, Russell Todd, Barbara Crampton, Paul Bartel, Dick Miller
COUNTRY	United States

Ever since the landmark *Dawn of the Dead*, the mall has been a "like totally awesome" setting for various horror films. *Chopping Mall* by far is the best post-*DOTD* and has been a favorite of mine for some time now. A group of teenage mall employees decide it would be a good idea to spend the night at their place of work for some carefree wild fun (as teens do). However, it just so happens that the mall has gone high-tech with robots that patrol the inside. The bots are programmed to not harm anyone but something goes haywire, turning them into cold steel killing machines. It's good-looking teens vs. metal in the ultimate showdown. Steve Mitchell and Jim Wynorski write a clever screenplay that thankfully leaves no padding to bog itself down. The result is a nonstop ride of action that comes fast and loud and never lets up until the finale. *Chopping Mall* is Wynorski's love letter to '50s B-horror with an '80s update, and his passion for these and films in general is evident in the details and inside gags that are littered in the film: See how many you can get. There are also some fun cameos such as Paul Bartel and Mary Woronov reprising their role as Paul and Mary Bland from *Eating Raoul*. Also, Dick Miller as Walter Paisley, another inside joke for horror fans. Also look for fan favorites Gerrit Graham, Angus Scrimm (the Tall Man), and Ace Mask. It also features not one but two scream queens, Barbara Crampton (*Re-Animator, Lords of Salem* etc) and Kelli Maroney (*Night of the Comet*). Both give great performances, and it's always a blast to see them in anything. I'm always impressed with how great the Killbots look; given this was an age before CGI and all of them had to be operated manually. What a pain that must have been. Sure the effects are dated but it only adds to the '80s charm. It does feature some very nicely done gore effects that any splatter punk would be impressed with. So if you're looking for a totally bitchin' movie that features action, blood, breasts, and killer robots set in a mall, this is your one stop shop for all this and more. It also features great film references that make repeat viewings a lot of fun! A must-see by anyone with eyeballs! *"Waitress, more butter."*

Interview with Writer/Director Jim Wynorski

MV: Was Mary Woronov and Paul Bartel reprising their roles from *Eating Raoul* originally in the script?

JW: *No, but Julie Corman, who produced it, already knew Paul and Mary, and she got them to come in and we just put the camera down and turned it on and just let them talk. Yeah, there were a couple scripted lines but everything else was adlibbed.*

MV: I'm sure you've been asked about a sequel?

JW: *My statement has always been watch the first one again, there can't be a Chopping Mall 2. Somebody right now is remaking Chopping Mall, I believe without the robots. It's like making Friday the 13th without Jason.*

MV: Is a Chopping Mall remake necessary?

JW: *It's not a film that you want to remake. Especially without the robots, and if they did it today they would probably use CGI robots and it would not be as good.*

Originally published on February 17, 2014, on Gorehound Mike's Blog (http://gorehoundmike.blogspot.com)

Chuck Cirino on Scoring *Chopping Mall*

As my first legitimate score I wasn't really sure I could deliver something that worked. But thanks to a blind passion for film scores in general I was able to muddle through and make some people happy . . . . Synthesizers and robots are the husbands and wives of horror and science fiction.

Christmas Evil, aka You Better Watch Out (1980)

DIRECTED BY	Lewis Jackson
WRITTEN BY	Lewis Jackson
STARRING	Brandon Maggart, Jeffrey DeMunn, Dianne Hull, Andy Fenwick, Brian Neville, Wally Morgan, Gus Salud
COUNTRY	United States

A factory toy worker named Harry (Brandon Maggart) is more than a little obsessed with Christmas and has alienated himself from everyone around him. After years of living inside his own head he finally snaps and vows to show people the Christmas spirit or else. Those who are expecting an ultra-bloody outing like *Silent Night Deadly Night* might be disappointed, as Jackson does something that makes his killer Santa movie totally different than any other. First off, Lewis focuses more on the inner workings of Harry, and it's actually a character study of a very lonely and, of course, disturbed yet sympathetic man. Second, while it does get bloody, this is not what I would call a full-on slasher, which might upset some but, for fans of something different, it's a breath of fresh holiday air. What really anchors this film is the brilliant performance by Brandon Maggart. He is skin-crawlingly creepy, yet there is an underlying sadness that he brings to the character, which makes him feel like a tragic anti-hero. Honestly, if it were anybody else in the role and I don't think it would have worked nearly as well. It also features an early role from character actor Jeffery DeMunn who's been in everything from *The Shawshank Redemption* to *The Walking Dead*. He's great, and it's not hard to see why his career took off the way it did. Overshadowed by other more successful holiday horror movies, *Christmas Evil* is finally getting the respect it deserves in the horror community and is a creepy and interesting character study wrapped up in a holiday bow. Required viewing.

TRIVIA: The favorite holiday film of director John Waters.

Actor Brandon Marrgart on Making *Christmas Evil*:

Jackson was dedicated to getting his film made. And, finally, he got it made. He certainly had a unique story to tell. For the budget he had he did a really good job. I understand there are many fans of the film as it is. It's seen by more soon-to-be fans every Christmas. Some critics didn't like the final scene where he is flying across the moon wishing everyone a "Merry Christmas. And, to all, a good night." Suddenly, for a brief moment, in his own mind, he was flying. And, off to do his job as the spirit of good on Christmas Eve. That was MY favorite scene. Go figure. And, it was difficult to market because it was not a "slasher" film. It was a psychological journey with a disillusioned man-child.

C.H.U.D. II: Bud the Chud (1989)

DIRECTED BY	David Irving
WRITTEN BY	Ed Naha
STARRING	Gerrit Graham, Brian Robbins, Bill Calvert, Tricia Leigh Fisher, Robert Vaughn, Larry Cedar, and Robert Englund (cameo)
COUNTRY	United States

C.H.U.D is certainly a weird movie and could easily fit into this book. However, its sequel is even weirder which is really saying something. The C.H.U.D.s from the previous film were rounded up by the military in order to use their blood for the purpose of chemical warfare. They decide to shut down the program and destroy the last remaining C.H.U.D. But of course this does not work out and Bud (Gerrit Graham) escapes, only to be frozen by Colonel Masters (Robert Vaughn), who plans on keeping him on ice just in case the program is re-opened. And after a series of misadventures involving Steve (Brian Robbins) and Kevin (Bill Calvert), two hapless students, the body of Bud is brought back to life and, boy is he hungry! Now it's up to a motley crew of teenagers and the military to stop him before he eats the entire town. *Bud the Chud* is more comedy than horror and the jokes fly fast and furious; problem is, they are hit-and-miss and some bits go on a little too long. I must admit I found myself snickering at some and outright laughing at others. It's also chock full of clever snarky social commentary. One of my favorites is the girl working out so she can have a smoke and order a pizza. The plot is not terribly original and is a patchwork of other films. For example, the idea of the military teaming up (or at odds) with local teenagers is something that's been done many times before, and Robert Vaughn's character, Colonel Masters, is pure *Dr. Strangelove*. Fans also can't help but feel like they're watching *Return of the Living Dead*. The biggest problem with the plot is it gets bogged down on its own goofy premise, often losing focus on major plot points. Gerrit Graham plays the title character, Bud and, of course, steals the show. He is perfectly OK with being zany and over the top. Any other actor might not have had the "chomps," I mean chops, to pull it off but his skill at character acting serves him well here. Look for some fun cameos by June Lockheart, Norman Fell, and in a small role as a Halloween party guest Freddy himself (out of makeup of course), Robert Englund. Blood and gore are very sparse with most of the violence taking place off-screen, so fans of blood-soaked cinema will be sorely disappointed. Even though *C.H.U.D. II* gets lost in its own wackiness it's saved by some good humor and biting satire by Ed Naha (*Dolls, Honey I Shrunk the Kids, Troll*), who is credited as M. Kane Jeeves, which plays up its B-horror status for all its worth. It might not be everyone's "taste" but it's trashy fun that is worth a devouring.

TRIVIA: Cynthia Garris, actress and wife of famed horror director Mick Garris, wrote the lyrics to the *Bud the Chud* theme song.

Color Me Blood Red (1965)

DIRECTED BY	Herschell Gordon Lewis
WRITTEN BY	Herschell Gordon Lewis
STARRING	Gordon Oas-Heim, Candi Conder, Elyn Warner, Pat Finn-Lee, Jerome Eden
COUNTRY	United States

The third film in splatter legend H.G. Lewis's unofficial Blood Trilogy, *Color Me Blood Red* is sadly not as fondly remembered as the first two. But, like any good work of art, it's always being rediscovered and experienced. Adam Sorg (Gordon Oas-Heim) is a hot tempered artist (aren't they all), but lately his work has been ice cold. His art dealer says he's lost his touch and he needs to inject some new blood onto his canvas. One day his girlfriend accidently cuts herself on a nail jutting out of his canvas and discovers she has the perfect shade of red coursing through her body. Inspiration hits him and he uses the blood in his art. All of a sudden his work is on top again, but how many bodies will it take for him to keep making art to die for? Lewis takes sinister delight in poking fun at the hypocrisy of the art world viewed through his own blood soaked glasses. He satirizes everything from the art to the critics and even the artists themselves while still retaining his campy low-budget splatter charms. It's very funny to think an artist would literally kill to make it in this business. As for the gore, it's the standard wonderful, messy, and effective work that his fans have come to expect. There is a nice nasty bit with a woman's guts hanging out as Sorga squeezes them, ejecting the precious iron-based medium he's working in. It's gleefully vile and intentionally tongue-in-cheek. Surprisingly, *Color Me Blood Red* is the best-paced film out of the trilogy and there is very little padding. I could have done without the annoying faux beatnik couple though. While not as famous as the previous films in the trilogy it has found its audience in recent years and has a solid following with fellow gore heads. Even the TV show *Tales from the Crypt* borrowed the idea for the episode *Easel Kill Ya* in the third season. A ghastly work of cinematic art and a fun companion to Roger Corman's much tamer *A Bucket of Blood*, this is far-out must-see for fans of H.G. Lewis and of campy Technicolor splatter fests. *"Holy bananas, it's a girl's leg!"*

Crawlspace (1986)

DIRECTED BY	David Schmoeller
WRITTEN BY	David Schmoeller
STARRING	Klaus Kinski, Talia Balsam, Barbara Whinnery, Tane McClure, Carole Francis, Sally Brown, Jack Heller
COUNTRY	United States

There are guilty pleasures and then there's *Crawlspace,* a deliciously sleazy and wonderful film by director David Schmoeller and produced in the heyday of Empire Studios. Karl (Klaus Kinski), a creepy man, rents rooms out to only attractive women. But inside a seemingly normal house lies a series of hidden passageways and rooms. As it turns out, Karl is the son of a Nazi who performed terrible human experiments. Now the disturbed man is carrying in his father's very dark footsteps. This is a film that I highly enjoy yet baffles me at the same time. The story and its main driving force seem to be sketchy at best with various plot holes, gaps in logic, and a lot remaining unclear. So why do I have such a fondness for this film? At the very core of this film is the amazingly unsettling villain Karl, who just oozes creepy from every pore in his body. His performance is profoundly unnerving, and as the film progresses, he somehow manages to up the eerie, and he carries the film through its somewhat uneven story. Not only is Mr. Kinski a brilliant casting choice but the overall film has a disturbed claustrophobic feeling that only increases as the film reaches a delirious fever pitch of unchecked sexual perversion and insanity. Also, using the atrocities of the Nazis as a template for a horror film is a nasty and refreshingly different concept when you consider the genre was still riding the wave of endless teen slashers. Further helping the film is a score from legendary composer Pino Donaggio, best-known for working on many Brian De Palma films including *Carrie* and *Dressed to Kill. Crawlspace* is so off-the-wall and one of my favorites from the golden age of Empire Studios. It's an incredibly bizarre, grimy little film that dares to be different and, even though it may not be perfect in terms of story, it's still entertaining and very much worth your time.

GOES WELL WITH: *Schizoid, Terror Trap*

TRIVIA: Director David Schmoeller and Klaus Kinski notoriously butted heads during the production and oftentimes Kinski refused to listen to basic directions like cut and action.

CAMEO: Director/writer David Schmoeller as the rejected tenant. His line calling him creep is not surprising as the pair did not get along well.

Creep (1995)

DIRECTED BY	Tim Ritter
WRITTEN BY	Tim Ritter
STARRING	Kathy Willet, Joel D. Wynkoop, Patricia Paul, Tom Karr, Asbestos Felt, Dika Newlin
COUNTRY	United States

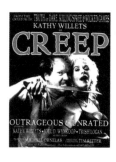

Discovering the films of Tim Ritter is like dumpster diving and finding some awesome and amazing gems and placing it proudly on your mantel, flaws and all, even when others don't understand why. As a child, Angus Lynch (Joel D. Wynkoop) and his sister Kascha (Kathy Willet) were sexually abused by their parents. Flash word and Angus is now a psycho killer having just escaped from jail. He seeks refuge at his sister's (now a sleazy stripper) house hoping to hide out until the heat is off. Meanwhile, hardboiled cop Jackie (Patricia Paul) is haunted by a recurring memory she had as a child after witnessing her mother being murdered by an unseen criminal. She's a tough woman who plays by her own set of rules, which often lands her in hot water with the Captain (Tom Karr), who is also her father. It's clear from the very first minute that Ritter has upped the weird factor and cranked it to eleven. The film seems to out strange itself at every single corner, and just when you think it couldn't get any more insane, guess what, it does! Think early John Waters meets Andy Milligan.

Writing-wise it's a step up from his earlier film *Killing Spree,* and we see an attempt (albeit crude) at character development. Also, it's nice to see that the film is at times intentionally tongue-in-cheek and the humor, at times, hits me right in the funny bone. Joel D. Wynkoop, a regular actor in Ritter's films, plays the main character of Angus Lynch. Sure his acting isn't great, but he has a great presence that makes it totally work for the film. *Deranged* producer Tom Karr also has a smaller but equally memorable role. Adult actress Kathy

Willets gives the film her voluptuous all in her rare legit film appearance and adds a weird dynamic to the film. However, the real break-out star is Dika Newlin, who has a very small but amazing role as the baby food killer. She's a Z-film national treasure in my opinion and I think when you see her you'll agree. This film, like his others, seem to inhabit a reality all its own. It languishes in a nightmare world of hyper-sexuality, brutal violence, and a level of perversion that is sure to endear any rabid horror fan to his films. Tim Ritter is the Ed Wood of shot-on-video gore and very much worth discovering.

Criminally Insane, aka Crazy Fat Ethel (1975)

DIRECTED BY	Nick Millard
WRITTEN BY	Nick Millard
STARRING	Priscilla Alden, Michael Flood, Jane Lambert, Robert Copple, George 'Buck' Flowers, Ginna Martine
COUNTRY	United States

I'm a sucker for '70s trash films so it came as a shock when I realized I had never seen Nick Millard's deep-fried horror film *Criminally Insane*. Morbidly obese Ethel (Priscilla Alden) is freshly released from a mental asylum and is hangry (hungry and angry) and armed with a cleaver: She will kill anyone who gets in the way of a meal. *Criminally Insane* feels like a movie that never really manages to rise above its own novelty, the novelty being Nick's large star, Priscilla Alden, as the crazed murderess. The plot is as basic as you can get with scenes that just go through the motions until it can get to a grisly murder. Millard also seems to not write women very well as every female in the film is terrible; take, for example, the prostitute sister who allows her awful boyfriend to treat her like garbage and, worse yet, beat her. When she asks why he does this he casually replies, "Because all women deserve it"—wow. I'm not often shocked by dialogue but this was icky. Still, even with a nonexistent plot that feels like one long fat joke, it's hard to actually outright hate it, and somehow Ethel has slaughtered and eaten her way into my black film-loving heart. It's also fun to see a young Buck Flowers star as a police detective. This is definitely a film that isn't to be taken too seriously, and fans of gutter trash from the era (which I am) will have a blast with this extremely odd film that serves up plenty of cheap thrills. Not great but worth making it a part of a balanced film diet.

Day of the Reaper (1984)

DIRECTED BY	Tim Ritter
WRITTEN BY	Tim Ritter, Joe Preuth (story by)
STARRING	Cathy O'Hanlon, Patrick Foster, Todd Nolf
COUNTRY	United States

Gore maverick Tim Ritter blazed a low-budget trail back in the video days and made a name for himself with his trademark twisted plots filled with gore, nudity, and overall pure insanity. As an ambitious teenager he put his love for horror in a little Super 8 film called *Day of the Reaper,* and through it and hard work, has built a career which he still proudly continues. A mysterious black-hooded cannibal killer is on the loose and is targeting five young girls who are on a vacation. It's really fascinating to watch a filmmaker's first effort, but it's even more interesting to watch it from someone who was only in junior high at the time. Keeping that fact in mind it would be easy for me to pick apart this film's carcass and nail Ritter's first effort to the cinematic cross, but I'm going to be a lot kinder than some snarky reviewers. Yes, the film is confusing and slowly paced with a plot filled with holes so large that you could drive a Mac truck through, not to mention the dubbing that may take the prize for worst ever. But as amateur as it is, it still shows creativity and sincerity that all later films would

have. On what had to have been a beyond-micro-budget the splatter is not actually that terrible and he took cues from his hero, H.G. Lewis, and used meat to give the gore a nastier look. As with his later films he sprinkles a lot of film references, including a clever wink to a personal favorite of mine, *Basket Case*. It amazes me that someone so young actually made a movie at all let alone something this ambitious, and while it's very crude, Ritter has my respect for having the passion and the guts to do it. Afterall, picture what you were doing in high school. Probably a film that can only be truly appreciated by hardcore Ritter fans that are curious as to the seeds of his cinematic madness.

TRIVIA: Tim Ritter took a job as a dishwasher to fund this film.

The eyeball at the end of the film was a ping pong ball made by Ritter's father.

Deadly Blessing (1981)

DIRECTED BY	Wes Craven
WRITTEN BY	Matthew Barr, Glenn Benset, Wes Craven
STARRING	Ernest Borgnine, Sharon Stone, Jeff East, Lisa Hartman, Lois Nettleton, Susan Buckner, Michael Berryman, Colleen Riley
COUNTRY	United States

Growing up in the country and living close to Lancaster, Pennsylvania, I can tell you this; the country is a beautiful place and is the closest thing to getting back to a time before the Internet, phones, and the countless things that distract us in our fast-paced everyday life. But it can also give you a feeling that underneath the surface of the picturesque landscape lurks something evil and even unholy. *Deadly Blessing* really taps into this. Doting couple Martha (Maren Jenson) and Jim Schmidt (Doug Barr) are living the simple life on a farm and own a pretty house complete with white picket fence. Shortly after the couple celebrates there one-year wedding anniversary tragedy strikes when a farming "accident" claims the life of Jim. Lana Marcus (Sharon Stone) and Vicky Anderson (Susan Buckner) rush from the city to visit their grieving friend. Soon after, the girls find themselves in a tangled web of religious mania and bloodshed, but is it man committing these wicked deeds or is it something supernatural? Several key things set this film apart from the rest, like blending the ever popular slasher genre with religious zealous overtones, a trend which was decades ahead of its time. It also does something almost totally unheard of in horror, which is populate the main cast with not only mostly females but also making them strong and resourceful and not just fodder for the killer's blade. Craven is perfectly in his element of terror and surprisingly, the most tense scenes take place during the day, employing simple yet effective tricks to build and maintain suspense all while misdirecting the audience. This film also gets a huge boost from its beautiful cinematography by Robert Jessup. He flawlessly captures the stark beauty contrasted with the eerie, which perfectly sets the film's driving story. As much as I enjoy *Deadly Blessing* it's by no means a masterpiece and suffers from some needless padding, coupled with a romantic subplot between Vicky and country boy Jim, which adds nothing to the story; instead I wish certain aspects of the story were explored in more depth. Without a doubt, this is Wes Craven's most underrated gem, coming out at a very prolific time in his career. Melding the body count genre with the horror of religious cults makes for some unnerving and interesting horror and, thanks to a re-release blu-ray, it's finally getting the attention it so desperately deserves. Not without its warts but an overall effective and different '80s flick.

Co-Writer Glenn M. Benest on *Deadly Blessing:*

Deadly Blessing was the first feature I wrote with my writing partner, Matt Barr. We went through a number of directors before we met Wes Craven, who directed a TV movie I adapted from a novel, "Summer of Fear." It was titled for NBC: "A Stranger In Our House." Once we hooked up with Wes everything went well. He wasn't well-known at that time, but he was on the way up. Once he was attached, we got the film made.

Actor Jeff East (John Schmidt) on *Deadly Blessing:*

Best experience with three gorgeous women and terrific supporting actors. Susan Buckner's a doll, Sharon Stone is a cool lady! Loved working with all the actresses, and Wes Craven is very kind.

Originally published on August 29, 2015, on Gorehound Mike's Blog (http://gorehoundmike.blogspot.com)

Death Bed: The Bed that Eats (1977)

DIRECTED BY	George Barry
WRITTEN BY	George Barry
STARRING	William Russ, Demene Hall, Julie Ritter, Linda Bond, Dave Marsh, Rosa Luxemburg, Ed Oldani
COUNTRY	United States

Death Bed is a pure off-the-wall film that I can honestly say is unlike any other film ever. The film follows the strange odyssey of a bed that is possessed by the spirit of a demon as told by our narrator who was an artist that became trapped inside a painting, doomed to forever remain with the bed in a creepy, nearly empty room. As luck would have it, a group of girls come for a weekend stay, and the hungry bed is ready for its three courses. The brother of one of the girls comes to find her only to discover the terrible secret of the death bed. As I mentioned above, this film manages to set itself totally apart from the pack—a feat that is rare. Barry's one and only cinematic opus flies in the face of the other, more outrageous, films being made at the time and also rejects the emerging slasher genre. Besides its wacky premise it has a lot of lofty ideas that are creative, and it gleefully blazes its own gonzo trail of insanity. It also has some very sharp tone changes being part art house film, part horror with some intentional tongue-in-cheek humor that seems to almost act as satire of the genre as a whole. Another thing is the very hyper-surreal atmosphere that Barry manages to create, and it really is like you're watching someone's bizarre nightmare. My main problem with the film is it takes an already thin premise and struggles to stretch it out to feature length, and the result is a film that starts to feel terribly repetitive and somewhat boring. The pre-CGI effects may seem crude, but for the time it was wildly inventive and very much adds to its low-budget odd charm. I also give the filmmakers credit for taking advantage of the wonderful shooting locations, especially the mansion, which sadly is no long standing. It further echoes the film's folk tale feeling. Sure it has its problems, but I gotta give major props to the film for being totally off-the-wall bonkers while also injecting some refreshingly different ideas and stunning art house imagery. It may be too uneven for the casual horror set but for the midnight crowd this bed is just right. *Death Bed* is the *Jaws* of bedroom furniture.

Death Spa (1989)

DIRECTED BY	Michael Fischa
WRITTEN BY	James Bartruff and Mitch Paradise
STARRING	Merritt Butrick, Ken Foree, Brenda Bakke, William Bumiller, Robert Lipton
COUNTRY	United States

Death Spa is a glorious mess of celluloid trash, but it's also a fun-fried slice of cheesy gold. Starbodies Health Spa is all the rage due largely to its state-of-the art computer system which, of course, controls the entire gym because what could go wrong there? Recently things start to go haywire and loyal customers are getting hurt and soon worse. All pain no gain is in store for clients unless Michael, the owner, can "work out" who or what is behind it. *Death Spa* firmly belongs in this book because of just how increasingly bonkers it gets. Flawed? Oh, you bet. This film shows potential with some interesting ideas, the problem is it gets bogged down in them and quickly loses its focus. It's further weighed down by its many subplots and needless padding. First off, there is the stock cop characters, they don't move the story forward and don't detect anything. Also, Michael and his budding romance with co-worker Laura is utterly pointless. Heaped onto that is a bizarre psychic that again does nothing to really further the story. Even with its glaring faults I still find this film pretty damn entertaining. It is at times weird, other times just surreal, but mostly it will leave you wondering what you're watching and later questioning your own sanity. Let's start with the cringe-worthy and very odd dialogue that gets a lot of laughs. Also, just to make things more interesting, there is a thick layer of homo eroticism all over the film, which foreshadows the shocking and head-scratching finale. The cast is actually pretty decent considering its low-budget status. Horror film favorite Ken Foree is featured, and it's always great to see him in a good splatter romp. Karyn Parsons makes a pre-*Fresh Prince of Bel-Air* appearance. The real scene stealer is Merritt Butrick who plays the twin brother. With his faux British accent and huge personality he makes a terrific bad guy. Sadly, this was his final movie. Even with a limited budget, the film still manages to showcase some nice splatter gags. There is a nice head-exploding bit that is quiet satisfying. Bad dialogue, a mish-mashie plot filled with ugly spandex, and zombie fish: what more could you want in a film?

Dementia, aka Daughter of Darkness (edited edition, 1955)

DIRECTED BY	John Parker
WRITTEN BY	John Parker
STARRING	Adrienne Barrett, Bruno VeSota, Ben Roseman, Angelo Rossitto
COUNTRY	United States

There are movies that are so criminally underrated and forgotten about. John Parker's totally weird art house film *Dementia* sadly falls into that category. *Dementia* follows a girl's hellish descent into the seamy sides of skid row, like a hellish film noir. What follows is a walking nightmare of surrealism and unchecked sexual repression spiraling into madness. You might be thrown by the over-the-top cheesy score but don't let that fool you; this is a great film and way of ahead of its time, exploring themes like sex, prostitution, and violence. The family drama that plays out in the middle of a cemetery is a brilliant metaphor that works as a scathing indictment on the happy house, *Leave it to Beaver*-style myth that so many films and TV shows perpetuated in the '50s. It also might be one of the first American films to show the impact of someone being shot rather than just cutting away, something Sergio Leone is often credited with much later on. Yes, the blood is very mild compared to today, but you have to understand this was back in 1955, in a pre-*Psycho* and *Night of the Living Dead* era. This film is also ahead of its time in terms of being art house when that was virtually unheard of. It skillfully blends the popular film noir genre with its visually stunning German Expressionist style mixed with Gothic overtones; the result is an unforgettable and groundbreaking work of art. Adrienne Barrett plays The Garmin, and sadly she would do only one other film before retiring from cinema. B-movie star Bruno VeSota (*Attack of the Giant Leeches, Wasp Women,* etc.) does a great job playing Rich Man, a very grimy sleaze ball. Fans of the classic MGM film *Freaks* will notice Angelo Rossitto as a newspaper man. Ahead of its time in both theme and its bold surrealist vision, it no doubt inspired films such as *Carnival of Souls* and David Lynch's *Eraserhead*. With various re-releases, thankfully this film is being rightfully re-discovered and loved for its bold and haunting style and taboo-breaking subject matter. So take a walk on the seamier side of the city and explore the darkest recesses of your unconsciousness.

TRIVIA: The recut edition, *Daughters of Darkness* is narrated by Ed McMahon—yes, The Ed McMahon.

The film became a lost classic until it was used in 1958's *The Blob* as the film that was being shown in the theater during the infamous blob attack scene under its re-title, *Daughter of Darkness*.

William Thompson photographed this film. He would also do Edward D. Wood Jr.'s infamous *Plan 9 from Outer Space* and *Glen or Glenda*.

Devil Bat, The (1940)

DIRECTED BY	Jean Yarbrough
WRITTEN BY	John Neville
STARRING	Bela Lugosi, Suzanne Kaaren, David O'Brien, Guy Usher, Hal Price, Yolande Donlan, Donald Kerr, Edmund Mortimer, John Ellis
COUNTRY	United States

If you can't enjoy a Z-grade movie with a giant fake killer bat, wow I don't even know how to finish that sentence . . . I adore movies like *The Devil Bat* and hopefully you do, too. A seemingly mild-mannered scientist named Dr. Paul Carruthers (Bela Lugosi) feels cheated out of money by the family of a big perfume company. He uses a giant bat to get his revenge. Without any bit of shame I admit I dearly love this Poverty Row cheapie. Its appeal is largely based on its wonderfully silly yet earnest plot and its *biting* sense of dark humor also makes this a stand-out, and you get the sense the filmmakers were clearly in on its own joke. It also hangs a lot on the performance by everyone's favorite silver *scream* icon, Bela Lugosi, who is clearly having fun in the role. Sure it's hokey, and yes it's an ultra-low-budget slice of camp, but it's also an extremely fun and engaging movie. *The Devil Bat* makes the perfect movie with a group of friends or to watch with a hangover.

TRIVIA: Much to the shock of the *Producers Releasing Corp.* the film was a huge hit for the small studio, so much so that they made a sequel, *Devil Bat's Daughter,* in 1946, and an unofficial remake entitled *The Flying Serpent* in 1946.

Devil Times Five, aka People Toys, aka Tantrums (UK title), aka The Horrible House on The Hill (1974)

DIRECTED BY	Sean MacGregor
WRITTEN BY	John Durren, Sandra Lee Blowitz, Dylan Jones (story)
STARRING	Gene Evans, Leif Garrett, Joan McCall, Dawn Lyn, Shelley Morrison, Sorrell Booke
COUNTRY	United States

If horror films have taught me anything it's that kids are evil and will probably kill you. Such is the case in *Devil Times Five*. Rich Papa Doc (Gene Evans), his trophy wife Lovely (Carolyn Stellar), and two other couples are all spending some time at his secluded winter home, partly for business and partly pleasure. A group of kids and a hippy-looking nun escape a bus crash not far from there and seek shelter from the blistering cold. The kids? Oh they've come from the local funny farm, and snow ball fights and hot cocoa are the furthest thing from their devilish minds. Can the adults escape, or will the kids give them a permanent time out? *Devil Times Five* is a film at odds with itself. On the one hand it's a strange little chiller with some icky moments. But it also tries to be a relationship drama, and the two don't blend well. It is possible, but neither the writing nor the director has the kind of skills to pull it off. The result is a film horribly padded, and audiences get treated to watching couples talk shop, fight, and oh yeah, sled. Even if it tests its viewer's patience there are some pretty weird goings-on, strange enough to justify being in this book. For example, Lovely, the horny trophy wife of rich Papa Doc tries to have her way with Ralph (John Durran), the mentally challenged handyman. It's a cheesy and humorous scene but it's also skin-crawling at the same time. When the film gets going fans of horror will be delighted by the nasty mayhem the kid brings down on the household. What really makes *Devils* stand out is the fact that the kid, or in this case kids, arc not agents of the devil, not possessed by demons, but real flesh-and-blood killers, which is much more disturbing in my book. Sadly, the concept is bogged down in horrible padding and failed attempts at character drama, when all fans want is a fun killer kid(s) movie. Still there are moments of great trashy '70s cinema and the ending is delightfully absurd and bizarre. I'd say watch it if you dig vintage cheese, but keep your expectations low.

Doom Asylum (1987)

DIRECTED BY	Richard Friedman
WRITTEN BY	Richard Friedman, Rick Marx
STARRING	Patty Mulligan, Kristin Davis, Ruth Collins, Harrison White, Dawn Alvan, Harvey Keith, Kenny L. Price
COUNTRY	United States

By the late '80s every aspect of the slasher sub-genre has been exhausted, every holiday under the sun a time of mayhem, and it was becoming a source of self parody, signaling the end of the already bled dry market. *Doom Asylum* sadly is one of the death rattles of the slice-and-dice films. I have a love/hate relationship with *Doom Asylum*: on the one hand it takes me back to my days of horror rental bliss, but as an adult I also see the glaring flaws that even video charm can't fully cover up. What I enjoy about this film is how it deals with the comedy; imagine *Kentucky Fried Movie* as a slasher film. Blood and jokes fly fast and a lot of humor is pretty good, at first. There are some really funny bits between the characters, especially Michael and Kiki. The incest bit is still quoted among friends. The cast is an interesting one featuring Penthouse playmate Patty Mulligan (*Frankenhooker*) giving a rather odd low-key performance. This film is also notorious for being *Sex and the City* star Kristin Davis' first feature film. Her performance won't win any awards but it's definitely a notch above everyone else. Cult actress Ruth Collins (*Psychos in Love, Prime Evil*) plays punk rocker Tina and is deliriously mad cap to the point of borderline annoying. There's over-the-top and then there's whatever the hell she's doing. Keeping in mind the shoestring budget the special effects and makeup are decent but still leave a lot to be desired, and the killer's face looks like a crude take on Freddy. Still, fans of the red, red kroovy will find enough blood and outrageous gore gags to keep them slated. Sadly though, whatever fun the first half of the film provides is quickly squashed by a host of problems. The first being the terrible padding in the form of a classic movie being shown throughout, with the good doctor watching and reacting to it (even when it makes no sense plot-wise). This was done because the producers literally ran out of money and had to inject filler to get the film to a scant seventy-nine-minute run time. It's super annoying and tries the viewer's patience quickly. I mean, I wanna watch this movie not something else. By this point even the jokes run painfully thin and the film sluggishly limps to its finale. *Doom Asylum* feels like an end of an era and a reminder that even the profitable slasher genre had its sell by date. Still I can't totally hate this film even with its host of problems and I'd say it's still worth a watch if only for the nostalgia factor (which it has in spades) and for some of the humor that does work. Hardcore '80s slasher fans who don't mind a bit of cheese will also enjoy it but sadly there is some lame filler to wade through.

Dr. Caligari (1989)

DIRECTED BY	Stephen Sayadian
WRITTEN BY	Stephen Sayadian, Jerry Stahl
STARRING	Madeline Reynal, Fox Harris, Laura Albert, David Perry, Gene Zerna, John Durbin, Jennifer Miro, Barry Philip
COUNTRY	United States

Take Cronenberg-style body horror, add the hyper-sexuality of John Waters, mix a good helping of horror fanzines like energy, and a generous amount of LSD. Blend on high. Once done, garnish with an eyeball, then take a sip and kiss your sanity goodbye as Stephen Sayadian's *Dr. Caligari* slowly melts your brain into a jellied paste. The plot (of which there is) concerns straightlaced Mr. Van Houten (Gene Zerna) who takes his wife to psychotherapy when her libido goes haywire. Meanwhile, the evil Dr. Caligari (Madeline Reynal) has more sinister plans for the poor girl, namely to use her as a human guinea pig for her own twisted sexual pleasures. Though it has nothing to do with the silent era masterpiece *The Cabinet of Dr. Caligari* except in name only (and stills used during the opening credits), it does retain some of the German Expressionism vibe, using similar off-kilter minimalistic set dressings which are often misshapen and purposely rough looking. It was something Elfman did successfully in the brilliant *The Forbidden Zone*. But I gotta say, Sayadian's film may just out crazy *Zone*, which is saying a lot if you've ever seen it. It features wonderfully twisted surreal imagery coupled with dialogue that is so severely warped yet cleverly written. But *Caligari* is not just weird for weird sake, as it's highly creative in its creation of a trippy pop art world that feels like a nightmare funhouse of repressed sexuality. And while we're on the subject, the film is overflowing with enough overt eroticism to make even the late great smut maestro Russ Meyer grin from ear to ear. Without a doubt, this has to be the weirdest and cleverest film to ooze its way out of the '80s . Required viewing for anyone seriously interested in underground films.

GOES WELL WITH: *The Forbidden Zone, Frankenhooker, Society*

Excision (2012)

DIRECTED BY	Richard Bates Jr.
WRITTEN BY	Richard Bates Jr.
STARRING	AnnaLynn McCord, Traci Lords, Roger Bart, Ray Wise, Malcolm McDowell, Ariel Winter, John Waters
COUNTRY	United States

The teen years can be unusually cruel for the misunderstood what with pressures at school, home life, and worst of all, other snotty teens. *Excision* explores the awkward life of a teenage girl and the horrors that come along with it, and the result is a mixed bag. Pauline (AnnaLynn McCord) is a weird and socially stunted girl who plans on being a surgeon someday. Her classmates hate her and it seems like things aren't any better at home with overbearing mom Phyllis (Traci Lords) and ineffectual dad Bob (Roger Bart). As she navigates through the hell of teen life her behavior gets increasing more disturbing as her strange nightmares start to bleed into her reality, blurring the two together with deadly results. First off, I love Bates' fearless sense of direction and he's not afraid to meld a typical teen comedy drama with crazy surrealist horror. It really takes guts to commit to that and keep from going overboard. The film also has surprising depth in its characters and they clearly are more fleshed out than your standard horror film. Just when you think you have someone pegged, you don't. The cast is also fantastic, with Traci Lords giving a wonderfully layered performance as Pauline's mother, Phyllis. Equally brilliant is Roger Bart, who sadly doesn't have a real chance to shine as the brow-beaten husband. Still, he is entertaining as always and he and Lords play off each other beautifully. The real break-out is AnnaLynn McCord, who walks a fine line of endearingly shy and mentally psychotic, all without going to campy or theatrical. John Waters, Ray Wise, and Malcolm McDowell all make deliriously amazing cameos. Sadly though, as strong as its concept, acting, and decent first act are, the film loses its focus and runs out of stream, and its point becomes somewhat unclear. Also, scenes in which Pauline talks to God as a way of an internal monologue are needless and only serve to further slow the film down. After a while it starts to feel like an overly long episode of *Daria* meets *Donnie Darko*. *Excision* is one of those very near genius films. All the ingredients are there; a great cast, a bold and interesting concept, and a clearly imaginative force at work with some great grotesque and visually stunning moments. However, an underdone screenplay holds it back from gaining the kind of cult status as say *May,* and it leaves me frustrated at the kind of film it could have been. Still, for Richard Bates Jr's first outing, it's impressive what he managed to accomplish out of the gate and I have the utmost respect for him regardless of a confused second and third act. Not a terrible film by any means and I'm willing to bet some of you may enjoy it. For me, however, it just narrowly made the grade.

Eyes of Fire (1983)

DIRECTED BY	Avery Crounse
WRITTEN BY	Avery Crounse
STARRING	Dennis Lipscomb, Guy Boyd, Rebecca Stanley, Sally Klein, Karlene Crockett, Fran Ryan, Rob Paulsen
COUNTRY	United States

Before the Blair Witch haunted the woods of Burkettsville or Black Philip tromped his way into our black hearts, two films (coming within a year of each other) took the witch genre in a new direction, which wasn't kid-friendly or ultra-cheesy. Those films were *Black Candles* and this film, *Eyes of Fire*. A preacher is accused of adultery and is cast out of the town along with a group of followers. It's a harsh existence as they face not only the hardships of surviving in the unforgiving land but also must fend off Native American attacks. Just when things seem to get settled for their party an evil force is awakened deep in the woods. Avery Crounse's film, *Eyes of Fire,* is a beautiful and haunting film that very much set the groundwork for *The Blair Witch Project, Lords of Salem,* and *The Witch*. It takes the witch out of kiddie movies like *Snow White* and into more serious adult works. The film is definitely a slow burn, and people who don't have patience may find this a bit boring, but the reward for sticking with it is a wonderfully creepy and, at points, downright disturbing thrill ride. Visually the film is remarkable and has an ominous quality that hangs heavily on every frame. Guy Boyd, future actor of such films as De Palma's *Body Double* and *Foxcatcher,* heads up a terrific cast of actors, all of which sell the story so well and give the material the respect it deserves. *Eyes of Fire* is a bizarre and wonderful folk horror film and a slice of Americana, and you can see how ahead of its time it really was. You can't take your eyes off this mesmerizing work of terror.

Fear No Evil (1981)

DIRECTED BY	Frank LaLoggia
WRITTEN BY	Frank LaLoggia
STARRING	Stefan Arngrim, Elizabeth Hoffman, Frank Birney, Paul Haber, John Holland
COUNTRY	United States

Remember that shy goth kid you went to school with? What if he was actually the son of the devil? This is the question posed in what has got to be one of the weirdest '80s teen horror entries. Two archangels, Rafael (John Holland) and Mikhail (Elizabeth Hoffman), were sent to Earth in forms of humans, Father Tom and Margaret. Their mission is to stop Lucifer from spreading his evil (and bad fashion, it seems) unto the world. Father Tom kills the devil, but before he dies he vows to be reborn. The devil then transforms into a man and Father Tom is locked up for murder. True to his word, his son is born and it's up to Mikhail and a second angel, Gabrielle (Kathleen Rowe McAllen), born as Julie, a typical teenage girl, to stop the devil's son before it's too late! This film has been a long-time guilty pleasure of mine and in my early blogger days I got a chance to briefly speak to director Frank LaLoggia. I quickly learned he's a colorful character that never took himself very seriously. For example, when

I asked for a quote to use at the end of my blog he gave me this rather odd gem: *"Hey dude! What the **** is this! You musta been smokin' some doggie drenched weed to actually like dis! If I were the director I'd go back to makin peezas!"*. By the way, the dashes were included by him. *Fear No Evil* is a refreshing change from the same old. From frame one it's crystal clear that LaLoggia was aiming high with some very lofty ideas with themes of religion, redemption, and evil. It also explores the psychological toll raising the son of the devil takes on the unknowing parents in a very brief montage. Indeed, a really interesting concept that I have never seen before or since. While the film is serious, it still lets itself play with the genre and have some fun. A highlight is the baptism scene and, of course, who could forget the death by dodge ball. I love the way he blends standard horror tropes with surreal art house even if it does feel wildly uneven at times. I'm not saying the film is without flaws, and even the director was quoted as calling it "outrageous" and "campy". The problem with the film is not the lack of good ideas, just a lack of budget, which even for the time was shoestring. This is painfully evident in the cheesy zombie makeup and the devil makeup at the end. It also doesn't help that during the finale the anti-Christ acts (or overacts) more like a whiny Cure reject than a strong and powerful dark lord. Fans of ultra-gore might be disappointed by the lack of real nasty stuff; however, when it does get bloody it's used in very disturbing and effective ways. The havoc at the Passions play, for example, is very well-done. Just another way it tries to be more than just a hack and stab film. In the era when slashers were done to death, Frank LaLoggia (then only twenty-six years old) made something wonderfully different. Even though it's low-budget and uneven tone I find this a neat and ambitious work from someone who obviously has a love for the genre.

TRIVIA: If the zombies seem out of place it's because the director was forced to add them to ride the wave of other popular films like *Dawn of the Dead*.

Final Terror, The (1983)

DIRECTED BY	Andrew Davis
WRITTEN BY	Jon George, Neill D. Hicks, Ronald Shusett
STARRING	Adrian Zmed, Lewis Smith, Joe Pantoliano, Daryl Hannah, Mark Metcalf, Rachel Ward, Ernest Harden Jr.
COUNTRY	United States

I love slashers as much as the next red-blooded horror fan, but unlike some, I don't watch them with nostalgia-tinted glasses; you know, the kind that upon wearing automatically allows you to omit glaring flaws and give them a free pass because they are "classics". *The Final Terror* was made in a time when many slashers were being endlessly cranked out, but this little gem seemed to get lost in the shuffle. A group of guys and girls go into the woods for some drinking, fooling around, and drug usage, in other words, typical young people activity. They quickly dismiss the warning about going beyond the designated camping area and, of course, pay the price for doing so. It's a deadly game of prey versus the hunted in this grim backwoods thriller. On the surface *Final Terror* seems like a very standard slasher romp. You have good-looking young people traveling into the woods for a good time and ignoring warnings about venturing where they shouldn't. You also have some fooling around and drug use. What sets Davis's film apart from the countless other slashers are a few key things. First, it melds the slasher genre with a survival film—something that was virtually unheard of then and even now is a rarity. The characters are also smarter than your average horror film and are more proactive; even the women have brains and are much more than objects of lust and fodder for the killer's weapon of choice. Its harsh and gritty tone reflects the survival element and, while there is some levity injected into it, it is mostly a dark film. I'm also surprised by the interesting cast assembled which includes Adrian Zmed, Mark Metcalf, a pre-*Matrix* Joe Pantoliano, and an early role for Daryl Hannah. For the most part the acting is really well-done and it's easy to see why a lot of these actors went onto having decent careers. The one sour note is Pantoliano playing Edgar. He goes way over the top, which seems out of step with the rest of the cast. Thankfully, his acting methods have matured a great deal since. *The Final Terror* has something for everyone. Lovers of traditional slashers will find enough familiar territory to enjoy it while more jaded fans will respect the refreshing change of pace. In recent years the film has finally found a wider audience due to a much overdue re-release. A slasher gem that was unfairly brushed aside at the time of its release is being re-discovered and is very much worth your time.

Flesh-Eating Mothers (1989)

DIRECTED BY	James Aviles Martin
WRITTEN BY	James Aviles Martin, Zev Shlasinger
STARRING	Robert Lee Oliver, Donatella Hecht, Neal Rosen, Valorie Hubbard, Terry Hayes, Louis Homyak
COUNTRY	United States

Yet another bizarre film oddity that came out in the wake of the horror video boom. I remember buying this film from a mom-and-pop rental shop that was going under. Roddy Douglas (Louis Homyak) is a local man-whore and, even though he's married, he beds every mother on his block. It seems he carries a strange unidentified venereal disease that causes the women to get an increased appetite for food and later crave human flesh. Now it's up to their children to stop them before they all end up on the menu. Yes, I was suckered in by the artwork and the great title, but it seems I might have been had. First off, the idea of an STD causing madness and violence was already done more effectively in David Cronenberg's *Shivers,* though I do like the change up, making the male the plague carrier rather than the woman. I could forgive the used plot, but sadly, the film takes itself just a tad bit too seriously and is yet another case of a film confused on what it's trying to be. On the one chewed hand it's an intentional tongue-in-cheek comedy play-

ing up its camp aspect, yet it also tries to be a domestic drama and corrupt police story. Honestly, how can you take the drama seriously when the plot is so off-the-wall? As far as the comedy goes some of the jokes work while others are eye-twitchingly bad. The acting is what you'd expect from this type of film, with some being decent, to others that you swear are simply reading off cue cards. Mickey Ross, who plays Officer McDormick, and his sidekick, coroner

Dr. Grouly, played by Michael Fuer are just awful, even for B-movie standards. I will say some of the teen actors are not bad; Valorie Hubbard, for example, is very natural. She would go on to a pretty good career playing bit parts in such things as the TV shows *Workaholics* and *American Horror Story*. Towards the halfway point the film has already outstayed its welcome and exhausted its humor. To highlight this, the mothers are at one point just aimlessly walking around cracking unfunny jokes. It's painfully clear that the film has run out of steam. Even with a premise that is stretched to its breaking point and unfunny humor it does have a certain camp value, especially when the film tries to get into domestic drama mode. You gotta love the moment when the Dad is holding up the chewed arm of his son who still has a catcher's mitt on. If you're craving a trashy, tasty little Z-grade morsel and don't mind an extra helping of cheese than this film might satisfy. Recommended for hardcore trash lovers only.

Actor Valorie Hubbard on Making *Flesh-Eating Mothers:*

Flesh-Eating Mothers was my first film. I didn't make a dime, but I had a blast shooting it, and I got recognized by people on the street for ten years after the fact. Weird. The funniest memory was the toothless/homeless guy on the street that said, "Yo, blondie. I seen you in that movie Man-Eating Mothers!!" I said, "Oh, did you see it on TV?" and he said, "No, girl. I paid to see that shit!!!"

Frankenstein's Army (2013)

DIRECTED BY	Richard Raaphorst
WRITTEN BY	Richard Raaphorst
STARRING	Robert Gwilym, Hon Ping Tang, Luke Newberry, Alexander Mercury, Joshua Sasse, Mark Stevenson, Karel Roden
COUNTRY	United States, Czech Republic, Netherlands

I have to say I have an automatic groan when I hear the words "horror" and "found footage." However, I was delightfully impressed by this steampunk fright action hybrid. Nearing the end of World War II Russian troops receive a distress call on the radio from a band of Russian soldiers under attack by Germans. As the men travel to their comrade's aid they discover the slaughtered remains, which lead them to a small town and a church that houses some horrifying secrets. Future filmmakers need to take note, this is how to do found footage correctly, as Raaphorst uses the normally played-out narrative device in both a creative way and one that makes sense storywise. It actually feels very organic rather than a hokey gimmick. I loved the fresh take on both the undead Nazi sub-genre as well as the Dr. Frankenstein mythos. Normally, trying to meld pulse-pounding action and horror is a tricky thing; however, *Army* does this seamlessly. Fans of the game *Wolfenstein* will get a certain rush of nostalgia, as (not sure if intentional) it feels like the game in the best possible sense. *Frankenstein's Army* is populated by some highly inventive and creepy creatures that are achieved by some obviously talented makeup and special effects people and, honestly, I haven't seen monsters this creative since the original *Hellraiser*. Furthermore, the dirty, grimy sets are incredibly done and really help craft a thick sense of dread, and at times unbearable claustrophobia. Wisely, the filmmakers never take the film too seriously with some sly dark humor to counter the more serious subject matter. Even some of the weaker moments and gaps in logic can easily be forgiven as the action is ever moving and very engaging. Sure it's a film that feels more like a video game, but if you're willing to go with it, it's a great deal of fun. My fellow splatter punks will also be happy, as the film serves up enough blood and guts and other grisly surprises to slate even diehard fans. And while it's not perfect, *Frankenstein's Army* remains a wonderfully nasty little action horror, and with a jolt of talent, brings life into several sub-genres while also breathing new life into the tired found footage plot device. So gather a group of friends, let the cold suds flow, and enjoy this nonstop thrill ride.

Ghastly Ones, The, aka Blood Rites (1968)

DIRECTED BY	Andy Milligan
WRITTEN BY	Andy Milligan, Hal Sherwood
STARRING	Veronica Radburn, Maggie Rogers, Hal Borske, Anne Linden, Richard Romanus, Carol Vogel, Don Williams
COUNTRY	United States

Like beer or fine wine, the films of Andy Milligan are an acquired taste. Some hail him as an underground genius while others simply write him off as an untalented Z-grade showman. Sure his movies are terribly inept in their construction; however, the very fact that his movies keep getting re-released and finding new audiences tells me I'm not alone in my love of Andy and his horror trash epics.

The Ghastly Ones is probably his most famous, or infamous. After their father passes away three sisters and their husbands spend the weekend at the old homestead as per the will. On the final day a trunk will be opened and the goods divided up amongst the girls. However, what seems like a carefree weekend stay turns blood-soaked as a murderer stalks them. Now the family and all their ghastly secrets will come spilling out, along with entrails. Now, I'm not going to make a

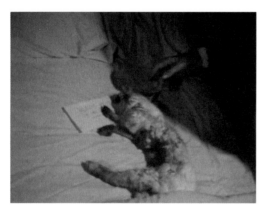

case that this is a great work of art because it's not; however, instead of picking apart every glaring flaw I'm going to point out the interesting things it has going for it that critics seem to miss or totally ignore. Andy wastes no time in dispensing gore and while it is crude, some are rather effective. For example, the scene where the girl is getting her limbs butchered is actually well-done considering the extremely low budget. Milligan's flare seems like it could easily fit in the constructs of a play, with its over-the-top theatrics and period costumes. It's, of course, a great deal of campy fun unofficial remake of *The Cat and the Carney,* done in a gross-out low-functioning fevered nightmare only Milligan could dream up. And I gotta say the twists and turns elevate it higher than a lot of horror coming out at the time. Not a masterpiece but I still love this gritty, nasty bit of cinema filth.

TRIVIA: *The Ghastly Ones* was a part of the now infamous Video Nasties List.

God Told Me To, aka Demon, aka God Told Me to Kill (1976)

DIRECTED BY	Larry Cohen
WRITTEN BY	Larry Cohen
STARRING	Tony Lo Bianco, Sandy Dennis, Mike Kellin, Sylvia Sidney, Deborah Raffin, Richard Lynch, Andy Kaufman
COUNTRY	United States

Larry Cohen is a director who always impresses me with his bold concepts and, even if you happen to dislike his films, you have to give the man credit for his wildly inventive storytelling. The busy streets of New York are rocked by a vicious and random mass shooting by a lone sniper perched high above the city streets, leaving many dead or wounded. Detective Peter Nicholas (Tony Lo Bianco), determined to find out why, boldly risks his safety and engages the gunman, and when asked for a reason behind the mass killing he simply and calmly states God told him to before leaping to his death. This is only the start of a rash of mass killings in the name of the almighty and Peter will stop at nothing to solve the deadly riddle. With the all-too-real tragic shootings Larry Cohen's '70s thriller is given a new disturbing dimension and all of the violence is wisely done in a very matter-of-fact fashion and leads to its gritty urban feel. Cohen assembles a stellar cast including veteran Tony Bianco who, in my opinion, is the perfect choice for the role of Dt. Nicholas. He thankfully plays the film totally straight without a single wink to the audience and it really helps keep the film grounded even when it gets ultra-weird. Oscar winner Sandy Dennis also turns in an understated yet solid performance and her signature quirk fits the film like a glove. And of course, cult icon and cinema treasure Richard Lynch gets in on the madness with a small but extremely memorable role. Even Andy Kaufman has a cameo in his first feature film appearance. *God Told Me To* is decently written and Cohen weaves a highly intense and interesting mystery with enough twists to keep you guessing at every turn, and I was engaged at every step. He also throws in some humorous religious satire that never gets heavy-handed. Sadly though, the story feels a tad bit unbalanced and worse yet, has a few sizeable plot holes. However, I'm more than willing to overlook the flaws because the film is a total psychotropic trip of crazy with one of the greatest endings in Grindhouse history. Cohen always has my undying respect for his creative works and, even if they are at times uneven, I'll gladly take that over mediocre Hollywood fare any day. See it and tell'em God told you to, or blame it on me— either way you'll have a blast with this off-the-rails little shocker that ranks as the craziest to come out of the decade.

Gruesome Twosome, The (1967)

DIRECTED BY	Herschell Gordon Lewis
WRITTEN BY	Allison Louise Downe
STARRING	Elizabeth Davis, Gretchen Wells, Chris Martell, Ronnie Cass, Rodney Bedell, Karl Stoeber, Dianne Wilhite
COUNTRY	United States

Lewis really lets his hair down in this lesser-known horror gore film. A seemingly harmless old lady runs The Little Wig Show with her son and stuffed cat. She lures college girls in with the phony promise of rooms for rent only to kill and later scalp them. A plucky girl named Kathy (Gretchen Wells), known in town for crying wolf, stumbles upon this scheme, but will anyone believe her? This movie literally starts out with talking foam heads (with Picasso-like faces) wearing wigs, which later get stabbed. It's a fun and clever way to not only introduce the movie, but it also sets the film's tone which is barking-mad bloody yet there is something innocent about it. It has a host of problems that even a Lewis fan like myself can't completely overlook. The film (like most of his) hasn't aged very well and its central concept of women causally buying and wearing wigs is something we in modern life just don't do. Also, the way they depict the mentally challenged son is pretty cringeworthy. What *Twosome* suffers most from, however, is its pacing, which can be a bit taxing at times. The story itself could have used a tighter focus as it tends to veer off at times. It's not all bad, thankfully, and there is enough kitschy charm, outrageous splatter, and just bizarre goings-on to make it entertaining despite its shortcomings. Basically, it's what I love about most H.G. Lewis films, which are high-energy fun, camp, and gore, yet in an endearing low-rent way. It is also full of black comedy and twisted irony, another trademark of Lewis's. And as I stated above, it retains a kind of innocence to it that adds to its retro charm. And as weird as it sounds, despite its murders it's never meanspirited, especially when you compare it to today's torture porn. *The Gruesome Twosome* may not be a well groomed film but it's just grimy gory and fun enough to warrant a watch.

Gut Pile (1997)

DIRECTED BY	Jerry O' Sullivan
WRITTEN BY	Jerry O' Sullivan
STARRING	Jeff Forsyth, Ron Bank, Edward Mastin, Bob Licata, Jerry O' Sullivan
COUNTRY	United States

The late '90s saw a resurgence in the horror genre and, like the video boom of the previous decade, many wannabe filmmakers picked up a camera and gathered their friends and decided to try their hand at making their own. Dan (Jeff Forsyth) goes hunting with a buddy and accidently shoots him. Rather than calling the police (and getting medical aid) he panics and buries the body and marks it with a stick. One year later he decides to go back there with a group of friends to party and hunt. They didn't suspect that their late friend was there with them in spirit, in the form of a scarecrow. One by one the group is hunted down. As the immortal Bard once said, *"What's in a name?"* Well, I admit I was totally sucked in by the lurid title *Gut Pile* and great cover art, which seemed to promise all sorts of messy fun. Problem is, it's not as fun as one might think. At a very small run time of just fifty-two minutes this film suffers from poor pacing. A good chunk of the first act is a crude attempt at humor mostly at the expensive of the character of Bob, and paper-thin character development. *Gut Pile* has a few interesting ideas and I do applaud the less is more approach; however, it quickly loses focus and is further sunk by lackluster writing. One major problem is the character motivation, or lack thereof. For example, not only does Dan return to the scene of the crime, he does so to have a fun, beer-soaked hunting weekend, the very act that caused the horrible tragedy. It would have made more sense to have the hunting accident occur during the hunting trip with the guys, providing much needed drama and in turn real character development. It would also explain why the scarecrow is after all of the hunters instead of just Dan. All of this might have been forgivable had the film not taken itself so seriously. It never lets itself take a step back and have fun with the genre. After all, you can make a good film while still injecting some humor even at its own expense, especially when working with a small budget. Worse yet, the monster only appears briefly and it feels shoe-horned in like an afterthought. You would think it would be more of a main focus. Flaws aside, it does have a certain home video charm that gives this gore hound a sense of nostalgia for the decade. For the obvious shoestring budget, there is some nicely done gore and some flying limb gags that I was very impressed with. In recent years it had a small but loyal cult following due in part by home video releases. I give props for the noble efforts of cast and crew, and with a re-worked script I think this could have been a pretty awesome flick. *Gut Pile* is worth checking out, if only for the '90s video vibes.

Help Me . . . I'm Possessed, aka The Possession (1976)

DIRECTED BY	Charles Nizet
WRITTEN BY	William Greer, Deedy Peters
STARRING	Bill Greer, Deedy Peters, Jim Dean, Tony Reese, Lynne Marta, Blackie Hunt, Dorothy Green, Pepper Davis
COUNTRY	United States

Help Me . . . I'm Possessed has no actual possessions but it's a dirty, hilarious, and spook-tastic movie experience. A strange man named Doctor Blackwood (Bill Greer) runs a sanitarium (which looks like a castle) in the middle of the desert. He is aided by his hunchback servant who has a fondness for whipping young girls. When a series of brutal murders occur near the castle the law is quick to knock on his door. But what they discover is more horrifying

than any flesh-and-blood killer. My brain feels like it was put through the blender, that's my thoughts as the credits rolled on this grimy dumpster fire of a movie. A mad scientist, creepy hunchback assistant, complete with kink and a spooky castle; it has it all. The film has a great Euro-trashy feel despite it being made in America.

Help Me starts out strong with an engaging mystery, lots of blood, and a healthy amount of mind-spinning weirdness. Pretty quickly, though, the film loses its focus and any logic is buried in its own silly incoherent plot. Thankfully, it squeaks by on its no-budget charms and there is enough splatter, nudity, bad acting, sleaze, and camp to keep things always entertaining despite its glaring shortcomings. Drive-in trash fans will find themselves possessed by this little gem.

TRIVIA: Actor Bill Greer had found success producing the TV show *Charles in Charge* as well as writing for it on occasion.

Ice from the Sun (1999)

DIRECTED BY	Eric Stanze
WRITTEN BY	Eric Stanze
STARRING	D.J Vivona, Ramona Midgett, Todd Tevlin, Angela Zimmerly, Jason Christ, Tracey Hein, Jessica Dodson
COUNTRY	United States

The late '90s and early 2000s were an interesting time for indie horror and art house. A young woman at the end of her rope is in the midst of committing suicide by cutting her wrists. She is contacted by a supernatural force to help with an epic struggle between heaven and hell. Now she is tasked with killing the ultimate evil force, but is she up to it? *Ice from the Sun* is no doubt an ambitious, high-energy film with glimmers of Ken Russell and Jörg Buttgereit.

The raw imagery and editing are great and seem to set the tone for the entire film. However, a few key things hold it back from succeeding. First off, let me address the elephant in the room; the actors are pretty bad. To be fair it's not like this is a huge-budget production of Shakespeare, and I try to give allowances, but it's really hard to get past it. And, while Stanze no doubt has some really interesting concepts, it's a case of a new filmmaker throwing everything onto the screen, and the end result is a deliriously convoluted plot. Making matters worse yet, at just shy of two hours, things tend to get tedious. I applaud Eric's bold attempt and he obviously tried for something more cerebral and dark than other films of the decade. I just wish the script had more direction and a shorter runtime. Not great but still worth checking out despite its problems.

Jug Face (2013)

DIRECTED BY	Chad Crawford Kinkle
WRITTEN BY	Chad Crawford Kinkle
STARRING	Sean Bridgers, Lauren Ashley Carter, Larry Fessenden, Kaitlin Cullum, Katie Groshong, Sean Young, Jennifer Spriggs
COUNTRY	United States

When you watch a horror film set in the backwoods, you're sure to get either deformed monsters or twisted hillbillies. If you've seen one you've pretty much seen them all. But *Jug Face* wisely takes the high ground and creates its own terrible mythos that will send shivers down your moonshine-drinking spine. *Jug Face* tells the story of a clan of people who must sacrifice certain members at the behest of an unseen force that dwells in the pit. How do they know who to kill you may ask; well, it's quite simple. A chosen man named Dawai (Sean Bridgers) makes the jugs (in a sort of trance) of its intended victim. Our heroin of the story, Ada (Lauren Ashley Carter), finds it's her face in the latest jug. To make matters worse, she has become pregnant to her brother while she is to be married to another member of the clan. In order to save herself and the life inside her she quickly hides the jug thinking nobody will ever know. Things go from bad to worse when people around her start to die, taken by the thing in the pit. As I said before, *Jug Face* takes the backwoods and, instead of filling them with killer rednecks or mutants or mutant rednecks chasing after big breasted co-eds, writer/director Chad Crawford Kinkle goes a more powerful and chilling route and shows us just how scary the woods of Tennessee can be. Right away Kinkle draws you into his world of ominous woods, an evil pit, magic, and sacrifice all without being campy or silly but deadly and frighteningly serious. It's a unique world with its own set of rules, yet it's also grounded in familiar settings and reality, which is so cleverly pulled off. A great deal of the film's punch is due to the extremely well written characters that, unlike most Hollywood horror films, are richly developed and fleshed out. We really begin to care about the two main characters and their plight, and of course, we don't want to see anything bad happen to them. Sean Bridgers, Lauren Ashley Carter, and a guest star appearance by Sean Young round out this amazingly talented cast. Everyone is just fantastic and gives credibility to the script by Mr. Kinkle. Director of photography Chris Heinrich shoots the Tennessee woods perfectly, making it almost one of the players in the film. With a keen cinematic eye, he really utilizes the sinister yet magical presence of the location, and the visual scope of the film heightens the storytelling which is what a great DP should do. *FEARNET.com* named this one of the best films of 2013, and I strongly agree with them. It takes a familiar trapping of a horror film and makes it smart thrilling and downright chilling to the bone, all without being silly or relying on gross-out gags (though gore hounds will be pleased). This is Kinkle's first feature film and something tells me he's going to be the next huge name in horror. So pull up a jug of shine and enjoy!

TRIVIA: The body parts in the film were from the Final Destination movies.

The hands making the face jugs in the film were not the actor Sean Bridgers, but Jason Mahlke's, who crafted all of the face jugs.

Interview with Director Chad Crawford Kinkle

MV: What was it about growing up in Tennessee that inspired you to make Jug Face?

CK: Being from a small town was one thing. And knowing people who practiced their own version of Christianity was another; like snake handling churches.

MV: How long was this story brewing inside your head?

CK: It had been in my head for about four years. I hadn't worked on it hardly at all. I only had the concept.

MV: Finding the right sculptor for the jugs was key for the film. How did you come to hire Jason Mahlke for the job?

CK: Once I started writing the screenplay, I read two books about face jugs and began collecting them. I have twenty-two now. But I knew I needed a current jade jug potter who could do portraits. I stumbled across Jason's work on eBay.

MV: Did Jason make a jug face of you?

CK: He did! We were testing out glazes and wanted to see what an actual throat slit on the jugs would look like. The slits were way too much. But we used my head.

MV: Did you always have Sean Young in mind for the role of the mother?

CK: I didn't, but Andrew van den Houten, the producer, mentioned her. I was standoffish at first, but could see her doing amazing job with the role.

MV: Being your first feature film, did Young, a seasoned actor, teach you a lot about working with actors?

CK: I learned a lot from all of the actors. They each have their own different set of needs in order to perform properly. It's about figuring out what that is . . . quickly!

MV: As a director, do you give your actors room to improv or is the written word gold, as they say?

CK: I'm always open to something better than what I've written. We had many discussions.

MV: One of the genius things about your film is you never see the evil in the pit. Were you every pressured by outside forces to deliver on a seen monster?

CK: We did have a creature suit that we shot. I always figured we would use it sparingly because the concept for the creature was that it wasn't totally a physical thing. We ended up using those shots as layers over Ada during her visions, which worked perfectly. If you pause the film, you can see it.

Interview conducted and written by Michael Vaughn, originally published January 28, 2014, on Gorehound Mike's Blog (http://gorehoundmike.blogspot.com)

Just Before Dawn (1981)

DIRECTED BY	Jeff Lieberman
WRITTEN BY	Jeff Lieberman, Mark Arywitz
STARRING	George Kennedy, Gregg Henry, Mike Kellin, Chris Lemmon, Ralph Seymour, John Hunsaker, Jamie Rose
COUNTRY	United States

The year 1981 was an interesting one for horror films, and there was a slew of highly original material coming out, along with a lot of formulaic but fun slashers that were still riding high from *Friday the 13th*, released just a year prior. Jeff Lieberman's *Just Before Dawn* falls nicely in between and is an altogether refreshing outing. Warren's (Gregg Henry) father bought a piece of wilderness, and he takes a group of friends up to have a carefree weekend of partying, drinking, and sex—you know, the usual young people activity. While up there they are warned by ranger Roy (George Kennedy) to stay clear of a certain part of the mountains they are planning on staying. But of course, in typical horror movie fashion, they lie and tell him they are going someplace else and totally disregard the wise advice, because after all, they don't want him spoiling their fun. But there is a legend in these parts, of a demon that stalks the wicked. I know I give Lieberman a hard time sometimes but I'm more than man enough to admit that I think *Just Before Dawn* is a damn good slasher film, and I'd say it's among my favorite of the decade. It may follow the standard body count road map but it also adds a wonderfully weird vibe, and Lieberman wisely play up the folklore aspects that help set it apart from the pack. The characters are also better developed than most slashers. Also, I like how both the beauty and the danger of the extreme wilderness is captured, further giving the film a more thick sense of dread. Another impressive element is the cast, with veteran actor George Kennedy playing against type as a ranger and amateur botanist. Cult actor Mike Kellin is also pretty good, in a small but memorable role as a crazy drunk. Sadly, this was among his last films before dying at only sixty-one years old. Oddly enough, his very last screen appearance would be another slasher, the fan favorite *Sleepaway Camp*. *Just Before Dawn* has gained a loyal cult following and I can certainly see why, with enough slasher tropes that fans have come to love yet attempts at something different to please more discriminating fans.

GOES WELL WITH: *The Redeemer, The Final Terror*

Killing Spree (1987)

DIRECTED BY	Tim Ritter
WRITTEN BY	Tim Ritter
STARRING	Asbestos Felt, Courtney Lercara
COUNTRY	United States

Do you hear that sound? It's just me scraping the bottom of the cinematic barrel. Make no mistake, that's not a bad thing, sometimes some cool films can be found languishing in that toxic sludge, just begging to be discovered. Tom Russo (Asbestos Felt) is a regular blue collar

guy that fixes airplanes for a living. His work is hard and the pay is terrible. This puts strain on his marriage to Leeza (Courtney Lercara) and, to make matters worse, Tom is insanely jealous of her, to the point where he demands she stay at home. One day he finds a diary chronicling her sexual escapades with various men. This pushes an already unstable Tom to the breaking point and he sets out to get his revenge on every man that his wife has been with.

Ritter's early effort, *Killing Spree* is quite unbelievable in its mad cap lunacy that was achieved on a budget that might put H.G. Lewis to shame. The major thing going for it is that Tim is clearly a horror buff and his earnest love for the genre helps gloss over its obvious flaws. It wears its grimy horror proudly on its blood-stained sleeve with no hint of irony or cynicism which makes it so much fun to watch. Surprisingly, Ritter shows some interesting visual flare using funky pink and purple lighting to highlight Russo's growing insanity. There is also a pretty neat surreal nightmare moment that I thought was clever. And like any good '80s splatter film the blood and guts fly fast and furious, coating everything and everyone in its path. The gore gags are crude, yes, but I've seen much worse, and the makeup effects are

rather ambitious and I have to give him props for at least attempting them. Even some of its humor managed to tickle my twisted funny bone, and other times I was laughing at the ineptitude of, well, everything. The great joy of this movie is just how nutso it is and its camp value is worth its weight in gold. Ritter even throws a nice little twist at the end which, again, works if you're willing to go along with the crazy premise. Ultra-eye-popping gore and '80s cheese that makes you long for the days when you could find these nasty little gems at your local mom and pop rental store. Tim Ritter's films should be a part of every trash fan's diet. A must watch, and remember, *"I hate pork chops!"*

Linnea Quigley's Horror Workout (1990)

DIRECTED BY	Kenneth Hall
WRITTEN BY	Kenneth Hall
STARRING	Linnea Quigley, Victoria Nesbitt, Amy Hunt, Cynthia Garris, Kristine Seeley, Jeff Bowser, Patricia Harras, Clive Hall
COUNTRY	United States

Toss out those old Jane Fonda tapes and get ready to raise the dead and drop some pounds with everyone's favorite scream queen, Linnea Quigley. The plot (of which there is), centers around Linnea (as herself) finding herself encountering zombies and a creepy killer all while burning those all-important calories. In the glut of shot-on-video horror that flooded the video market you'll be hard pressed to come across something as totally random and awesomely cheesy as *Linnea Quigley's Horror Workout*. You may wonder why this film even exists in the cinematic landscape and, to be honest, it seems I can't wrap my mind around it either, but I can say without a hint of irony that I enjoy *LQHW*. Yes, its painfully cheesy with an ultra-low budget, but if you're willing to embrace the gimmick there is a lot of fun to be had. And obviously everyone working on this knew what they were making and it retains a playful tongue-in-cheek quality. This coupled with a late '80s early '90s video nostalgia makes it extremely watchable even if it's totally pointless. So if you're in the mood for some mindless bit of weirdness that crawled out of the video era, this is certainly an entertaining, albeit trashy, film.

TRIVIA: The multi-talented Cynthia Garris (wife of director Mick Garris) not only acts in the film but she is also credited as choreographer.

Love Me Deadly (1973)

DIRECTED BY	Jaques Lacrete
WRITTEN BY	Jaques Lacrete and Buck Edwards
STARRING	Lyle Waggoner, Mary Wilcox, Christopher Stone, Timothy Scott, Michael Pardue, Dassa Cates, Terri Anne Duvails
COUNTRY	United States

Ever wonder what a '70s soap opera would be like if the story centered on a woman with a lustful desire for the dead? Well the painfully retro oddity of *Love Me Deadly* answers that question and so much more. Lindsey Finch (Mary Wilcox) is a young, pretty woman with grace and style. She could have any steamy hunk she desires; only she doesn't want them hot, just cold and dead. We later learn her sexual appetite for the undead stems from memories of her father. It is something that has left her frigid and unable to have normal healthy sexual relationships. She soon learns of a sort of cult that meets and revels in their love for the cold flesh, and they're not above killing people to get donors. The main issue I have with this movie is that despite its necrophilia theme it never takes it far enough to be truly renegade art. Don't go there at all if you're not willing to push the film and the audience to the extreme. What baffles me is, who exactly was this film aimed towards? Despite some murder and a creepy cult it's not really a horror film because it takes a back seat to the less interesting character conflict; however, its subject matter is too perverse to be considered a drama. Whatever the intended audience was you can be sure that the camp value and cheesy '70s vibes is strong, which is painfully clear from the horrible opening theme song. The movie is not without a few good shockers such as the twist when we find out what happens to daddy Finch and the link between Lindsey's obsession with both the dead and men that look like her father. Also, the death of the male prostitute who meets a horrible end is on the disturbing side. I'm also surprised by its bold choice to feature male full frontal which is something even movies today rarely do. It truly baffles me how a film like this managed to get legit actors. Lyle Waggoner (*Wonder Woman*), Christopher Stone (*Howling, Cujo*) and Timothy Scott (*Lonesome Dove, Vanishing Point*, etc.) all had decent careers or would go on to much better things. The acting for the most part is pretty decent although the leading lady, Mary Wilcox, gives off a strange Karen Black quality that just doesn't work and is anything but subtle. Fans of Philippine horror will no doubt recall her in *Beast of the Yellow Night*. It would be much later when director Jörg Buttgereit would make *Nekromantik* which is the final word in loving the undead. *Love Me Deadly* had some good ideas but it fails to do anything bold with them, and the end result is something as dead and lifeless as the corpses in the film. Not a good movie by any stretch but it is just bonkers enough to be included in this book. For true lovers of '70s trash only.

Mad Love (1935)

DIRECTED BY   Karl Freund

WRITTEN BY   Maurice Renard (novel), P.J Wolfson, John L. Balderston

STARRING   Peter Lorre, Colin Clive, Frances Drake, Edward Brophy, May Beatty,
Sarah Haden, Henry Kolker

COUNTRY   United States

Sure, Universal is the final word in classic horror films; however, MGM made some fine films that delved into some very dark, macabre subject matter; in this case, madness and obsession. Dr Gogol (Peter Lorre) is a brilliant surgeon who does what he can to protect life; however, the irony is that he has a strong lustful desire for sadism and death. As his kooky drunk maid says, "He likes dead things." Every night he gets intense pleasure from viewing his favorite actress, Yvonne Orlac (Frances Drake), perform in a very lurid (considering the time) show at 'Théâtre des Horreurs' which is modeled after the Grand Guignol in Paris. Much to his dismay he learns that this will be Yvonne's final show and she is looking forward to being a good wife to Stephen Orlac (Colin Clive), her husband, who is a concert pianist. Their plans for happily ever after are literally derailed when Mr. Orlac's train has a horrible accident, leaving him alive but his hands badly damaged. She must turn to Gogol and, through a risky experiment, is able to transplant his damaged hands from ones belonging to a murderer named Rollo (Edward Brophy), a knifethrower in a circus who killed his girlfriend. Soon Stephen finds himself with a killer urge and a penchant for knifethrowing. What is the mad secret of Dr.Gogol? I discovered this film some time ago and I'm amazed and saddened at how little attention it gets. The subject matter is ahead of its time and is possibly the first one featuring a fan obsessed with an actor/performer—a staple of the horror and thriller genre that still thrives to this day. It also explores a man's lust that turns horribly twisted which is incredible bold, especially considering this was a made in Post Code Hollywood. The talented cinematographer-turned-director (having previously done *The Mummy* for Universal) Karl Freund does an incredible job and his skill behind the camera is truly stunning. His style in this is akin to German Expressionism, and his inventive camera work on this was said to inspire cinematographer Gregg Toland on *Citizen Kane*. The cast is wonderful and full of great actors that horror fans will no doubt be familiar with. Peter Lorre plays the mad doctor and his performance is among the finest of his career. There are things he does with just a look or a gesture that still send chills down my spine. Colin Clive, who will forever be remembered for shouting "It's ALIVE!" in *Frankenstein,* plays the poor pianist and it is among his best work. Frances Drake proves that she can hang with the big boys and holds her own, playing a character that is both vulnerable and at times strong. When I first saw this I was both surprised and delighted by the biting dark sense of humor, and it's full of irony. For example, Rollo, the murderer, survives the train crash unharmed only to face the guillotine. Dr. Gogol saves lives yet is obsessed with death. These are just other examples of the great writing. Way ahead of its time both in story and the progressive way it handled its subject matter, *Mad Love* is a deeply twisted and subversive film that pushed the boundaries in every way it could.

Manipulator, The (1971)

DIRECTED BY	Yabo Yablonsky
WRITTEN BY	Yabo Yablonsky, John Durin (story)
STARRING	Mickey Rooney, Luana Anders, Keenan Wynn
COUNTRY	United States

The Manipulator may very well be the strangest American horror movie to crawl its way out of the pot-hazed '70s. A psychotic former makeup man kidnaps a woman and keeps her in an old prop house. There he forces her to act out scenes as if he's directing her in his latest masterpiece film.

It baffles me why Mickey Rooney, a person very vocal about his distaste of horror films, would actually act in one, a rather crappy over-the-top one at that. Surely he didn't need the money, as he had been acting since childhood and steadily till he died in 2014. His performance is desperately hammy and certainly it was a job he didn't enjoy doing. But it's Rooney himself that makes this otherwise tired stagey film watchable (just), and he's genuinely creepy in it. Also, how can you not love watching him do a bizarre little jig complete with cowboy hat and false nose? What keeps this film from being truly amazing is its one room setting which makes one feel like you're watching a terrible play rather than a film. With an expanded story and locations to break things up this would have been a lot better. Besides some wonderfully weird moments with Rooney it's an utterly forgettable and tedious attempt at surreal horror mixed with dark comedy.

Mausoleum (1983)

DIRECTED BY	Michael Dugan
WRITTEN BY	Robert Barich, Robert Madero
STARRING	Bobbie Bresee, Marjoe Gortner, Norman Burton, Laura Hippe, Sheri Mann, Maurice Sherbanee, LaWanda Page
COUNTRY	United States

After *The Exorcist* puked its way into horror film history, a slew of rip-offs were quickly (and cheaply) made to cash in on its mega-success. Movies like *Abby* and *Beyond the Door* were low-rent films but pretty entertaining nonetheless. *Mausoleum* proves that sometimes rip-off's can be just as entertaining for all the wrong reasons. Susan Nomed (Bobbie Bresee) lost her mother at the tender age of ten and, while at her funeral, she is mysteriously drawn to a mausoleum where she discovers a sinister evil is waiting inside for her. Flash forward to Susan at age thirty: She has a

wonderful house, a handsome husband, and wealth—she seems to have it all. However, her life becomes very strange when she is taken over by an evil force. Now it's up to her shrink to save her before it's too late. *Mausoleum* is certainly a great big mess of a movie but it's also one of the craziest demon movies to come out on the heels of *The Exorcist*. Now, for what works in this film's favor: What is striking right from the start is the style—its creepy green and pinkish-purple hues remind me of early Mario Bava. It really gives it an Italian horror vibe which makes it much more interesting and never drab. The whole plot is a tangled mess of needless convolution and posses-sions that were done much better in other films. And the overacting is so bad it's sublime in its awfulness. One scene that is unintentionally hilarious is when Susan is being hypnotized in her therapist's office. She goes full-blown nutso and then demonically possessed faster than you can say "pea soup." Its low budget really shows as well, with some laughable demon makeup and some crappy special effects. However, there is some nice wire work showing people levitated, but even that is ruined when you notice the wire. Splatter fans will not be disappointed, as this film features some very nicely done gore gags, even if they are a bit crude. Obviously, director Quentin Taran-tino is a huge fan, as this film was a part of his Grindhouse tour. Deliriously wonderful in its manic plot, cheesy effects, and laughable over-the-top acting, featuring enough sex and gore to make your head spin 360 degrees! In the world of *Exorcist* knock-off's this is pretty damn enjoy-able, cheese and all.

Mother's Day (1980)

DIRECTED BY	Charles Kaufman
WRITTEN BY	Charles Kaufman, Warren Leight
STARRING	Nancy Hendrickson, Deborah Luce, Tiana Pierce, Fredrick Coffin, Peter Fox
COUNTRY	United States

Troma is one of those studios where the marketing seems way more fun than the actual product, with a few exceptions (*The Toxic Avenger*). *Mother's Day* is an early outing for Kaufman and puts their stamp on the emerging slasher genre. Abbey (Nancy Hendrickson), Jackie (Deborah Luce), and Trina (Tiana Pierce) were best friends in college, and their little clique was known as the rat pack, pulling pranks and generally having a good time. They make a promise to remain in touch and every year the girls take a surprise vacation that each girl takes turns planning. This year the girls decide it would be fun to go camping deep in the woods. But they are not alone, and soon they are kidnapped by two thugs and their mother for depraved fun. *Mother's Day* starts promising with a nasty kill and a nicely done montage that cleverly provides character exposition. However, the film bogs itself down in plot holes, stretches of needless padding, and takes itself far too seriously with a terribly heavy-handed message at the end. It's also wildly uneven in both story and tone. The setup and the added element of a psycho matriarch seems like it will put a sleazy new spin on the backwoods psycho genre, but sadly that is wasted and it never goes far enough to be different or memorable. The scene where the boys do a bizarre form of role-playing with the girls for their mother's amusement before raping them is surprisingly tame. It baffles me why Kaufman led us down the sleaze road if he was not willing to go all the way and push boundaries. Even nudity is kept to a bare minimum. Still, the film isn't a total waste of time and features an amazingly grimy set design that is so filthy you swear you can smell it. The details in these sets give a lot of production value on what I can only assume was a micro-budget. It also has some dark comedy like the girls being tied to exercise equipment as a way of making them symbolically just a household tool. The other saving grace of the film is Fredrick Coffin, who is amazingly creepy as the slow-witted deranged brother Ike. Splatter fans looking for low-rent thrills might be disappointed in a film that seems to hold itself back despite a promising setup. The end result is a confused film that is horribly uneven and worse yet, it takes itself way too seriously. This is one bad mother.

Nail Gun Massacre, The (1985)

DIRECTED BY	Bill Leslie, Terry Lofton
WRITTEN BY	Terry Lofton
STARRING	Rocky Patterson, Ron Queen, Beau Leland, Michelle Meyer
COUNTRY	United States

The horror video boom produced a lot of horror movies to fill a demanding video rental market. Some were good, some bad, and some, like the one we're about to talk about, garbage goodness. A gang of construction workers savagely rape a young woman. Not long after that the peace of a small town in Texas is rocked when a mysterious figure with a nail gun dispatches people. Now it's up to the local sheriff and the town's doctor to solve the case before the hardware-happy killer nails more victims. *Nail Gun Massacre* is often trashed by reviewers for its mile-high list of film ineptitude. And while it has a whole host of issues, I come here not to trash this film but to praise it (sort of). I look at this movie as a self-aware parody of other slashers of the time, most obviously *The Texas Chainsaw Massacre*.

This film features some of the weirdest and, at times cringeworthy dialogue of any slasher. Some examples include the doctor, who is helping (and seemingly leading) the investigation, has this gem to say in regards to the woman who was brutally raped: "She still might be a little bitter about it." Um, yah think so? Or the local redneck store owner: "Do you remember when you could sit outside and not worry about mosquitoes and killers?" It's very clear that the filmmakers are having a laugh at them-

selves and the genre as a whole. It's also an extra-cheesy slice of '80s horror that has something for every horror hound. Lots of sex and nudity? Check. A bizarre serial killer with painfully bad one-liners? Check. Blood and violence? Double check. The pacing is good with the violence flying as fast as the nails themselves. Even if you don't like the film you have to admit you never get bored with it. Knowing that they had not the money nor talent to make a serious slasher they wisely decided to play up the camp, poking fun at the genre. Bill Leslie and Terry Lofton must have done something right as the film has a loyal cult following ironically held in the same regard as the very horror films they were having a laugh at. *The Nail Gun Massacre* is a great way to kill some brain cells and perfect for any movie night.

Neon Maniacs (1986)

DIRECTED BY	Joseph Mangine
WRITTEN BY	Mark Patrick Carducci
STARRING	Clyde Hayes, Leilani Sarelle, Donna Locke, Victor Brandt, David Muir, Marta Kober, James Acheson
COUNTRY	United States

When your '80s horror film starts with a slow jazz credit sequence you know you're in for something... well, not great. A collection of weird creatures in various costumes have invaded San Francisco leaving behind a trail of carnage. Natalie (Leilani Sarelle), unaware of this, is out partying with friends when everyone but her is slaughtered by these strange fiends. Now it's up to her and her horror film-obsessed sidekick to try and stop the undead killing machines before the whole city is painted red. *Neon Maniacs* is a film I so badly wanted to like because it seems to have all the right elements for a cheese-tastic film perfect for Saturday night unwind. However, sadly it's not nearly as great as the title and posters might lead you to believe. First off, the film tries hard to bring a degree of drama to the mix; now that's not a bad thing per se but the attempt feels haphazard and extremely ill-advised considering we're dealing with ridiculous monsters running amok. That may have been forgivable but it's also just plain dull in spots, suffering from loads of scenes that only pad out the film, and the titular villains are missing for a chunk of time, leaving the audience wallowing in needless subplot. It also doesn't help when the filmmakers raise a lot of questions yet never even attempt at answering them. Like, what's with the cards at the beginning? The whole affair feels rushed and sloppy, and a lot of issues may have stemmed from the film's troubled production. I will give the film credit for some interesting makeup designs (even though some are horribly dated) and some decent gore. The concept is different, but it still does not make up for an overall limp screenplay that tries to be part drama but forgot to have it just be a fun slasher film. Not big on my list; however, I know people who enjoy this, so it's worth a rent but keep your expectations on the low side.

Outing, The, aka The Lamp (1987)

DIRECTED BY	Tom Daley
WRITTEN BY	Warren Chaney
STARRING	Deborah Winters, James Huston, Andra St. Ivanyi, Red Mitchell, Damon Merrill, Barry Coffing, Raan Lewis
COUNTRY	United States

When I popped in *The Outing*, originally titled *The Lamp*, I thought to myself, why have I not heard of this weird little horror film about an evil killer genie? Well, close to ninety minutes later, I got my answer. Three of the world's worst thieves break into an old woman's house after her supposed fortune, but instead of riches they find an old lamp that hides an evil inside it. It's released and, three dead drama school drop-outs later, the lamp is taken to a museum. Dr. Wallace (James Huston), who is tasked with studying the object, just so happens to have a teenage daughter named Alex (Andra St. Ivanyi). During a class field trip to the same museum (plot convenience anyone?) Alex and her friends have the bright idea to stay overnight after everyone has left. Little do they know they are trapped inside with an accident evil. What struck me about this film right from the start was how incredibly unremarkable and bland it was considering a premise that is refreshingly different. The film seems to have a hard time figuring out what exactly it is, a supernatural horror film or a slasher-style body count. It tries for a mixture of the two but fails miserable on both counts. Worst of all, it seems to totally ignore its own mythos, which takes a back seat to pointless melodrama and romantic subplot that does nothing to move the story forward. Not to mention a slew of plot holes and ridiculous nonsense such as a bathtub in the specimen room of the museum. I think a lot of things could be forgivable had the filmmakers attempted to have some fun with the genre, but alas, the material is taken just a bit too seriously for its own good. I will say the film picks up in the last act with some decade kills but sadly it's too little too late to make the film salvageable. Having an interesting concept is great but not when it bogs itself down in needless padding and a confused and contrived plot with an ending that is just plain lazy. The Outing is an utterly forgettable horror film that is not worth your time.

Ozone: The Attack of the Redneck Mutants (1987)

DIRECTED BY	Matt Devlen
WRITTEN BY	Brad Redd
STARRING	Scott Davis, Blue Thompson, Brad McCormick, Janice Williams, Luther Webb, Dick Durr, Rhonda Rooney
COUNTRY	United States

Get yer butt in a seat, grab a cold one, and get ready for some good ol' fashioned redneck splatter film courtesy of director/producer Matt Devlen. A hole in the ozone layer transforms the folks of a small hick town into savage slime-spewing maniacs. You know you're in for a rare treat when the film's opening shot is of an outhouse. As you may have guessed this isn't exactly a classic. The story lacks direction and the characters are not very likable or well-developed. But I think the biggest issue is the pacing, which really stretches out the first act with scenes that go on way too long. There is also some totally bonkers random stuff added in for good measure. The old lady killing the chicken (fake blood splatter included) comes to mind or the redneck stand-up. Despite all this I found myself oddly amused, even entertained. Its redeeming quality comes from its ultra-grimy, low-budget gore and camp, which this film has in spades. And while we're on the subject of carnage, surprisingly this film features some decent practical effects, given its dime store budget. I also respected the fact that it doesn't take itself too seriously and it's obviously in on its own joke. You may be scraping the bottom of the toxic barrel with Ozone but it's a delightfully weird treat for fans of Troma-style outrageousness. Recommended for true trashy bad movie fans. "Hush your mouth and eat!"

Parents (1989)

DIRECTED BY	Bob Balaban
WRITTEN BY	Christopher Hawthorne
STARRING	Randy Quaid, Mary Beth Hurt, Sandy Dennis, Bryan Madorsky, Deborah Rush, Graham Jarvis, Helen Carcallen
COUNTRY	United States

The multi-talented Bob Balaban directs this horror satirical comedy that takes a bite out of 1950s culture in this sorely overlooked late-'80s gem. The year is 1954, and Nick (Randy Quaid) and Lily Laemle (Mary Beth Hurt) move themselves and their ten-year-old son, Michael (Bryan Madorsky), to their own little slice of suburban paradise. Things aren't so blissful for Michael who is introverted and seems to live in a world totally of his own. He slowly becomes convinced something is rotten with his parents and the leftovers they serve every night. Is it all in his active imagination or is something more sinister cooking? Keeping with the theme of the movie, one can look at it like movie stew. Take one part dark comedy, season with '50s food satire, mix in some art house flavor, and finally a dash of tried and true horror show and you get *Parents*. Balanban may have bitten off more than he could chew; trying to make all these things mesh well together, and the result is a somewhat uneven outing. However, it's still enjoyable despite this. Part of what holds this film together is its unnerving quality done in subtle yet effective moments. For example, the early scenes between Quaid's character and son Michael is so simple yet totally creepy. Balanban also knows just how to rack up the tension and permeate the entire film with an off-kilter feeling. Like a David Lynch master work the film blends a hypersexual and twisted surreal art house sensibility which I think audiences and critics just weren't prepared for, probably going in expecting a silly horror comedy. *Parents* explores the idea that the rose-colored glasses of the '50s family life might be deeply rotten at its core, and with its psycho-sexual surreal nature coupled with dark comedy it makes for a truly different horror outing. It's so good you'll likely come back for seconds.

TRIVIA: Bob Balanban would reunite with cast member Deborah Rush when he directed her in an episode of the cult hit *Strangers with Candy*.

GOES WELL WITH: *Society*

Private Parts (1972)

DIRECTED BY	Paul Bartel
WRITTEN BY	Philip Kearney, Les Rendelstein
STARRING	Ayn Ruymen, Lucille Benson, John Ventantonio, Laurie Main, Charles Woolf, Stanley Livingston, Ann Gibbs
COUNTRY	United States

Paul Bartel was legendary in the Corman School. He wrote, acted in, and directed some of the most iconic films to come out of the '70s and '80s, including the full throttle satirical action film *Death Race 2000*, the campy cult classic *Lust in the Dust*, not to mention a personal favorite *Eating Raoul*. However, it's the equally great yet criminally overlooked *Private Parts* that is deserving of some attention. Cheryl (Ayn Ruymen) is a young girl who ran away from her small Ohio town for the big city. She has had a falling out with her roommate and, instead of going back home, she looks up her Aunt Martha (Lucille Benson), who owns an old creepy hotel. She talks her aunt into letting her stay for a little while in exchange for helping out around the place. Cheryl quickly discovers, however, that everyone staying in the decaying hotel is more than a little strange, and Martha herself is off her rocker. Things go from strange to deadly when she meets a mysterious young man named George (John Ventantonio), a photographer who seems to have an obsession with her. Of course nosey Cheryl ignores her aunt's warning about exploring the hotel alone and she may just discover all the skeletons hiding throughout. Right away the film wastes no time in crafting a thick sense of strange sexual perversion and dread which only seems to escalate as the things progress. In terms of sleaze, violence, and just plain bizarre goings-on it has an Italian Giallo-like feeling, something really interesting for an American film. It is very much akin to Roman Pulanski's *The Tenant,* but this film pre-dates it by four years. Indeed, a lot of similar eerie tones and themes are echoed in both. It's not what you would call plot heavy, leaving some questions unanswered; however, there is enough mystery, suspense, and just downright nutty characters to keep the audience in a trance wondering what is around the next twisted bend. Bartel brilliantly mixes some intentional tongue-in-cheek humor to help perfectly balance the more unsettling aspects. In the vault of forgotten but amazing films *Private Parts* is maybe the most overlooked, but its ideas were ahead of its time, offering a pre-*Halloween* body count slasher while also providing the template for such films as *The Shining.* Its undercurrent of sexual repression, dark desires, and frank depictions of fetishes is something that was very much unheard of at the time, especially in American cinema. I hope more people seek out this film because it's very much an unnerving and sleazy little romp with a wicked sense of humor and a great finale.

Q, aka Q: The Winged Serpent (1982)

DIRECTED BY	Larry Cohen
WRITTEN BY	Larry Cohen
STARRING	Michael Moriarty, Candy Clark, David Carradine, Richard Roundtree, James Dixton, Tony Web, Malachy McCourt
COUNTRY	United States

Godzilla has Tokyo and now New York City has the Aztec God Quetzalcoatl, or Q to his friends. New York City is in a panic as a giant bird-like creature is savagely attacking people. Meanwhile, Detective Shepard (David Carradine) is investigating a series of bizarre ritualistic murders, which leave the bodies skinned totally clean, and a thug named Jimmy (Michael Moriarty) accidentally stumbles upon the bird's nest. Jimmy soon teams up to help Shepard, for a price. Now it's up to Shepard and police to stop the bird from taking a bite out of the Big Apple. Larry Cohen pays a loving homage to the B-monster films of the '50s as well as the amazing stop-motion of Ray Harryhausen in this highly insane but entertaining little horror flick. Like I've said in my other Cohen reviews he's definitely a big idea guy who always has something altogether different and exciting up his sleeve, which is what I find

most endearing about his work. However, *Q* suffers from numerous holes in the plot with big story points glossed over. In sharp contrast, he focuses heavily on minor details like Jimmy Quinn's demands, which ultimately proves moot and does nothing to move the story forward. But it's not all bad and has a lot of redeeming qualities. The greatest thing in this film by far is Michael Moriarty who gives a surprisingly layered performance as a two-bit criminal and has enough charisma to go from sympatric to utterly lonesome effortlessly. When you manage to outshine David Carradine you're doing something right. Part of the film's charm is the wonderfully effective stop-motion animation used for the creature and, while it may look dated, I think it further drives home the B-monster movie vibes of yesteryears. Also, the practical effects are quite good especially considering the low budget. At the end of the day the weak points in *Q* can be easily forgiven due to its mad cap and creative plot, solid acting, and of course it's tribute to films like *King Kong* and *The Beast from 20,000 Fathoms*. Once again, even with its rocky foundation Cohen still makes me love his charming and inventive film despite its flaws. And, I mean, come on, how can you not love a giant Aztec god soaring around New York? Once again, Larry, my hats off to you, now call off your creature, please.

Larry Cohen on *Q*

Birds Nest: On Filming at the Chrysler Building

As it's quite clear, Q was shot in New York City and we wanted the Chrysler Building more than anything else, because that was where the giant bird makes its nest and I was refused by them six times and I kept going back and offering them more money and trying to make it more attractive for them and eventually they broke down and let us do it, so we were allowed to shot on the top level, but they didn't know we were going to climb the ladder and go up into the needle and into the highest parts of the building which was eighty stories above the street, and all I could hope for was that no one who managed the building came up to see what we were doing.

Technical Challenges

When I climbed up there I really didn't believe that the crew would follow me, it was a very narrow rookity ladder going up, and no other way up or down, and then we got to the next level and then the ladder going further up and then further up after that and finally as it narrowed into the very tip of the needle only one person could go up there at a time. Eventually I got David Carradine up there to fire a machine gun off of it, but we could feel the building swaying back and forth in the wind and it was an odd feeling being up that high, and we had no money to build the top of the Chrysler so we had to shoot at the real place and we had to bring the cables up and the cameras, the lights, and the sound equipment, everything on ropes being hauled up into the tip of the building. We even brought up a pigeon wrangler, because there was none up there so we had to bring our own, the guy brought them in boxes and released them and when we were finished with them, well the carrier pigeons would fly back to New Jersey on their own. I didn't have to provide them with any transportation.

Lights Out

One day we were up there and it ran into the early evening and all the lights started to go on in the city and the night was starting to fall and there was a power failure and we were plunged into darkness. So there we were on the platform because that's all that the top of the Chrysler Building is when you get up high, all those triangular openings that you see on the side of the building are not walled with glass, they're completely open so you can just step right off the building and drop eighty some floors, and I was hoping it wasn't going to be me. We were all up there in the dark and I said to everybody 'Don't move from where you are, don't take another step,' I had everybody hold hands and wait for the lights to come on. We waited about twelve, fifteen minutes and the lights came back on. It was breathtaking though, because in the darkness the entire view of the city stretched all around us was even more magnificent because we were in the pitch-blackness ourselves.

Wrapping Up

We were up there for three or four days and hired steeple jacks who are guys who make their living repairing sky scrapers. They have the same mental capacity as window washers who can crawl around outside the eightieth or ninetieth floor of a building without losing their balance. These steeple jacks put on police uniforms and got in the baskets we had out there hanging around the building and they fired machine guns out of the basket, they weren't afraid of the heights. I didn't share their lack of fear. I was always worried I was going to fall off the building, I even had a stunt man walk behind me holding onto my belt just to make sure I wouldn't fall. But we made it through and I must commend David Carradine and Michael Moriarty and the crew for having the courage to go up there.

Redeemer, The, aka Class Reunion Massacre (1978)

DIRECTED BY	Constantine S. Gochis
WRITTEN BY	William Vernick
STARRING	Damien Knight, Jeannetta Arnette, Nick Carter, Nikki Barthen, Michael Hollingsworth, T.G Finkbinder
COUNTRY	United States

Released the same year as *Halloween*, *The Redeemer* feels like a slasher made by someone straight out of an asylum. Seriously. The graduating class of 1967 is holding their class reunion in the now abandoned high school. If that wasn't creepy enough the former students are shocked to find they are the only ones there. But it seems there is another uninvited classmate who's about to give them all a lesson in salvation and pain. There have been a slew of slasher films set in school or class reunions; however, this really has to be the weirdest out there. As you might have guessed *Redeemer* is not a good film and is plagued by the same pitfalls as many others. For starters, the setup is drawn out way too long and suffers from many gaps in logic and holes in the plot. But of course, Gochis' perverse little film plays by its own set of rules. Its low-budget charms stem from it's-so-bad-it's-great moments and deliriously strange and mostly nonsensical plot that has a religious bent to it. Gore hounds hoping for a good old-fashioned splatter fest will be pleased, as the film has an array of gruesome kills, most of which are brilliantly executed. This film felt like a much bigger ambitious project that, for whatever reason, was never fully realized, with many important things left totally unanswered. Still this film is wildly entertaining and perfect if you're looking for a refreshingly bizarre alternative to the more popular body entries in the genre. *The Redeemer* is highly recommended if only for its no-shame insanity, creepy moments, and grimy off-beat charms.

Refrigerator, The (1991)

DIRECTED BY	Nicolas Jacobs
WRITTEN BY	Nicolas Jacobs, Christopher Oldcorn, Philip Dolin
STARRING	Dave Simonds, Julia McNeal, Phyllis Sanz, Angel Caban, Nena Segal, Jaime Rojo, Alex Trisano,Karen Wexler
COUNTRY	United States

In the world of off-beat horror basically anything can come to life and kill you, from gym equipment, elevators, and yes, even the ice book isn't safe. A young couple moves into a cheap New York apartment in alphabet city and discover there is something odd with . . . wait for it . . . their refrigerator. When people start to disappear they must begin to wonder if it has to do with this seemingly common household device. The film starts off with high energy and humor with a hooker being eaten by the titular appliance, but sadly the delightfully wacky opening does not reflect things to come. With a premise like this you'd think it was a wonderfully gore-soaked tongue-in-cheek horror romp; however, that is not the case. Jacobs clearly is out of his depths, and what should be a fun and irreverent film plays out more like a strange melodrama sprinkled with a few scenes of actual killing. And like I've seen a thousand times, a filmmaker takes an already thin premise and painfully extends it for a feature length runtime. But maybe worst of all, the film never lets the inherent humor shine through. What we are left to do is wade through a lot of nonsense until occasionally something interesting happens. Though I have to admit the ending was great and I wished the whole film was on the same level. It really baffles me what the filmmakers were thinking with a film like *The Refrigerator,* which aims to be high art and surreal but comes off more boring and confused. If you're looking for a fun tasty midnight snack of a film this ice box is empty.

GOES WELL WITH: *Death Spa*

CRAZY CONNECTIONS: Director Nicolas Jacobs also worked on the popular kids show *Reading Rainbow.*

Ruins, The (2008)

DIRECTED BY	Carter Smith
WRITTEN BY	Scott B. Smith
STARRING	Jonathan Tucker, Jena Malone, Laura Ramsey, Shawn Ashmore, Joe Anderson, Sergio Calderon, Jesse Ramirez
COUNTRY	United States

Based on a book of the same title by Scott Smith, *The Ruins* is a prime example of how a really interesting film can be ruined by terrible marketing. I will admit that on the surface this seems like just another horror film about teens interloping in places they shouldn't be. However, surprisingly it's more richly developed and has a lot of genuine terror. Two young couples are soaking up some fun in the sun in Mexico. While relaxing poolside they meet a German tourist, Mathias (Joe Anderson), who tells them he is going to visit his brother at the Mayan ruins, totally off the map, and according to him, very VIP. He offers to take them with him and, being young and adventurous, they agree to go. After a taxi ride and a short hike they get to a hidden entrance that leads them to a rather impressive Mayan temple. However, they are not alone, and a group of villagers seem hell-bent on keeping them at the temple site and, as if it couldn't get worse, an even worse fate awaiting them in the ruins. When I first saw this film I was expecting to hate it, thinking it was just another film about hot people in danger in a foreign land. Boy was I wrong. Smith, the author of the original source material, also wrote the script, and what we get is nonstop action and horror with plenty of twists and turns that will leave you guessing till the last frame. Besides a small section at the beginning the whole film takes place in one location—the Mayan temple. Any film that confines itself to one set runs the risk of getting stagey, yet *Ruins* surprisingly doesn't and, in fact, the single location only serves to heighten the tension. What I really admire about this film is its fresh and original concept. You won't find any masked serial killers, monsters, or vampires, yet the shocks are still ever present and find a way to get under the audience's skin. This film also features something rare in movies of this type—smart women who are more than simply victims to get randomly nude, scream, and die. They are smart, proactive, and actually move the story along. The effects are very well-done, tastefully blending CGI (that aged pretty well) and practical makeup. While the splatter isn't huge there are some very nasty and skin-crawling moments that thankfully look masterfully done. The year 2008 saw a lot of terrible remakes and just awful horror films. Sadly, *The Ruins* got somehow lumped into these and forgotten about. I hope that someday the film finds its audience and takes its place as the modern classic that it is.

Satan's Black Wedding (1975)

DIRECTED BY	Nick Millard
WRITTEN BY	Nick Millard
STARRING	Greg Braddock, Ray Myles, Lisa Milano, Barrett Cooper, Lisa Pons, Don Lipsey
COUNTRY	United States

Nick Millard, the director of *Criminally Insane*, takes a bite out of the vampire genre in this highly weird little flick. After his sister kills herself, a Hollywood actor named Mark (Greg Braddock) investigates further, not being totally satisfied with the police findings. Now doing his own detective work he discovers the shocking secret behind the Satan's unholy union. It really takes a special kind of director who can take vampires, Satanism, and incest and make every single thing so totally unremarkable. Yet Millard is far than up to the task as evident with this snooze fest of a horror flick. Like his previous horror outing, *Criminally Insane*, the plot is thin and stretched to the max making its just-over-an-hour run time feel so much longer with lots of needless filler. The mystery of the film doesn't work, as no real clues are provided, leaving the big reveal thoroughly unsatisfying. Even the editing is terrible as scenes that you think are important just suddenly end and other scenes wildly bounce back and forth giving no real context for the viewer. Sadly, the film is so bad it's not even redeemable, for example, for its built-in camp value. When digging up a vampire for a fun evening of entertainment this one is best left in the coffin.

Septic Man (2013)

DIRECTED BY	Jesse T. Cook
WRITTEN BY	Tony Burgress
STARRING	Jason David Brown, Molly Dunsworth, Julian Richings, Timothy Burd, Stephen McHattie, Nicole G. Leier
COUNTRY	United States

Maybe the grimmest thing every to crawl out of celluloid, *Septic Man* makes me so thankful I can't smell a movie. A town's water has been contaminated, causing mass disease and panic. It gets so bad everyone is evacuated; everyone, that is, expect for poor Jack (Jason David Brown), the septic man who is tasked with fixing the problem and restoring the town to normal. *Septic Man* was a film that a friend and fellow writer highly recommended, and I have to say I can see why. Cook takes what could easily be high camp and instead weaves a horrifying and uncomfortable film. Burgess's screenplay is simple yet effective with real humanity and harrowing moments that get at the very core of its audience. We know very little about Jack or his wife Shelley (Molly Dunsworth) but, due to some good writing, it doesn't stop us from relating to them on some level and in turn caring about them as characters. A film like this hinges on the actors, and fortunately the performances are solid. Playing the title character is Jason David Brown and he's both believable and sympatric in the role of the hapless and tragic hero. And even when he's transformed into something hideous we still can't help but root for him. The true break-out, though, has to be Timothy Burd, who plays the most off-putting villain I've seen in quite a while, and thankfully goes just far enough without being hammy. It's also worth noting that the special effect work is top-notch, especially when you consider they were working on what I'm assuming was a modest budget. And of course Jason's humanity shines through the layers of grotesque prosthetics making for the perfect amalgamation of actor and makeup. Cook strikes just the right balance of monster film and human drama with just a hint of political satire; something that is not easy to do. A wonderfully unnerving film that is gross-out disgusting and utterly brilliant. Warning: you might need a shower after this one.

Actor Timothy Burd on His Role as Lord Auch

Getting into Character

Septic Man afforded me the time to develop a comfortable position in all regards. I had the script for a fortnight before photography began. The story always comes first when I read a script for the first time. While the needs of the story unfold, they release and influence an innate understanding of that need within me . . . scene by scene, how to support the characters I come in contact with unfold. By understanding the influences and motivations of the other characters, coupled with an in-depth backstory to my own, (and it was in-depth), I receive the attitude best suited to their needs and act accordingly. In other words, my attitude is created by the influences of their needs.

In Retrospect

Considering the variable input from all departments of a film, I'm of the mind that when the right people come together, magic is felt in the air and that gets transferred into the product as well. Septic Man? It started with the title! No film has ever made me gag before *Septic Man!*

She Freak (1967)

DIRECTED BY	Byron Mabe, Donn Davison (uncredited)
WRITTEN BY	David F. Friedman
STARRING	Claire Brennen, Ben Moore, Lee Raymond, Felix Silla, Claude Earl Jones, Madame Lee, Sandra Holcomb
COUNTRY	United States

Something Weird Video was one of the cornerstones of my underground film education. Through them I discovered trashy gems like *Blood Feast, Blood Freak,* and many others. It's also where I first watched this little nugget of weird. Jade Cochran (Claire Brennen) is a snobbish waitress in a local hick grease spoon rebuffing local men (including her sleazy boss) and *waiting* for her chance to get out and make something of her life. As fate would have it a carnival promoter named Ben Thomas (Ben Moore) stops in for a bite and, when she learns of his job, she starts seeing a way to get out of her horrible existence. Her boss doesn't like this idea and fires her, and she soon lands a job with the show. Jade wastes no time in stirring up trouble with the carnies and freaks while working (and sleeping) her way up the food chain. However, certain folks don't like this and teach her a deadly lesson. It's no secret that this is an unofficial remake of the landmark MGM horror film *Freaks.* My major bone with *She Freak* is not just that it's a horrible knock-off of a classic film but it's incredibly lazy. This film has more padding than a Victoria Secret store. Does the audience really want to see tons of stock footage of carnival prep? Worst yet, it does nothing with the human oddities, which seems really odd considering this is a horror film. It also drops the ball with building interesting characters and even introduces some and then quickly forgets about them. Some people say Claire Brennen was miscast because, let's face it, she's not that good-looking; however, I must disagree with that, and I'd even say casting her was one of the few things right with the film. She just oozes that kind of undeserved self-confidence and entitlement that sadly some people have. Her faux southern accent further drives the point home. Surprisingly, her acting is decent considering the material. What's frustrating is the untapped potential this film showed. It should have been a glorious gory Technicolor updating of a classic shocker but suffers from horrible padding, lazy writing, and an ending that has none of the horror that the original packs. Still it does have a certain sleazy charm, but don't expect much from this broken down ride of celluloid. For hardcore trash fans and carnival lovers only!

Society (1989)

DIRECTED BY	Brian Yuzna
WRITTEN BY	Rick Fry, Woody Keith
STARRING	Billy Warlock, Devin DeVasquez, Evan Richards, Tim Bartell, Heidi Kozak, Ben Meyerson, Charles Lucia
COUNTRY	United States

The rich are different from us, and in Brian Yuzna's seminal classic he takes that statement in a horrifying direction. Bill (Billy Warlock) is a normal teen born into wealth and privilege. He seemingly has it all; money, friends, a hot girlfriend. But all that comes crashing down when he discovers something is horribly rotten underneath the golden façade. What Bill learns is more terrifying than he could ever have imagined. Yuzna comes out swinging with his directorial debut. *Society* is a wonderfully dark comedy and social satire wrapped up in a gory late '80s horror film. It's incredibly high-concept and proves that the horror genre can have lofty ideas and social commentary without alienating its core fan base or becoming too preachy. What also sets this apart besides its premise is that it boldly explores a nightmare that oozes and overflows with Freudian sexuality, which makes for an altogether different and, at times, uncomfortable viewing. But of course, as I stated above, the film also sprinkles dark humor to keep everything nice and balanced, because after all it's still at its core a fun horror outing. The practical effects are some of the best of the decade. Legendary artist Screaming Mad George and a whole host of hardworking makeup people help give the film its over-the-top surreal quality, matching the tone perfectly. Flaws sure, but considering this was Brian's first feature it's an incredible feat and one that is still enjoyed decades later. A sly, wickedly funny, class system "alle-gory" that still holds up well today. Required viewing.

Brian Yuzna on a Possible Sequel:

I've actually been working not on a remake but a sequel called Society *Bitches. I thought it would be fun to do a movie that all took place in these clubs on Sunset Blvd. There, clubs always have the red carpet and the bouncers that let people in and it's very exclusive, and then if you actually get in the club they won't let you in the V.I.P section, and if you get into the V.I.P section there's a more V.I.P section (laughs) where really famous people go, and then there's clubs people don't even know about. So I thought it would be really funny to follow some social climbing girl with her friends who get deeper and deeper in the club scene one night. She finds once you get behind the final doors it's actually the shunting. It's the idea that someone learns how terrible it is but just wants to be a part of it. In the original Billy Warlock is just shocked by what's going on and disgusted this girl would be like someone who knew how corrupt it is but just wants to get into that exclusive place. I don't have a script yet or the financing but I'm working with one of the original producers of* Society.

Actor Tim Bartell on *Society*

On Getting the Role
After getting the part, I remember initially being a little freaked out reading the script. Especially my character going through the shunting. I drove to my agents and said, "Um, there's going to be everybody licking my body in this." He talked me into going through with it. But I was still a little nervous.

On the Infamous Shunting Scene
And the shunting is of course what stands out for me about the shoot. I remember lying on that couch, screaming and crying as I was being sacrificed to Society . . . half naked, covered in slime with lots of people fondling me and licking me. I had made the mistake of telling one of the crew that I was a big Ingmar Bergman fan. In between takes he would lean in and say, "Tim, Bergman called! He's very proud of you." But I really went for it as an actor. I wanted to make my death uber painful to watch. And I succeeded. Directed Brian Yuzna later told me that while he was editing my death, he had a visit from one of the actors from Night of the Living Dead. The actor was so disturbed by my performance he left the editing bay. I was really proud of that. Brian decided that my death had to be lightened a little. He cut and trimmed, brought down my screaming and added some waltz type music under the scene, so it wouldn't play too heavy. Which was probably a wise directional decision. I had screamed so much over the course of the day we shot most of the shunting, I lost my voice. We shot a little more the next day but I did the part, sans my voice. The whole thing was, frankly, a little creepy to play at times. You know you're in a film, it's just a part. But I'm crying, screaming, begging for my life, everyone is laughing and growling at me like animals. I got a little overwhelmed at one point. I thought it was just the pain in my legs, because I was crouching then inside couch, with the prosthetic version of my body attached to my neck. My legs were really sore. I got a break and an extra came up to me and said, "It's hard isn't it?" He didn't mean my legs, he meant just playing this whole weird scene. His acknowledging that really made me feel a lot better. But I don't regret the experience at all. I have nothing but the fondest memories of it, even the shunting.

Something Weird (1967)

DIRECTED BY	Herschell Gordon Lewis
WRITTEN BY	James F. Hurley
STARRING	Elizabeth Smith, Tony McCabe, William Brooker, Mudite Arums, Larry Wellington, Roy Collodi, Jeffery Allen
COUNTRY	United States

Something Weird is certainly a very apt title for this blazingly off-the-meds and lesser-talked-about outing from cult director and Godfather of Gore Herschell Gordon Lewis. Mitch (Tony McCabe) is a victim of a horrible (and hilariously cheap-looking) accident leaving his face burnt beyond repair. However, it also left him with the curious ability to channel ESP, and soon he has an encounter with a haggy old witch not unlike the one from *H.R. Pufnstuf*. She says she will give him back his handsome face if . . . wait for it . . . he will sleep with her on a regular bases. Lucky for Mitch she can morph into a good looking young lady and soon, with his face restored, Mitch cashes in on his psychic powers. Soon the police and the government want to tap his gift in order to solve a string of senseless and savage killings. And there's also a ghost and kung fu thrown in for good measure. Oh boy, is this film a great big wonderful mess. It's wildly incoherent in terms of story bouncing from one ridiculous subplot to another, features plot holes so large its like you've missed chunks of footage, and dialogue so far out it'll have you questioning your own sanity. Now that I got that out of the way let me tell you why this so-bad-it's-great film is worth taking a trip down psychedelic lane. Say what you will about H.G. Lewis's outpoint, he always tried something different and, even if you happen to dislike his work, you have to give him some credit for never playing it safe. This is by a mile his most strange film and sadly one of his most overlooked as well. Surprisingly this film is a lot tamer in the splatter department than his other films, especially his infamous *Blood Trilogy,* but what it lacks in eye-popping gore it makes up for in pure '60s camp and kitsch. It's like they took four or five different films, chopped them up, added a heaping helping of magic mushrooms, put them in a blender, and the result is this wonderfully absurd horror hybrid. Fans of lower-than-low-rent shockers with wacky dialogue and loads of cheese will find this a magical and addictive movie that is oh so fun with a group of like minded trash junkies. Ghosts, horny witches, and yes, even a killer blanket are just some of the brain melting z-grade treats in store from the maestro of the macabre.

Spider Baby, aka The Maddest Story Ever Told (1967)

DIRECTED BY	Jack Hill
WRITTEN BY	Jack Hill
STARRING	Lon Chaney Jr., Carol Ohmart, Quinn K. Redeker, Beverly Washburn, Sid Haig, Jill Banner, Mary Mitchel
COUNTRY	United States

When Universal's very own *Wolfman,* Lon Chaney Jr., sings the opening credit song you just know you are in for something really weird and altogether brilliant. After the death of his master Titus W. Merrye Bruno (Lon Chaney), a devoted servant is in sole charge of both the estate and his two daughters, Elizabeth (Beverly Washburn) and Virginia (Jill Banner), and various other family members (some hidden), including Ralph, played by future Rob Zombie regular Sid Haig. The members of the family suffer from a rare disease where they revert back to a primitive wild state. Bruno receives a letter that informs him Merrye's relatives, Emily (Carol Ohmart) and Peter (Quinn K. Redeker), plan to take possession of both the estate and the children. They are accompanied by a lawyer and his secretary Ann Morris (Mary Mitchel)

Now they must spend a night in a haunted-looking house with all sorts of creepy crawlers and, of course Virginia, who loves to play a deadly game of spider. Cinema treasure Jack Hill directed what I consider to be the most perfect love letter to classic Universal horror with this spooky film that has rightfully taken its place in cult cinema history. I like to describe it like taking a wild ride through one of those great old fun houses; it's amusing, a little bit cheesy, but it still delivers creepy enjoyment and by the end leaves you satisfied and ready to revisit it all over again. Hill injects a lot of carefully planned out sight gags, inside references, and intentional tongue-in-cheek humor, which is why the film still finds an audience. It also has genuine moments of both fright and heart. You also can't help but be in awe of the beautiful photography that really brings out the spine-chilling classic horror charms and eerie atmosphere of films gone by. Lon Chaney Jr. gives his all as Bruno, but sadly you can see he is not in good health and in a lot of scenes he is sweaty and his voice is gruff. Sadly, just six years after the film's release he passed away at only sixty-seven years old. Genre favorites Carol Ohmart (*House on Haunted Hill*) and Sid Haig also shine, but it's the break-out roles of the creepy sisters played by Beverly Washburn and Jill Banner that manage to steal every scene they are in. Washburn and Banner give appropriately odd performances and it can't be denied that they have a great chemistry together. This outrageous film plays as a loving homage to older horror films but has a wonderfully twisted and satirical edge. It's no wonder this film continues to inspire other filmmakers and find new followers.

Starry Eyes (2014)

DIRECTED BY	Kevin Kolsch, Dennis Widmyer
WRITTEN BY	Kevin Kolsch, Dennis Widmyer
STARRING	Alex Essoe, Amanda Fuller, Noah Segan, Pat Healy, Maria Olsen, Marc Senter, Shane Coffey, Nick Simmons
COUNTRY	United States

With the glut of unoriginality in Hollywood the true breath of fresh air comes from the indie filmmakers who are taking over the horror mantle from the masters and giving us unique visions, unbound by hopes of big profits and focus group bullshit. Sarah (Alex Essoe), like many young girls in Hollywood, is working a dead end job and going on countless auditions just hoping to land a juicy part. Her world is forever transformed when she is called in for a role for a film titled *The Silver Scream*. Soon she discovers a secret underworld of the elite and it tests just how far she would go to be famous. I often get asked for recommendations on recent horror films and I always mention 2014's *Starry Eyes.* Writer/directors Kevin Kolsch and Dennis Widmyer craft a cerebral horror film that serves up plenty of grisly twists and turns and gross-out moments all while avoiding the pitfalls of clichés horror sadly standard today. Characters are well fleshed out and to a large degree are relatable. It also cleverly plays as a satire on the film business and its cutthroat nature. *Starry Eyes* is a film that hangs a lot on its performances, especially the lead, and thankfully we get a real pro. Actor Alex Essoe gives a star-making performance as Sarah, and she brings to the character a depth that is lacking in her peers. I've said this to many people, this is going to be someone who has the makings of a huge movie star. She certainly has the talent to go far, and any production—horror or otherwise— would be lucky to have her. Stylishly disturbing with some dark comedy mixed in for good measure, *Starry Eyes* is an incredible work from horror masters in the making. Required viewing.

GOES WELL WITH: *Maps to the Stars*

Interview with Actor Alex Essoe (Sarah)

MV: What was your first impression of Starry Eyes?

AE: Love at first read. It read like a movie I would love to see, and the character of Sarah just lit me up. She came right off the page for me immediately.

MV: Everyone who sees you in this is blown away by the intensity you bring to Sarah. What was your process to get into that difficult headspace?

AE: I don't usually feel compelled to discuss process unless it's in a general sense, mostly because I think it sort of ruins the fantasy. Although I will say that my process was different depending upon which scene we were doing, and breathing and relaxation are tantamount no matter what.

MV: Was it hard to switch off at the end of an intense day of shooting?

AE: There was something about playing Sarah that I found cathartic, so it wasn't difficult to let go of it at the end of the day. We also had such long days with so many intense or physically demanding scenes that I wouldn't have the energy to take it home with me, anyway.

MV: I read that you enjoyed the makeup process. Do you feel it helped enhance your performance?

AE: One hundred percent. The makeup was so masterfully done and believable; it did so much to inform the role, especially the physicality. Even little things like the long nails or the chapped lips really aided me in getting lost in circumstances.

MV: How true does this movie ring in terms of the struggles of any artist trying to make it in the film business?

AE: Quite true indeed. I think anyone pursuing success in the arts, especially on a mainstream level, is beset on all sides. You need focus and drive as much as talent and a thick skin without becoming bitter. There is instability, insecurity, rejection, and doubt, but if you're prepared for this, and have a solid sense of who you are and what you want, I'm confident you can avoid a fate like Sarah's.

MV: Since the film, have you had much feedback from your peers in terms of them being able to relate to aspects of your character's strife?

AE: Oh, totally, specifically in the beginning. Most actors know an Erin or a Danny, and plenty of them have wanted to pull their hair out after an audition.

Originally published on September 8, 2015, on Gorehound Mike's Blog (http://gorehoundmike.blogspot.com)

Street Trash (1987)

DIRECTED BY	James Muro
WRITTEN BY	Roy Frumkes
STARRING	Mike Lackey, Bill Chepil, Vic Noto, Pat Ryan, Mark Sferrazza, Nicole Potter, James Lorinz, Bernard Perlman
COUNTRY	United States

Street Trash belongs to one of those rare ultra-weird, ultra-high energy, goopy meltdown movies made during the mid- to late-'80s, which includes Peter Jackson's *Bad Taste* (1987) and Frank Henenlotter's *Brain Damage* (1988). A sleazy liquor store owner, trying to make a quick buck, breaks out a crate filled with bottles of booze called *Tenafly Viper*. Problem is anyone who drinks it (mostly bums in the area) melts into a giant nasty puddle. Shot like a live-action comic book, this in-your-face horror comedy pulls zero punches and doesn't just cross the line of good taste, it gleefully dances over it. It's dirty, grimy, and delightfully gross-out, and hey, it even manages to sneak in some character development and social commentary for good measure. Smartly, the toxic liquor is used as merely a clever plot device in order to kick off other story points and characters. But of course everyone recalls the film's amazing meltdown moments, which are done in all their far-out, neon-colored, gloppy goodness. The gore itself is wonderfully done and really holds up well, especially considering the film's budget. I also have to give huge props for the inventive camera work, which really gives the film its style. *Street Trash* is an unexpected treat and it really deserves its status with Grindhouse buffs. Melting bums, vomit, and necrophilia are just a few whacked-out surprises that await you in this ultimate cult clas-sick! Highly recommended, even required viewing.

GOES WELL WITH: *Toxic Avenger, Bad Taste, Dead Alive*

Stuff, The (1985)

DIRECTED BY	Larry Cohen
WRITTEN BY	Larry Cohen
STARRING	Michael Moriarty, Andrea Marcovicci, Scott Bloom, Garret Morris, Paul Sorvino, Danny Aiello
COUNTRY	United States

Junk food: We're all guilty to a degree in eating it—some, like myself, try to limit that and others enjoy it often. But hey, we're all human and a bite or two won't kill us, right? Well in Larry Cohen's horror film *The Stuff* our favorite dessert might be a cooked-up commie scheme that really will kill us. A new taste sensation has hit the country in a major way. It's creamy; it's gooey; it's The Stuff, and everyone from humans to pets can't get enough of it, and soon it replaces whole meals. It seems that this doesn't sit well with its competitors, and David "Mo" Rutherford (Michael Moriarty), a former FBI agent, is hired as an industrial spy to gain information on how The Stuff is made so they can copy and re-package the product for themselves. He is helped by Nicole (Andrea Marcovicci), the ad woman who launched the highly successful ad campaign. But it seems something's not right with the tasty treat and together they work to solve the mystery of the highly addictive product. *The Stuff* first and foremost is a satirical film that examines people's addictions to junk food and the way we mindlessly consume it even though it's not very good for us. It also goes a step further and looks at big business and how slick ads dupe us into buying it all with a big smile on our faces. And I think it works very well as a satire. However, as a horror vehicle it tends to feel a bit uneven. The story itself also gets muddled with pesky plot holes and padding that tend to slow or stop the film dead in its tracks. For example, Jason doesn't actually further the plot and only services to showcase how people are being mind controlled. Chocolate Chip Charlie (Garret Morris) is a character that is introduced quickly, dropped only to appear long enough for plot convenience, again not really furthering the plot. But I'm not here to give the business to *The Stuff* because even with some problems it's still wildly entertaining, and I really respect its bold and high concept which is refreshingly different than the glut of slashers and sequels that clogged the genre at the time. It also plays like a love letter to Cold War paranoia flicks as *The Blob* and *Invasion of the Body Snatchers* of the 1950s with a nice update and a clearly fun tongue-in-cheek manner. I can even see how this film as being way ahead of its time and even more relevant now than when it was first released. Again, I'm not suggesting this is a bad film, and despite its flaws it has an edge over a lot of films made at the time, and it's worth checking out. *"Are you eating it or is it eating YOU?"*

Director Larry Cohen on *The Stuff*

Promoting The Stuff
I wanted to promote the picture in a different way than any other movie. I wanted the studio, which is New World, after Corman had sold the company—Corman had nothing to do with this picture, it was under new management and they didn't have much vision . . . I wanted them to advertise The Stuff *on television in fifteen second spots as a real product, an ice cream substitute, and show the packaging, and so people would go to the supermarket to buy it and they would find out that there was no such product and this would go on for a week or so and then after that we would put on the trailer which would be the horror movie trailer that reveals that* The Stuff *was a substance that would eat you up alive, and I thought that the fact that we set everybody up to think it was a real product and then reveal it was a movie would get a laugh and make people want to go see the film, but the studio didn't want to try anything unusual. I also tried to get them to put, in a few locations, an ice cream in the package and serve it to the customers at the theaters and they wouldn't do that either because they were afraid the insurance would not be covered for anybody that got poisoned or sued them because of indigestion or something else, so they wouldn't put out an ice cream product, they just let it come out in ordinary fashion and we did all right. We got wonderful reviews but I think we would have been able to create a blockbuster out of it if we had gone out and used my ideas of promoting* The Stuff.

TerrorVision (1986)

DIRECTED BY	Ted Nicolaou
WRITTEN BY	Ted Nicolaou
STARRING	Gerrit Graham, Mary Woronov, Diane Franklin, Jon Gries, Bert Remsen, Chad Allen, Jennifer Ricards, Sonny Carl Davis
COUNTRY	United States

Long before Full Moon Pictures there was Empire Pictures. Empire was the Wild West of movie productions, and they had a renegade spirit that would not be felt until Troma hit the scene. The result was sometimes bad, but other times they were mind-explodingly great films, like the one I'm about to talk about.

The Puttermans are those weird next-door neighbors you grew up with, you know the kind that had to have the latest and greatest everything? The newest addition to the household is a giant satellite dish for maximum boob tube enjoyment. However, the family gets much more than they bargained for when the dish brings back a creature from outer space. Now it's up to the youngest, Sherman Putterman (Chad Allen), to stop it before it devours the entire family. Simply put, *TerrorVision* is a gift for the film gods and endlessly entertaining. As soon as the amazingly bizarre credit theme song by The Fibonaccis plays you know you're in for a totally whacked-out ride. What Nicolaou crafts is a wonderfully over-the-top love letter to '50s B-movies wrapped up in clever '80s satire. It features all the trappings; a cheesy monster, clueless parents, and more aware children, and even a well-endowed horror hostess (obvious Elvira send up). The way-out fashions and hair-dos are lampooned and it takes delight in poking fun of the decade in a self aware way. Italian production and art designer Giovanni Nataluccii does a stunning job turning the Putterman house into a hypersexual, almost surreal funhouse. It's really very striking. I can say without a doubt you'd have a hard time finding a better assembled cast of talented character actors. Former punk rocker and Warhol star Mary Woronov plays Suzy Putterman, and Gerrit Graham plays her husband Stan. Mary and Gerrit are always fun to watch perform and they have a weird but nice chemistry together. Playing the children are '80s mainstay and su-

per-talented Diane Franklin (*Better off Dead*) and newcomer Chad Allen. It also features some great supporting roles from Jon Gries and Bert Remsen. Being Ted's first feature you can see some cracks in the film. Mainly how uneven it is story wise in certain areas. Still it's not enough to really detract, as the film has an entertaining high energy that keeps it from being boring. *TerrorVision* is all the fun and charm of an old cheesy monster film with a wild candy colored '80s update that will have you craving seconds and even thirds.

Thrill Killers, The (1964)

DIRECTED BY	Ray Dennis Steckler
WRITTEN BY	Ray Dennis Steckler, Gene Pollock, Ron Haydock (additional dialogue)
STARRING	Ray Dennis Steckler, Liz Renay, Gary Kent, Carolyn Brandt, Herb Robins, Ron Burr, Titus Moede, Laura Benedict
COUNTRY	United States

I'm dusting off yet another neglected treasure made by schlock master Ray Dennis Steckler whose films have been featured on the hilarious original run of *Mystery Science Theater 3000,* so you might imagine my shock when I found this film to be not only watchable but entertaining. Three patients escape from a mental asylum and wreck blood havoc on random people in California. Right off the bat the film wastes no time in establishing its brutally dark tone as evident of the random and senseless killing of a Greek family man (who moments earlier we were introduced to as a family man in a voice-over). It perfectly sets the stage for what I can only describe as a little seething ball of hate and grime. Steckler was notorious for trying to work outside of the constructs of the Hollywood system and this is certainly a film that tries hard to break free of studio norms. This is highlighted by some inventive camera work which helps to add the dread and suffocating feeling the film induces. It's of course not a perfect film and suffers cheesy dialogue, flat characters, and some drawn out scenes. Ray, as always, casts himself wisely—it's not of the hunky hero but the ring leader of the escaped psychos. And it actually works really well, because (and no disrespect to the late director) he certainly had a menacing look and his acting is for the most part solid. B-legend Gary Kent plays Gary and does a great job hamming it up for the camera as the axe-carrying psycho and, as a stunt man, he literally threw himself into the role. It would be easy for me to pick apart every little flaw in this film but I think all of that is greatly overshadowed by a very dark and foreboding tone and its raw and in-your-face approach to its violence. Indeed, when you look at films today you can begin to see how this film was ahead of its time, and this is one of the rare times a full on decapitation (not cut away or shown in shadow a la *Straight Jacket*) was shown on screen. Worth your time if only for its strange offbeat anti-Hollywood system attitude and in-your-face brutality, and its at times unintentional '60s kitschy camp value.

Tourist Trap (1979)

DIRECTED BY	David Schmoeller
WRITTEN BY	David Schmoeller, J. Larry Carroll
STARRING	Chuck Conners, Jocelyn Jones, Jon Van Ness, Tanya Roberts, Robin Sherwood, Keith McDermott, Shailar Coby
COUNTRY	United States

Dolls, dummies, vent figures . . . they're all creepy as hell in my book, and in David Scmoeller's shocker masterpiece you can add mannequins to that list. A group of carefree young people have car trouble at a local tourist trap run by an old-timer named Slausen (Chuck Conners). It seems they are stuck indefinitely until they can get it fixed. To say the place is a tad bit strange is putting it mildly, and what's up with the all-too-realistic mannequins? But being stranded in this deserted twilight zone is the least of their worries as people start disappearing. *Tourist Trap* is another gem from Empire Pictures era and certainly ranks up there with *Dolls* and even *Re-Animator* in terms of an effective horror film. Schmoeller takes his audience on a nonstop ride filled with nightmare logic and unsettling set pieces that will impress even the most jaded fright fans. The whole look of dread and eeriness is a testament to the amazing work of Robert A. Burns who sadly passed way before his time. Not only did he do the art design on this but did double duty as the special effects creator. He uses simple yet highly effective tricks all done practically—for you younger readers this was all per CGI. Besides *Texas Chainsaw*, this is his best work. A famous critic once said this film was boring: Well, I'm not sure what movie he was watching because this film is anything but. Right from minute one the film doesn't let up on the scares and the constant feeling of dread that spirals into a pure walking nightmare of shock and delirium. Wisely the film doesn't go too goofy, keeping it simple and not getting into campiness. Since this film, many others have tried to use mannequins in a creepy way but none capture the perverse haunting quality of *Tourist Trap*. So if you're like me and think dolls, vent figures, and in this case, mannequins are all things from hell, you'll love this nonstop horror ride. Just tell'em Mike sent yah!

Trailer Park of Terror (2008)

DIRECTED BY	Steve Goldmann
WRITTEN BY	Timothy Dolan
STARRING	Nicole Hitlz, Jeanette Brox, Lew Temple, Ed Corbin, Myk Watford, Ricky Mabe, Cody McMains, Michelle Lee, and Trace Adkins
COUNTRY	United States

Nothing seems to underwhelm film fans more than the words "direct-to-video," especially horror fans. However, sometimes a little gem seems to slither its way into my black heart; such is the case with *Trailer Park of Terror*. Norma (Nicole Hitlz) lives in a trashy trailer park with hopes of getting out and making something of herself. She is dating a nice young man and they plan to marry. It seems Norma is finally going to have her happily ever after with her Prince Charming. Tragedy strikes, however, when her man is cruelly murdered by some local redneck thugs. Upset, she decides to leave for good but is stopped by a mysterious man who offers her a Faust-like bargain to get her bloody revenge. Flash forward more than twenty years later: A group of teenage misfits from a church group are traveling through a stormy night when they get hit by a car. They have no choice but to go to the local trailer park for help, but discover the terror waiting for them. Steve Goldmann puts a Southern fried spin on the zombie genre and nearly makes a masterpiece in the process. The film knows exactly how to measure out the horror and the tongue-in-cheek humor, which can be very tricky in a film like this. It also manages to make the dead-tired zombie genre feel fresh again with an interesting concept, mixing in a curse element, which is something that is not done in many undead films. There are also some highly creative set pieces that really play up the premise and add to the already palpable mood. Casting wise they may have played it safe, but I think Lew Temple plays a great hillbilly baddie and Trace Adkins makes a fun cameo as the devil himself. Thankfully, the special makeup effects are extremely well done, giving the film a more polished professional look. Sadly, the film falls for a lot of the clichéd horror pitfalls and tropes like the stormy night and car trouble. The characters are also terribly flat and again bring nothing new to the table. And while I enjoyed some of the more over-the-top moments I thought it got just a tad bit too self-indulgent and worse yet, it quickly loses its focus at times. Sadly, it also suffers from some holes in the plot and gaps in logic. Still it's a fun enough horror film with some glimmer of greatness. With its bloody hillbilly tongue jammed firmly in its skeletal cheek this film acts like a wild haunted house ride with plenty of frights and laughs abound. It just nearly misses becoming a certified cult classic.

Truth or Dare? A Critical Madness (1986)

DIRECTED BY	Tim Ritter
WRITTEN BY	Tim Ritter
STARRING	John Brace, Mary Fanaro, Bruce Gold, A.J McLean, Mona Jones, Rick Paige, Bruce Paquette, Joel D. Wynkoop, Asbestos Felt
COUNTRY	United States

Who doesn't remember that childhood game of truth or dare? That wonderful kids game often played at parties or sleepover's. In this blood soaked little gem from Tim Ritter the innocent game is turned on its head with deadly consequences. Mike Strauber (John Brace) is a typical guy who has a steady job and a lovely wife. One day, however, he catches her having an affair, which sets off a chain reaction of madness and murder. Beware any brave soul willing to play this psycho's game. *Truth or Dare?* This is a perfect film for someone

starting out on Tim Ritter films. All his trademarks are present such as outrageous gore, nudity, and mentally disturbed people. It also includes his patented offbeat wacky dialogue and plot holes the size of he Grand Canyon—you know, the very things that make Ritter's movies the strange and charming creatures that they are. The plot is refreshingly not about bubble headed teens, and using the child's game as a motif is a novel idea. It also amps up the action with some nice explosions and decent stunt work. Not without its flaws, but it's a perfectly servable sleazy slasher with ample amount of cheese, tongue-in-cheek humor, and of course, what horror film wouldn't be complete without some excessive nakedness? If you're looking for an '80s body-count film but you're tired of the same old, play this game, if you dare!

TRIVIA: A.J of the Backstreet Boys plays a small role as young Mike in the flashbacks.

It's reported that actor Elijah Wood is a fan of this film.

Tusk (2014)

DIRECTED BY	Kevin Smith
WRITTEN BY	Kevin Smith
STARRING	Justin Long, Michael Parks, Genesis Rodriguez, Haley Joel Osment, Johnny Depp, Ralph Garman, Harley Quinn Smith, Lily-Rose Melody Depp
COUNTRY	United States

Kevin Smith is a director I feel gets a raw deal. Either fans hate him for doing the same thing or, when he tries to grow as an artist and take on a different genre, they blast him for not doing his usual stuff. Well, I for one, think his first foray into horror, *Red State,* was an amazingly tense and disturbing little flick that is very much worth your time. *Tusk,* his second venture into the fright genre is not only just as good, but in my opinion better. Popular podcaster Wallace (Justin Long) travels to Canada to interview (or rather mock) a viral video sensation nicknamed "The Kill Bill Kid." However, to his dismay, the kid he was to interview died, and now he is stuck without a story. That is, until he finds a flyer from a man promising a wealth of anecdotes. This peaks his curiosity and he meets Howard Howe (Michael Parks), a charismatic older gentlemen who has some incredible yarns to spin and soon has Wally transfixed. But it seems Howe has something more sinister in mind than telling tall tales. *Tusk* reminds me of those wonderfully odd films that would ooze out of 42nd street theaters in the '60s and '70s. Smith stitches together a pitch-black horror comedy, yet it's not just weird to be weird, and features his typically spot-on screenplay that takes the time to flesh out his characters and provide real motivations even when the things gets totally far out. Surprisingly, the film is also at times genuinely harrowing with some truly heartbreaking moments, and I'm okay admitting the end still gets to me. As I said, I very much enjoyed *Red State,* but my one minor compliant was it had virtually zero comic relief, but this time around Smith perfectly balances the disturbing quality with some smartly written comedy delivered to perfection by the cast. And speaking of, the actors are brilliant, with Justin Long giving perhaps his best performance to date. He effortlessly sways from being a total douche to terribly charming and later sympathetic. But it's the velvet voiced cinema legend Michael Parks that really steals the show, and he is perfectly suited to play the deranged Howard Howe. Like Long his range is wide and he throws himself wholeheartedly into the role. Even Johnny Depp has a zany role as a detective. Smith once again proves he can totally surprise his audience with a well written and layered film that is totally off the wall and refreshingly different. Haters will always hate but for those willing to give it a chance *Tusk* is a howling good time.

Voices, The (2014)

DIRECTED BY	Marjane Satrapi
WRITTEN BY	Michael R. Perry
STARRING	Ryan Reynolds, Gemma Arteton, Anna Kendrick, Jacki Weaver, Ella Smith, Stanley Townsend, Sam Spruell
COUNTRY	United States

I think we all talk to our pets, because after all, they're our companions; however, they don't talk back, unless you're the guy in *The Voices*. Jerry (Ryan Reynolds) is socially awkward and, as we quickly discover, very disturbed young man that starts working at a factory. His attempt to fit in and later woo an attractive woman turns disastrous, and he goes to the only friends he has, his cat and dog, both of who talk to him. At the black heart of it *The Voices* is a blistering dark comedy that works to a certain degree, but the jokes at times feel ham-fisted to the audience. It also attempts to be a straight up psycho thriller but that too suffers from a less-than-subtle screenplay with our anti-hero Jerry at an eleven on the crazy meter right off the bat, leaving little room for character growth. It is further dragged down by gaps in logic, wildly uneven tone and plot holes, and clichés. For example, Jerry's childhood back story is meant to be harrowing, but it instead comes off predictable, like something we've seen many times before. Even the talking pet loses its charm really fast. On the plus side, Ryan Reynolds gives a wonderfully layered performance seemingly modeled after Anthony Perkins a la *Psycho,* and in fact the film is even not-so-subtly name-checked. If one thing somewhat anchors this film it is Reynolds' charisma, which he brilliantly sways from quirky and endearing to downright disturbing. I will say this film does offer some genuinely strange and unnerving moments and had the filmmakers kept with this tone I think it would have fared a lot better. On some levels *The Voices* works as a dark comedy, but with its uneven tone and an underdeveloped script filled with clichés it fails to bring anything truly new to the table. And that comes straight from the dog's mouth.

Zombeavers (2014)

DIRECTED BY	Jordan Rubin
WRITTEN BY	Jordan Rubin, Al Kaplan
STARRING	Rachel Melvin, Cortney Palm, Lexi Atkins, Hutch Dano, Rex Linn, Peter Gilroy, Jack Weary, Bill Burr, John Mayer
COUNTRY	United States

First-time director Jordan Rubin comes out of the gate with a stillborn horror comedy featuring possibly the most loathsome group of characters ever assembled. A group of girls go into the small town to get away from it all, but instead of finding a relaxing weekend they encounter scummy boyfriends and, almost worse yet, rabid, crazed beavers. I went into *Zombeavers* with an open mind expecting a funny, bloody, and clever romp in the vein of the original *Piranha*. This film had the makings of a smart, humorous horror outing playing up the nature run amok subgenre, but sadly, its one flimsy joke premise falls flat. What we get is a horribly clichéd cast of awful two dimensional characters that, frankly, you want to die from the very start. Any tiny bit of sympathy or depth is thrown right out the window with every cringeworthy line they utter. Now I know what you're thinking, this is a film called *Zombeavers*—obviously it's not high art; however, similar projects like *Black Sheep* and *Shaun of the Dead* took possibly silly plots and elevated them with brilliant direction and of course, three dimensional characters that you actually gave a damn about. The so called comedy in the film is just as lazy with grade school jokes, and of course, they make the beaver sex pun often because that's the kind of humor this movie aims for. It also dances between being in on its own joke and also taking itself a bit too seriously, and worst yet, hacks a tepid romance subplot further slowing things down. This brings me to my next point which is the horrible pacing. The plot takes its sweet time and makes the already scant runtime of seventy-one minutes feel double that. In fact, the first real beaver attack (not counting the little snippet at the beginning) doesn't take place until almost halfway through. The one thing I can say about this film is it does feature some decent practical effects but even that gets a bit wonky when we get into Werebeavers. I wish I could say that *Zombeavers* is at least a so-bad-it's-fun flick, but its horrible characters, tepid plot, and cringeworthy humor makes it a choir to watch. What could have been a cult classic ends up being just a humorless creature with no bite. Avoid!

CHAPTER 8

Sci-fi, a phrase coined by the late great Forest J. Ackerman, is an interesting genre as, like fantasy (and horror to a degree), it's almost limitless in what direction it can go and how much it can "get away with". This makes for some wonderfully whacked-out moments. Featured within are the big-butted space aliens in Jackson's gore-gasmic *Bad Taste* and the drug-seeking aliens of *Liquid Sky*. But if you're looking for something more cerebral you might want to try Nicolas Roeg's *The Man Who Gell to Earth* or the brilliant and trippy *Coherence*. It may not be the longest chapter in the book but the films are certainly entertaining and diverse. Everything from cyberpunk, to trashy z-grade movies, to more thought-provoking fare, there is just about something for everyone's tastes. I went back and forth with including some terrible B-sci-fi from the '50s but ultimately I decided I wanted to go with films less predictable and talked about. Because the last thing I want to bring you guys is things by the numbers, because yes, some of these movies are bad, but they are interesting nonetheless. And hey, we got David Bowie inside, and how could you not love that?

Sci-Fi

964 Pinocchio, aka Screams of Blasphemy (1991)

DIRECTED BY	Shorzin Fukui
WRITTEN BY	Shorzin Fukui, Makoto Hamaguchi, Naoshi Goda
STARRING	Haji Suzuki, Onn-chann, Koji Otsubo, Kyoko Hara, Kota Mori, Rakumaro San'yutel, Anri Hayashi
COUNTRY	Japan

Cyberpunk is a really interesting subgenre that gained a lot of popularity with 1999's *The Matrix*, but it's been around much longer than that. Sex, blood, and android surgery are just the tip of the iceberg for this strange independent film. Set in the distant future, a sex robot, number 964 Pinocchio (Haji Suzuki), is not "up to snuff," so he is given a lobotomy and sent out into the world, confused and unable to speak. He befriends a girl named Himiko (Onn-chann), who we later learn is mentally disturbed. The two  form a bond, but suddenly the company that made Pinocchio wants him back, like it or not. What is striking right away are Fukui's visual style and his constantly interesting camera work, which is ever evolving and engaging to its audience. The film explores some deep-rooted issues, and the whole film can easily be viewed as a metaphor for a disposable society that treats people as objects, like Pinocchio that can feel and, to a degree, even reason, yet is used just for sexual gratification. The madam looking through a catalogue of other "robo-studs" further pounds this idea home. Also there is the major theme of memory erasing and having what makes you special completely wiped away. Whatever your take is on the film and the deeper meaning, it's hard to deny it has a strong visual language with some unique concepts and disturbing imagery. And its story and tone takes a sudden left turn, which is jarring and is best described as Ridley Scott's *Alien* on LSD. But like so many films it has strong concepts but drops the ball big time story-wise. I would have liked the relationship between Pinocchio and Himiko expanded, which would make what precedes it all the more powerful and heart-wrenching. It also quickly loses its focus and scenes tend to go on way too long, making it tedious, and it's hard not to reach for the fast forward button. Fukui's film is a high-flying, gross-out, surreal, roller coaster ride that harkens back to old school Peter Jackson, and it has some very strong ideas. Unfortunately, the film could have used a stronger script that explored the characters and its own ideas with more depth, instead of padding it needlessly. Still it's different enough to recommend but it's frustrating to think how good it could have been with some changes.

Bad Taste (1987)

DIRECTED BY	Peter Jackson
WRITTEN BY	Peter Jackson
STARRING	Peter Jackson, Terry Potter, Craig Smith, Mike Minett, Doug Wren, Peter O'Herne, Dean Lawrie, Ken Hammon
COUNTRY	New Zealand

Before Peter Jackson made huge-budget films and won multiple Oscars, he started out making low-budget, ultra-weird, indie films. *Bad Taste* was his first feature and he does triple duty as writer, director, and actor (playing a duel role no less). Lord Crumb (Doug Wren) is head of a race of aliens and owner of a chain of restaurants on his planet. The taste of human flesh is all the rage in the galaxy, and Crumb must keep up with the trend. So they head to a small town to get all the samples they need. Who are you going to call when evil E.T.s are invading Earth? Why, you get in touch with The Astro Investigation and Defense Service, comprising of Barry (Peter O'Herne), Frank (Mike Minett), Ozzy (Terry Potter), and bumbling Derek (Peter Jackson), of course.

Now it's aliens versus humans in a knock-out, drag-out fight for the very survival of the planet. The brilliant poster art for *Bad Taste*, an alien giving the middle finger, perfectly embodies the film's cinematic anarchy. What viewers are in store for is a nonstop thrill ride of sheep-exploding action, humor, and buckets of over-the-top gore. It's not hard to trace

the genius of Jackson from his very first feature, and style-wise it lays the groundwork for every single film he's done since. The writing is sharp-witted and does a fine job of maintaining its wacky premise without going too overboard but still retaining its tongue-in-cheek humor. While not as splatter-soaked as his later outing *Dead Alive,* this certainly has its share of full throttle blood and fun gore gags. Surprisingly the makeup effects hold up fairly well, especially considering it was done on a budget that wouldn't even be catering on one of his films nowadays. Sure Peter Jackson is an A-list director, but a big part of me hopes he secretly wears a *Bad Taste* t-shirt under his finely tailored suit and jacket, keeping it close to his heart like it has been for me for many years now. If you wanna see the beginning of a genius and a bloody good sci-fi comedy look no further. The Bastards have landed.

Being, The (1983)

DIRECTED BY	Jackie Kong
WRITTEN BY	Jackie Kong
STARRING	Martin Landau, Marianna Gordon, Bill Osco, Ruth Buzzi, Dorothy Malone, Johnny Dark, Kinky Friedman
COUNTRY	United States

"The ultimate terror has taken shape!" screams the tagline for this early '80s sci-fi dumpster baby. In a small town in Idaho toxic waste transforms a local boy into a savage killing machine. Meanwhile, a local cop discovers something weird is going on and no one, including the mayor, believes him. Soon enough the terror invades the town and nobody can deny its murderous existence. Critics seem to take great pleasure in racking this movie over the celluloid coals. I have no disillusions about this film and it's hard to actually argue the points the naysayers make. Still, I can see past its flaws and enjoy it for what it is; trashy, outlandish '80s cheese with a painfully low budget. It wonderfully pays tribute to B-monster films of the past, and it wears its camp status proudly on its toxic-stained sleeve, its tongue always planted firmly in its cheek. Obviously it wasn't aiming for high art and it takes delight in poking fun of itself and the genre as a whole. The drive-in scene, for example, is clearly taking pot shots at its own low-budget shortcomings while also incorporating it into the story such as it is. Future Oscar winner Martin Landau gives it his all and, God bless him, he never winks or mugs for the camera. Given the material, he is actually not bad. Veteran actor Ruth Buzzi really shines as the prudish wife of the major. Bill Osco, our hapless hero, gives an awkward and wooden performance, as does his on-screen girlfriend played by Marianna Gordon. I can begrudgingly see the critics' points, but I also enjoy this slithering toxic terror for its campy horror goodness, and in a time when slashers were all the craze it's always interesting when someone attempts something altogether different. Fans of the so-bad-it's-wonderful, drive-in, grime-house will enjoy this offbeat radioactive sci-fi horror film.

TRIVIA: *Easter Sunday* was the film's original title.

Boy and His Dog, A (1975)

DIRECTED BY   L. Q. Jones

WRITTEN BY   L. Q. Jones, Harlan Ellison (based on the novel by)

STARRING   Don Johnson, Susanne Benton, Jason Robards, Charles McGraw,
Alvy Moore, Tim McIntire, Ron Feinberg, Tiger the dog as 'Blood'

COUNTRY   United States

When I finished watching this bizarre and dark sci-fi film I had to ponder if a movie like this could have ever been made in a post-kid friendly *Star Wars*, which stormed into theaters just a mere two years after its release. Thankfully, time was on its side, and we have *A Boy and His Dog*, an engaging post apocalyptic "tail". Vic (Don Johnson) and his dog Blood (voiced by Tim McIntire) do their best to survive a harsh wasteland ravaged by war. Vic, who hasn't had sex in a while, chases a girl, Quilla (Susanne Benton), to the underground where he finds they want him for a rather strange purpose. Apparently moviegoers were ready for a bleak dystopian future film, as people were still reeling from Watergate, cold war tensions, and men returning home from Vietnam. The film mixes blisteringly dark humor and biting social commentary all wrapped up in a high-concept sci-fi story. To my delight it is wildly creative and stretches its modest budget with some nicely done production designs, and much like *Star Wars*, features a dirty broken-down vision of the future. In such a short amount of time the filmmakers perfectly establish the gritty, burnt-out world and characters who are rich in development. Pacing is brisk, and it features enough action to keep one glued. The story and tone take a dramatic shift once Vic is taken to the underground, and it crosses into the strange, even surreal, which only adds to the already nutty plot. A young pre-*Miami Vice* Don Johnson heads up an amazing cast, which features some outstanding veteran actors, including Charles McGraw and Ron Feinberg, to name a few. *A Boy and His Dog* certainly reflects the time it was made, and I applaud the film for its edgy, darkly humorous outlook, with an ending that is both oddly tender yet jarring as hell. Watch it in your fallout shelter.

TRIVIA: A sequel was in the works which would pick up where the film ends and feature a female hero. Sadly, it was scrapped.

The popular game *Fall Out* was heavily influenced by *A Boy and His Dog*.

Coherence (2013)

DIRECTED BY	James Ward Byrkit
WRITTEN BY	James Ward Byrkit, Alex Manugian (story by)
STARRING	Emily Baldoni, Maury Sterling, Nicolas Brendon, Hugo Armstrong, Elizabeth Gracen, Lorene Scafaria
COUNTRY	America, Britain

James Ward Byrkit comes out swinging with his feature film debut, which really bowled me over and made me think about it long after the credits rolled. A group of friends get together for a dinner party while a comet is passing by. All things seem to be going smoothly until a series of strange events occur, leaving a trail of paranoia in its wake. If it's a great mind-melting cerebral science fiction thriller you're in the mood for *Coherence* is an unexpected treat. I like to say from the start, this is a movie you need to have your whole brain on while watching, and it's also one you'll want to watch at least twice to fully get every little detail and foreshadowing sprinkled throughout. Pay especially close attention to the dinner scene, because it contains a lot of clues that can easily wiz by you. What impressed me was how Byrkit presents a highly interesting and multi-layered story with characters that seem totally real and not one dimensional. This leads me to the second strength of this film, which is its fantastic cast, and their ease and naturalism in front of the camera really helps sell the incredibly weird, twisting, turning plot. I also thought it was a wise choice to have the film shot on handheld's and giving the actors the freedom to improve lines, which further gives everything a very realistic feel to an otherwise out-there story. This is certainly something that you can pick apart and quickly dismiss as convoluted, but for those willing to fully embrace the premise you will be fully rewarded by a well plotted and thought-provoking exploration. Life choices and the pain of regret are just some of the interesting subtext cleverly weaved into the core of the screenplay. I can't say enough great things about this movie, which is a smart, totally engrossing ride that left me reeling by the end and thinking about it weeks after I watched it. Highly recommended.

eXistenZ (1999)

DIRECTED BY	David Cronenberg
WRITTEN BY	David Cronenberg
STARRING	Jennifer Jason Leigh, Jude Law, Ian Holm, Willem Dafoe, Don McKellar, Sarah Polley, Christopher Eccleston
COUNTRY	Canada

The late '90s and early 2000s was an exciting time for gamers and nerds (myself included), for it was the dawn of the Internet, and game systems like Playstation 2 and Xbox were just hitting the market for an ever hungry audience. Leave it to someone like David Cronenberg to tap into this world of detached gaming and violence fused with his patented brand of body horror. Set in the future where virtual reality games are not just entertainment but a way of life. A group of people are gathered to test a new game by legendary designer Allegra Geller (Jennifer Jason Leigh), but before they can get started someone in the audience makes an attempt on her life. Now aided by a public relations manager named Ted (Jude Law) they must figure out who is behind it and why. The problem is it's getting harder to tell what's reality and what's game. I'm always stunned by how great this film is yet how criminally underrated it is. Cronenberg creates a multi-layered sci-fi neo-noir and it also plays like a clever allegory for game culture. Upon re-watching it was I blown away by not only how well it aged, but with the explosion of gamers it feels more relevant now then when it was made. For example, a key location is an old ski lodge that acts as a secret headquarters. Jude Law's character asks, 'What if people actually want to ski?' to which Leigh replies, 'Nobody physically skis anymore.' Now, keep in mind this was way before Nintendo would come out with their *Wii Ski*. It also is a sly cautionary tale about the dangers of blurring the line between this world and the virtual one, a danger that is all too real. Of course Cronenberg adds his signature grotesque images, which are highly bizarre and wonderfully creative. Surprisingly the CGI has aged well and thankfully most of the effects work was done practically. The acting is great, with Oscar-nominated Jennifer Jason Leigh and Jude Law giving this extremely weird movie some balance. And of course, a short but memorable role from Willem Dafoe. *eXistenZ* is a seriously amazing film and something that is endlessly watchable. Required viewing.

Hardware (1990)

DIRECTED BY	Richard Stanley
WRITTEN BY	Richard Stanley
STARRING	Carl McCoy, Iggy Pop, Dylan McDermott, John Lynch, Stacey Travis, Lemmy, William Hootkins, Paul McKenzie
COUNTRY	United States, Britain

Hardware ushered in the first feature film by South African-born Richard Stanley who would soon became a name in the realm of cult cinema. Mo (Dylan McDermott) brings his artist girlfriend Jill (Stacey Travis) a robot head, but little do they know it's installed with a military program, hell bent on destroying everything in its sight. Playing out like a twisted gear-and-wire-laden cyber fetish Richard Stanley's neo-punk masterpiece smashes the mold of other dystopian films. Unlike more recent films the pacing is purposely slow at the start, establishing an almost overwhelmingly bleak tone and a thick sense of atmosphere, which only grows as the film progresses. It's obvious that Stanley has a keen sense of visuals, and it one-up's other similar genre pictures with its slick style and attention to detail in set design. Boldly, he takes things a step further, exploring adult themes of sex and voyeurism—something rarely dealt with in science fiction at the time. Character actor Dylan McDermott heads up an amazing cast, with solid performances from Stacey Travis, and an unforgettable one by William Hootkins, who is so unnerving he manages to out-scary the killer robot. It also features rock icons Iggy Pop and the late great Lemmy of *Motorhead* fame. At the time of its release critics unfairly blasted the film for ripping off films like *The Terminator* and *Alien,* yet David's film has a decided edge, injecting much a grittier burnt-out punk vibe while aiming for something more cerebral and adult oriented. *Hardware* is a refreshingly different and trippy sci-fi horror that deserves its cult status. Required viewing.

Liquid Sky (1982)

DIRECTED BY	Slava Tsukerman
WRITTEN BY	Slava Tsukerman, Anne Carlisle, Nina V. Kerova
STARRING	Anne Carlisle, Paul E Sheppard, Susan Doukas, Otto von Wernherr, Bob Brady, Stanley Knapp, Jack Adalist
COUNTRY	United States

Hmmm . . . . How would I describe *Liquid Sky*? Take *Blade Runner* minus the budget, add a good helping of psychotropic drugs and punk glamour, and you have a nice little cocktail to fry your senses. Tiny invisible aliens come to New York City, not to conquer or learn but rather to score heroin. The intergalactic junkies soon discover that the human orgasm is better than the drug and find a way to harvest it. *Liquid Sky* is a wonderfully brain-melting experience that brilliantly mashes the New York-New Wave Punk scene of the early '80s with drug culture, all wrapped up in a gooey, hyper-surreal science fiction film. Right from frame one Tsukerman shows off an array of bold and experimental visual designs which may feel dated by today's CGI-based landscape; it is still pretty interesting, and of course fits the funky neon world that is created. I have to say I was totally blown away by the film's two leading ladies. Anne Carlisle is just amazing, especially considering she does double duty playing not only Margaret but gender-bending Jimmy. They even have a scene together, carefully edited of course. She has such an ease in front the camera as well as nature beauty. Paula Sheppard, best-known for her role in the cult film (and a personal favorite) *Alice Sweet Alice*, really nails the role of Adrian, the drug-addicted girlfriend of Margaret. Like Carlisle she gives the role her all and never quite crosses the line of camp. Anyone expecting a funny sci-fi film in the style of *Vegas in Space* may be disappointed, as the film is a brutally stark and at times hypnotic look at drug usage, much like *Trainspotting* would do more than a decade later. It's not to say the film doesn't have its campy moments, but I liked how it never went too overboard and it features some deliciously frank dialogue, which is pretty ballsy even by today's standards. *Liquid Sky* explores the era of crazy hair and punk anarchy, but I also see this as having a strong female empowerment message, which becomes very evident by the final act. Anyone nostalgic for the truly outrageous '80s will enjoy this bat-shit-crazy midnight classic.

GOES WELL WITH: *Jubilee, The Man Who Fell to Earth*

Man Who Fell to Earth, The (1976)

DIRECTED BY	Nicolas Roeg
WRITTEN BY	Paul Mayersberg, Walter Tevis (based on novel by)
STARRING	David Bowie, Rip Torn, Candy Clark, Buck Henry, Bernie Casey, Jackson D Kane, Rick Riccardo, Hilary Holland
COUNTRY	United States

The entire rock and roll world mourned the loss of the star man himself, David Bowie. *The Man Who fell to Earth*, based on the novel by Walter Tevis, marked his first feature film and it's an incredible one. A mysterious man comes in the form of Thomas Newton (David Bowie) with the sole mission to bring water to his dying planet. He brings with him the patents that make billions to aid in his mission. Things change, however, when he meets a young lady named Mary-Lou (Candy Clark). My head was spinning the first time I experienced Nicolas Roeg's genre-bending film. For the casual viewer this definitely will seem long and at times confusing with its fragmented narrative which sways wildly all over the place. But for the adventurous film lover this is a wonderful sci-fi drama that acts like a satire of American culture, and Bowie's Christ-like figure makes for the perfect religious allegory. It should come as no big shocker that this film is beautiful-looking and at times almost hypnotic. Roeg was after all a cinematographer before he stepped into the director's shoes. David Bowie is of course totally electric as the stranger from outer space, and his quiet enigma perfectly embodies not only the character but the film itself. Candy Clark and Rip Torn also give great performances. *The Man Who Fell to Earth* is a stylish, strange, and whirlwind of a film which is cerebral and challenging to its audience. Required viewing.

Mosquito, aka Sketters (1995)

DIRECTED BY	Gary Jones
WRITTEN BY	Tom Chaney, Steve Hodge, Gary Jones
STARRING	Gunnar Hansen, Rob Asheton, Steve Dixon, Tim Lovelace, Mike Hard, Rachel Loiselle, Kenny Mugwump
COUNTRY	United States

Before we dive into this luscious cornucopia of cheese, I must confess that I have a huge weakness for '50s science fiction—the good, the bad, and the unbelievably ugly. Oh, and giant insects? I'm already planted on the seat, junk food in hand, and eyes transfixed on the tube. *Mosquito* is of course a tribute to these films and then some. Aliens crash land in a national park and spawn giant mosquitoes that, you guessed it, go on a bloodthirsty rampage. A motley crew of misfits must band together to stop the invasion of the flying kind, before they put the whole world on the menu. You'll need more than a rolled up newspaper to get rid of these intergalactic pests. Director Gary Jones is clearly a science fiction fan, and his first feature is a delightfully cheesy love letter to films like *Them*. But it also works on its own strengths as well. Jones wisely walks a fine line between the goofy and the serious, never letting one outweigh the other, and it strikes a nice balance. Also, its humor works for the most part with only a few sour notes. The late great Gunnar Hansen gives a solid performance and plays it without any sense of irony nor does he phone it in. Rob Asheton of *The Stooges* fame makes his feature film debut and, even though he hams it up, you can tell he's clearly having a blast, and I think he does a fine job. Gary Jones' previous experience in the FX department certainly comes in handy, and the better-than-expected effects give the film a much needed polish to a clearly low budget. Sure, some of the effects haven't aged very well, but it doesn't detract from the entertainment value in the least. Once the film kicks into gear there are plenty of great action scenes, and they even give Hansen a nice call back to his Leatherface days. And really, who doesn't want to see Gunnar killing giant bugs with a chainsaw? And unlike the films they pay homage to there is some nice splatter to make it enjoyable for the gore fans. *Mosquito* may have its interstellar DNA in other films of the past but it puts an entirely fresh spin on it. It's not only hilarious but its action is fast and furious with some nudity and gore thrown in for good measure. An enjoyable B-movie that harkens back to the good old days with a decidedly nasty '90s upgrade, fans will want to sink there proboscis into this vastly underrated little gem which sadly doesn't get enough 'buzz.'

Mutant Action, aka Acción mutante (1993)

DIRECTED BY	Álex de la Iglesia
WRITTEN BY	Álex de la Iglesia, Jorge Guerricaechevarría
STARRING	Álex Angulo, Antonio Resines, Frédérique Feder, Juan Viadas, Karra Elejalde, Saturnino García, Fernando Guillén
COUNTRY	Spain

In a future overrun by the rich and the good looking, a rag tag terrorist group calling themselves *Mutant Action* emerges to stir shit up. But it seems the group bungles just about every task they are given. Now with their leader Ramon (Antonio Resines) released from a five-year sentence they plot to kidnap an heiress for

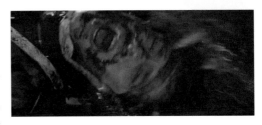

a hefty sum of money. But can this motley crew actually pull it off? The best way to describe this film is, blend the clever high-energy splatter of Peter Jackson's *Bad Taste* and the broken-down future of *Mad Max* done like a Carlos Ezquerra comic book. It's easy to understand why writer/director Álex de la Iglesia has been referred to as the Spanish Terry Gilliam. Like Gilliam he showcases a flair for the weird, visual-driven films that not only explore the outsider but celebrate them. It also cleverly satirizes the media, high society, and even acts as a kind of parody to action films in general. And it's these sardonic views that give the film its strongest aspects. However, as great as the beginning is, a major plot shift serves to squash any chance of future character development; it's like you get to know these people only to see them exit just as quickly. Despite this there is enough action and quirky set pieces to keep things entertaining. Clever writing, bizarre set pieces, and dark satirical humor help save it from imploding. If you're looking for a fun, gonzo sci-fi action flick with a Spanish kick look no further. Highly recommended.

TRIVIA: Look out for a clever nod to Lon Chaney's *Phantom of the Opera*.

Spanish artist Carlos Ezquerra is best known for co-creating *Judge Dredd* in 1977. He also did uncredited work on *Wizard*.

Timecrimes, aka Los cronocrímenes (2007)

DIRECTED BY	Nacho Vigalondo
WRITTEN BY	Nacho Vigalondo
STARRING	Karra Elejalde, Candela Fernández, Bárbara Goenaga, Nacho Vigalondo, Juan Inciarte
COUNTRY	Spain

I'm always pretty skeptical when it comes to films about time travel, because for the exception of a handful of great titles, they are mostly overly confusing and often clunky. Thankfully, this is not the case with Spanish director Nacho Vigalondo's first feature film, *Timecrimes*. It's a typical lazy Saturday for everyday joe Hector (Karra Elejalde), until he spies something strange in the woods. He goes out to investigate only to find the dead body of a young woman, and he is promptly stabbed by a mysterious man with a bandaged face. This triggers a chain reaction that leads to time travel. I purposely kept my plot description vague because I don't want to spoil the least bit of story. Nacho Vigalondo comes out of the gate swinging with this highly intelligent sci-fi thriller that is well plotted and stylish. Going in I figured this would be a twisting and turning plot much like *Primer*; however, to my delight it's fairly easy to follow. Of course this is something you really need to watch a few times to get every little detail you may have missed on first viewing. I will say the end will split fans, as it isn't what some may consider satisfying. At first I thought it was anti-climactic but after thinking about it I'm of the opinion it actually works well. If I had one complaint I would have liked to see the story more fleshed out, and certain plot points felt rushed. *Timecrimes* is a high brow and strange science fiction that is both gripping and absorbing.

Visitor, The (1979)

DIRECTED BY	Giulio Paradisi
WRITTEN BY	Robert Mundi, Luciano Comici, Giulio Paradisi (story), Ovidio G. Assonitis (story)
STARRING	Lance Henriksen, Shelley Winters, John Huston, Glen Ford, Sam Peckinpah, Joanne Nail, Paige Conner, Franco Nero as Jesus Christ
COUNTRY	Italy, United States

The Visitor has to take the prize for the craziest movie to slither its way out of Italy in the '70s, which is really saying something. A young girl named Katy (Paige Conner) has been endowed with alien powers, which she often uses for less than angelic purposes. When a new maid named Jane (Shelley Winters) comes to work for Katy's mother she soon learns where her true destiny lies. Mash together a handful of films like *The Omen, The Bad Seed, The Exorcist,* and dose it with some LSD, and you may come close to this highly weird space, horror, and spiritual hybrid that will have you questioning your own sanity by the end. This film definitely lives up to its reputation as a strange blending of other more successful genre films, and therefore has been quickly dismissed as unoriginal. While the film does pay homage to many different movies it deserves to be taken on its own merits, of which there are many.

The plot as incoherent, as it moves at a fairly brisk pace with enough action, twists, and turns to keep this mess entertaining. The cast is just stunning and I'm always amazed how the filmmakers managed to assemble a cast like this. John Houston, Glen Ford, and Sam Peckinpah, not to mention Shelley Winters—that's just for starters. It's really incredible to see all these people acting in one mind-bending sci-fi epic. Progressive rock band Tangerine Dream provides a fitting trippy and ear-purring soundtrack that perfectly fits the film's out-of-this, world offbeat nature. *The Visitor* may not be everyone's cup of tea; however, those looking for a mesmerizing and cerebral film may just find this a strange yet refreshing treat. Even though it suffers from an uneven plot and borrows heavily from other more successful projects it is still wildly entertaining in its own right. I highly recommend this to anyone really wanting to go off the cinematic deep end. Plus it has space Jesus played by Franco Nero—what more could you ask for?

Without Warning (1980)

DIRECTED BY	Greydon Clark
WRITTEN BY	Lyn Freeman, Daniel Grodnik, Steve Mathis, Bennett Tramer
STARRING	Jack Palance, Martin Landau, Neville Band, Cameron Mitchell, Tarah Nutter, Ralph Meeker, Larry Storch
COUNTRY	United States

Fans of bad movies will no doubt know the name Greydon Clark, whose films have been featured not once but twice on *Mystery Science Theater 3000*. A group of kids go off for a carefree trip in the woods. However, it's not a psycho killer they need to worry about, but rather the killer flying alien discs. Before I get into my review I want to say I enjoy so-bad-they're-good movies, especially ones involving aliens, so I was excited to finally watch *Without Warning*. But sadly this is just plain awful. The first act is solid, with a lot of brisk paced action that is chock full of gory goopy flying aliens (that look hilarious); however, all the B-fun of the beginning is quickly dissolved by the second act. It's not hard to tell this film was written by multiple people, as it feels like a haphazard jigsaw of ideas that just don't mesh well. For example, the main heroin blurts out a tearful anecdote about her dead mother, something completely out of the blue. Worse yet, unlike *Mosquito*, Clark doesn't play up the B-homage aspects and the result is a painfully dull outing. Actors Martin Landau and Jack Palance are truly hammy but help to keep things at least somewhat entertaining. A massive re-write that is more focused and some injection of fun would have saved this utterly forgettable sci-fi schlock fest. For hardcore trash fans only but otherwise just watch *Slither*.

TRIVIA: The final film of Ralph Meeker, best remembered for roles in such films as Stanley Kubrick's war epic *Paths of Glory* and the classic film noir *Kiss Me Deadly*.

$75,000 of the film's very modest budget went to actors Jack Palance and Martin Landau.

Film debut of David Caruso.